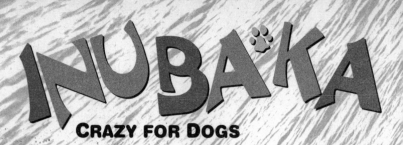

# INUBAKA

## CRAZY FOR DOGS

12

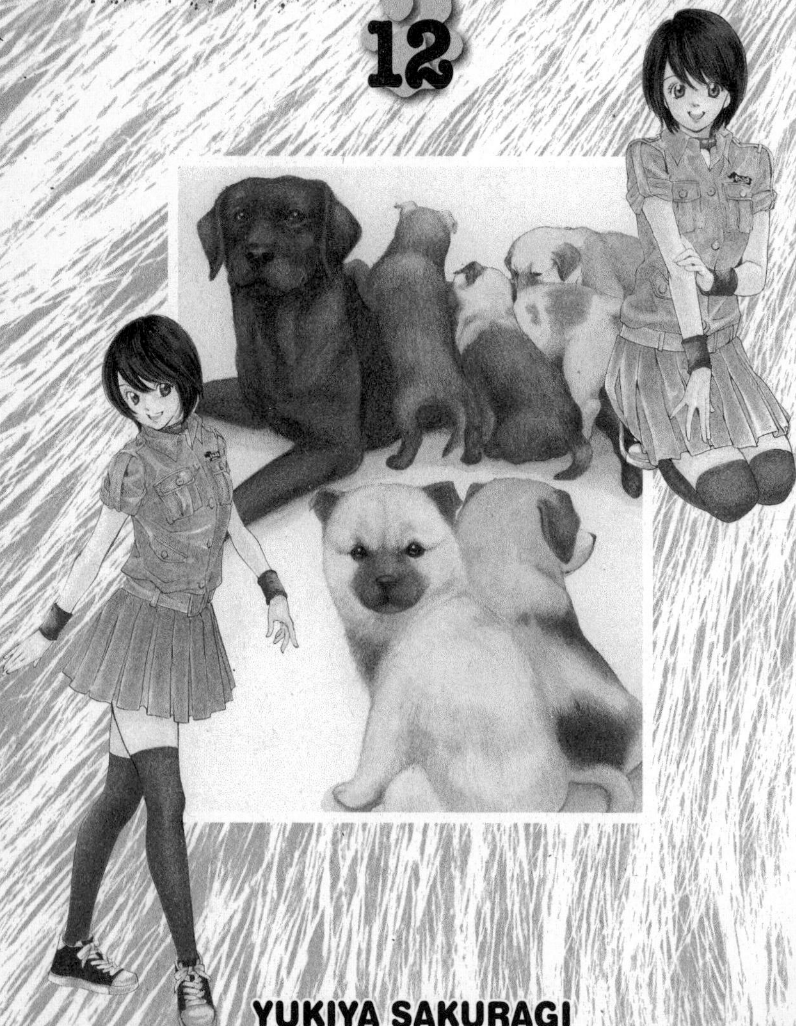

YUKIYA SAKURAGI

# Contents

## Story thus far

*Teppei is the manager of the recently opened pet shop Woofles. He intended to breed his black Labrador Noa with a champion dog, but instead Noa was "taken advantage of" by an unknown and unfixed male dog!*

*The unknown dog's owner was Suguri Miyauchi and her dog was a mutt named Lupin. Suguri is now working at Woofles to make up for her dog's actions.*

*Suguri's enthusiasm is more than a little unique. She has eaten dog food (and said it was tasty), caught dog poop with her bare hands and caused dogs to have "happy pee" in her presence. Teppei is starting to realize that Suguri is indeed a very special girl.*

*Woofles main store manager Show Kaneko visits Teppei's store and encourages Suguri to enter a K-9 Freestyle (dog dancing) competition where the winner gets to perform during a professional baseball game. He is excited about this great opportunity to promote Woofles. Suguri is unsure at first, but when Miho Sawatari from WAN KAW, the rival store, makes fun of her "mutt" she decides she has to win, and do so with Lupin! Thus begins Suguri and Lupin's daily training. Surprisingly, Lupin gets better day by day, and Suguri tries to keep up with his enthusiasm, but answering to Lupin's demands brings Suguri to the point of exhaustion. Teppei suggests they live separately until the competition. When he takes Lupin in he discovers some of his unusual behavior...*

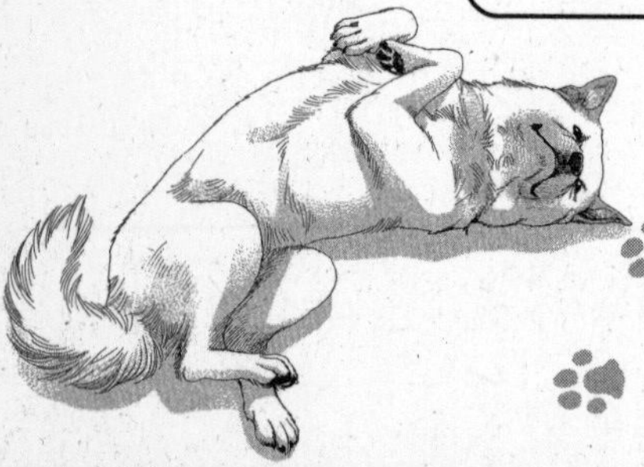

# CHARACTERS

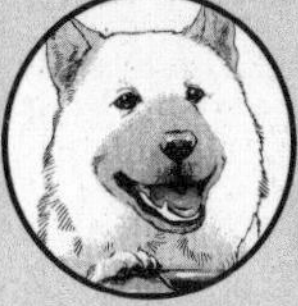

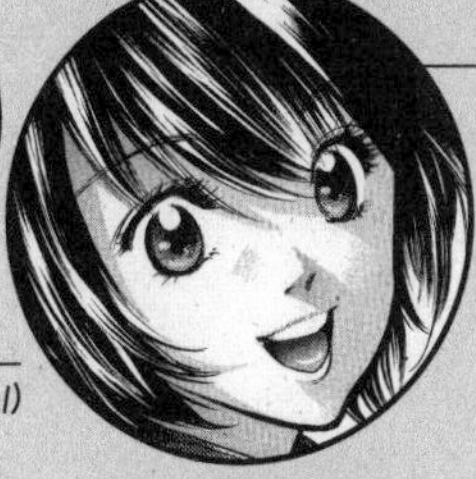

## Suguri Miyauchi

*She seems to possess an almost supernatural connection with dogs. When she approaches them they often urinate with great excitement! She is crazy for dogs and can catch their droppings with her bare hands. She is currently a trainee at the Woofles Pet Shop.*

**Lupin**

♂ *Mutt (mongrel)*

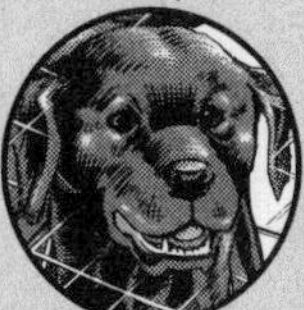

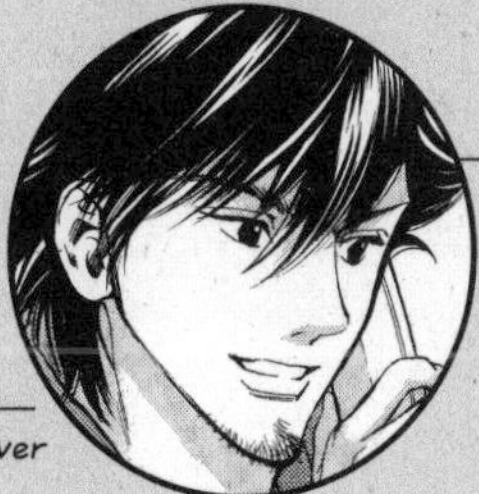

## Teppei Iida

*He is the manager of the recently opened pet shop Woofles. He is aware of Suguri's special ability and has hired her to work in his shop. He also lets Suguri and Kentaro crash with him.*

**Noa**

♀ *Labrador retriever*

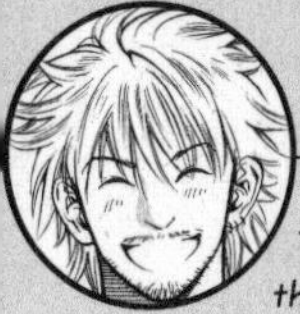

## Kentaro Osada

*A buddy of Teppei's from their high school days. He's on the staff at Woofles' second store.*

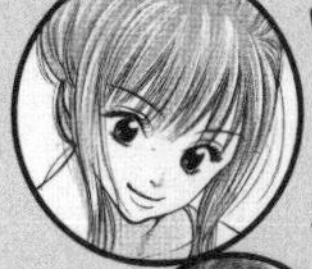

## Momoko Takeuchi

*Woofles Pet Shop (second location) pet groomer. At first she was a girl with many problems and she rarely smiled. But after meeting Suguri, she's changed, and the two are now best friends.*

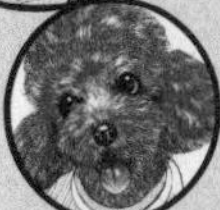

**Mel**

♀ *Toy poodle*

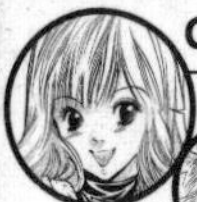

**Chizuru Sawamura**

*Waitress at hostess club*

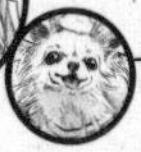

**Melon**

♂ *Chihuahua*

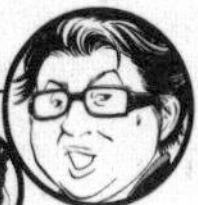

**Hiroshi Akiba**

*Civil servant*

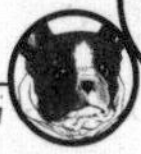

**Zidane**

♂ *French bulldog*

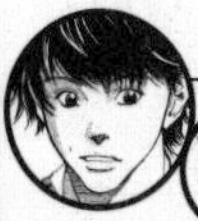

**Kim Hyeon-Jun**

*International student*

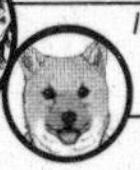

**Chanta**

♀ *Shiba*

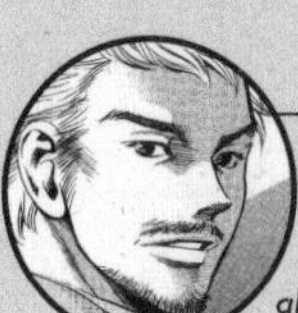

## Show Kaneko

*He is the manager of the main Woofles store and is Teppei's boss. He is very passionate about the business and makes TV appearances from time to time.*

**Woofles**

## Yasumin Sendo

*Mysterious sexy-cute dancer-*
*A dancer hired by Wan Kaw for the K-9 Freestyle Competition.*

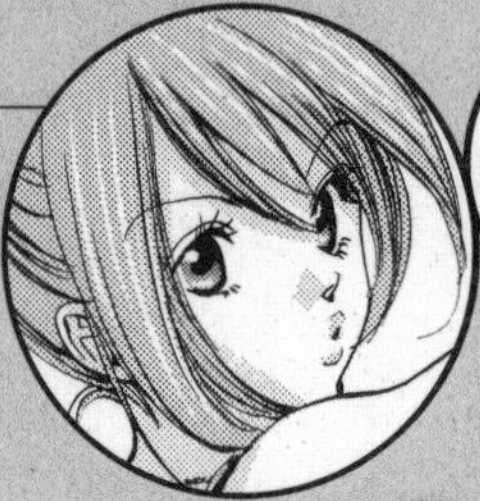

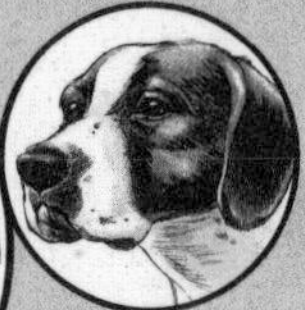

## Carlos

♂ *English pointer*

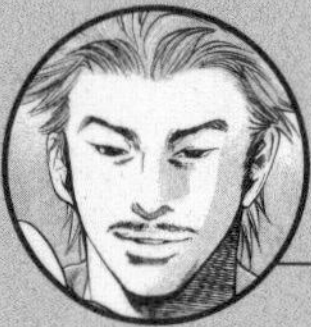

## Haruomi Nishina

*Yasmin's dog-dancing trainer*

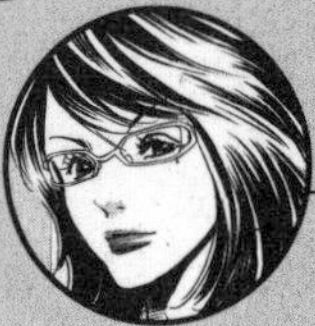

## Miho Sawatari

*Pet shop Wan Kaw's executive director*

## Motoshi Hibino

*General manager of pet shop Wan Kaw*

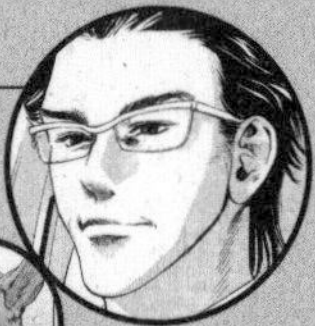

## Sabrina

♀ *Miniature pinscher*

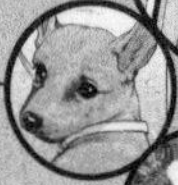

## Ann

♀ *Papillon*

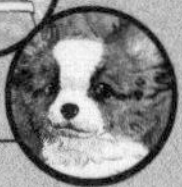

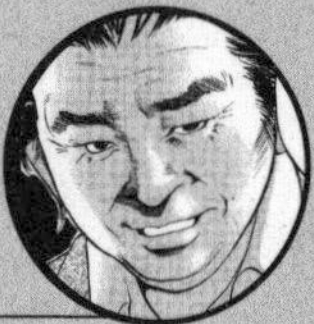

## President of KAW KAW

*President of major online shopping site and investor in pet shop Wan Kaw*

**WAN KAW**

## Kyoko Furuya

*Suguri's dog-dancing trainer*

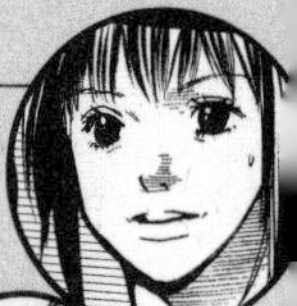

## Henry

♂ *German shepherd*

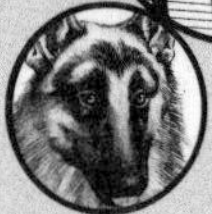

## Kanako Mori

*A piano instructor-*
*She teaches piano on the second floor c*
*the same building as Woofles. She loves her dog Czerny-cha so much that even Suguri is surprised.*

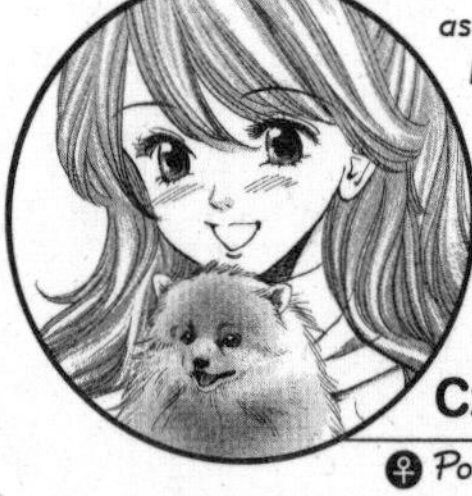

## Czerny

♀ *Pomeranian*

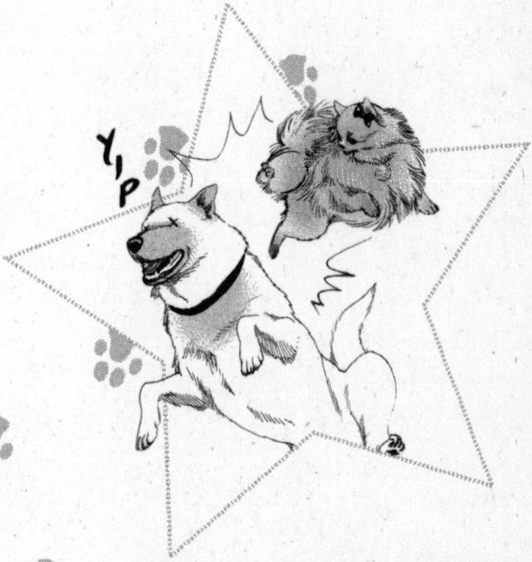
YIP

INUBAKA

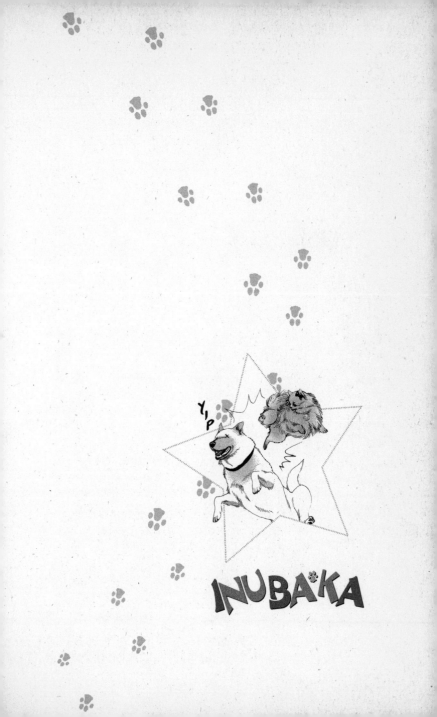

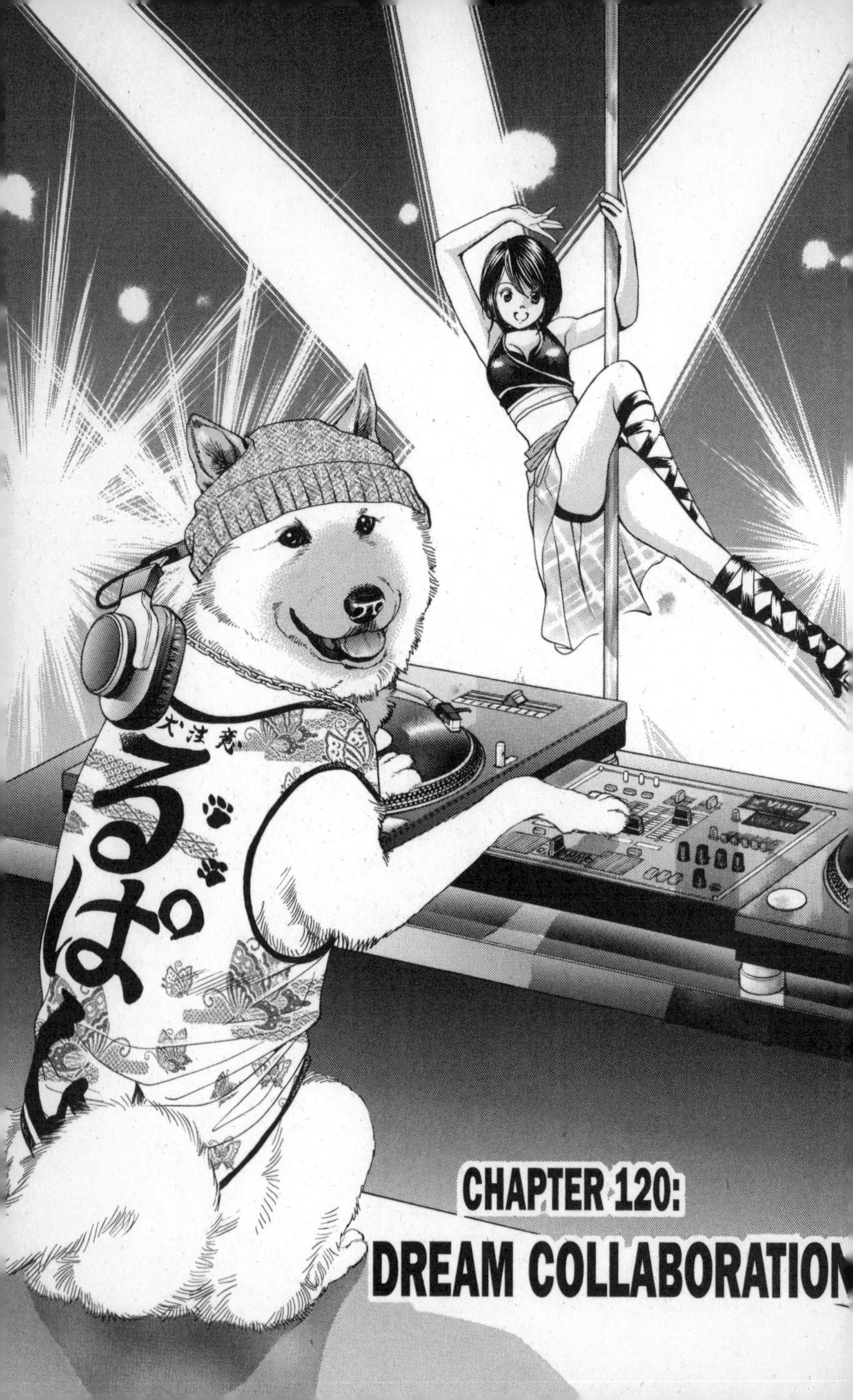

# CHAPTER 120: DREAM COLLABORATION

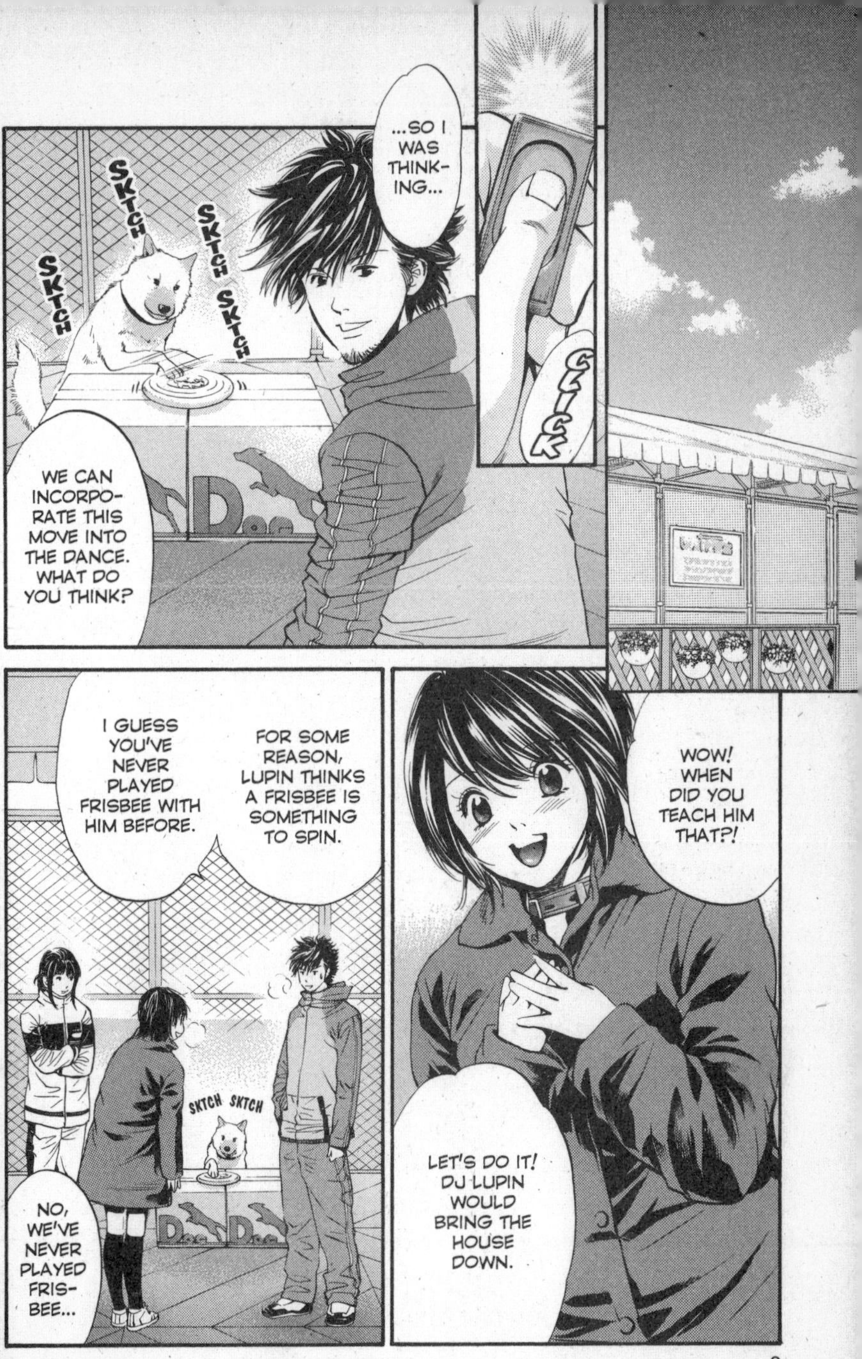
CLICK
...SO I WAS THINKING...
SKTCH SKTCH SKTCH SKTCH SKTCH
WE CAN INCORPORATE THIS MOVE INTO THE DANCE. WHAT DO YOU THINK?
WOW! WHEN DID YOU TEACH HIM THAT?!
LET'S DO IT! DJ LUPIN WOULD BRING THE HOUSE DOWN.
FOR SOME REASON, LUPIN THINKS A FRISBEE IS SOMETHING TO SPIN.
I GUESS YOU'VE NEVER PLAYED FRISBEE WITH HIM BEFORE.
SKTCH SKTCH
NO, WE'VE NEVER PLAYED FRISBEE...

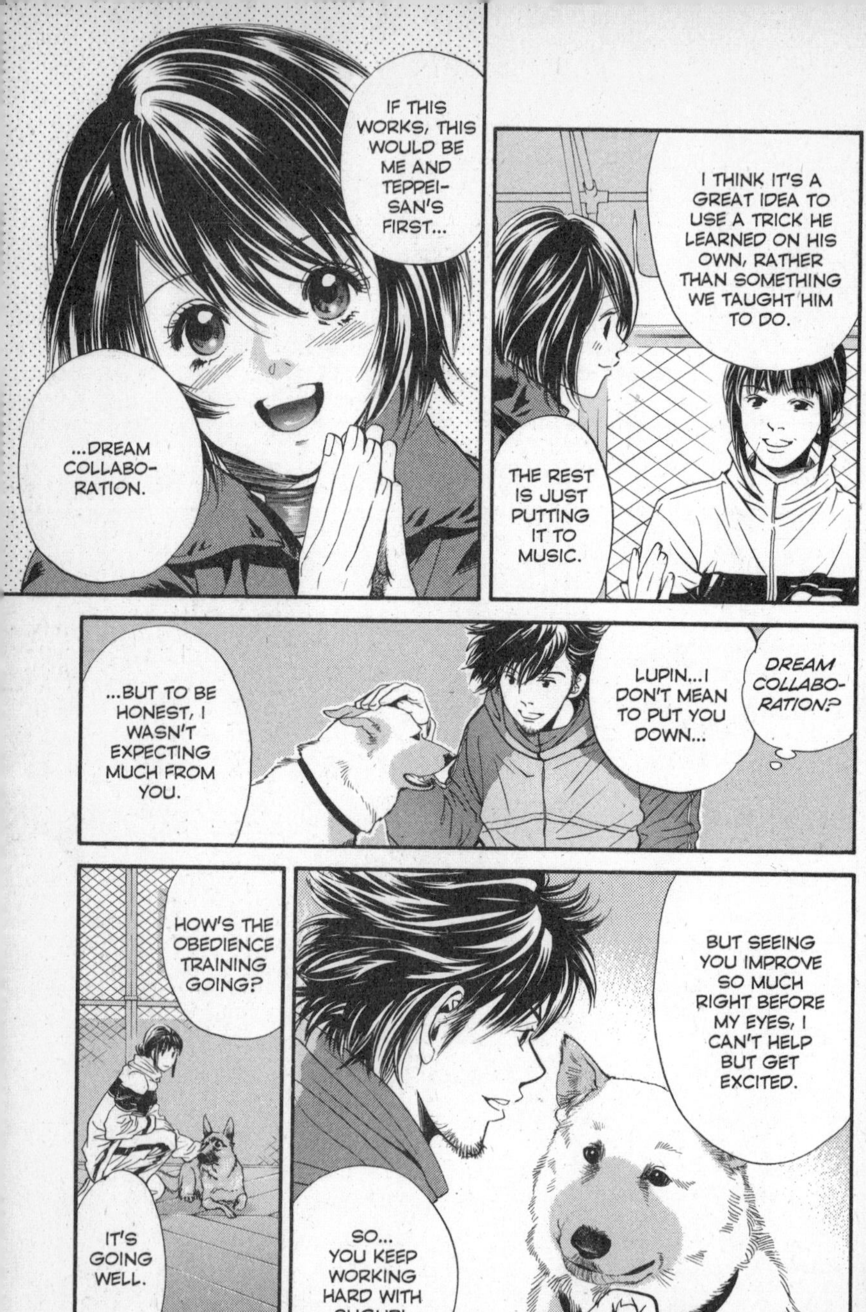
I THINK IT'S A GREAT IDEA TO USE A TRICK HE LEARNED ON HIS OWN, RATHER THAN SOMETHING WE TAUGHT HIM TO DO.
THE REST IS JUST PUTTING IT TO MUSIC.
IF THIS WORKS, THIS WOULD BE ME AND TEPPEI-SAN'S FIRST...
...DREAM COLLABO-RATION.
*DREAM COLLABO-RATION?*
LUPIN...I DON'T MEAN TO PUT YOU DOWN...
...BUT TO BE HONEST, I WASN'T EXPECTING MUCH FROM YOU.
BUT SEEING YOU IMPROVE SO MUCH RIGHT BEFORE MY EYES, I CAN'T HELP BUT GET EXCITED.
SO... YOU KEEP WORKING HARD WITH SUGURI, OKAY?
HOW'S THE OBEDIENCE TRAINING GOING?
IT'S GOING WELL.

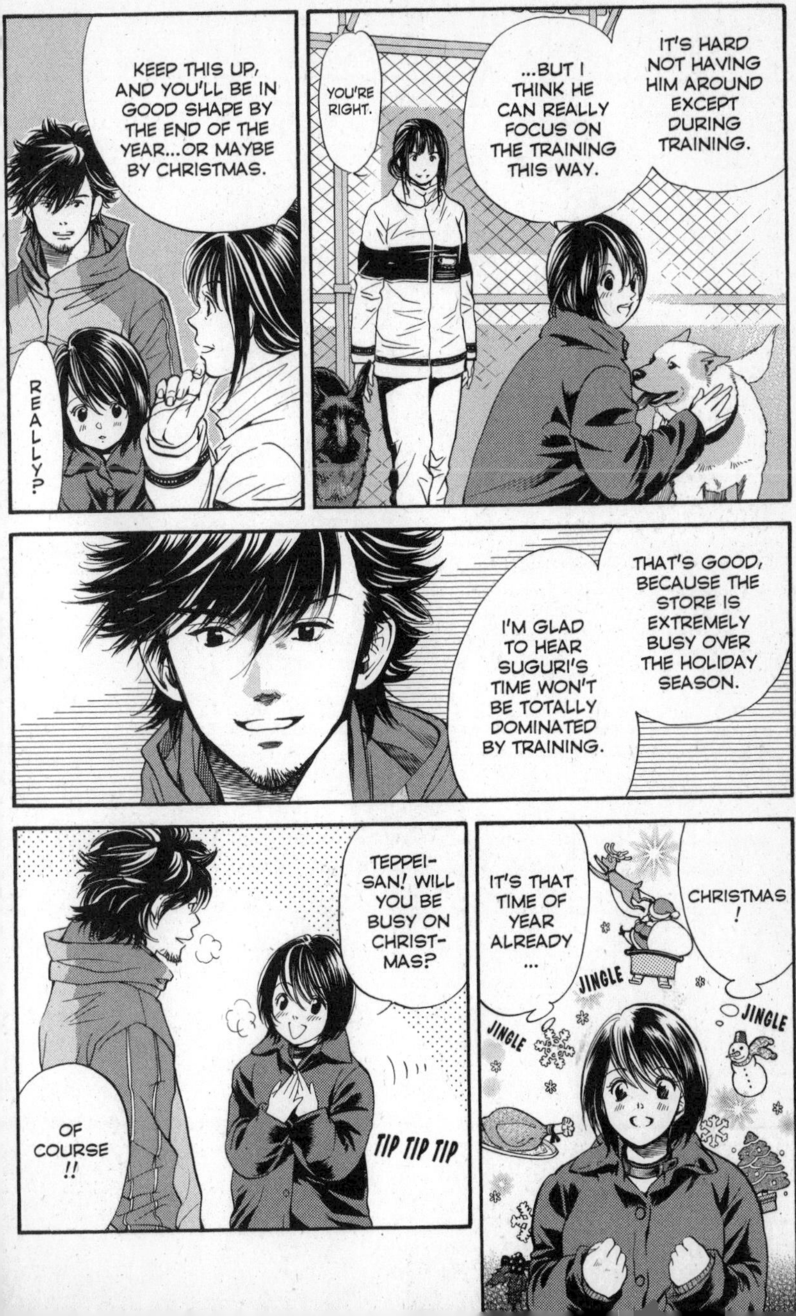
IT'S HARD NOT HAVING HIM AROUND EXCEPT DURING TRAINING.
...BUT I THINK HE CAN REALLY FOCUS ON THE TRAINING THIS WAY.
YOU'RE RIGHT.
KEEP THIS UP, AND YOU'LL BE IN GOOD SHAPE BY THE END OF THE YEAR...OR MAYBE BY CHRISTMAS.
REALLY?
THAT'S GOOD, BECAUSE THE STORE IS EXTREMELY BUSY OVER THE HOLIDAY SEASON.
I'M GLAD TO HEAR SUGURI'S TIME WON'T BE TOTALLY DOMINATED BY TRAINING.
CHRISTMAS!
IT'S THAT TIME OF YEAR ALREADY...
JINGLE
JINGLE
JINGLE
TEPPEI-SAN! WILL YOU BE BUSY ON CHRISTMAS?
TIP TIP TIP
OF COURSE!!

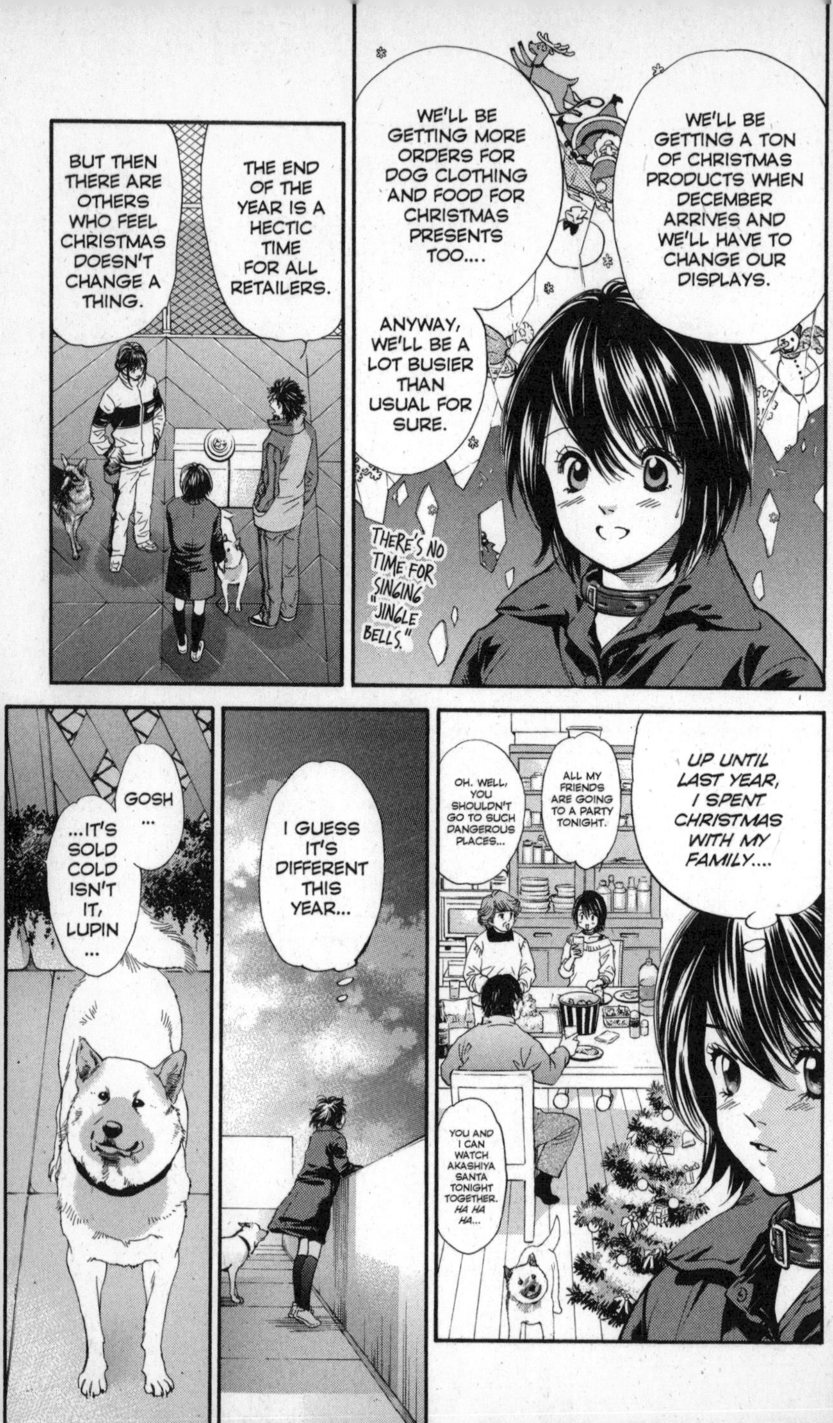
WE'LL BE GETTING A TON OF CHRISTMAS PRODUCTS WHEN DECEMBER ARRIVES AND WE'LL HAVE TO CHANGE OUR DISPLAYS.
WE'LL BE GETTING MORE ORDERS FOR DOG CLOTHING AND FOOD FOR CHRISTMAS PRESENTS TOO....
ANYWAY, WE'LL BE A LOT BUSIER THAN USUAL FOR SURE.
THERE'S NO TIME FOR SINGING "JINGLE BELLS."
THE END OF THE YEAR IS A HECTIC TIME FOR ALL RETAILERS.
BUT THEN THERE ARE OTHERS WHO FEEL CHRISTMAS DOESN'T CHANGE A THING.
UP UNTIL LAST YEAR, I SPENT CHRISTMAS WITH MY FAMILY....
ALL MY FRIENDS ARE GOING TO A PARTY TONIGHT.
OH. WELL, YOU SHOULDN'T GO TO SUCH DANGEROUS PLACES...
YOU AND I CAN WATCH AKASHIYA SANTA TONIGHT TOGETHER. HA HA HA...
I GUESS IT'S DIFFERENT THIS YEAR...
GOSH ...
...IT'S SOLD COLD ISN'T IT, LUPIN ...

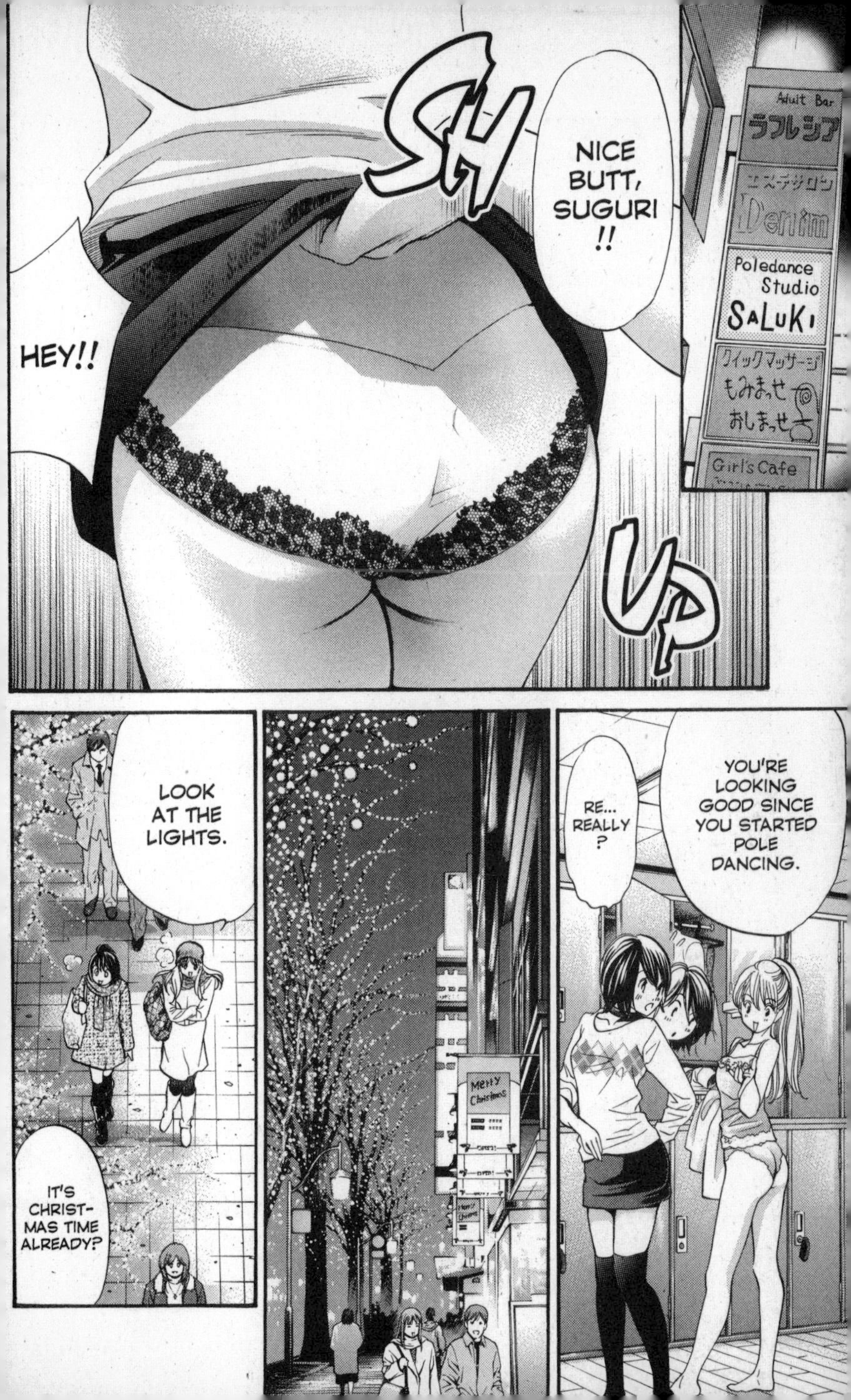
Adult Bar
ラフレシア
エステサロン
Denim
Poledance Studio
SALUKI
クイックマッサージ
もみまっせ
おしまっせ
Girl's Cafe
NICE BUTT, SUGURI!!
SH
UP
HEY!!
YOU'RE LOOKING GOOD SINCE YOU STARTED POLE DANCING.
RE... REALLY?
Merry Christmas
LOOK AT THE LIGHTS.
IT'S CHRISTMAS TIME ALREADY?

ARE YOU GOING ON A DATE WITH TEPPEI-SAN OR SOMETHING FOR CHRISTMAS?
I WISH. WE HAVE TO WORK. APPARENTLY IT GETS SUPER BUSY.
THAT'S NO FUN. YOU SHOULD AT LEAST GET HIM A PRESENT OR SOMETHING.
YEAH... YOU'RE RIGHT ...
HOW ABOUT...
...YOUR VIRGINITY ...?
CHI... CHIZURU-CHAN!
HEE HEE HEE
WHY NOT?! WHAT ARE YOU SAVING YOURSELF FOR?
IT'S NONE OF YOUR BUSINESS.
BESIDES, I'M FOCUSED ON THE DOG DANCE TRAINING RIGHT NOW.
WHAT A SHAME. YOU HAVE A REALLY SEXY BUTT NOW.

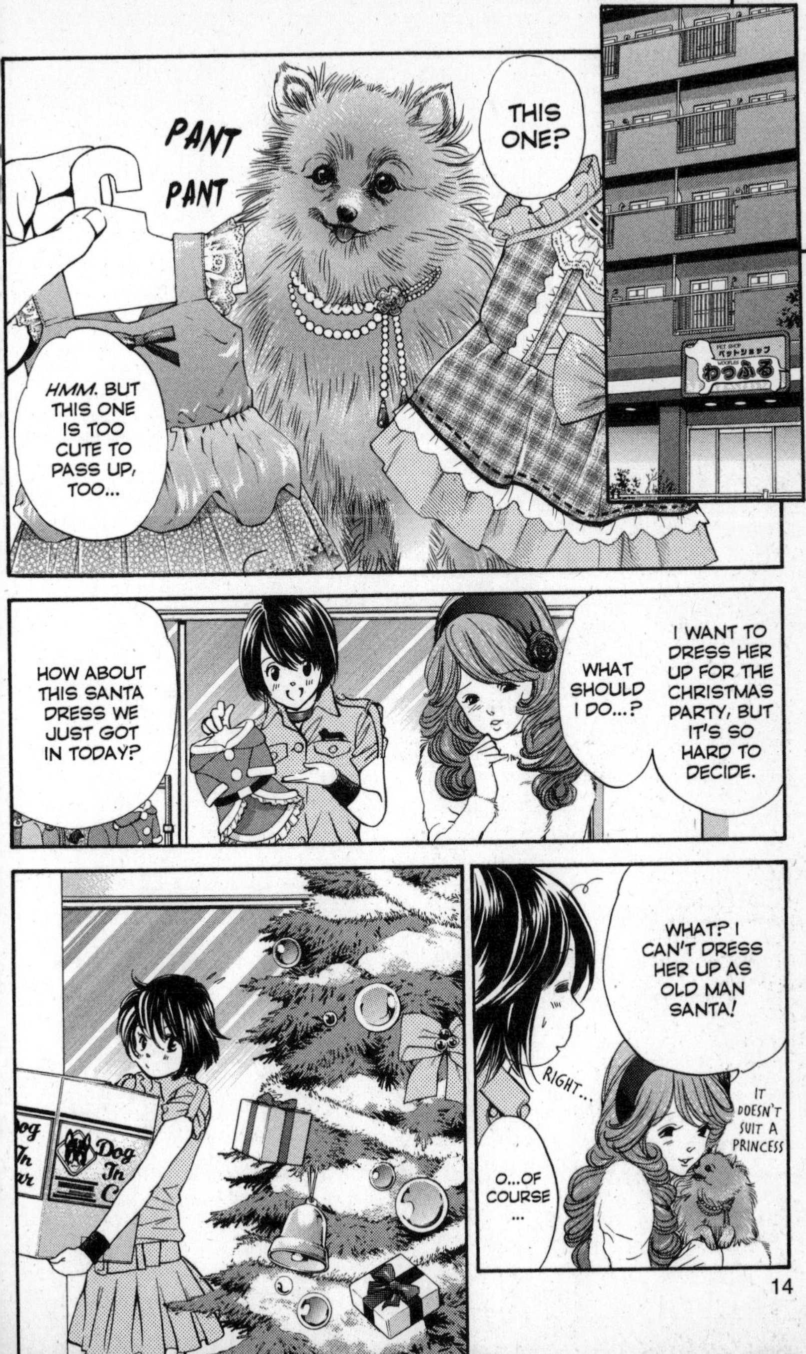
わっふる
THIS ONE?
PANT
PANT
HMM. BUT THIS ONE IS TOO CUTE TO PASS UP, TOO...
I WANT TO DRESS HER UP FOR THE CHRISTMAS PARTY, BUT IT'S SO HARD TO DECIDE.
WHAT SHOULD I DO...?
HOW ABOUT THIS SANTA DRESS WE JUST GOT IN TODAY?
WHAT? I CAN'T DRESS HER UP AS OLD MAN SANTA!
IT DOESN'T SUIT A PRINCESS
RIGHT...
O...OF COURSE ...

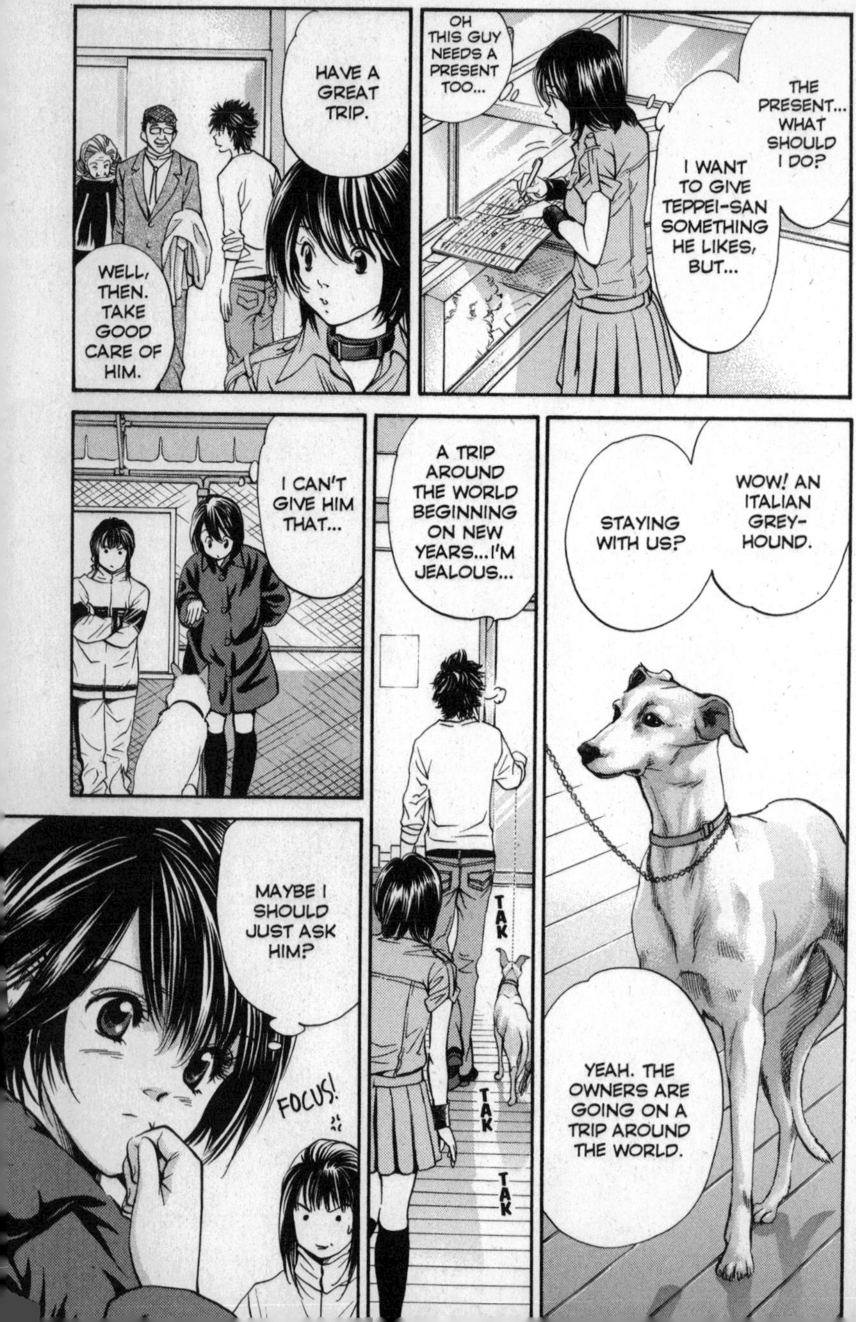
THE PRESENT... WHAT SHOULD I DO?
I WANT TO GIVE TEPPEI-SAN SOMETHING HE LIKES, BUT...
OH THIS GUY NEEDS A PRESENT TOO...
HAVE A GREAT TRIP.
WELL, THEN. TAKE GOOD CARE OF HIM.
WOW! AN ITALIAN GREY-HOUND.
STAYING WITH US?
YEAH. THE OWNERS ARE GOING ON A TRIP AROUND THE WORLD.
A TRIP AROUND THE WORLD BEGINNING ON NEW YEARS...I'M JEALOUS...
TAK
TAK
TAK
I CAN'T GIVE HIM THAT...
MAYBE I SHOULD JUST ASK HIM?
FOCUS!

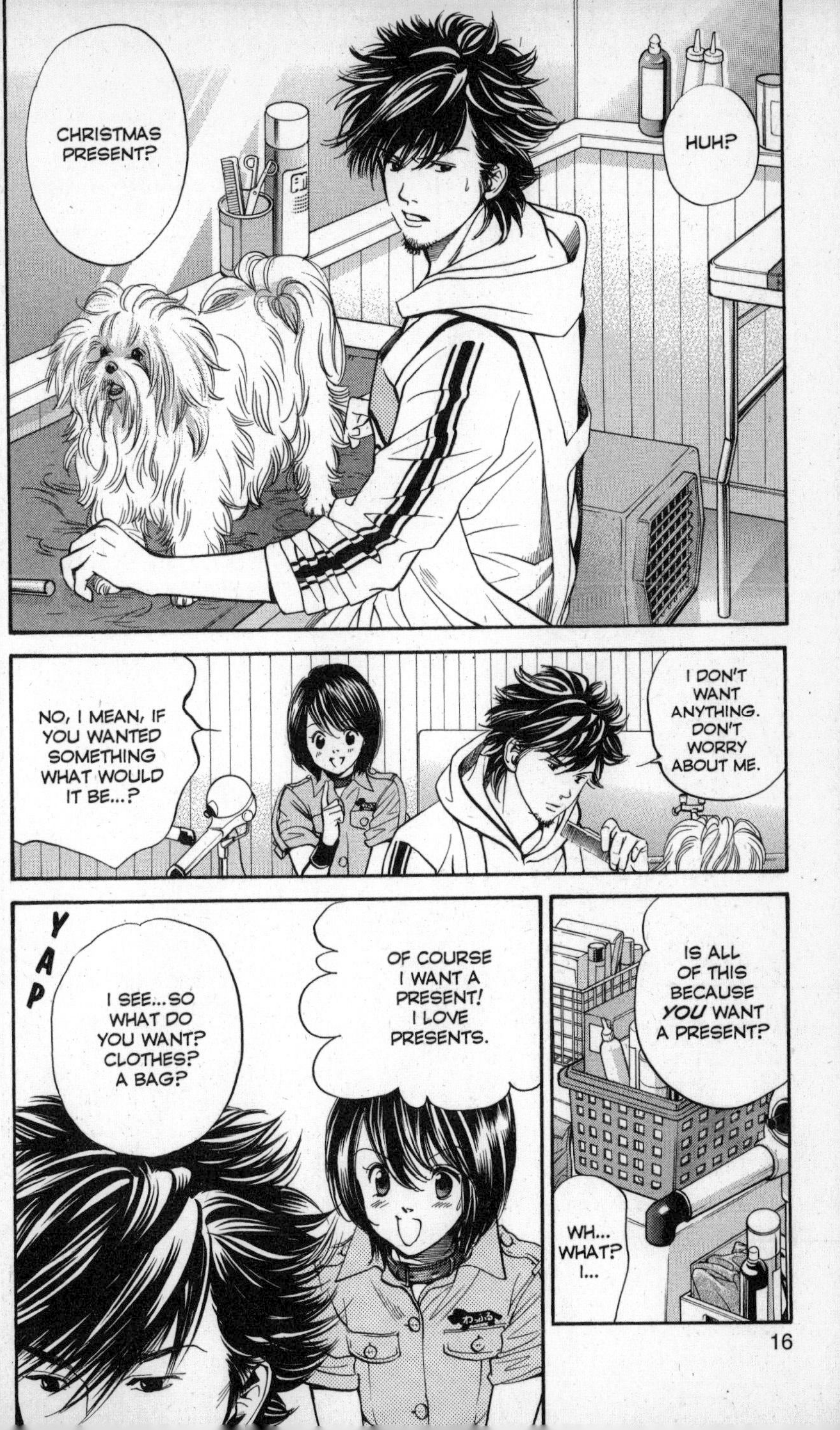

HUH?
CHRISTMAS PRESENT?
I DON'T WANT ANYTHING. DON'T WORRY ABOUT ME.
NO, I MEAN, IF YOU WANTED SOMETHING WHAT WOULD IT BE...?
IS ALL OF THIS BECAUSE *YOU* WANT A PRESENT?
WH... WHAT? I...
OF COURSE I WANT A PRESENT! I LOVE PRESENTS.
I SEE...SO WHAT DO YOU WANT? CLOTHES? A BAG?
YAP

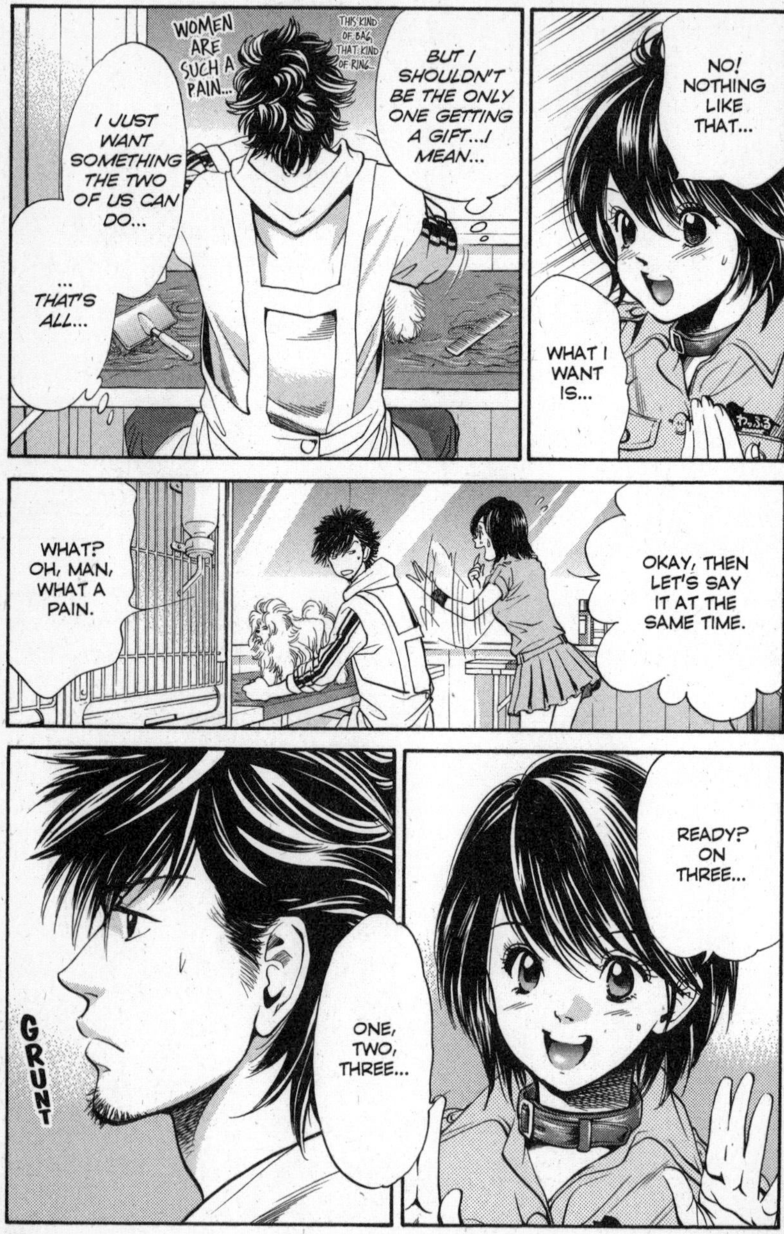
NO! NOTHING LIKE THAT...
WHAT I WANT IS...
BUT I SHOULDN'T BE THE ONLY ONE GETTING A GIFT...I MEAN...
THIS KIND OF BAG, THAT KIND OF RING...
WOMEN ARE SUCH A PAIN...
I JUST WANT SOMETHING THE TWO OF US CAN DO...
... THAT'S ALL...
OKAY, THEN LET'S SAY IT AT THE SAME TIME.
WHAT? OH, MAN, WHAT A PAIN.
READY? ON THREE...
ONE, TWO, THREE...
GRUNT

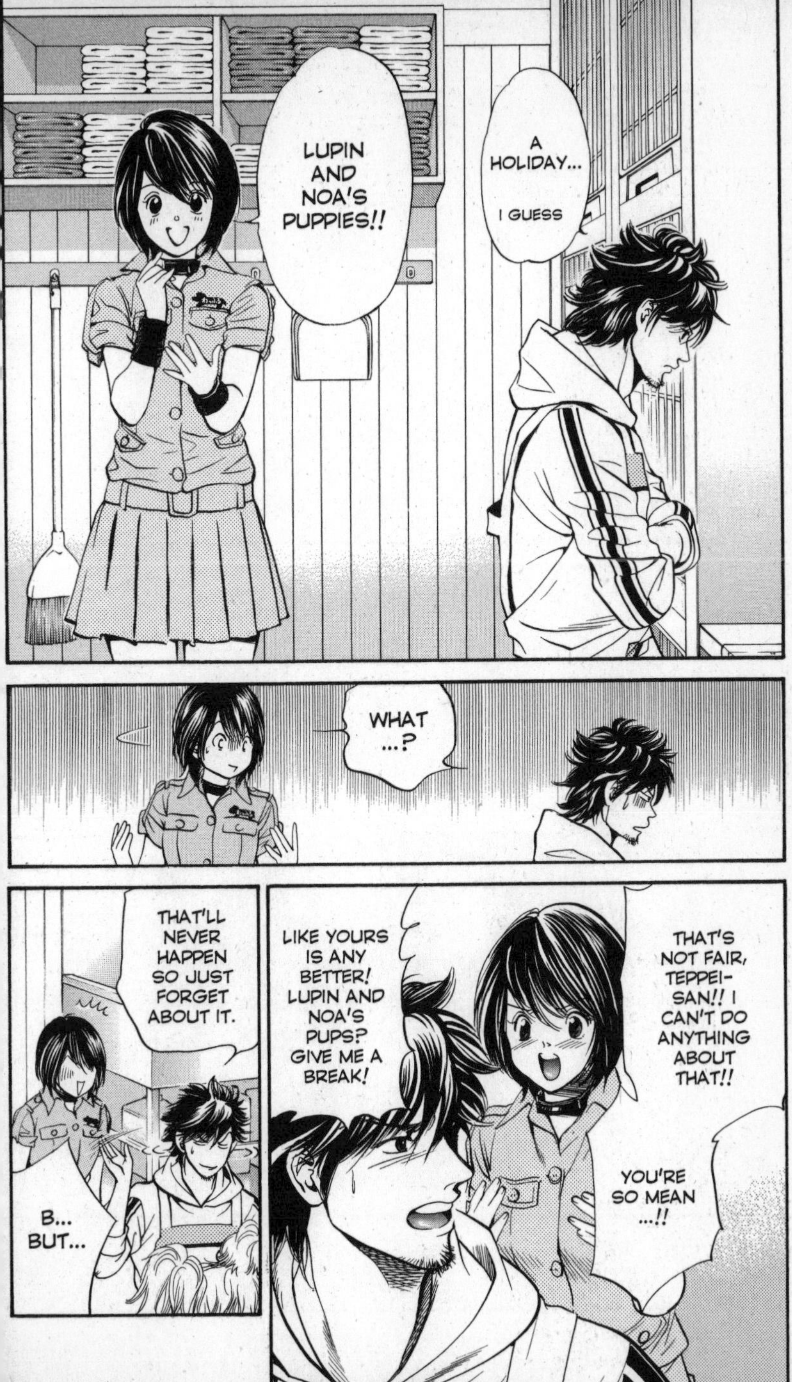
A HOLIDAY... I GUESS
LUPIN AND NOA'S PUPPIES!!
WHAT ...?
LIKE YOURS IS ANY BETTER! LUPIN AND NOA'S PUPS? GIVE ME A BREAK!
THAT'S NOT FAIR, TEPPEI-SAN!! I CAN'T DO ANYTHING ABOUT THAT!!
YOU'RE SO MEAN ...!!
THAT'LL NEVER HAPPEN SO JUST FORGET ABOUT IT.
B... BUT...

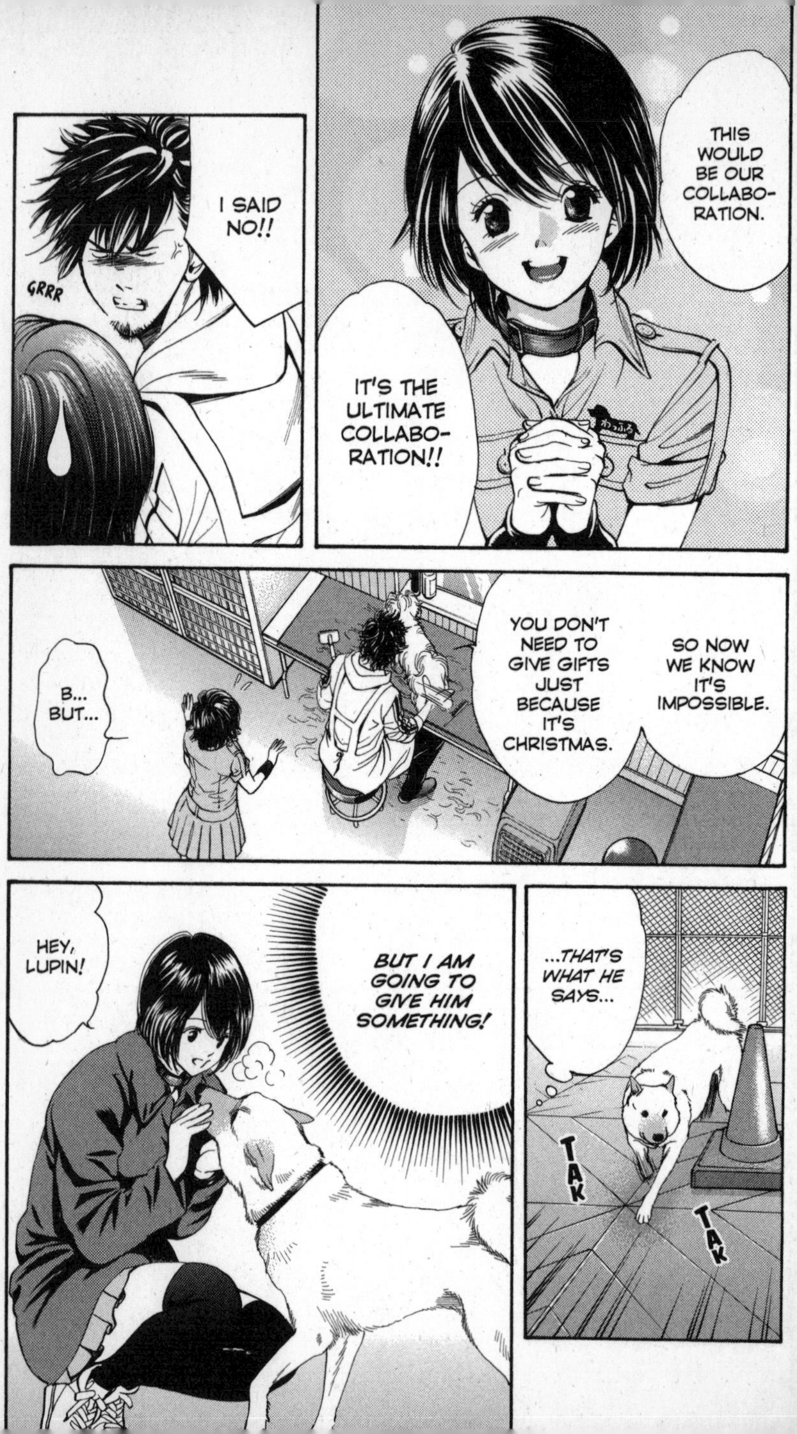
THIS WOULD BE OUR COLLABO-RATION.
IT'S THE ULTIMATE COLLABO-RATION!!
I SAID NO!!
GRRR
SO NOW WE KNOW IT'S IMPOSSIBLE.
YOU DON'T NEED TO GIVE GIFTS JUST BECAUSE IT'S CHRISTMAS.
B... BUT...
...THAT'S WHAT HE SAYS...
TAK
TAK
BUT I AM GOING TO GIVE HIM SOMETHING!
HEY, LUPIN!

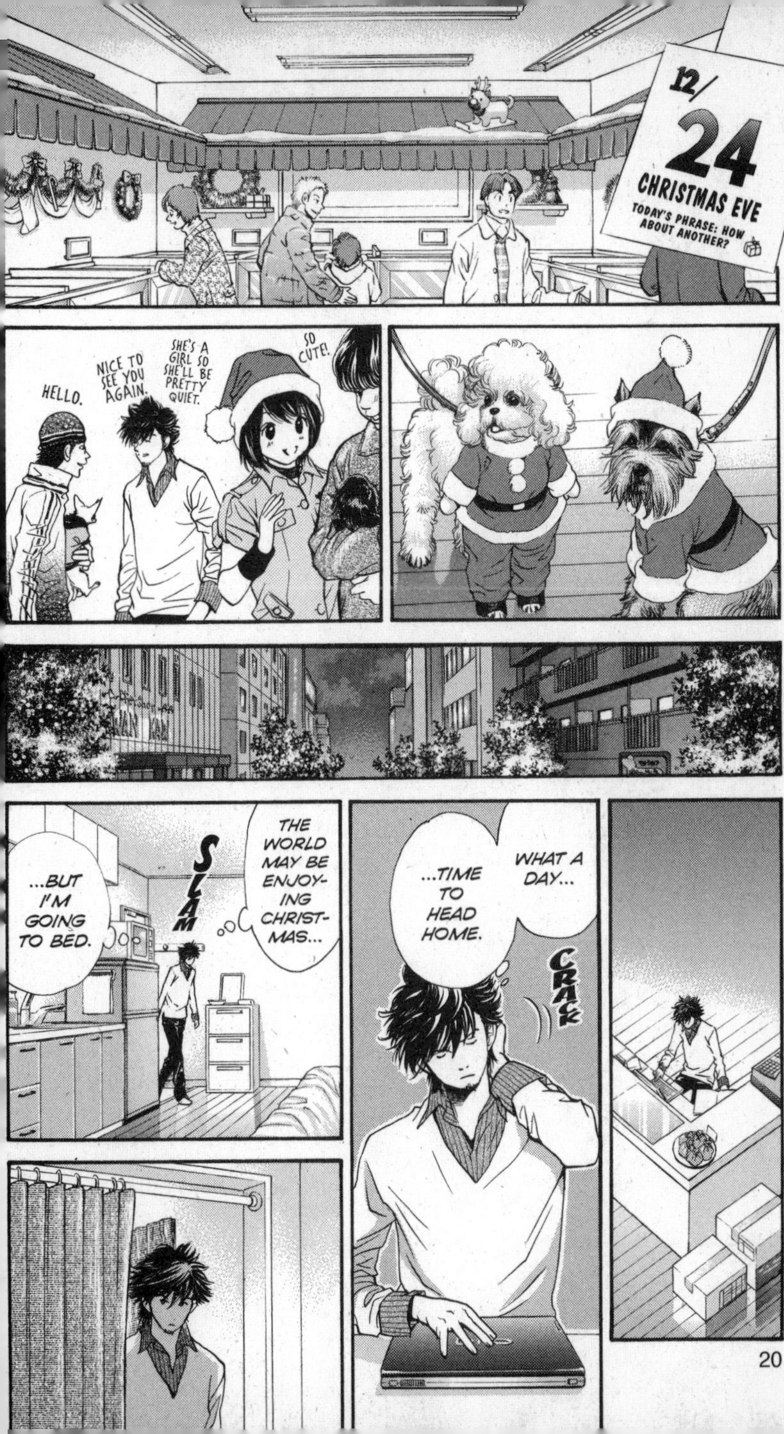
12/
24
CHRISTMAS EVE
TODAY'S PHRASE: HOW ABOUT ANOTHER?
SO CUTE!
SHE'S A GIRL SO SHE'LL BE PRETTY QUIET.
NICE TO SEE YOU AGAIN.
HELLO.
WHAT A DAY...
...TIME TO HEAD HOME.
CRACK
THE WORLD MAY BE ENJOYING CHRISTMAS...
SLAM
...BUT I'M GOING TO BED.

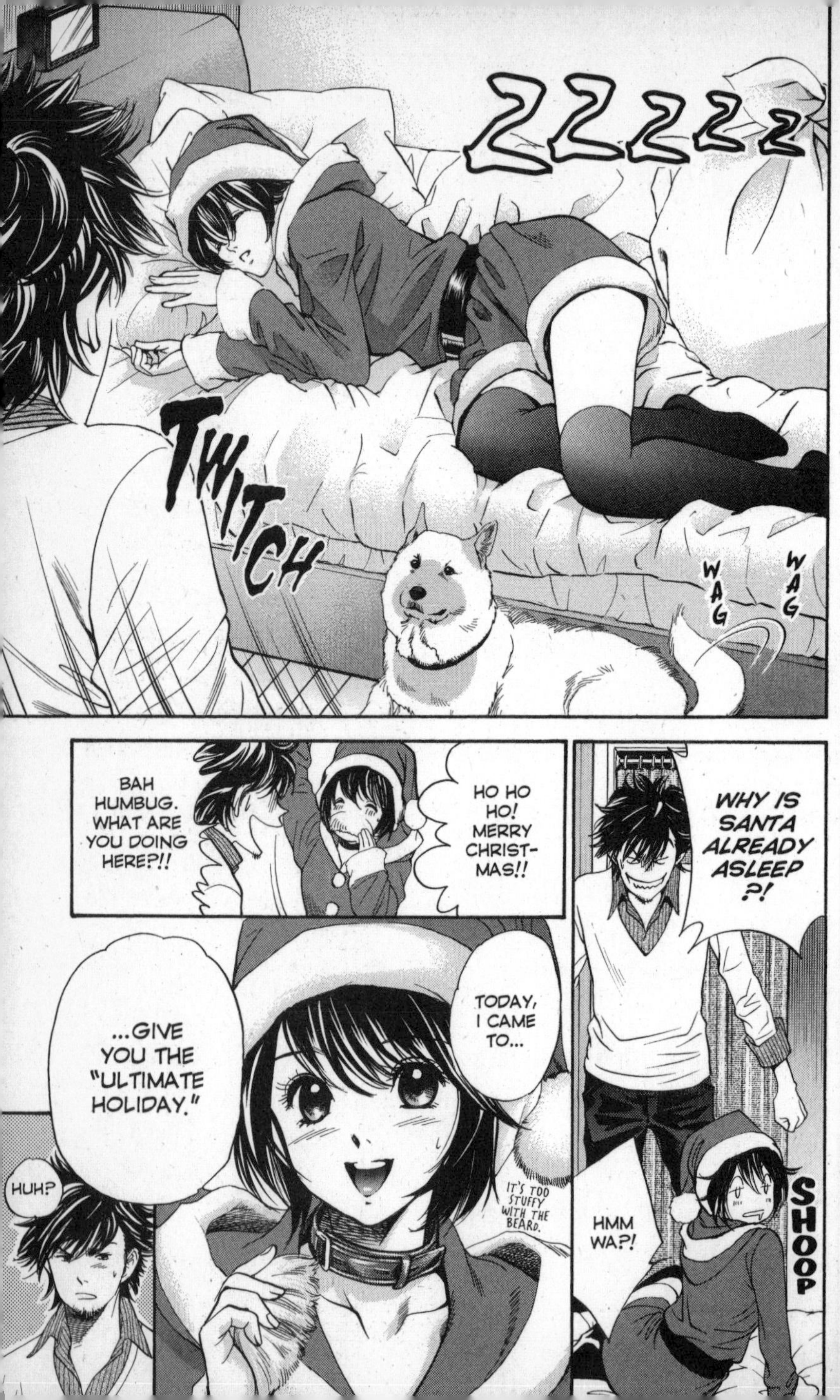
ZZZZZZ
WAG WAG
TWITCH
WHY IS SANTA ALREADY ASLEEP ?!
SHOOP
HMM WA?!
HO HO HO! MERRY CHRIST-MAS!!
BAH HUMBUG. WHAT ARE YOU DOING HERE?!!
TODAY, I CAME TO...
IT'S TOO STUFFY WITH THE BEARD.
...GIVE YOU THE "ULTIMATE HOLIDAY."
HUH?

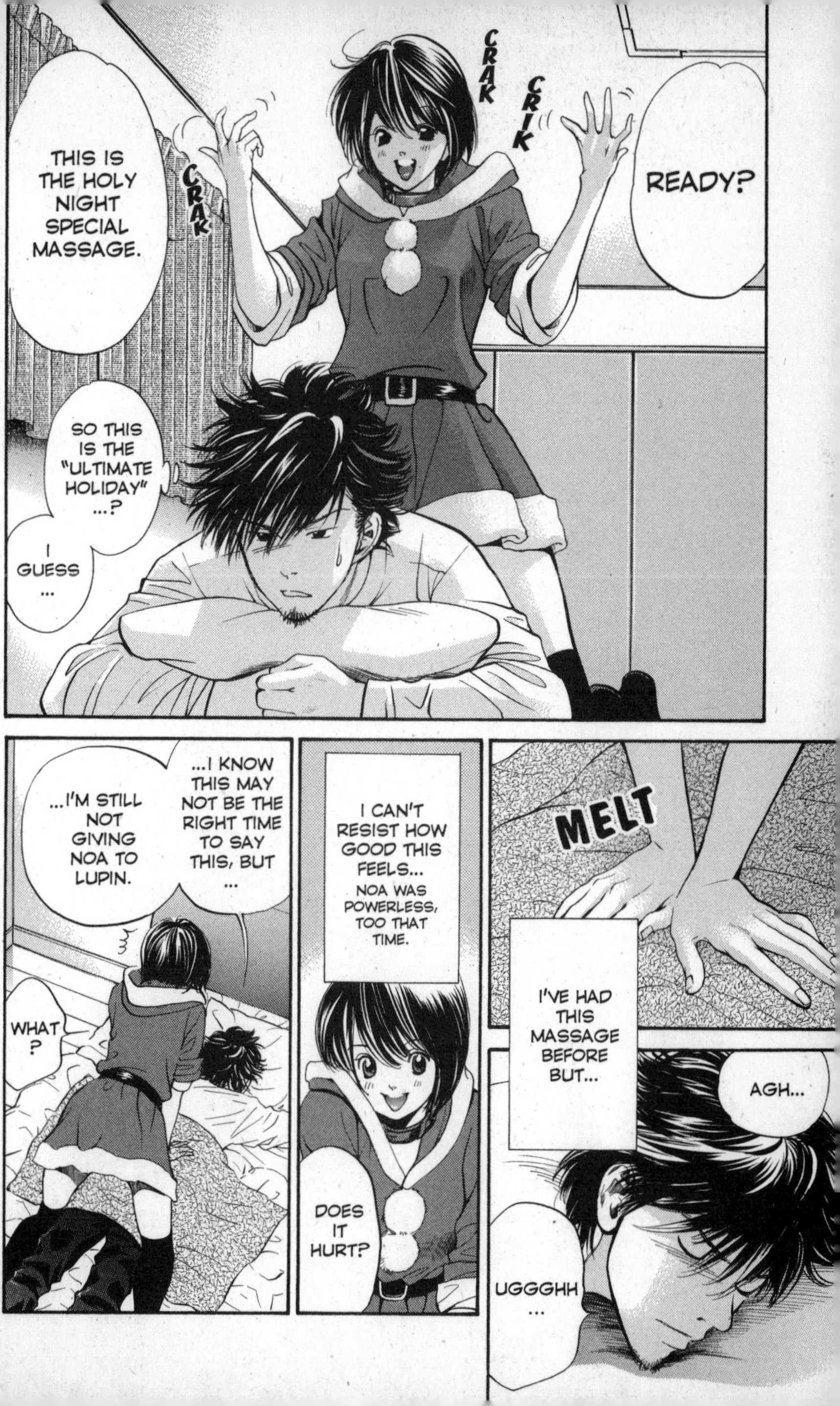
READY?
CRAK
CRIK
CRAK
THIS IS THE HOLY NIGHT SPECIAL MASSAGE.
SO THIS IS THE "ULTIMATE HOLIDAY" ...?
I GUESS ...
MELT
I'VE HAD THIS MASSAGE BEFORE BUT...
AGH...
UGGGHH ...
I CAN'T RESIST HOW GOOD THIS FEELS... NOA WAS POWERLESS, TOO THAT TIME.
DOES IT HURT?
...I KNOW THIS MAY NOT BE THE RIGHT TIME TO SAY THIS, BUT ...
...I'M STILL NOT GIVING NOA TO LUPIN.
WHAT ?

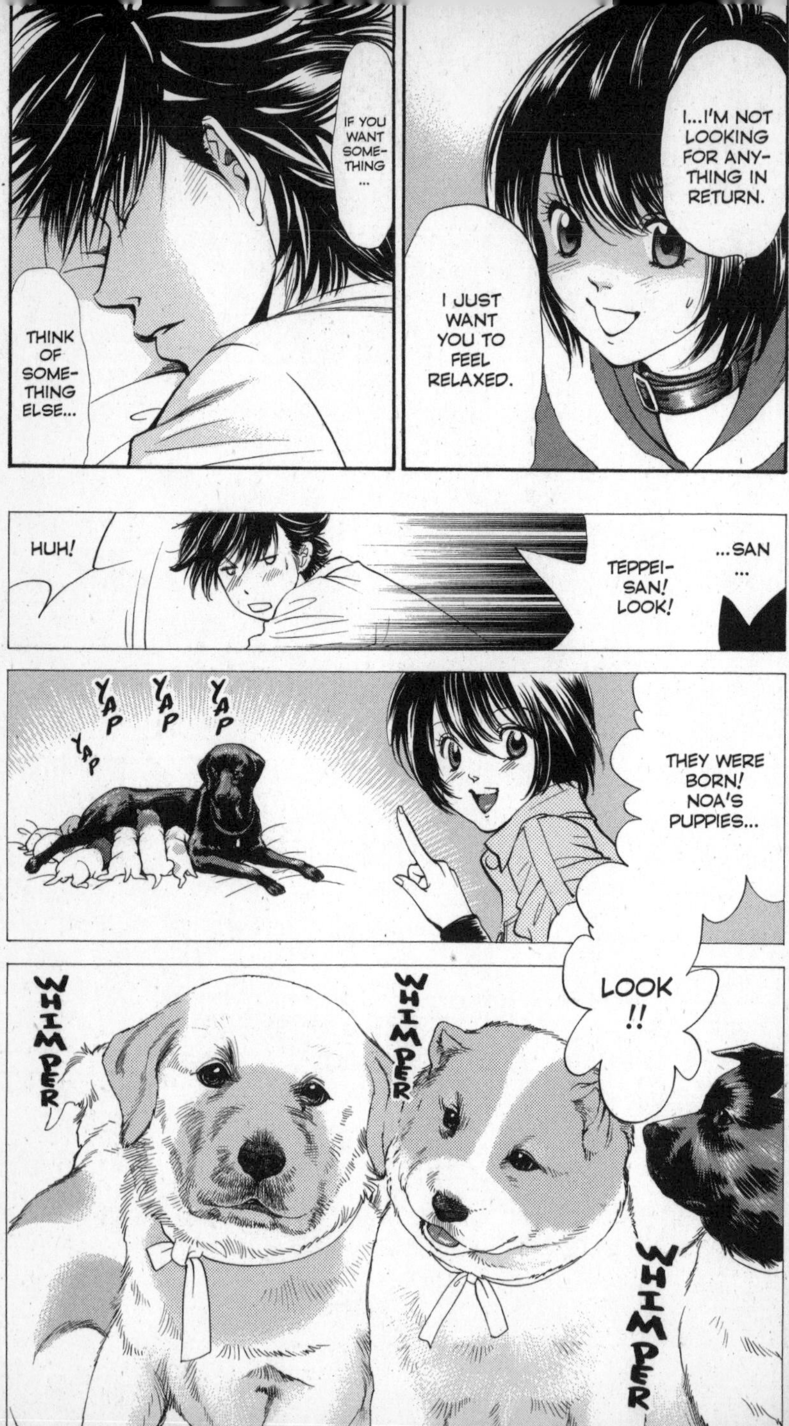

I...I'M NOT LOOKING FOR ANYTHING IN RETURN.
I JUST WANT YOU TO FEEL RELAXED.
IF YOU WANT SOMETHING...
THINK OF SOMETHING ELSE...
...SAN ...
TEPPEI-SAN! LOOK!
HUH!
THEY WERE BORN! NOA'S PUPPIES...
YAP
YAP
YAP
YAP
LOOK !!
WHIMPER
WHIMPER
WHIMPER

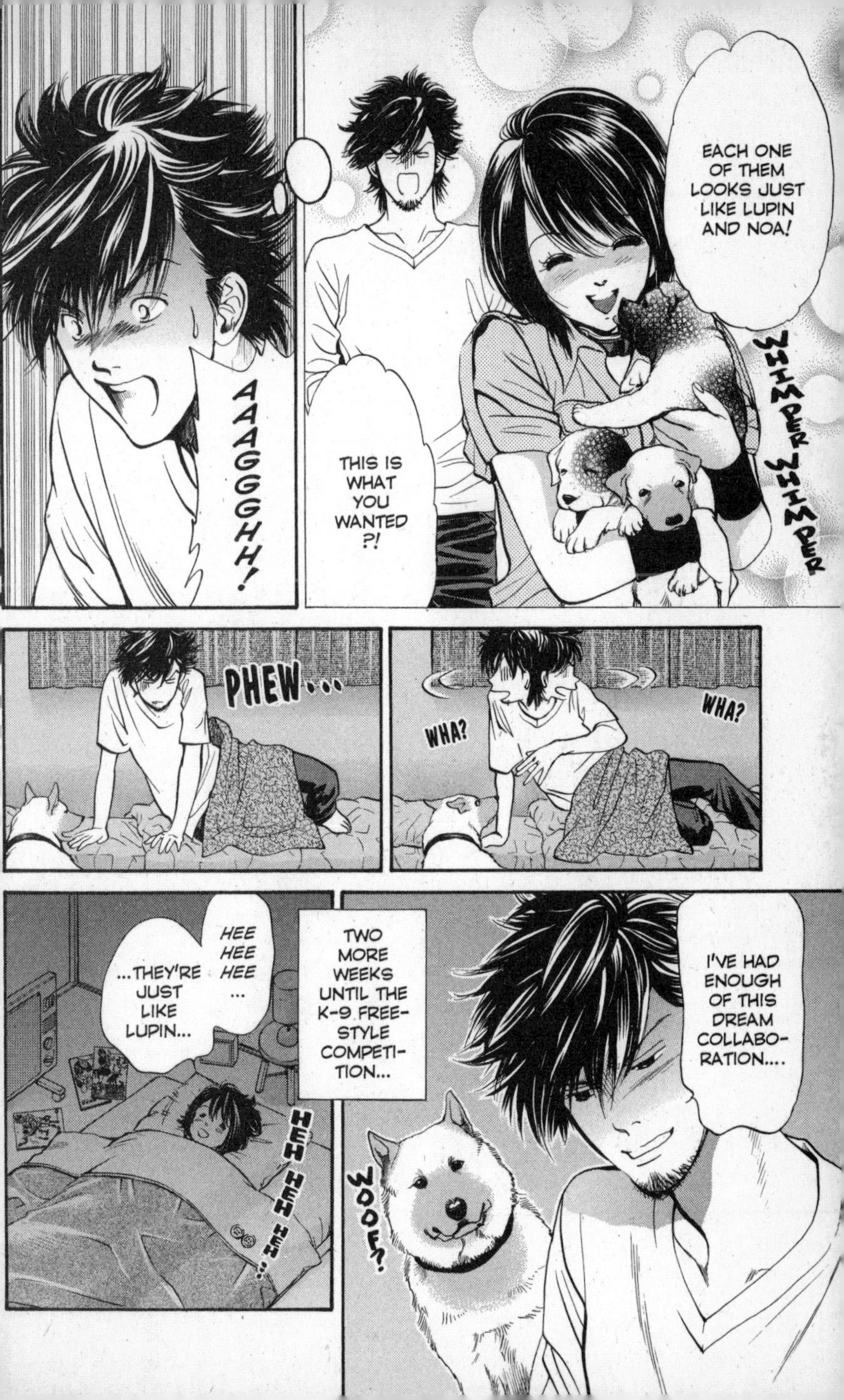
EACH ONE OF THEM LOOKS JUST LIKE LUPIN AND NOA!
WHIMPER WHIMPER
THIS IS WHAT YOU WANTED ?!
AAAAGGGHH!
WHA?
WHA?
PHEW...
I'VE HAD ENOUGH OF THIS DREAM COLLABO-RATION....
WOOF?
TWO MORE WEEKS UNTIL THE K-9 FREE-STYLE COMPETI-TION...
HEE HEE HEE ...
...THEY'RE JUST LIKE LUPIN...
HEH HEH HEH...

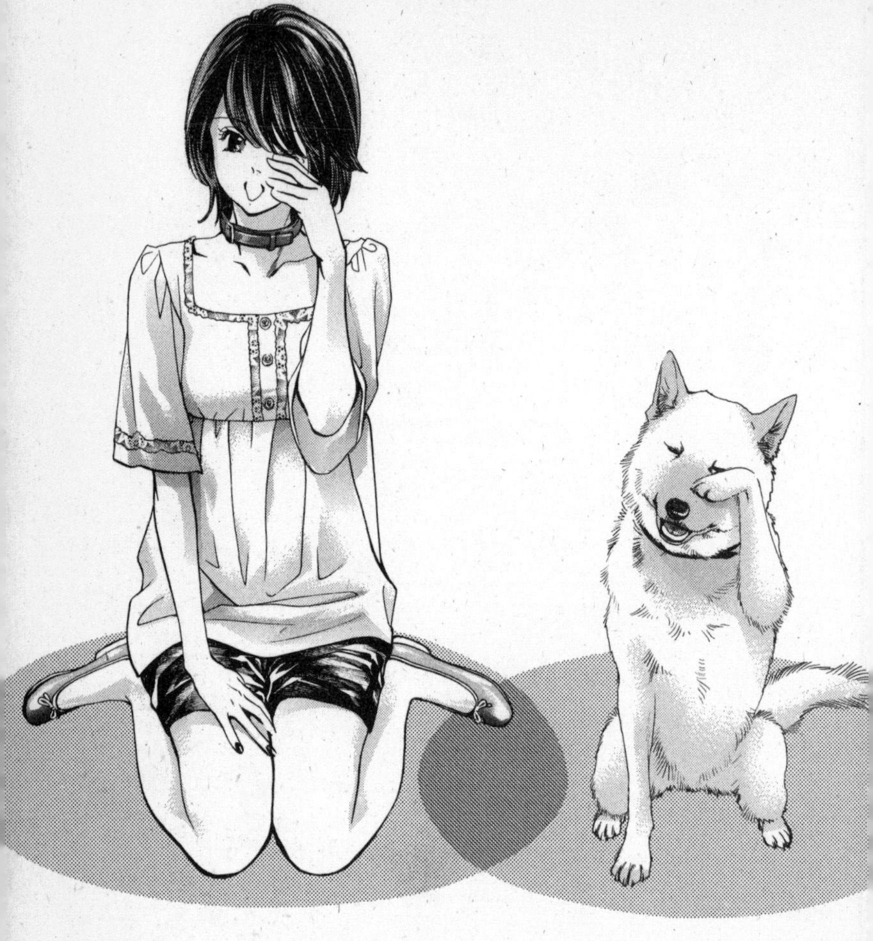

# CHAPTER 121: LUPIN'S TALENT

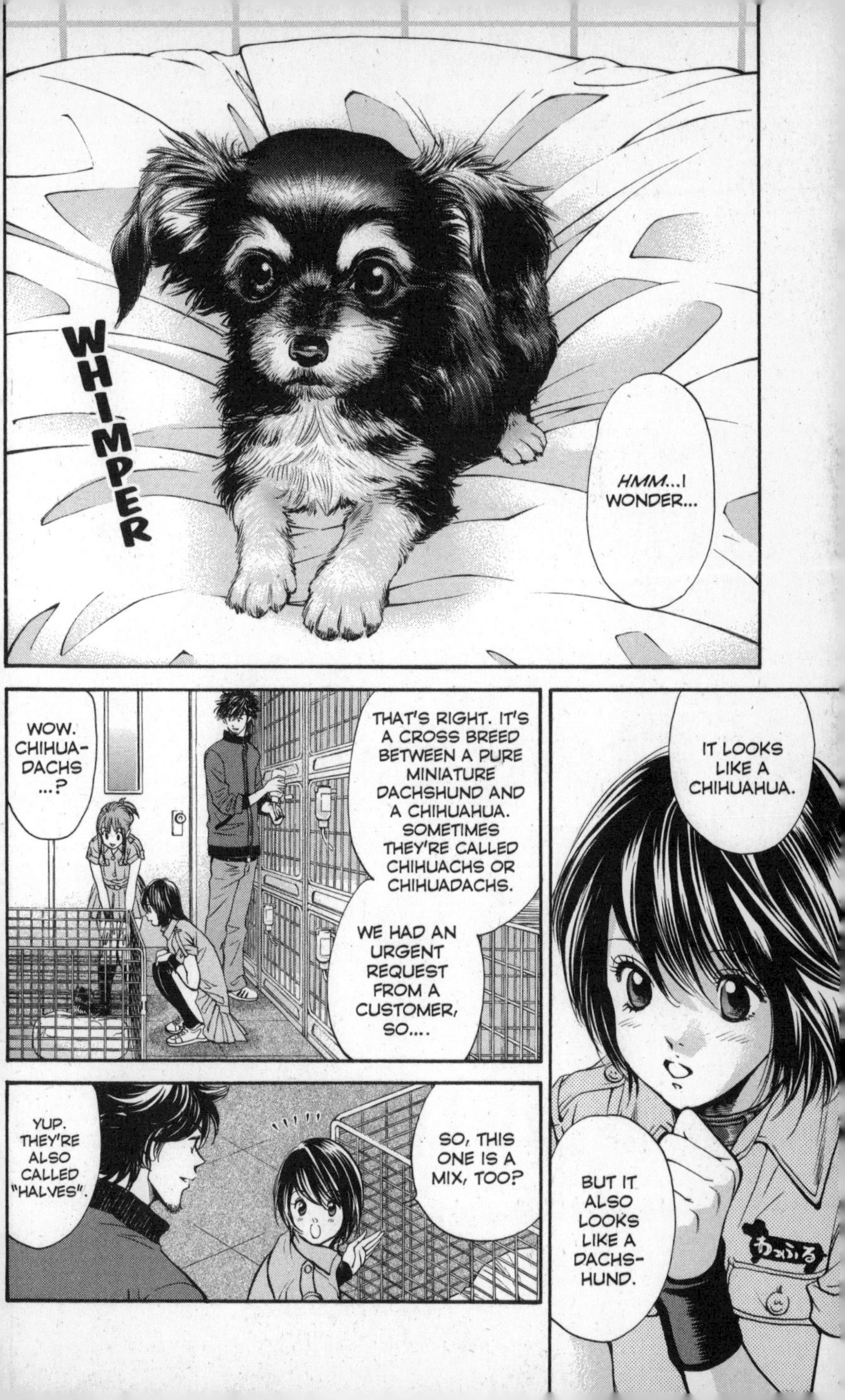
HMM...I WONDER...
WHIMPER
IT LOOKS LIKE A CHIHUAHUA.
BUT IT ALSO LOOKS LIKE A DACHS-HUND.
THAT'S RIGHT. IT'S A CROSS BREED BETWEEN A PURE MINIATURE DACHSHUND AND A CHIHUAHUA. SOMETIMES THEY'RE CALLED CHIHUACHS OR CHIHUADACHS.
WOW. CHIHUA-DACHS ...?
WE HAD AN URGENT REQUEST FROM A CUSTOMER, SO....
SO, THIS ONE IS A MIX, TOO?
YUP. THEY'RE ALSO CALLED "HALVES".

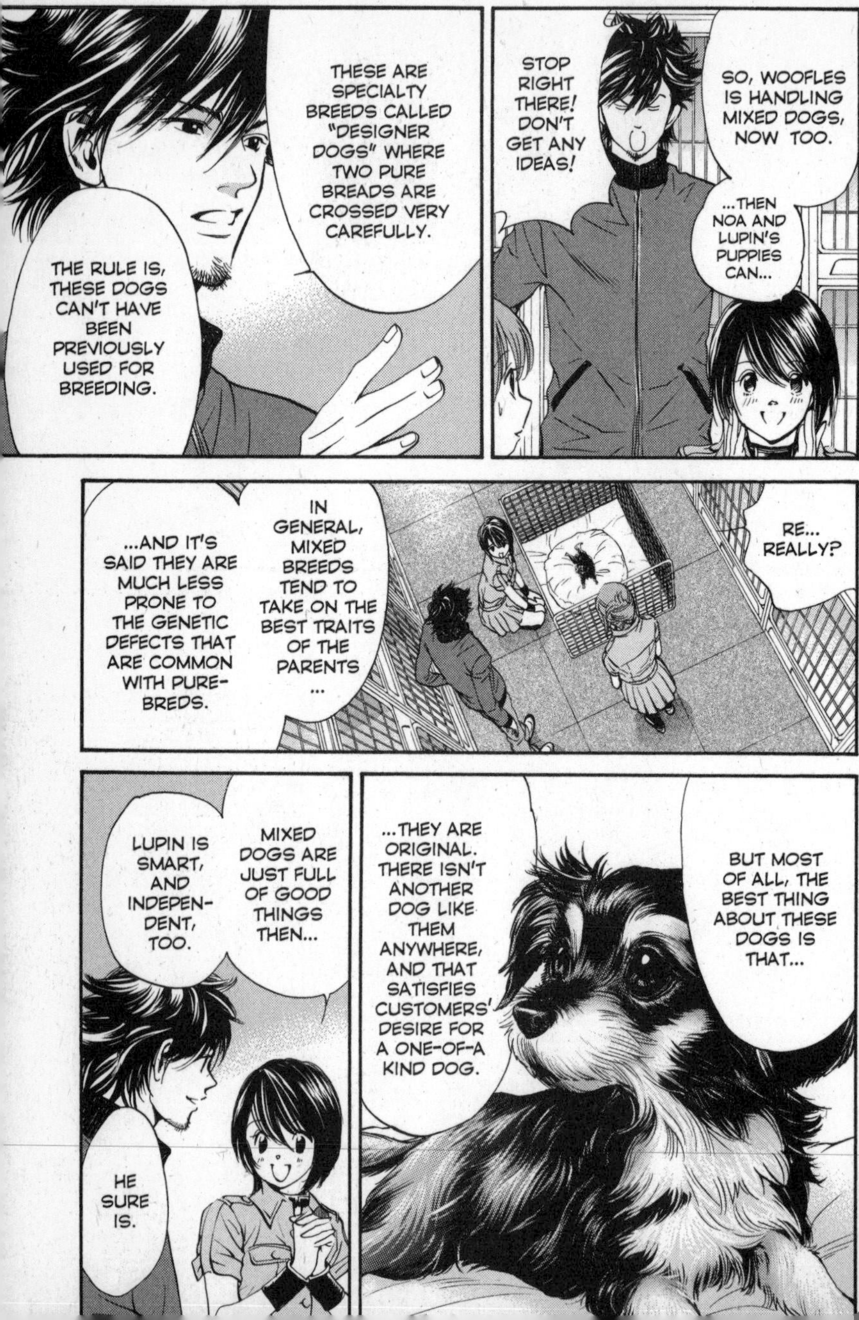
SO, WOOFLES IS HANDLING MIXED DOGS, NOW TOO.
...THEN NOA AND LUPIN'S PUPPIES CAN...
STOP RIGHT THERE! DON'T GET ANY IDEAS!
THESE ARE SPECIALTY BREEDS CALLED "DESIGNER DOGS" WHERE TWO PURE BREADS ARE CROSSED VERY CAREFULLY.
THE RULE IS, THESE DOGS CAN'T HAVE BEEN PREVIOUSLY USED FOR BREEDING.
RE... REALLY?
IN GENERAL, MIXED BREEDS TEND TO TAKE ON THE BEST TRAITS OF THE PARENTS ...
...AND IT'S SAID THEY ARE MUCH LESS PRONE TO THE GENETIC DEFECTS THAT ARE COMMON WITH PURE-BREDS.
BUT MOST OF ALL, THE BEST THING ABOUT THESE DOGS IS THAT...
...THEY ARE ORIGINAL. THERE ISN'T ANOTHER DOG LIKE THEM ANYWHERE, AND THAT SATISFIES CUSTOMERS' DESIRE FOR A ONE-OF-A KIND DOG.
MIXED DOGS ARE JUST FULL OF GOOD THINGS THEN...
LUPIN IS SMART, AND INDEPEN-DENT, TOO.
HE SURE IS.

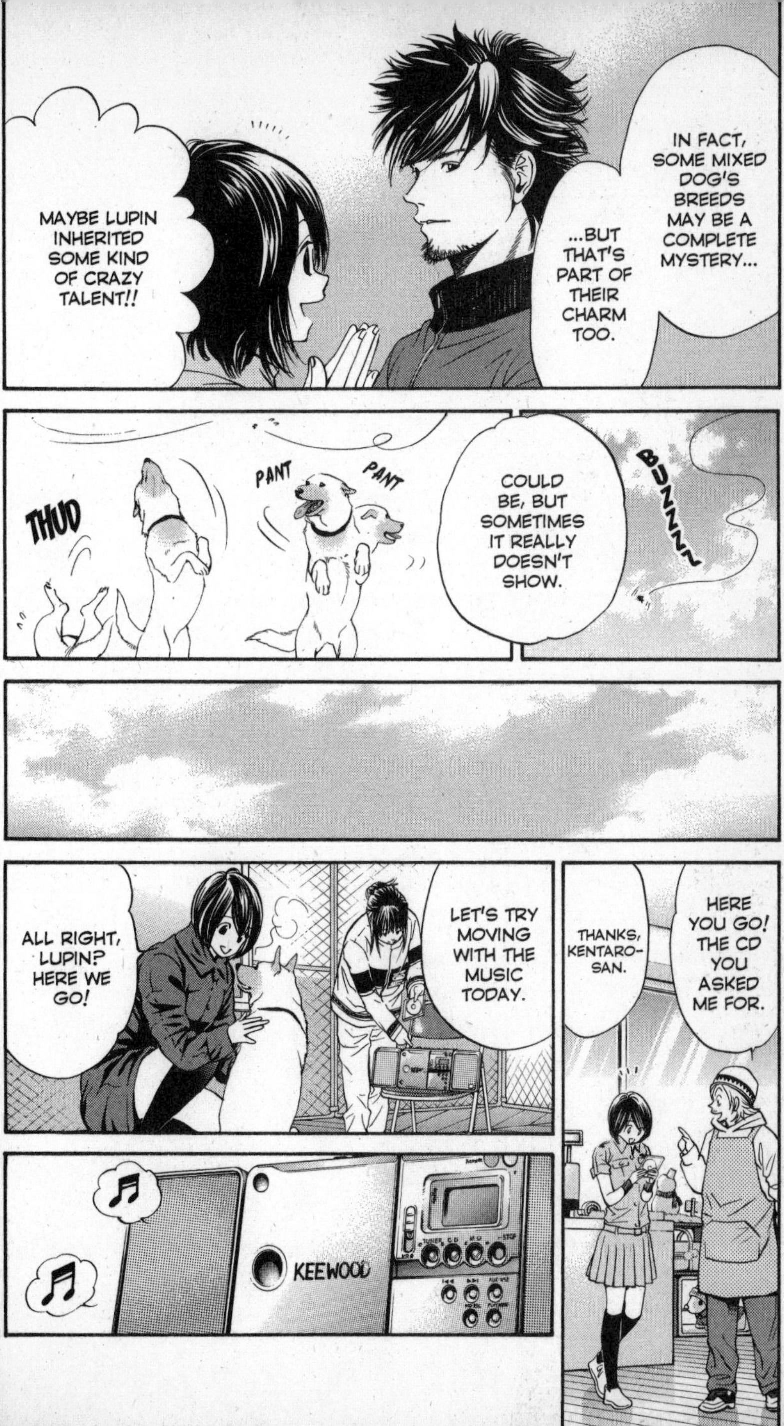

IN FACT, SOME MIXED DOG'S BREEDS MAY BE A COMPLETE MYSTERY...
...BUT THAT'S PART OF THEIR CHARM TOO.
MAYBE LUPIN INHERITED SOME KIND OF CRAZY TALENT!!
BUZZZZ
COULD BE, BUT SOMETIMES IT REALLY DOESN'T SHOW.
PANT
PANT
THUD
HERE YOU GO! THE CD YOU ASKED ME FOR.
THANKS, KENTARO-SAN.
LET'S TRY MOVING WITH THE MUSIC TODAY.
ALL RIGHT, LUPIN? HERE WE GO!
KEEWOOD

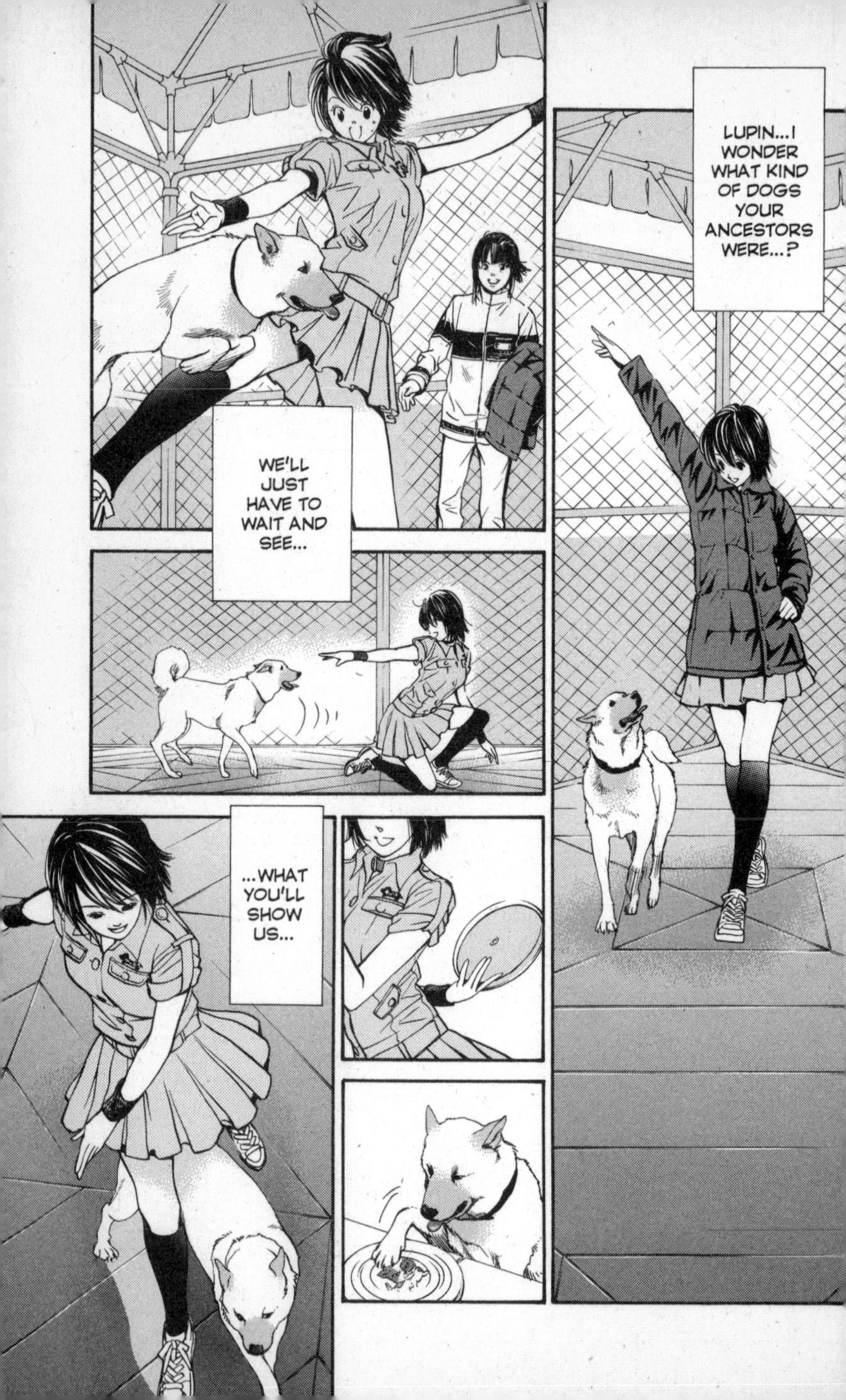
LUPIN...I WONDER WHAT KIND OF DOGS YOUR ANCESTORS WERE...?
WE'LL JUST HAVE TO WAIT AND SEE...
...WHAT YOU'LL SHOW US...

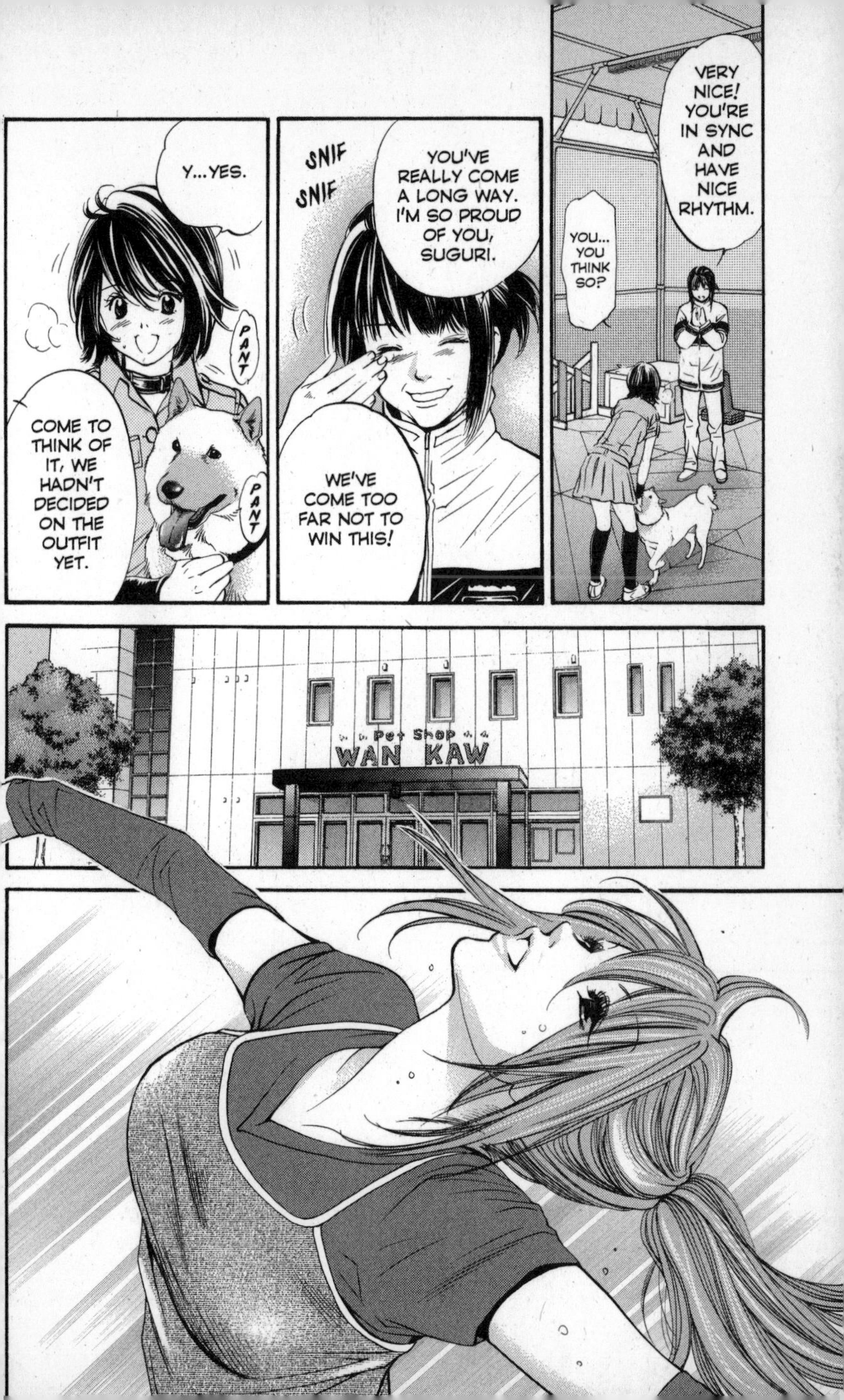
VERY NICE! YOU'RE IN SYNC AND HAVE NICE RHYTHM.
YOU... YOU THINK SO?
SNIF
SNIF
YOU'VE REALLY COME A LONG WAY. I'M SO PROUD OF YOU, SUGURI.
WE'VE COME TOO FAR NOT TO WIN THIS!
Y...YES.
PANT
PANT
COME TO THINK OF IT, WE HADN'T DECIDED ON THE OUTFIT YET.
Pet Shop
WAN KAW

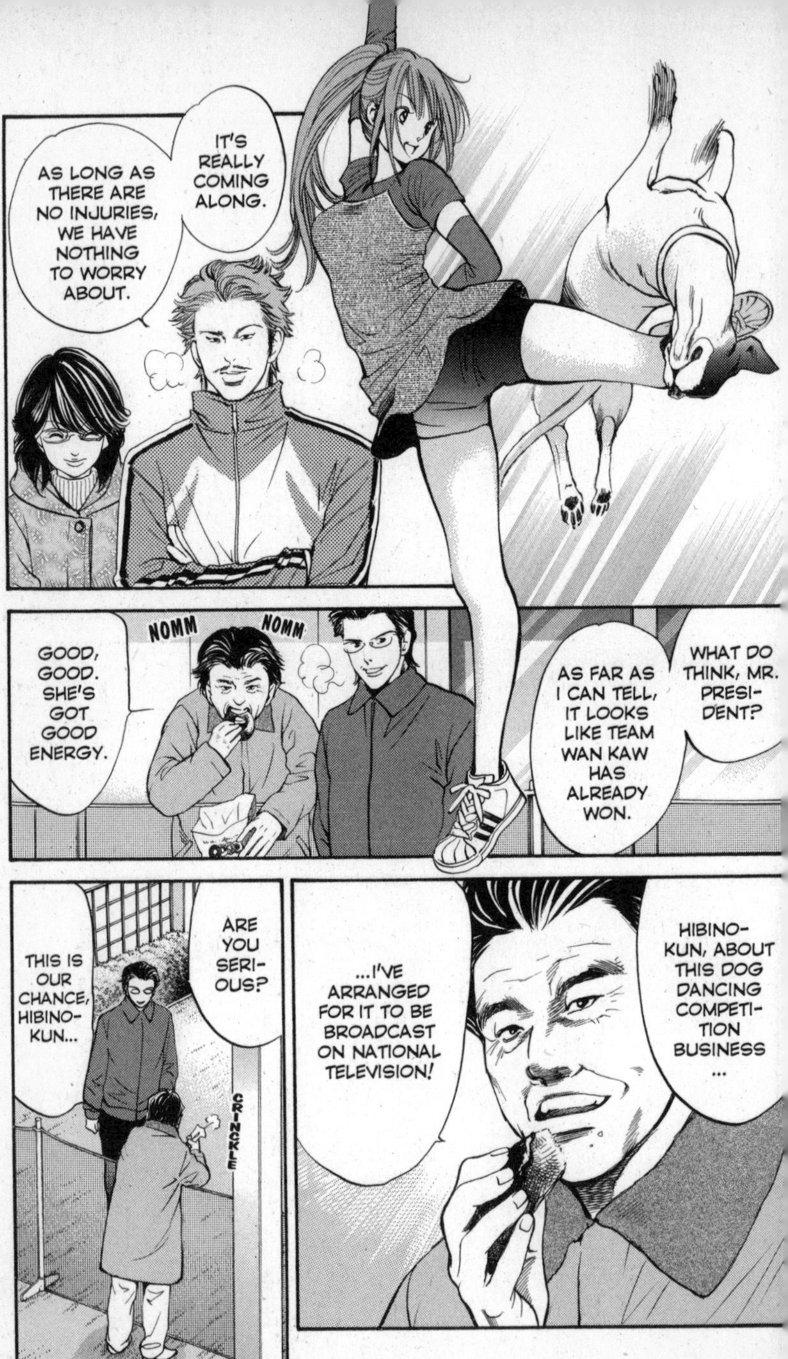
IT'S REALLY COMING ALONG.
AS LONG AS THERE ARE NO INJURIES, WE HAVE NOTHING TO WORRY ABOUT.
WHAT DO THINK, MR. PRESIDENT?
AS FAR AS I CAN TELL, IT LOOKS LIKE TEAM WAN KAW HAS ALREADY WON.
NOMM NOMM
GOOD, GOOD. SHE'S GOT GOOD ENERGY.
HIBINO-KUN, ABOUT THIS DOG DANCING COMPETITION BUSINESS...
...I'VE ARRANGED FOR IT TO BE BROADCAST ON NATIONAL TELEVISION!
ARE YOU SERIOUS?
CRINKLE
THIS IS OUR CHANCE, HIBINO-KUN...

WE'VE COME TOO FAR NOT TO WIN THIS THING. I'M COUNTING ON YOU TO MAKE THE WAN KAW NAME FAMOUS WITH THIS.
DON'T LET ME DOWN...
PAT
DON'T WORRY.
SHE'LL DO IT FOR US.
LE
A
P
PET SHOP
ペットショップ
WOOFLES
わっふる
ペットホテル・美容 ☎03(○○××)○××○
WHAT? YOU'RE GOING HOME?
YEAH, I THINK I BETTER GO HOME FOR NEW YEAR'S AT LEAST ...
WHAT ABOUT YOU, SUGURI ?
FSSHH
CLANK
WELL...

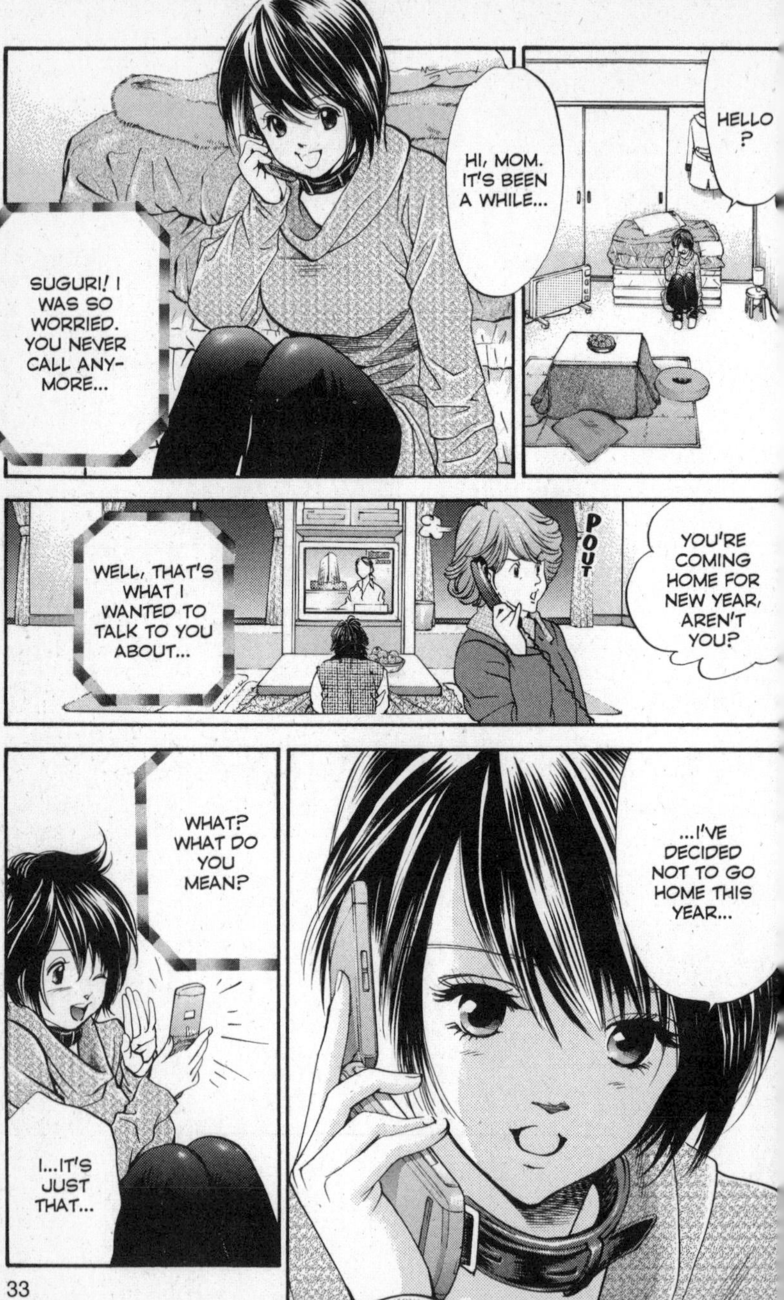
HELLO?
HI, MOM. IT'S BEEN A WHILE...
SUGURI! I WAS SO WORRIED. YOU NEVER CALL ANY-MORE...
YOU'RE COMING HOME FOR NEW YEAR, AREN'T YOU?
POUT
WELL, THAT'S WHAT I WANTED TO TALK TO YOU ABOUT...
...I'VE DECIDED NOT TO GO HOME THIS YEAR...
WHAT? WHAT DO YOU MEAN?
I...IT'S JUST THAT...

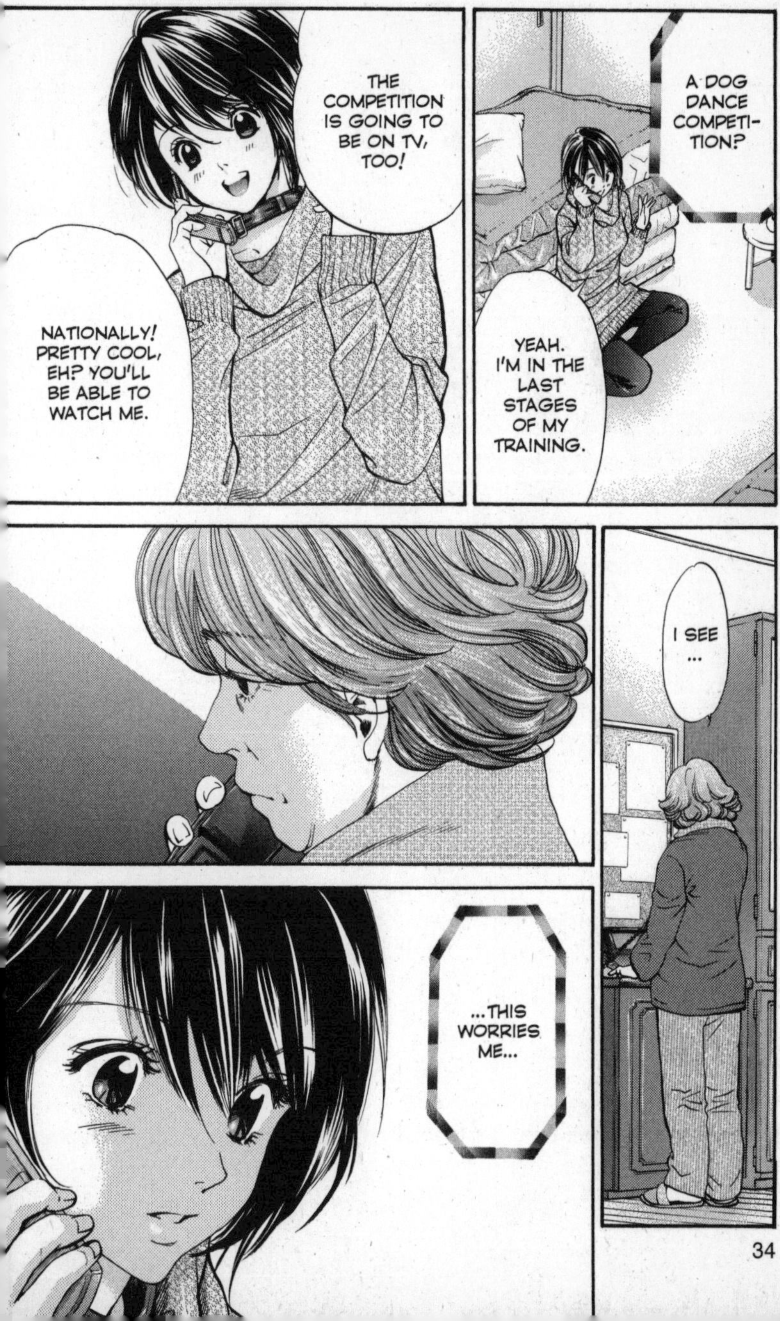
A DOG DANCE COMPETITION?
YEAH. I'M IN THE LAST STAGES OF MY TRAINING.
THE COMPETITION IS GOING TO BE ON TV, TOO!
NATIONALLY! PRETTY COOL, EH? YOU'LL BE ABLE TO WATCH ME.
I SEE ...
...THIS WORRIES ME...

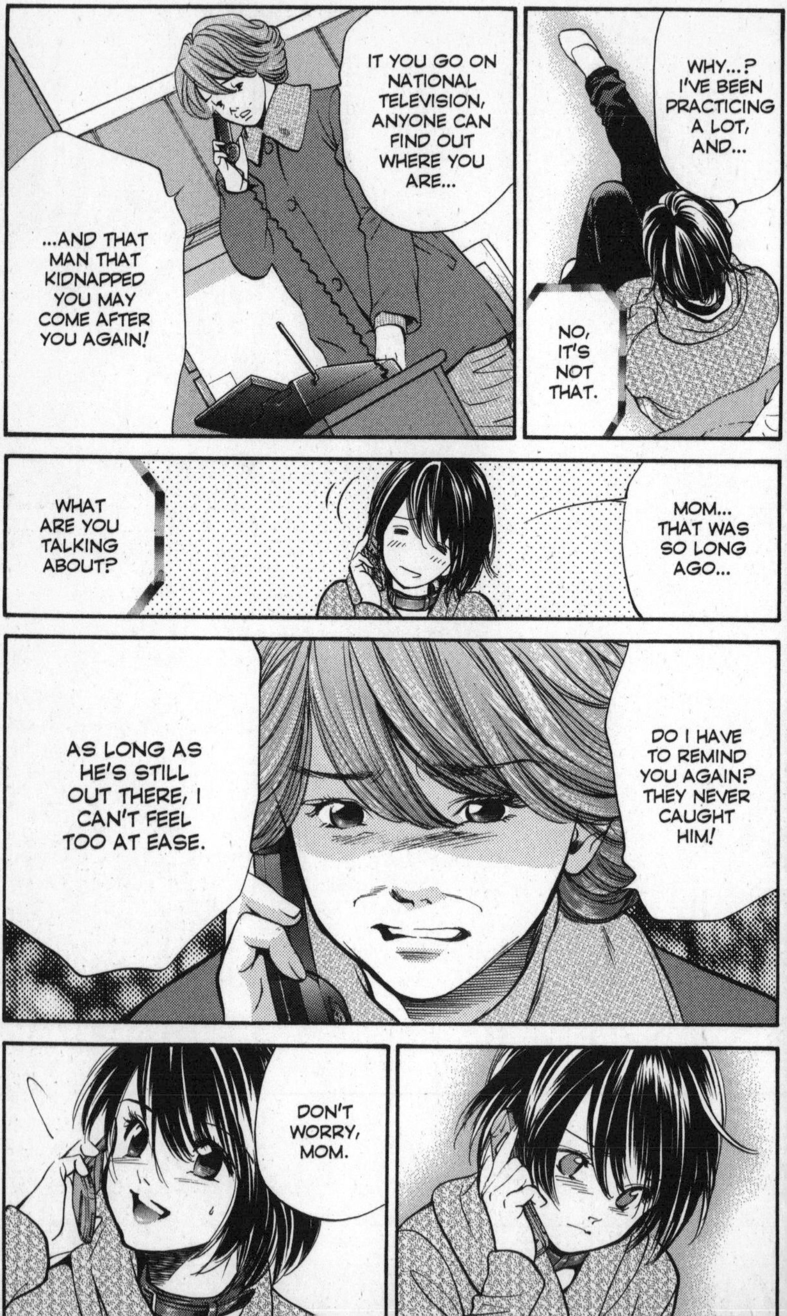
WHY...? I'VE BEEN PRACTICING A LOT, AND...
NO, IT'S NOT THAT.
IT YOU GO ON NATIONAL TELEVISION, ANYONE CAN FIND OUT WHERE YOU ARE...
...AND THAT MAN THAT KIDNAPPED YOU MAY COME AFTER YOU AGAIN!
MOM... THAT WAS SO LONG AGO...
WHAT ARE YOU TALKING ABOUT?
DO I HAVE TO REMIND YOU AGAIN? THEY NEVER CAUGHT HIM!
AS LONG AS HE'S STILL OUT THERE, I CAN'T FEEL TOO AT EASE.
DON'T WORRY, MOM.

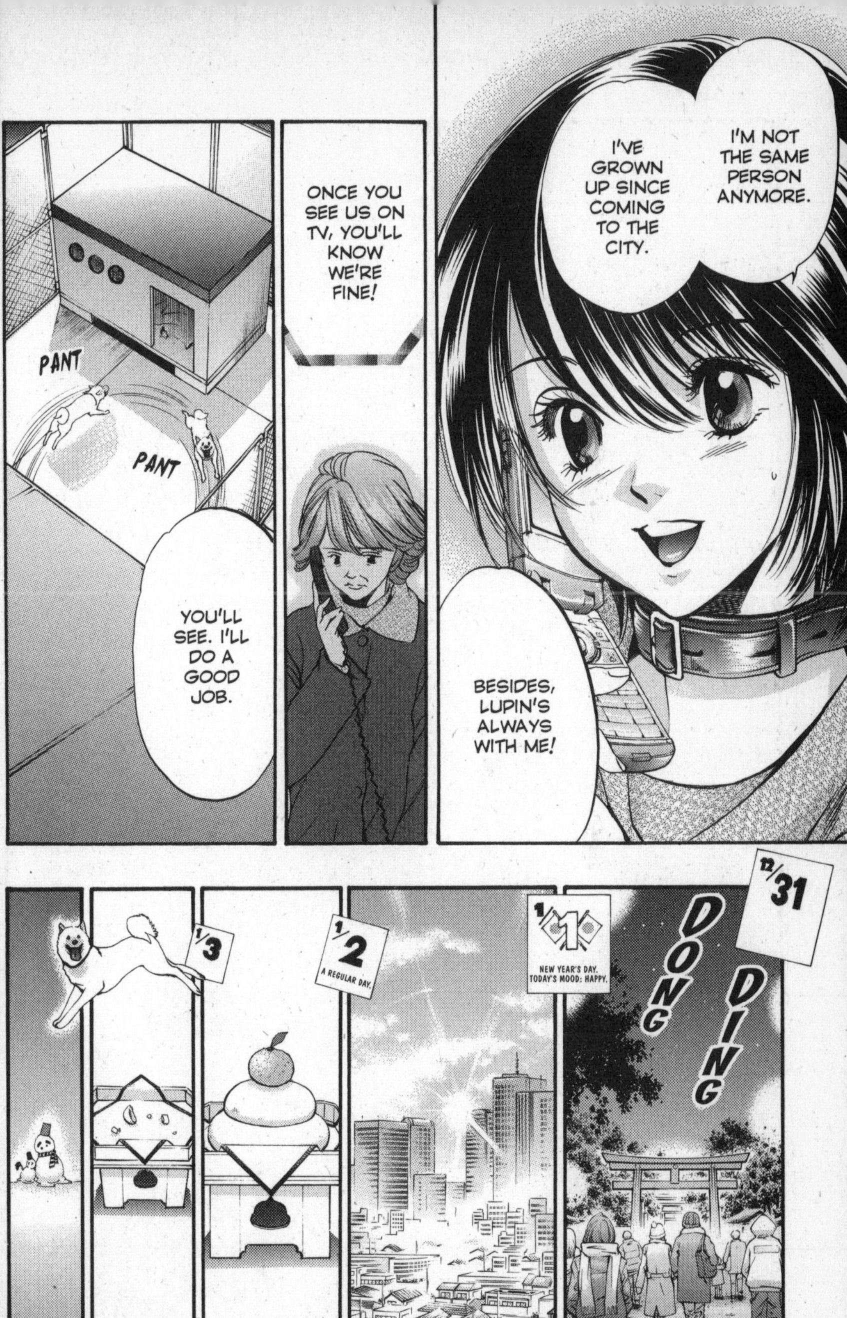
I'M NOT THE SAME PERSON ANYMORE.
I'VE GROWN UP SINCE COMING TO THE CITY.
BESIDES, LUPIN'S ALWAYS WITH ME!
ONCE YOU SEE US ON TV, YOU'LL KNOW WE'RE FINE!
PANT
PANT
YOU'LL SEE. I'LL DO A GOOD JOB.
12/31
DING
DONG
1/1
NEW YEAR'S DAY. TODAY'S MOOD: HAPPY.
1/2
A REGULAR DAY.
1/3

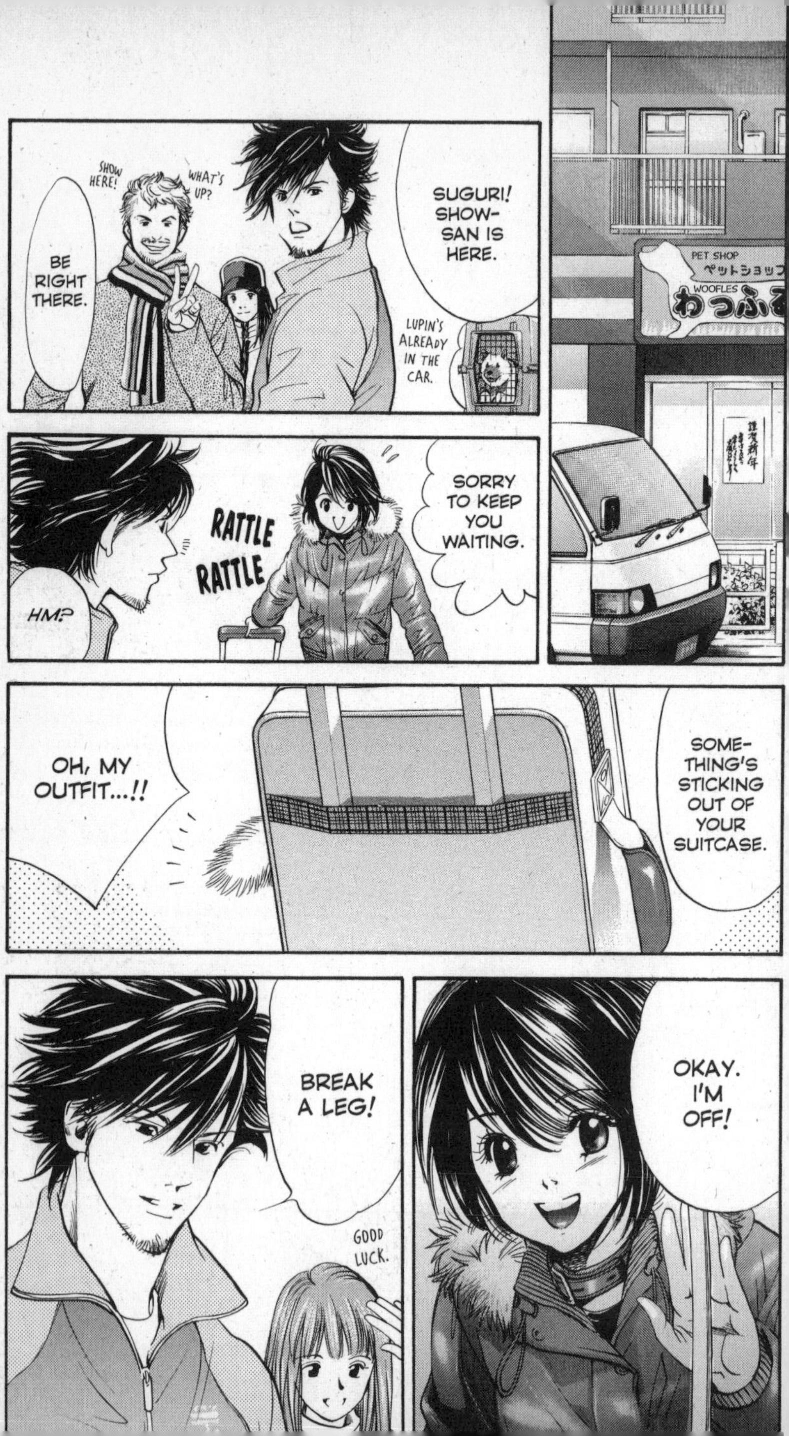
PET SHOP
WOOFLES
SUGURI! SHOW-SAN IS HERE.
LUPIN'S ALREADY IN THE CAR.
WHAT'S UP?
SHOW HERE!
BE RIGHT THERE.
SORRY TO KEEP YOU WAITING.
RATTLE RATTLE
HM?
SOME-THING'S STICKING OUT OF YOUR SUITCASE.
OH, MY OUTFIT...!!
OKAY. I'M OFF!
BREAK A LEG!
GOOD LUCK.

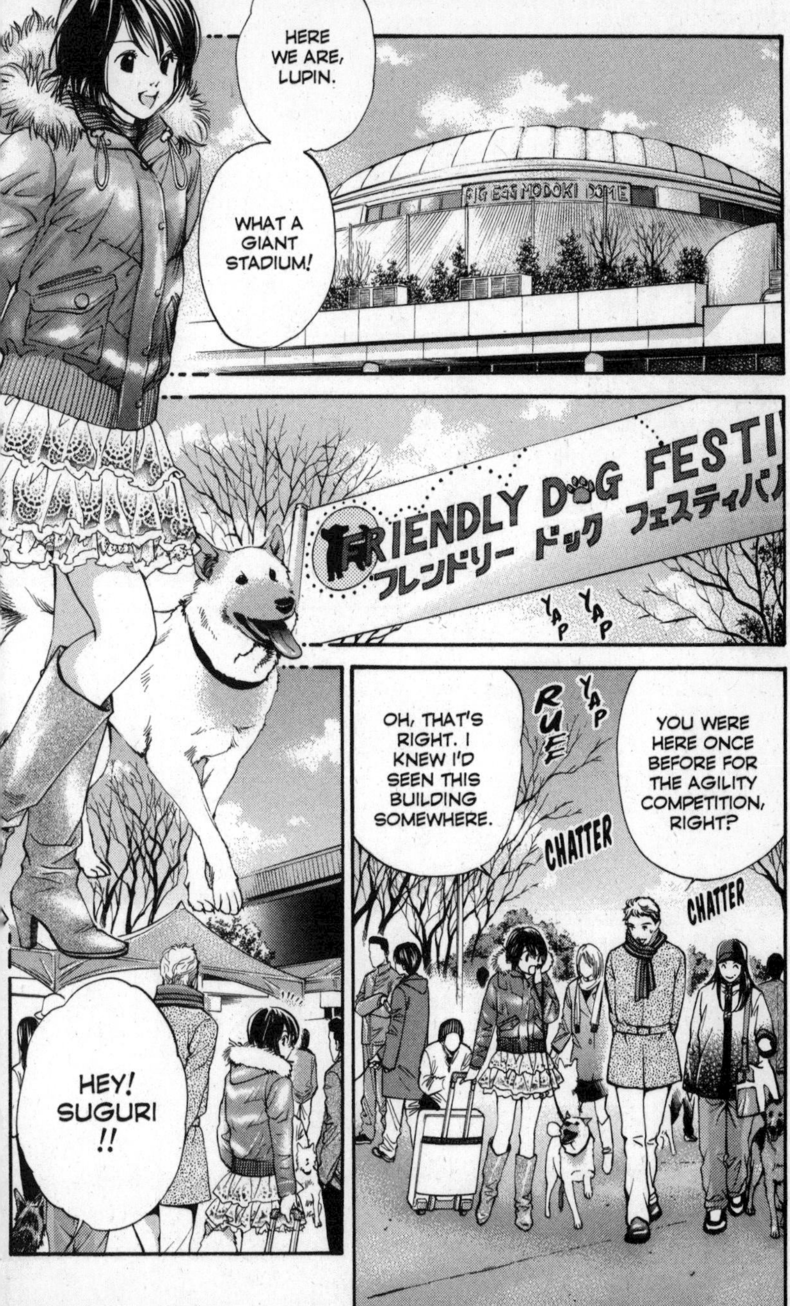
HERE WE ARE, LUPIN.
WHAT A GIANT STADIUM!
BIG EGG MODOKI DOME
FRIENDLY DOG FESTI
フレンドリー ドック フェスティバ
YAP YAP
YOU WERE HERE ONCE BEFORE FOR THE AGILITY COMPETITION, RIGHT?
YAP
RUFF
OH, THAT'S RIGHT. I KNEW I'D SEEN THIS BUILDING SOMEWHERE.
CHATTER
CHATTER
HEY! SUGURI!!

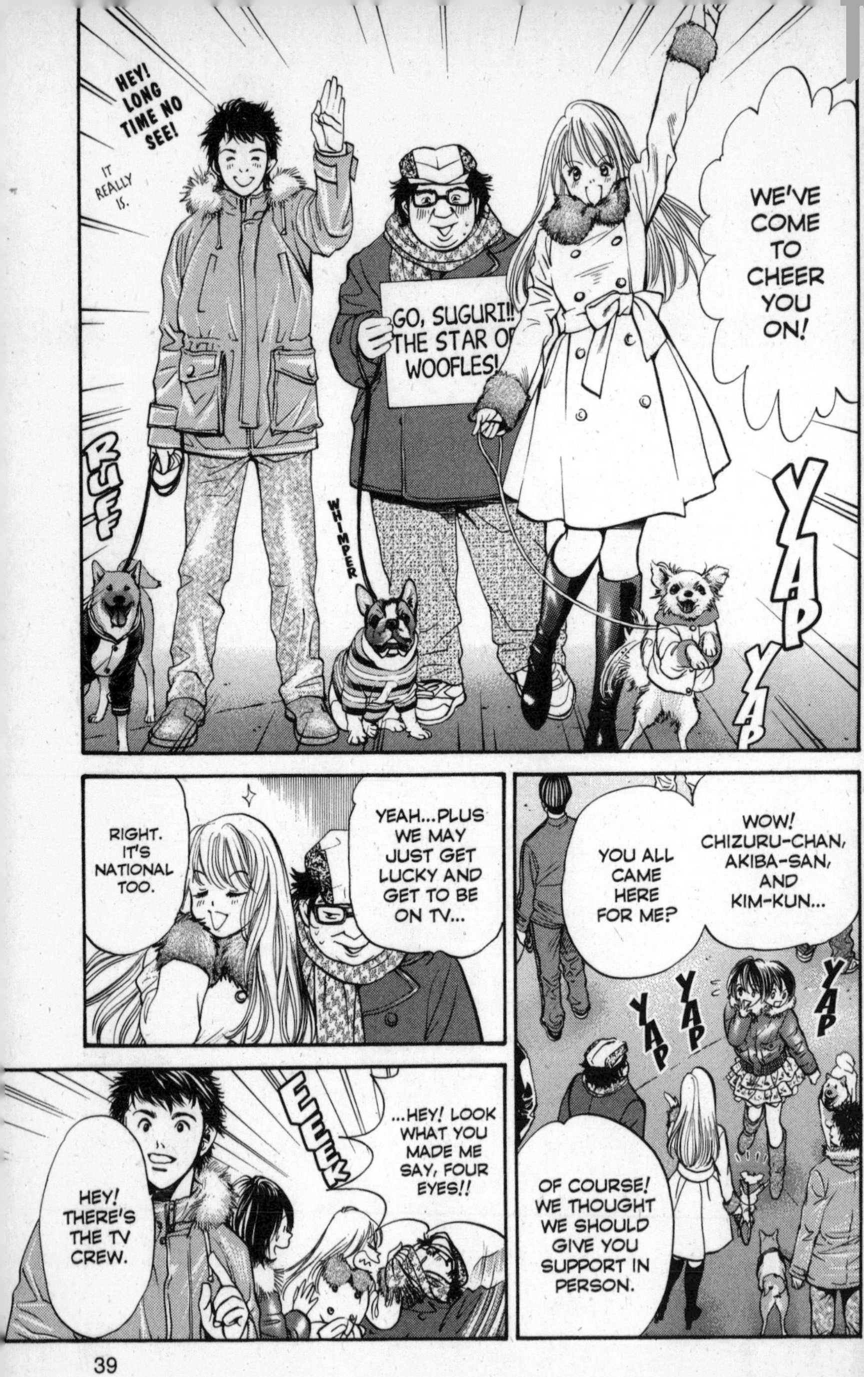
WE'VE COME TO CHEER YOU ON!
YAP
YAP
YAP
GO, SUGURI!! THE STAR OF WOOFLES!
WHIMPER
HEY! LONG TIME NO SEE!
IT REALLY IS.
RUFF
WOW! CHIZURU-CHAN, AKIBA-SAN, AND KIM-KUN...
YOU ALL CAME HERE FOR ME?
YAP
YAP
YAP
OF COURSE! WE THOUGHT WE SHOULD GIVE YOU SUPPORT IN PERSON.
YEAH...PLUS WE MAY JUST GET LUCKY AND GET TO BE ON TV...
RIGHT. IT'S NATIONAL TOO.
...HEY! LOOK WHAT YOU MADE ME SAY, FOUR EYES!!
EEEEK
HEY! THERE'S THE TV CREW.

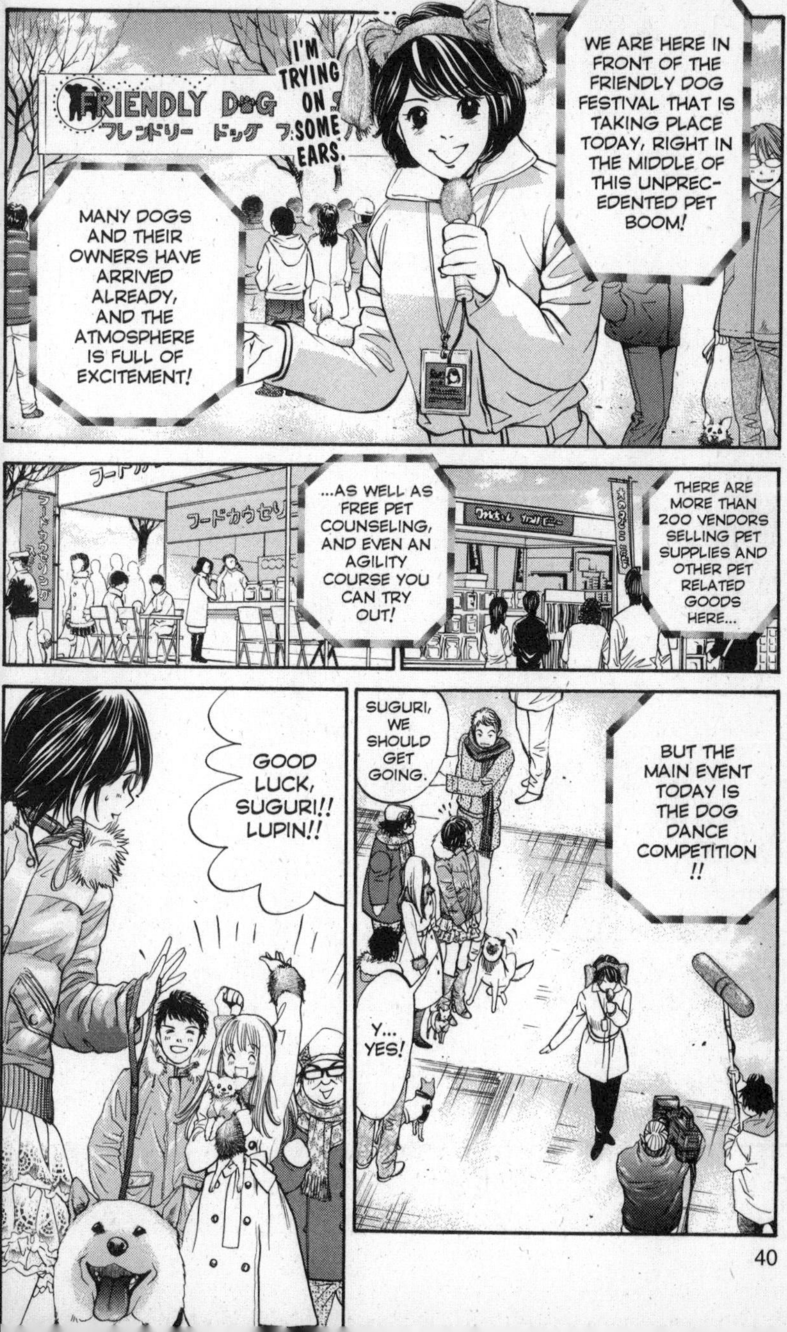
WE ARE HERE IN FRONT OF THE FRIENDLY DOG FESTIVAL THAT IS TAKING PLACE TODAY, RIGHT IN THE MIDDLE OF THIS UNPRECEDENTED PET BOOM!
I'M TRYING ON SOME EARS.
FRIENDLY DOG
MANY DOGS AND THEIR OWNERS HAVE ARRIVED ALREADY, AND THE ATMOSPHERE IS FULL OF EXCITEMENT!
THERE ARE MORE THAN 200 VENDORS SELLING PET SUPPLIES AND OTHER PET RELATED GOODS HERE...
...AS WELL AS FREE PET COUNSELING, AND EVEN AN AGILITY COURSE YOU CAN TRY OUT!
BUT THE MAIN EVENT TODAY IS THE DOG DANCE COMPETITION!!
SUGURI, WE SHOULD GET GOING.
Y... YES!
GOOD LUCK, SUGURI!! LUPIN!!

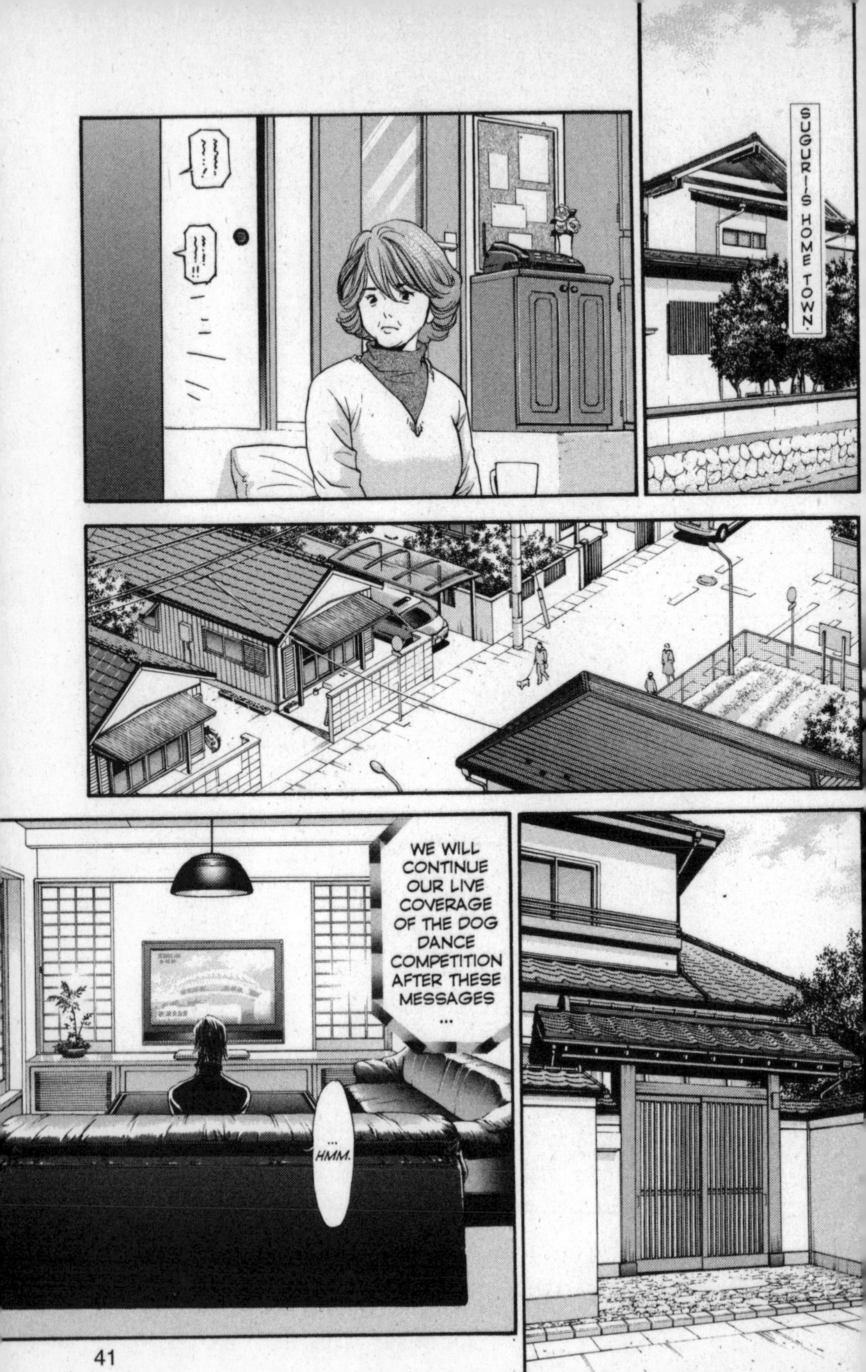
SUGURI'S HOME TOWN.
WE WILL CONTINUE OUR LIVE COVERAGE OF THE DOG DANCE COMPETITION AFTER THESE MESSAGES ...
... HMM.

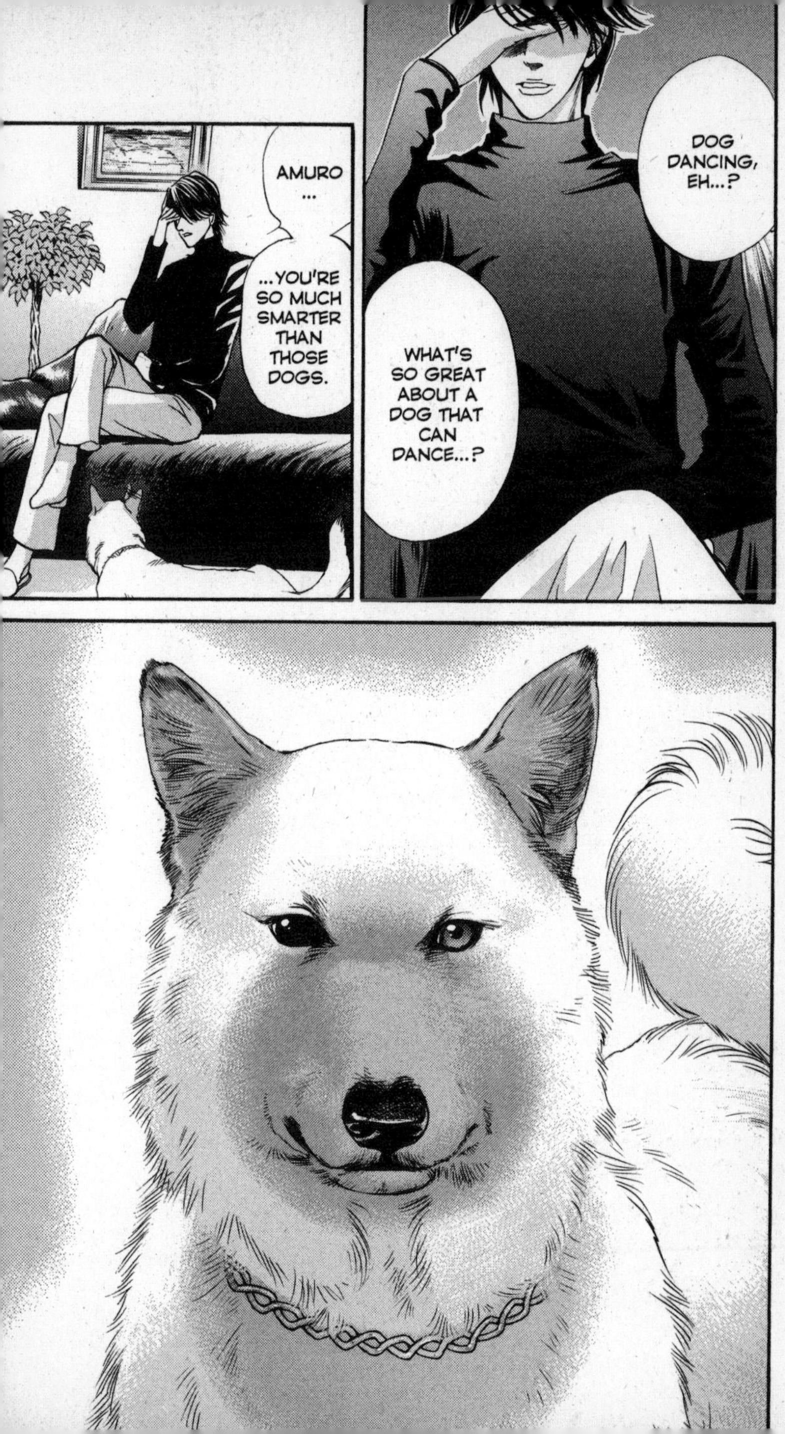
DOG DANCING, EH...?
WHAT'S SO GREAT ABOUT A DOG THAT CAN DANCE...?
AMURO ...
...YOU'RE SO MUCH SMARTER THAN THOSE DOGS.

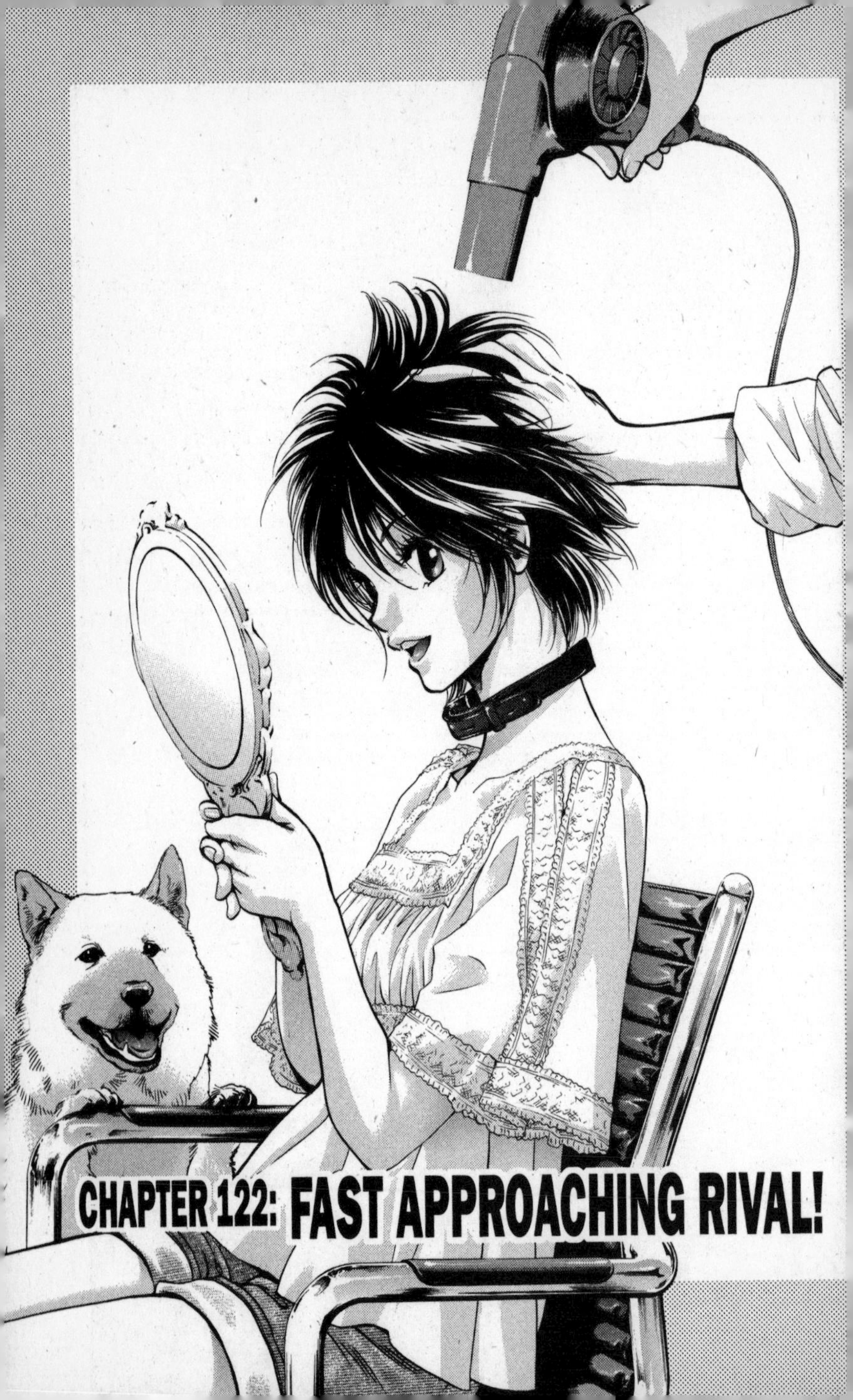
CHAPTER 122: FAST APPROACHING RIVAL!

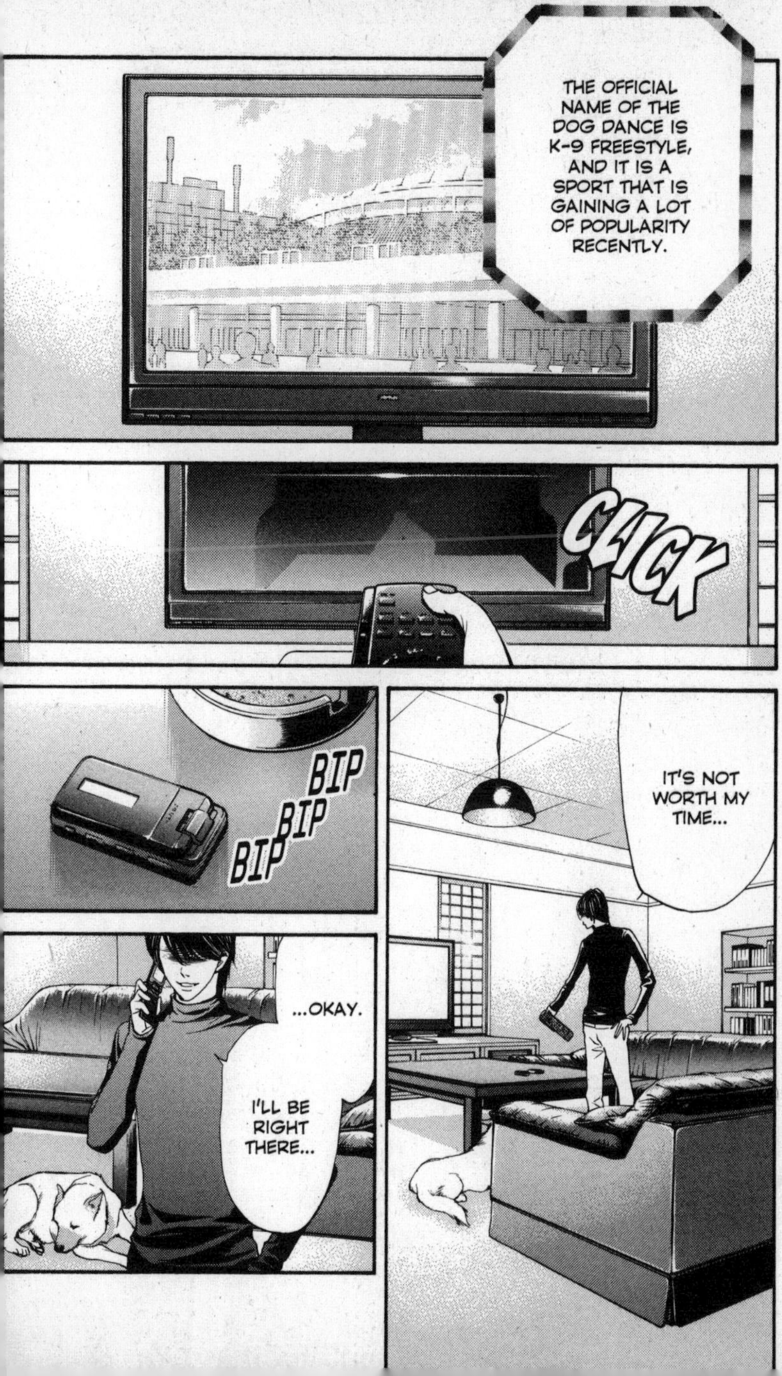
THE OFFICIAL NAME OF THE DOG DANCE IS K-9 FREESTYLE, AND IT IS A SPORT THAT IS GAINING A LOT OF POPULARITY RECENTLY.
CLICK
IT'S NOT WORTH MY TIME...
BIP BIP BIP
...OKAY.
I'LL BE RIGHT THERE...

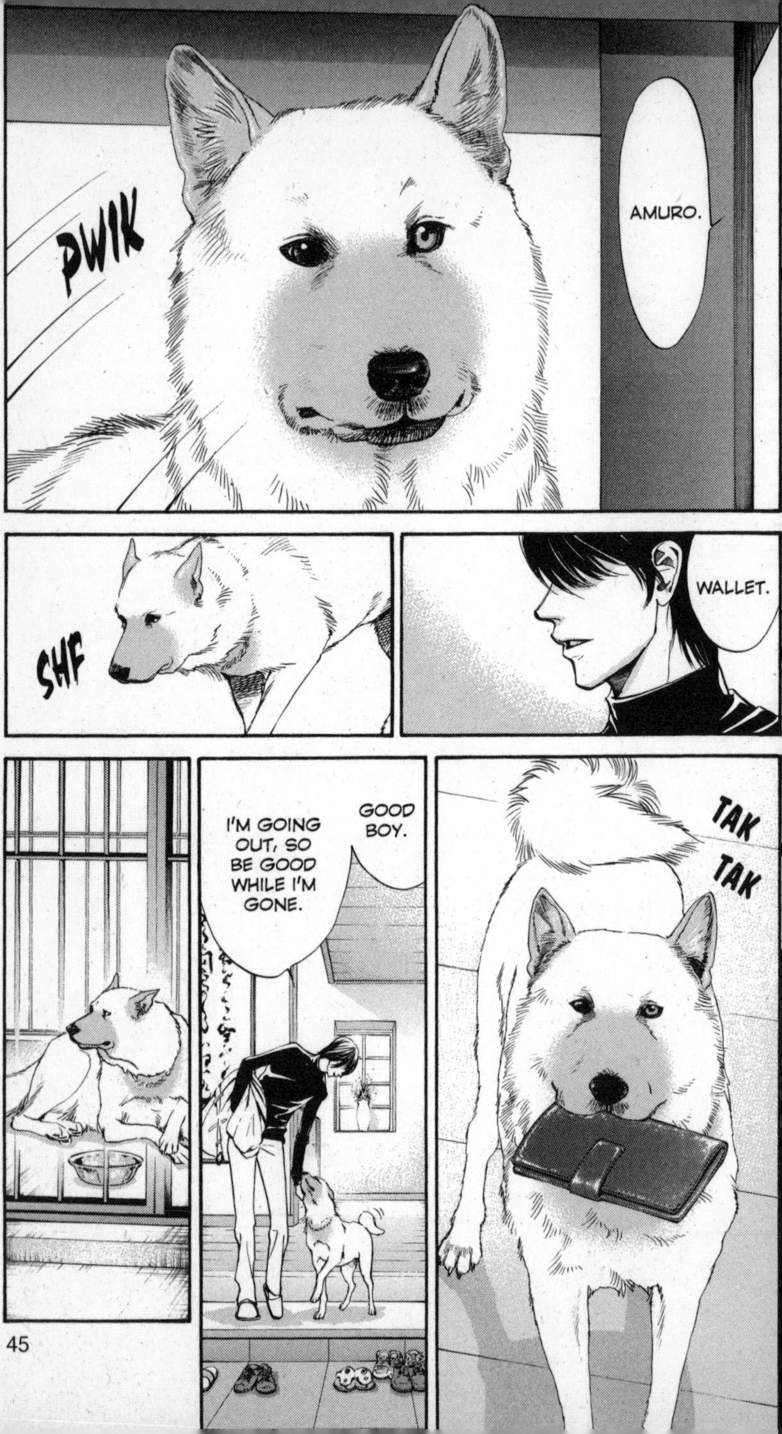

AMURO.
PWIK
WALLET.
SHF
TAK
TAK
GOOD BOY.
I'M GOING OUT, SO BE GOOD WHILE I'M GONE.

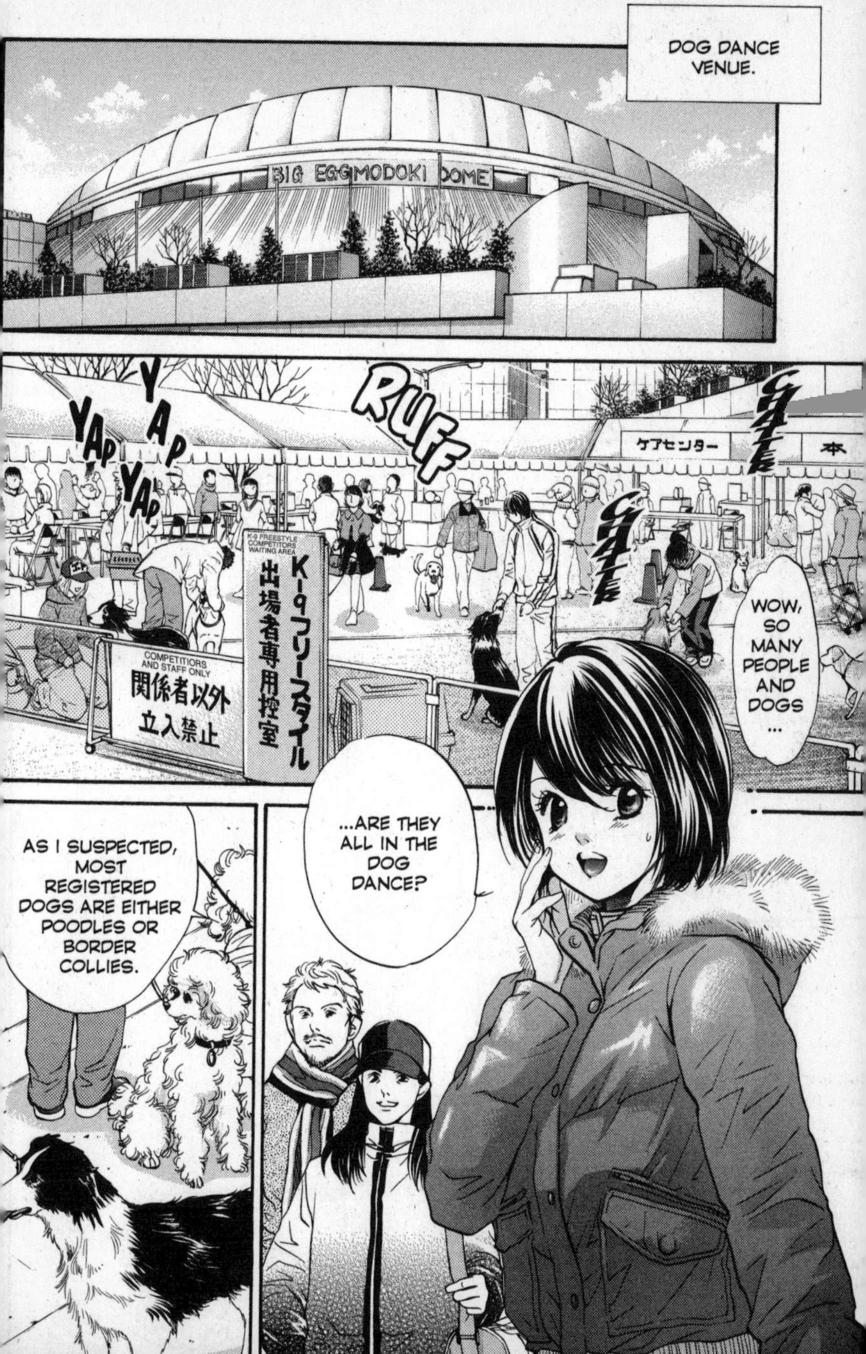
DOG DANCE VENUE.
BIG EGGMODOKI DOME
ケアセンター
本
RUFF
YAP
YAP
YAP
K-9 FREESTYLE COMPETITORS WAITING AREA
K-9フリースタイル出場者専用控室
COMPETITIORS AND STAFF ONLY
関係者以外立入禁止
WOW, SO MANY PEOPLE AND DOGS ...
...ARE THEY ALL IN THE DOG DANCE?
AS I SUSPECTED, MOST REGISTERED DOGS ARE EITHER POODLES OR BORDER COLLIES.

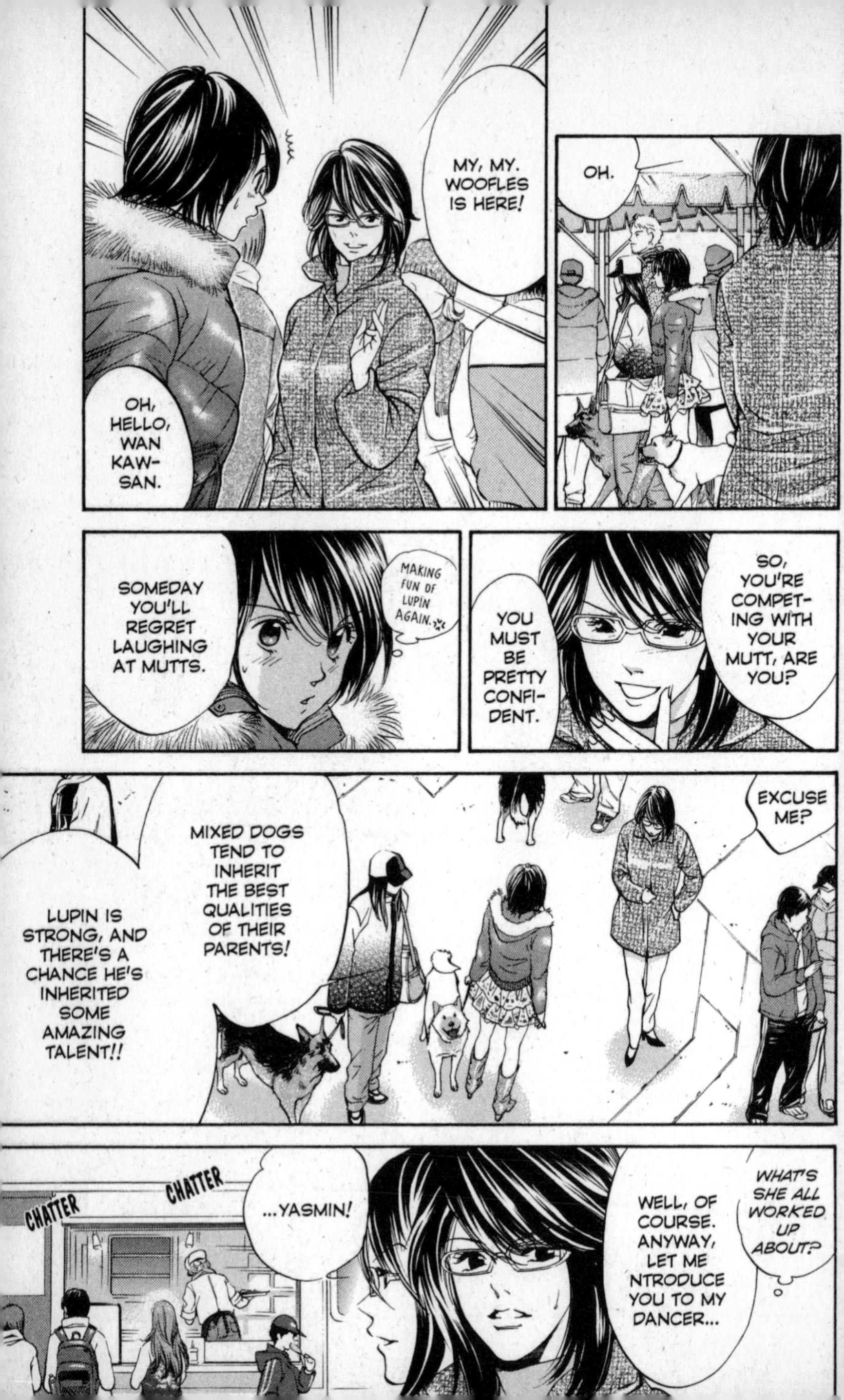
OH.
MY, MY. WOOFLES IS HERE!
OH, HELLO, WAN KAW-SAN.
SO, YOU'RE COMPETING WITH YOUR MUTT, ARE YOU?
YOU MUST BE PRETTY CONFIDENT.
MAKING FUN OF LUPIN AGAIN.
SOMEDAY YOU'LL REGRET LAUGHING AT MUTTS.
EXCUSE ME?
MIXED DOGS TEND TO INHERIT THE BEST QUALITIES OF THEIR PARENTS!
LUPIN IS STRONG, AND THERE'S A CHANCE HE'S INHERITED SOME AMAZING TALENT!!
WHAT'S SHE ALL WORKED UP ABOUT?
WELL, OF COURSE. ANYWAY, LET ME NTRODUCE YOU TO MY DANCER...
...YASMIN!
CHATTER
CHATTER

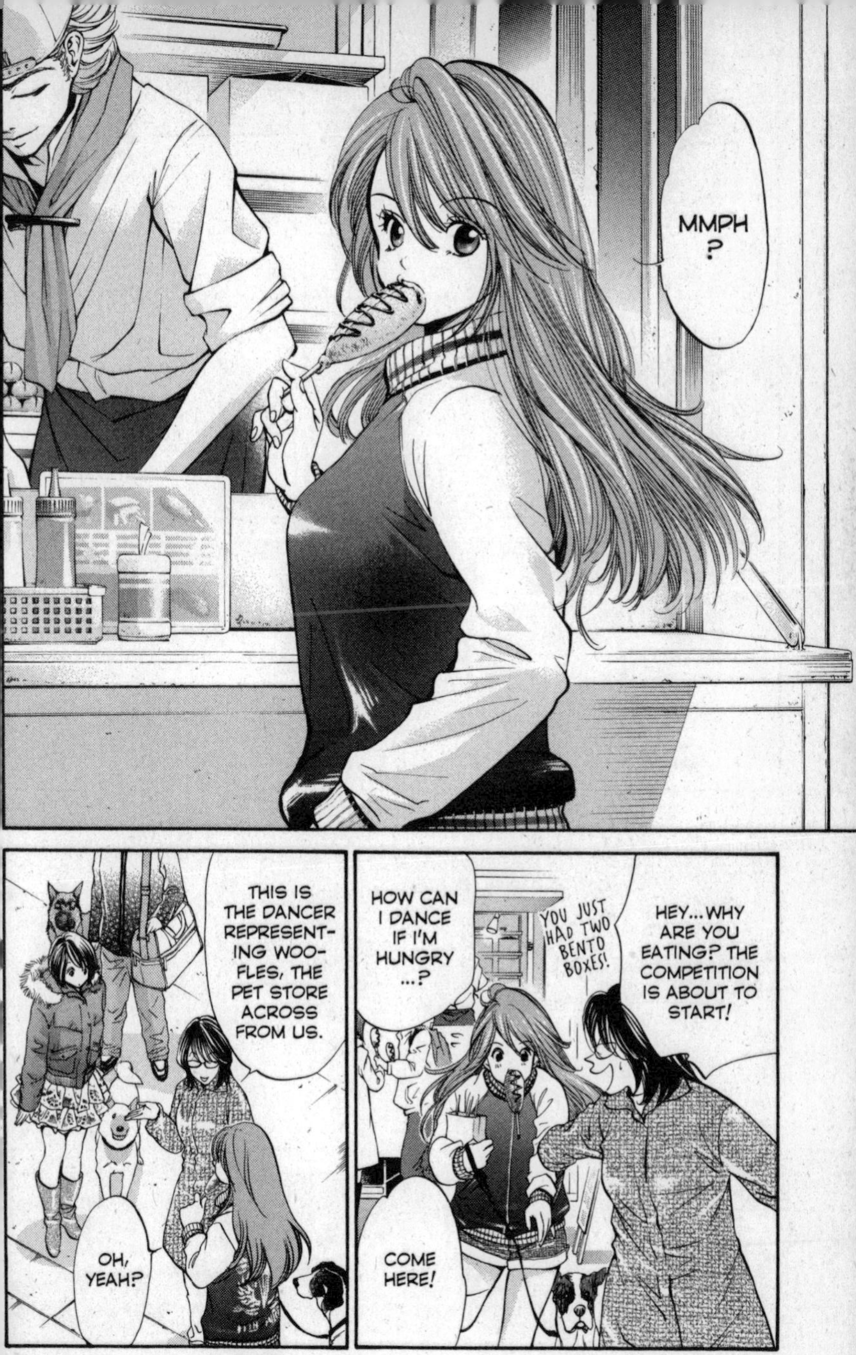
MMPH ?
HEY...WHY ARE YOU EATING? THE COMPETITION IS ABOUT TO START!
YOU JUST HAD TWO BENTO BOXES!
HOW CAN I DANCE IF I'M HUNGRY ...?
COME HERE!
THIS IS THE DANCER REPRESENT-ING WOO-FLES, THE PET STORE ACROSS FROM US.
OH, YEAH?

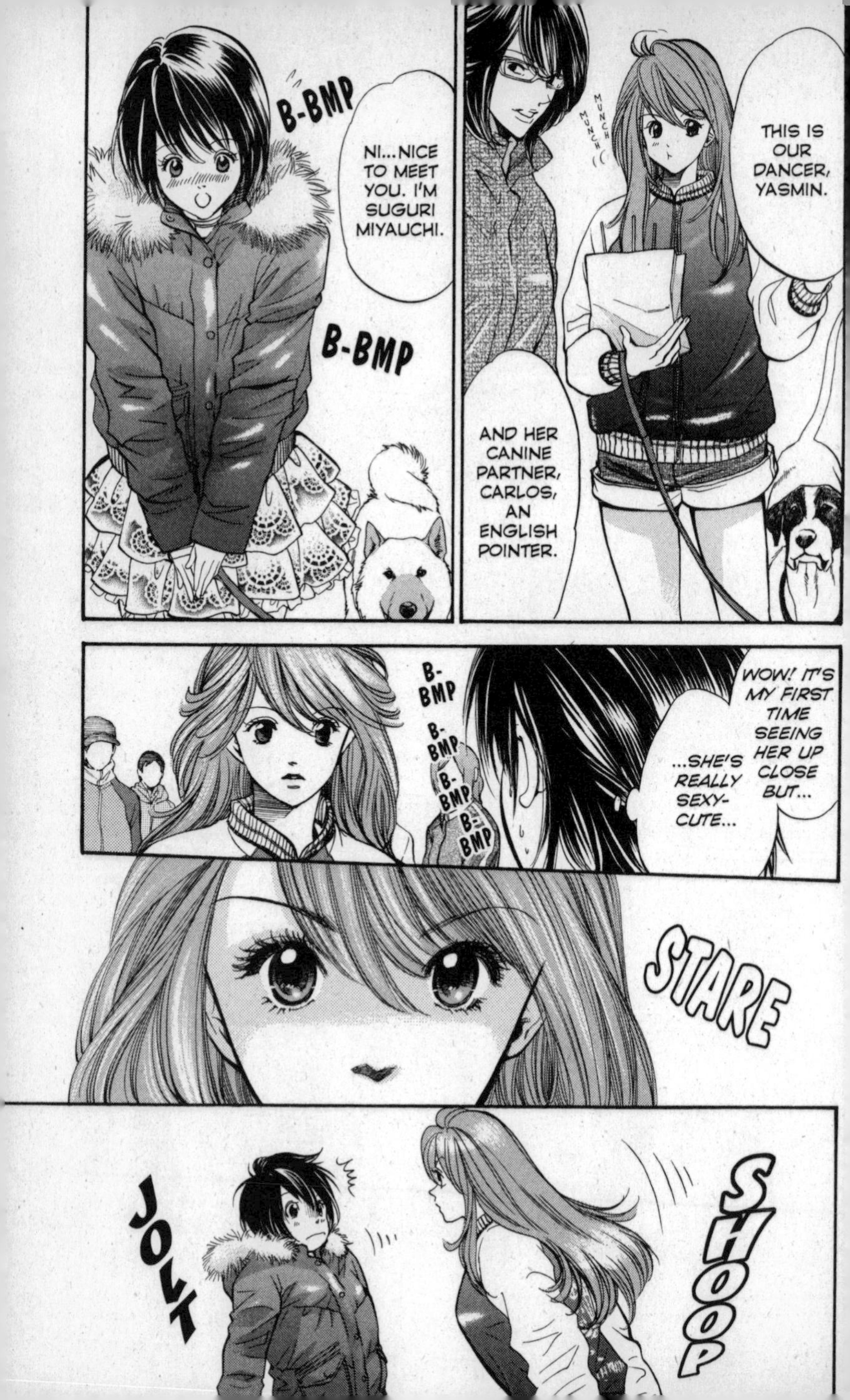
THIS IS OUR DANCER, YASMIN.
MUNCH MUNCH
AND HER CANINE PARTNER, CARLOS, AN ENGLISH POINTER.
NI...NICE TO MEET YOU. I'M SUGURI MIYAUCHI.
B-BMP
B-BMP
WOW! IT'S MY FIRST TIME SEEING HER UP CLOSE BUT...
...SHE'S REALLY SEXY-CUTE...
B-BMP
B-BMP
B-BMP
B-BMP
STARE
SHOOP
JOLT

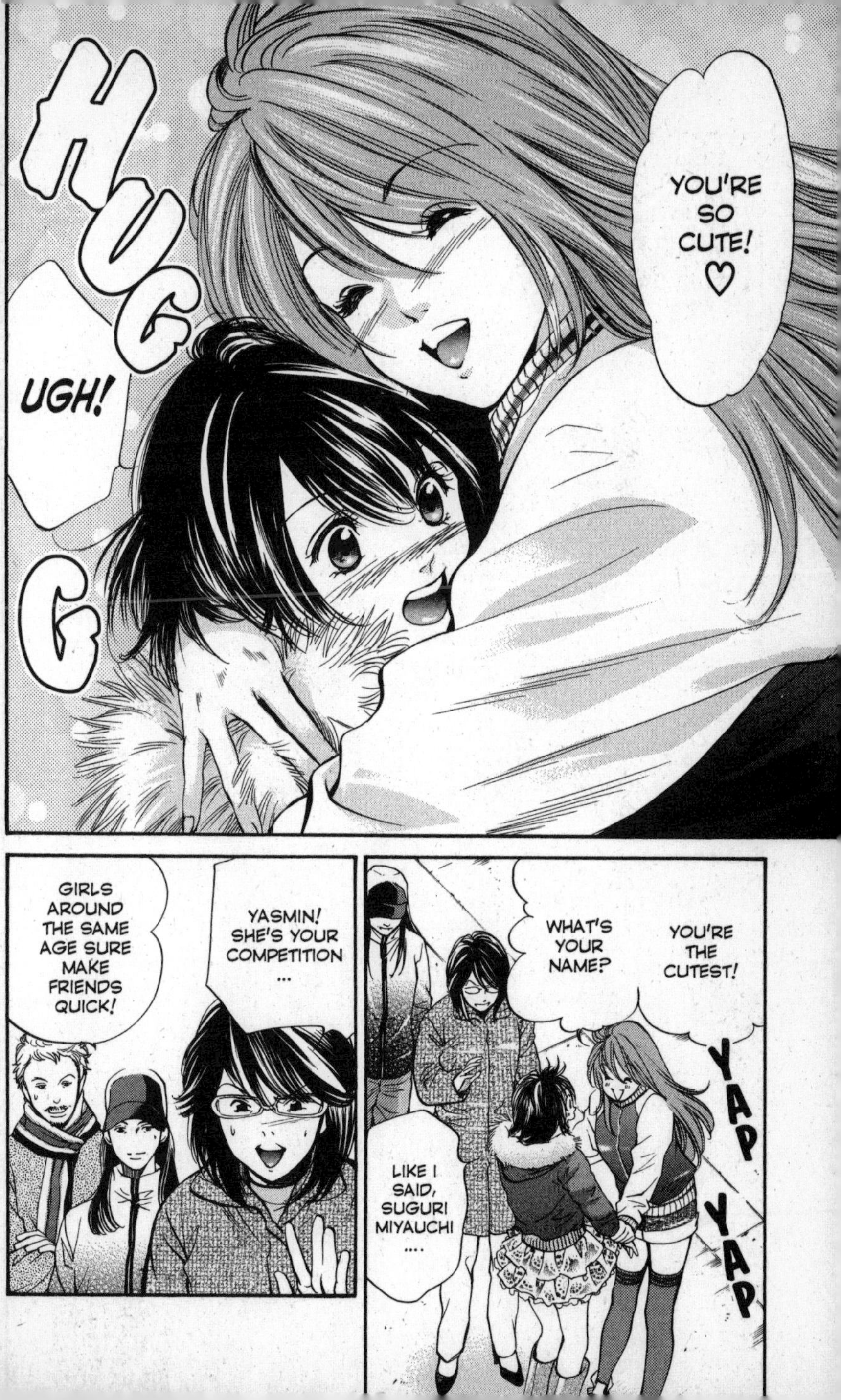
YOU'RE SO CUTE! ♡
HUG
UGH!
G
YOU'RE THE CUTEST!
WHAT'S YOUR NAME?
YAP YAP
LIKE I SAID, SUGURI MIYAUCHI ....
YASMIN! SHE'S YOUR COMPETITION ...
GIRLS AROUND THE SAME AGE SURE MAKE FRIENDS QUICK!

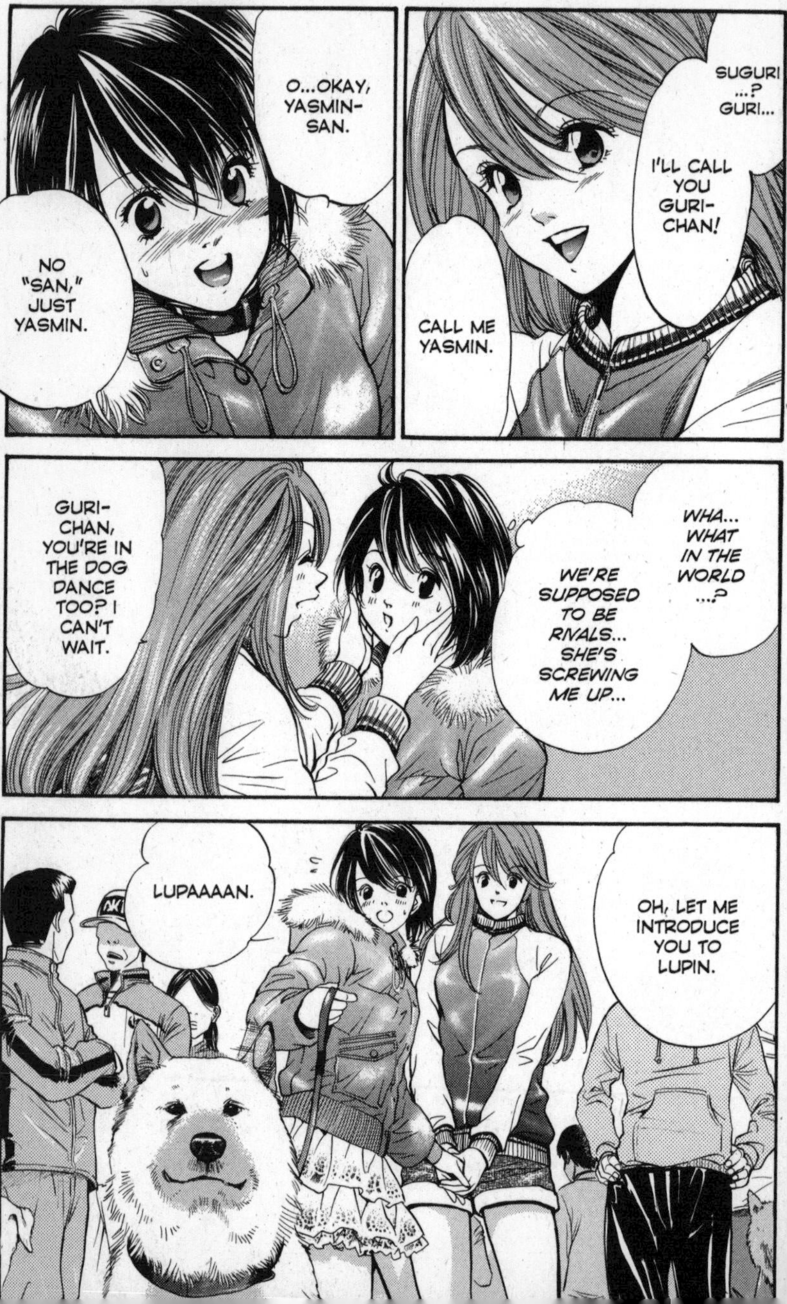
SUGURI ...? GURI...
I'LL CALL YOU GURI-CHAN!
CALL ME YASMIN.
O...OKAY, YASMIN-SAN.
NO "SAN," JUST YASMIN.
WHA... WHAT IN THE WORLD ...?
WE'RE SUPPOSED TO BE RIVALS... SHE'S SCREWING ME UP...
GURI-CHAN, YOU'RE IN THE DOG DANCE TOO? I CAN'T WAIT.
OH, LET ME INTRODUCE YOU TO LUPIN.
LUPAAAAN.

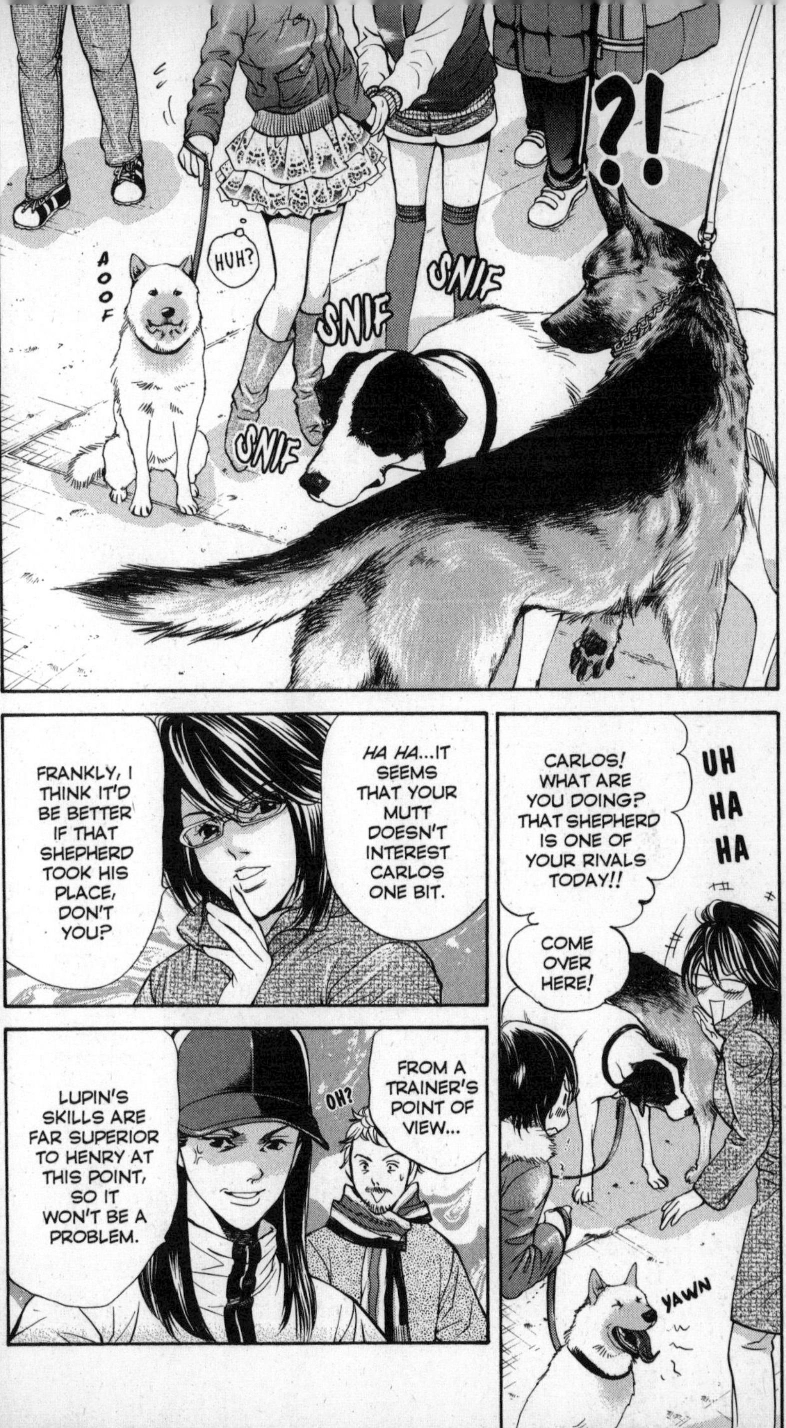
?!
SNIF
SNIF
HUH?
AOOF
SNIF
UH HA HA
CARLOS! WHAT ARE YOU DOING? THAT SHEPHERD IS ONE OF YOUR RIVALS TODAY!!
COME OVER HERE!
YAWN
HA HA...IT SEEMS THAT YOUR MUTT DOESN'T INTEREST CARLOS ONE BIT.
FRANKLY, I THINK IT'D BE BETTER IF THAT SHEPHERD TOOK HIS PLACE, DON'T YOU?
FROM A TRAINER'S POINT OF VIEW...
OH?
LUPIN'S SKILLS ARE FAR SUPERIOR TO HENRY AT THIS POINT, SO IT WON'T BE A PROBLEM.

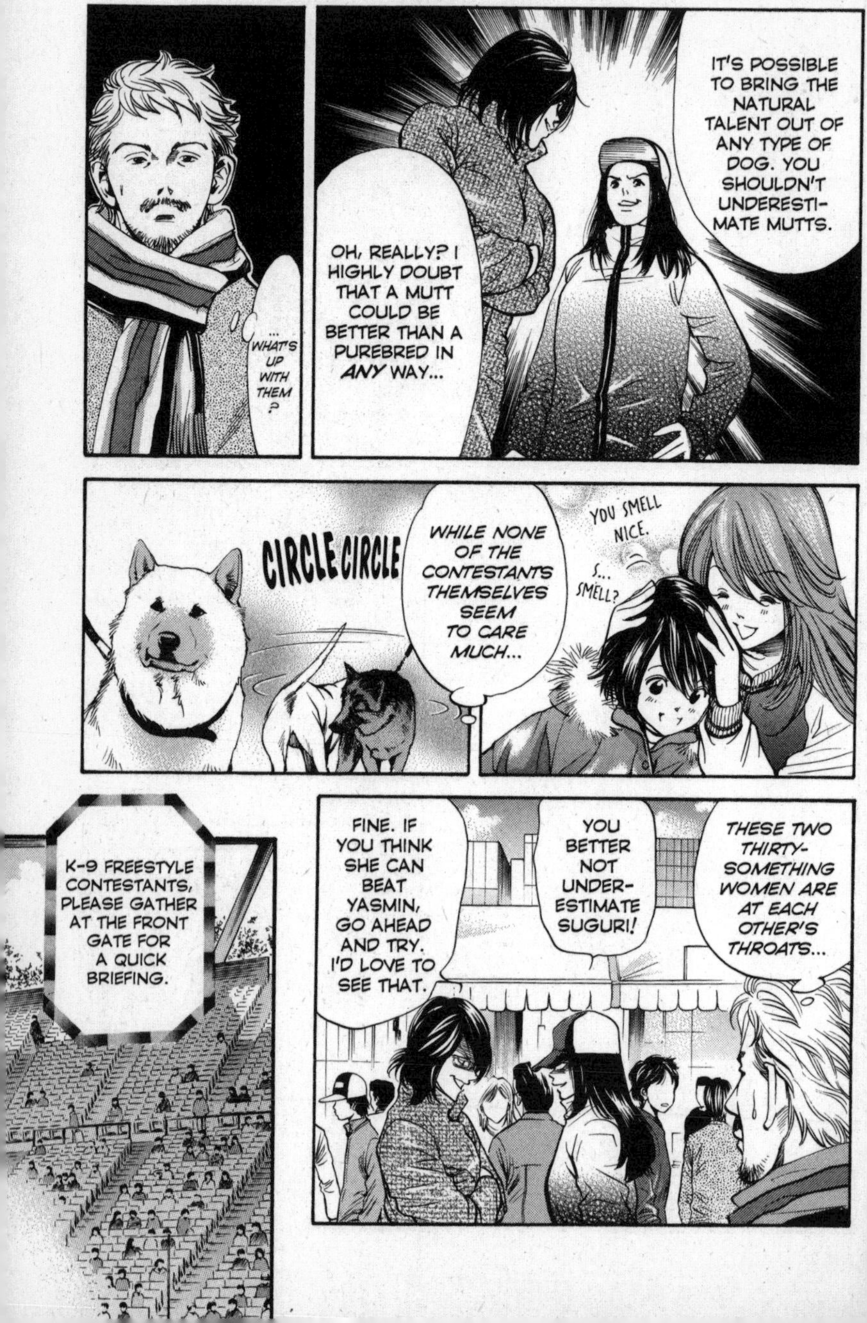
IT'S POSSIBLE TO BRING THE NATURAL TALENT OUT OF ANY TYPE OF DOG. YOU SHOULDN'T UNDERESTI-MATE MUTTS.
OH, REALLY? I HIGHLY DOUBT THAT A MUTT COULD BE BETTER THAN A PUREBRED IN *ANY* WAY...
...WHAT'S UP WITH THEM?
YOU SMELL NICE.
S... SMELL?
*WHILE NONE OF THE CONTESTANTS THEMSELVES SEEM TO CARE MUCH...*
CIRCLE CIRCLE
*THESE TWO THIRTY-SOMETHING WOMEN ARE AT EACH OTHER'S THROATS...*
YOU BETTER NOT UNDER-ESTIMATE SUGURI!
FINE. IF YOU THINK SHE CAN BEAT YASMIN, GO AHEAD AND TRY. I'D LOVE TO SEE THAT.
K-9 FREESTYLE CONTESTANTS, PLEASE GATHER AT THE FRONT GATE FOR A QUICK BRIEFING.

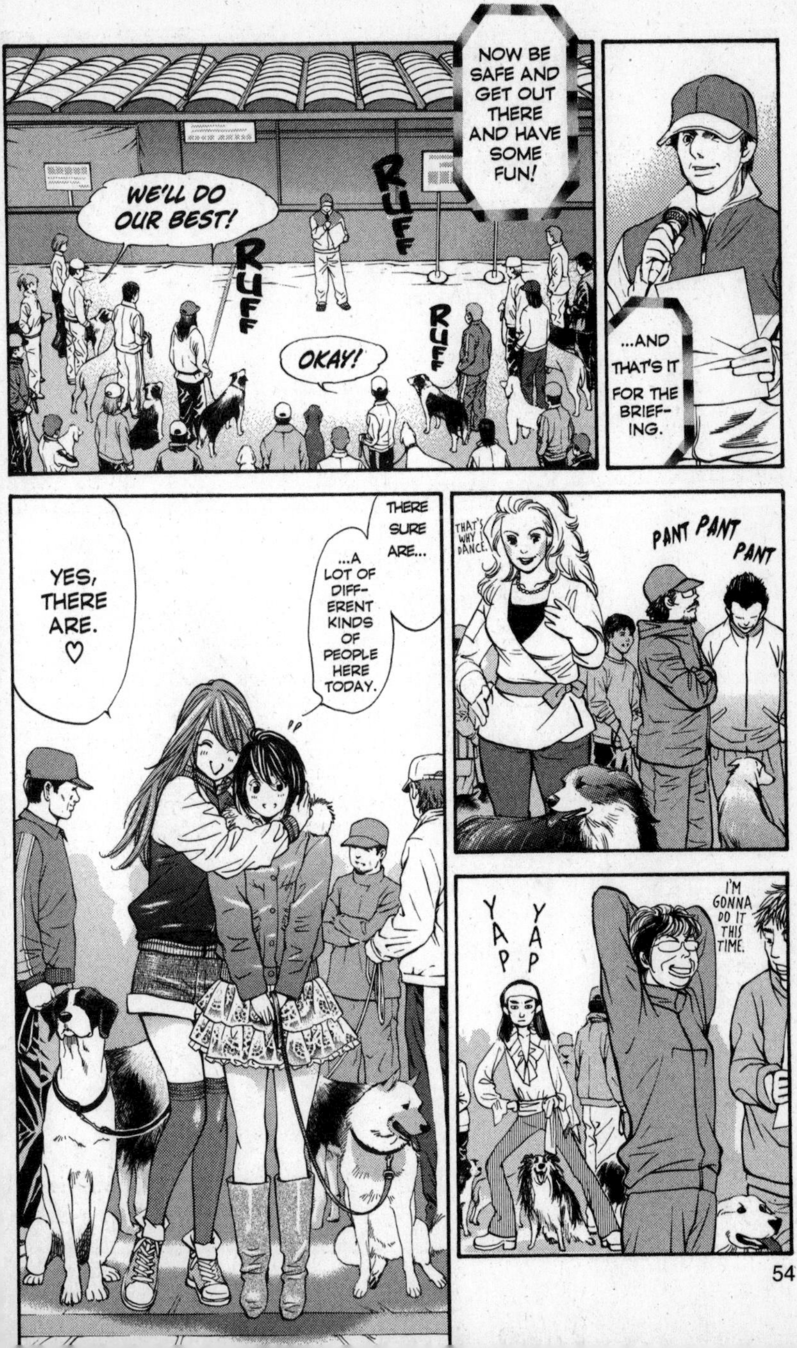
NOW BE SAFE AND GET OUT THERE AND HAVE SOME FUN!
...AND THAT'S IT FOR THE BRIEFING.
RUFF
WE'LL DO OUR BEST!
RUFF
RUFF
OKAY!
PANT PANT PANT
THAT'S WHY I DANCE.
I'M GONNA DO IT THIS TIME.
YAP YAP
THERE SURE ARE...
...A LOT OF DIFFERENT KINDS OF PEOPLE HERE TODAY.
YES, THERE ARE. ♡

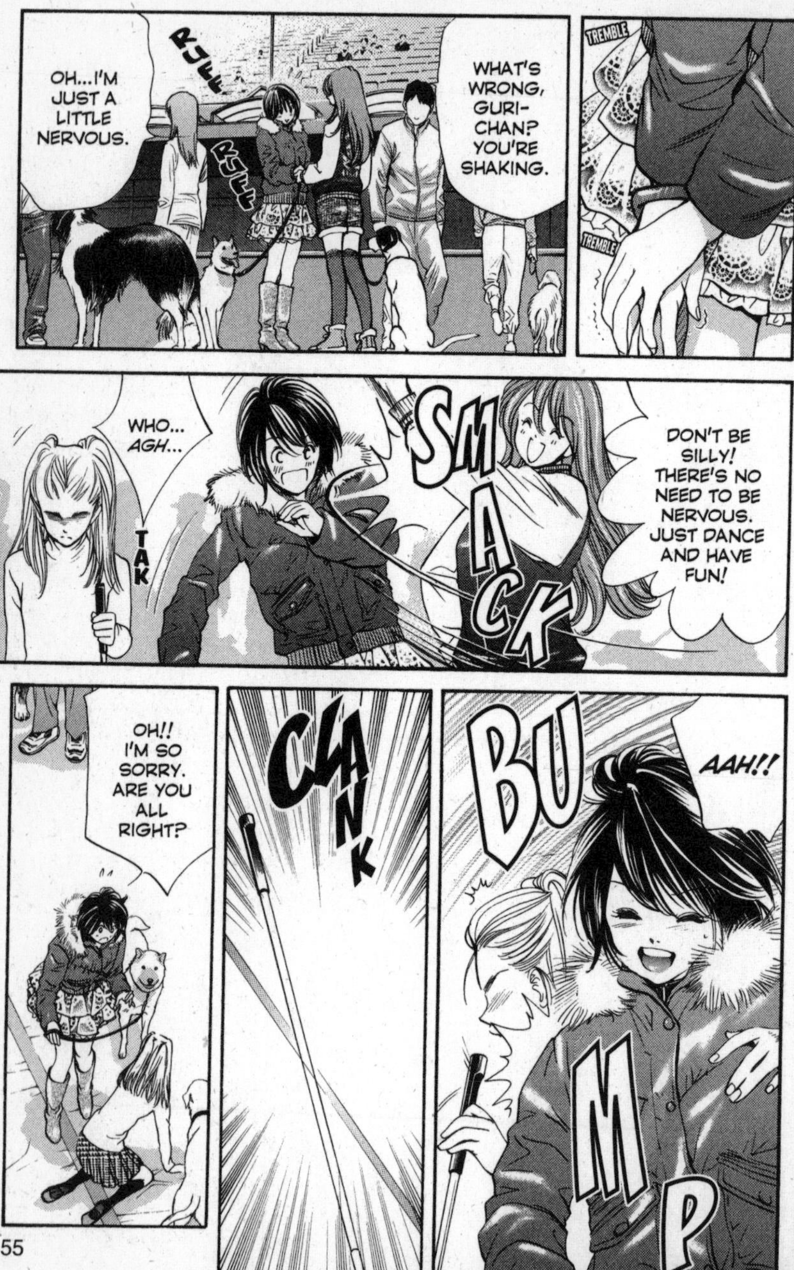
TREMBLE
TREMBLE
WHAT'S WRONG, GURI-CHAN? YOU'RE SHAKING.
RUFF
RUFF
OH...I'M JUST A LITTLE NERVOUS.
DON'T BE SILLY! THERE'S NO NEED TO BE NERVOUS. JUST DANCE AND HAVE FUN!
SMACK
WHO... *AGH...*
TAK
TAK
*AAH!!*
BUMP
CLANK
OH!! I'M SO SORRY. ARE YOU ALL RIGHT?

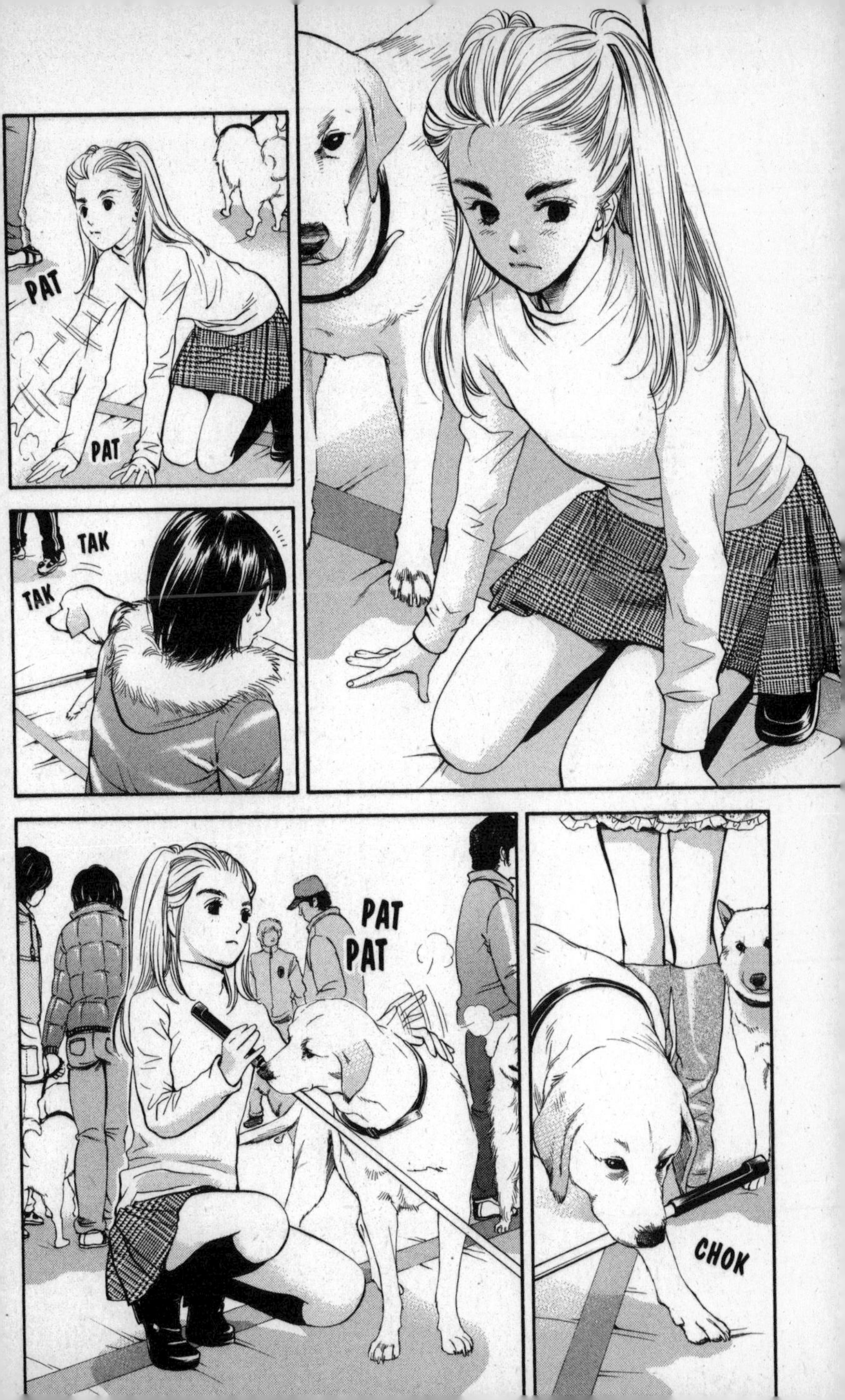
PAT
PAT
TAK
TAK
CHOK
PAT
PAT

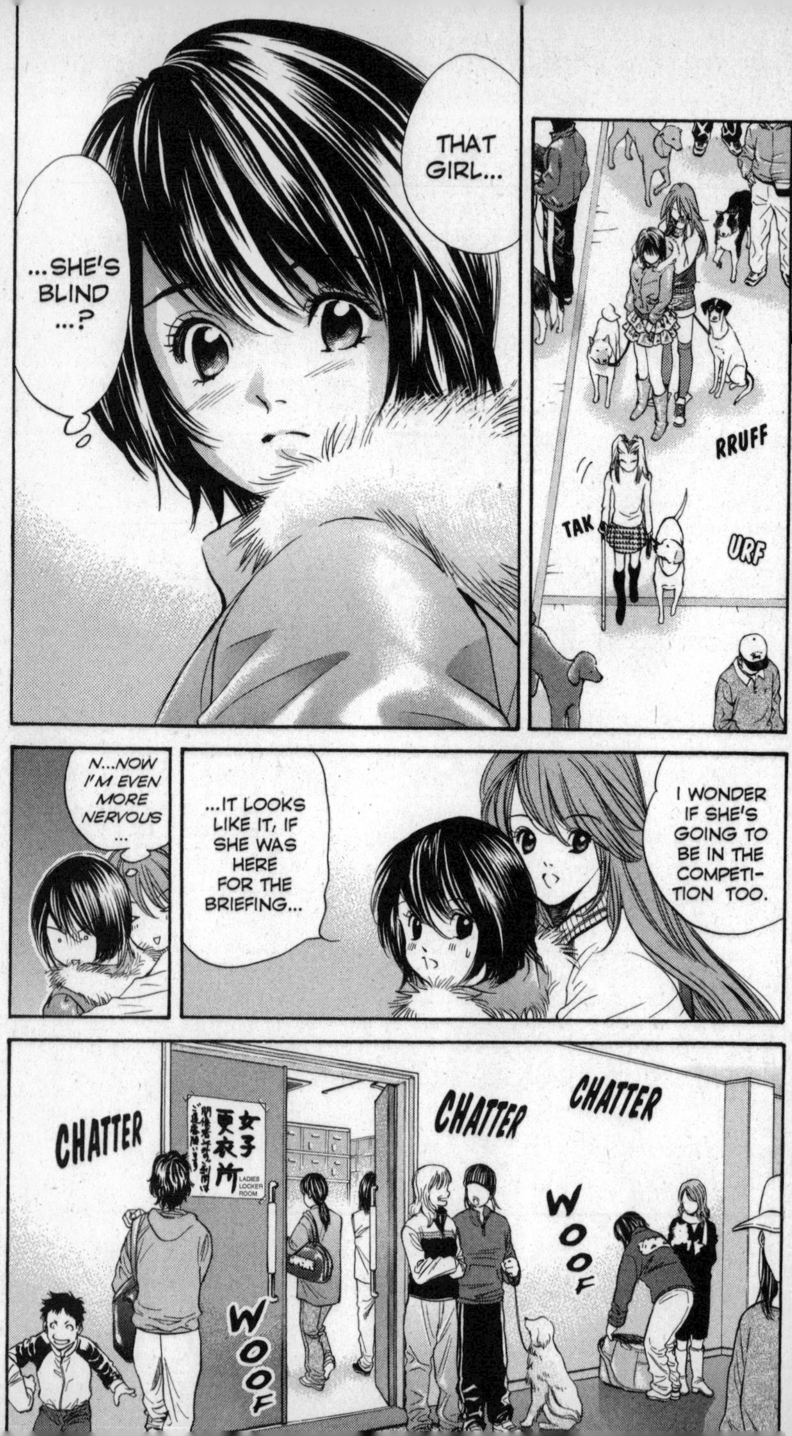
RRUFF
TAK
URF
THAT GIRL...
...SHE'S BLIND ...?
I WONDER IF SHE'S GOING TO BE IN THE COMPETITION TOO.
...IT LOOKS LIKE IT, IF SHE WAS HERE FOR THE BRIEFING...
N...NOW I'M EVEN MORE NERVOUS ...
CHATTER
CHATTER
WOOF
女子更衣所
LADIES LOCKER ROOM
CHATTER
WOOF

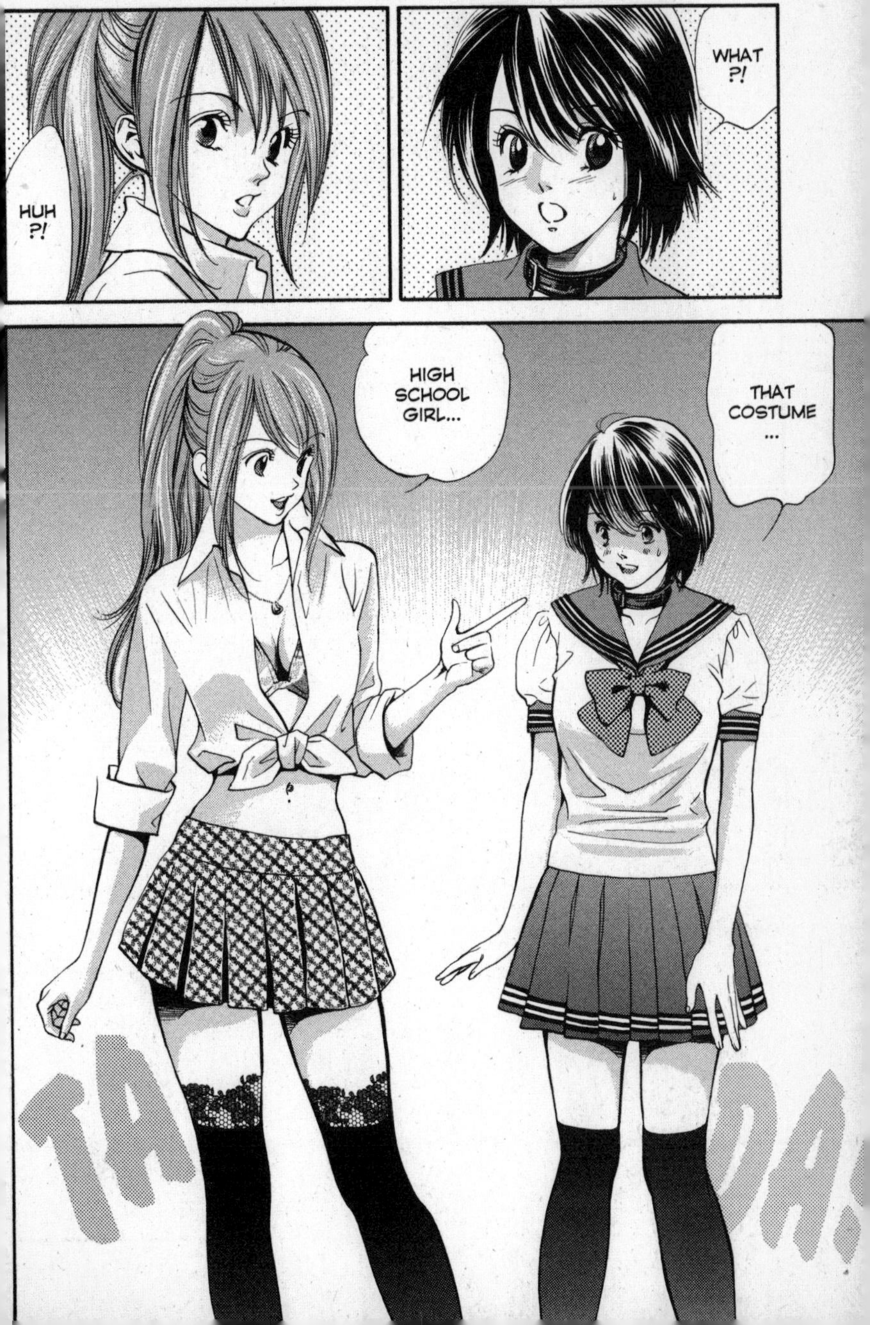
WHAT ?!
HUH ?!
THAT COSTUME ...
HIGH SCHOOL GIRL...
TA DA!

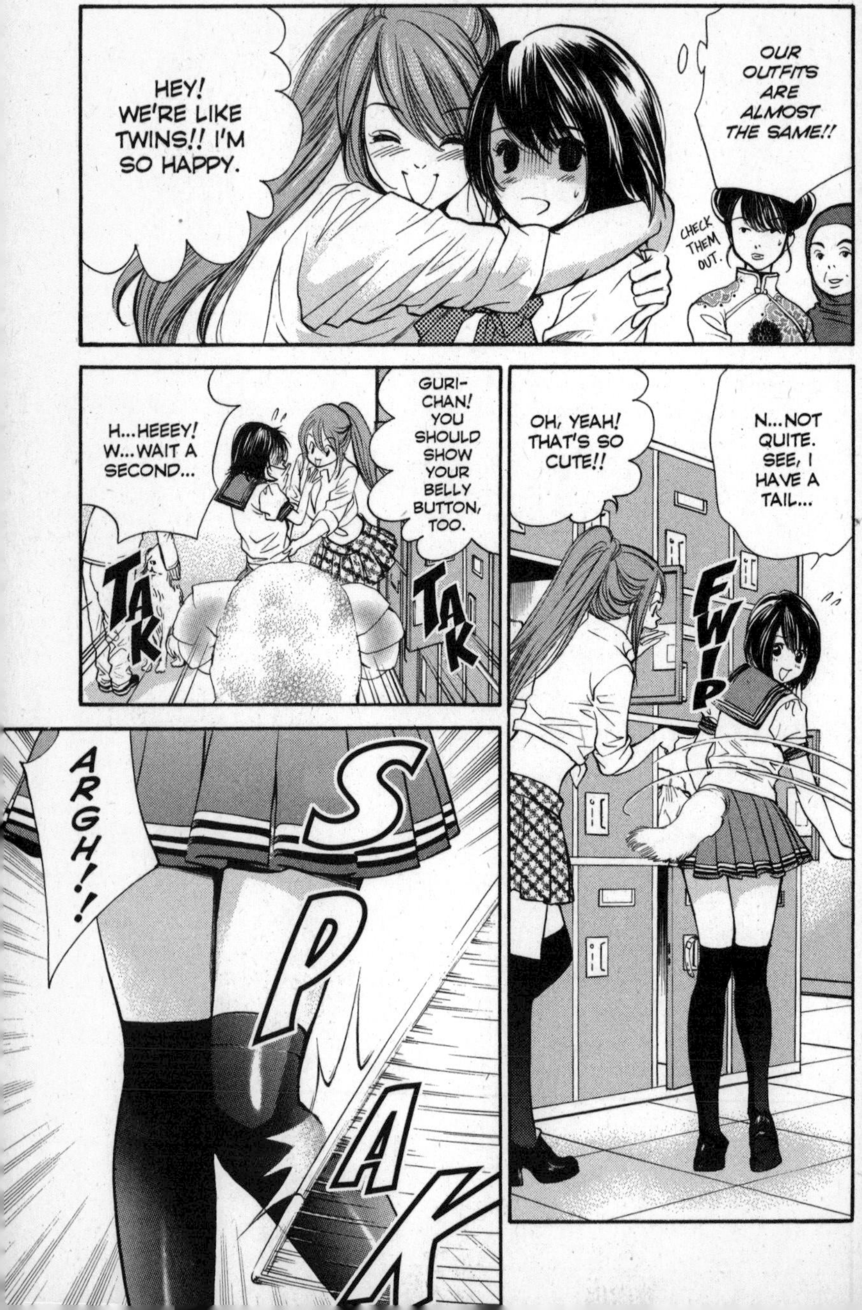
OUR OUTFITS ARE ALMOST THE SAME!!
CHECK THEM OUT.
HEY! WE'RE LIKE TWINS!! I'M SO HAPPY.
N...NOT QUITE. SEE, I HAVE A TAIL...
OH, YEAH! THAT'S SO CUTE!!
FWIP
GURI-CHAN! YOU SHOULD SHOW YOUR BELLY BUTTON, TOO.
TAK
H...HEEEY! W...WAIT A SECOND...
TAK
SPAK
ARGH!!

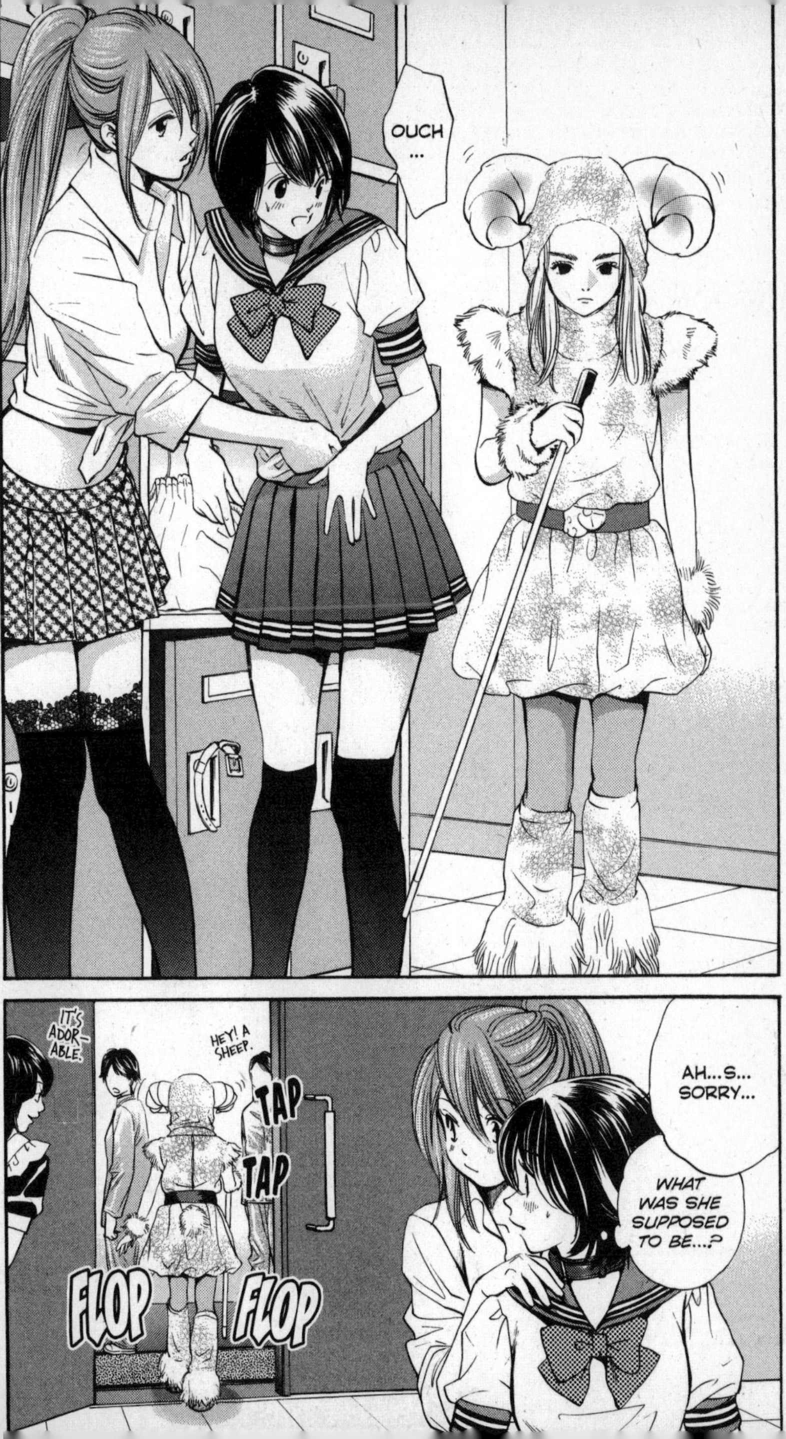
OUCH ...
AH... S... SORRY...
WHAT WAS SHE SUPPOSED TO BE...?
TAP TAP
HEY! A SHEEP.
IT'S ADORABLE.
FLOP FLOP

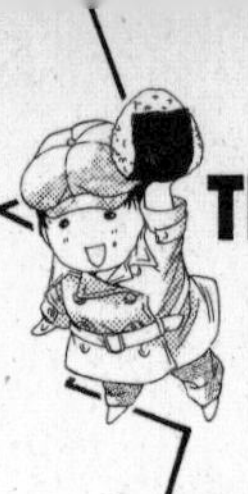

# THE ADVENTURES OF DETECTIVE RICE BALL!

HELLO! DETECTIVE RICE BALL HERE! I'VE BEEN APPEARING SINCE CHAPTER 117 (OFFICIALLY CHAPTER 116). KANUMISO...I MEAN...YASMIN SENDO. AS SOME OF YOU MAY HAVE ALREADY REALIZED, YASMIN IS THE MAIN CHARACTER OF ONE OF MASTER YUKIYAN SENSEI'S PREVIOUS WORKS, "YASMIN'S DANCE." FOR THOSE WHO DON'T KNOW IT, HERE'S SOME BRIEF BACKGROUND INFORMATION.

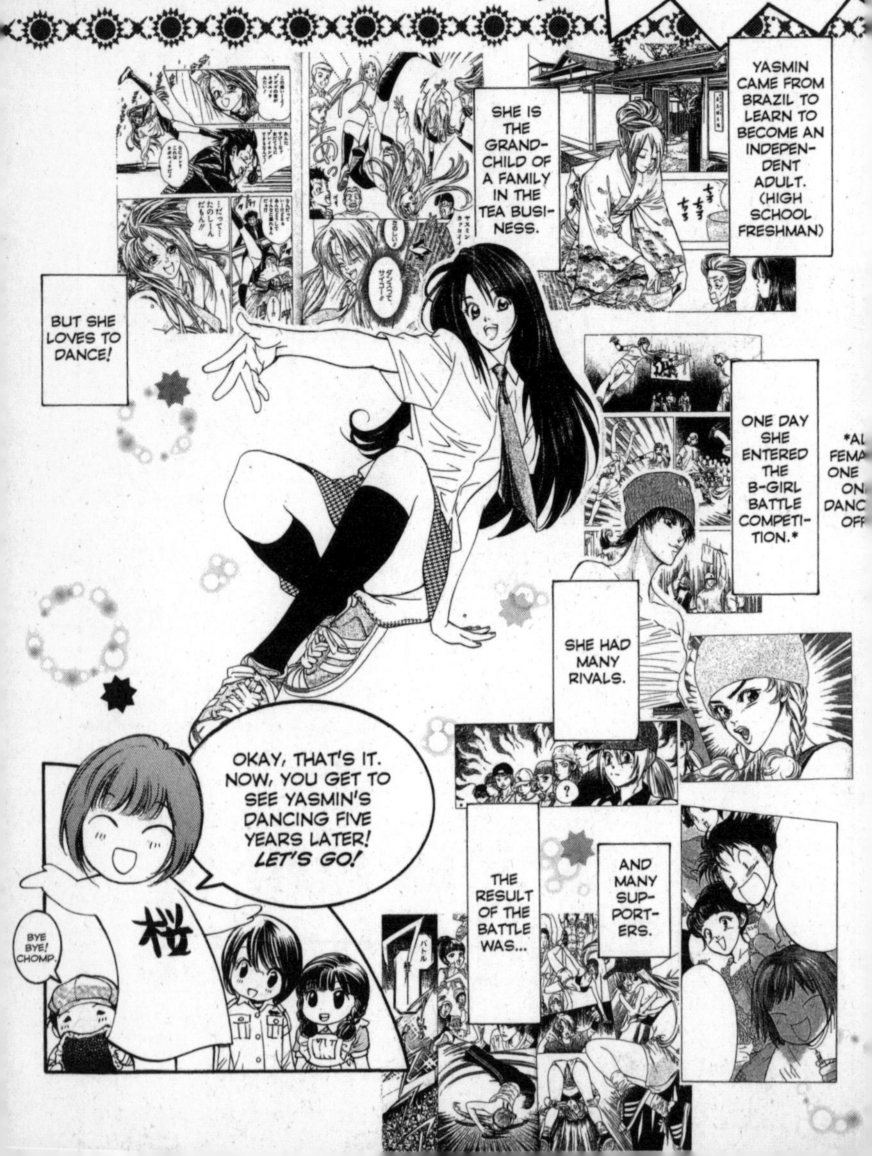
YASMIN CAME FROM BRAZIL TO LEARN TO BECOME AN INDEPENDENT ADULT. (HIGH SCHOOL FRESHMAN)
SHE IS THE GRANDCHILD OF A FAMILY IN THE TEA BUSINESS.
BUT SHE LOVES TO DANCE!
ONE DAY SHE ENTERED THE B-GIRL BATTLE COMPETITION.*
SHE HAD MANY RIVALS.
OKAY, THAT'S IT. NOW, YOU GET TO SEE YASMIN'S DANCING FIVE YEARS LATER! *LET'S GO!*
AND MANY SUPPORTERS.
THE RESULT OF THE BATTLE WAS...
BYE BYE! CHOMP.

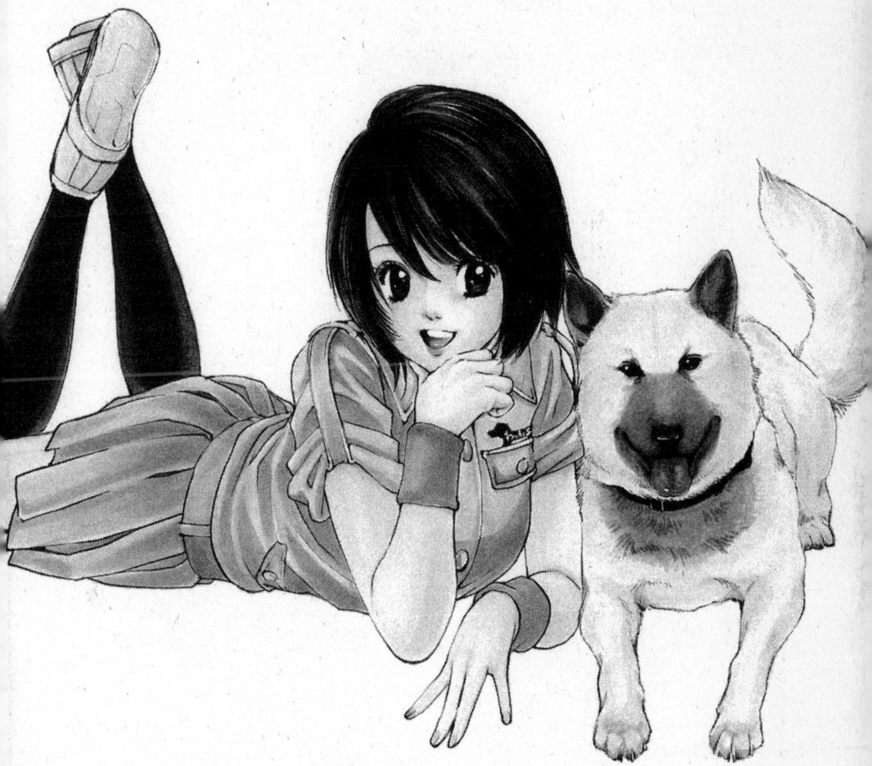

# CHAPTER 123:
# YASMIN'S DANCE

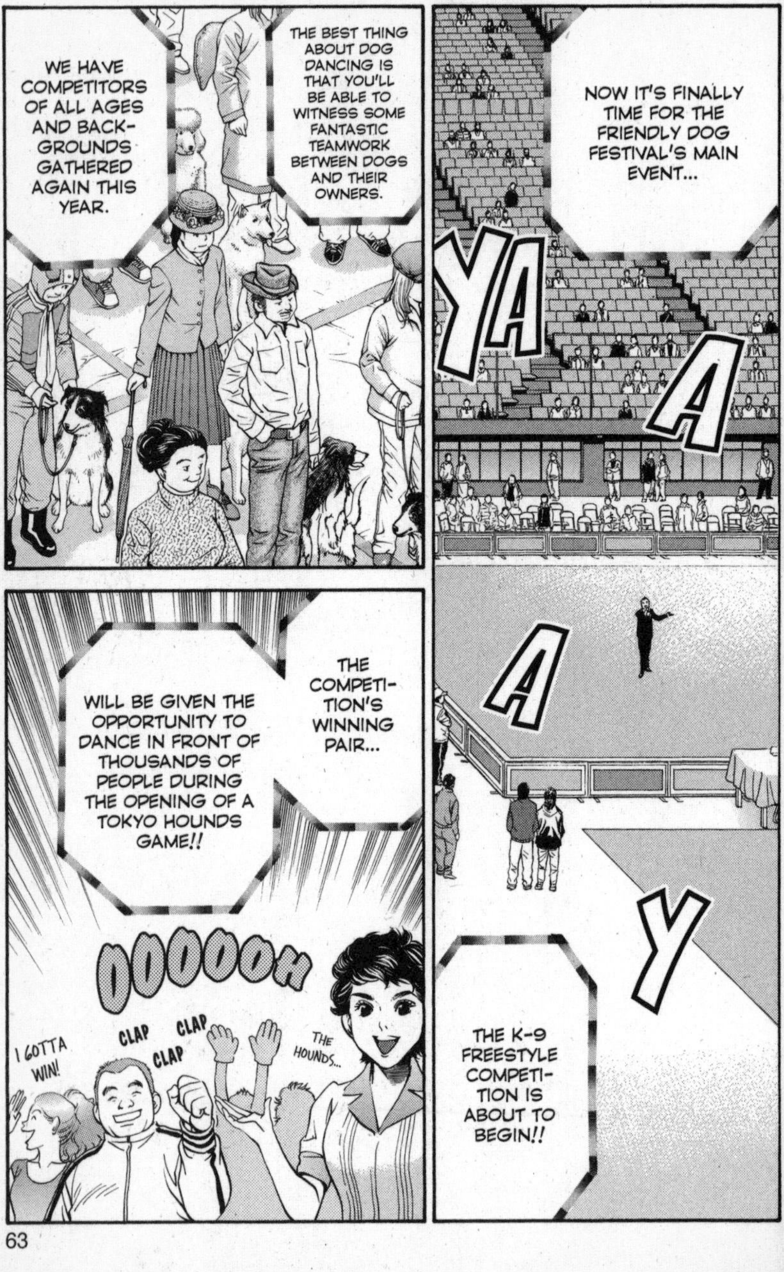
NOW IT'S FINALLY TIME FOR THE FRIENDLY DOG FESTIVAL'S MAIN EVENT...
YAAAY
THE K-9 FREESTYLE COMPETITION IS ABOUT TO BEGIN!!
THE BEST THING ABOUT DOG DANCING IS THAT YOU'LL BE ABLE TO WITNESS SOME FANTASTIC TEAMWORK BETWEEN DOGS AND THEIR OWNERS.
WE HAVE COMPETITORS OF ALL AGES AND BACKGROUNDS GATHERED AGAIN THIS YEAR.
THE COMPETITION'S WINNING PAIR...
WILL BE GIVEN THE OPPORTUNITY TO DANCE IN FRONT OF THOUSANDS OF PEOPLE DURING THE OPENING OF A TOKYO HOUNDS GAME!!
OOOOOH
THE HOUNDS...
CLAP
CLAP
CLAP
I GOTTA WIN!

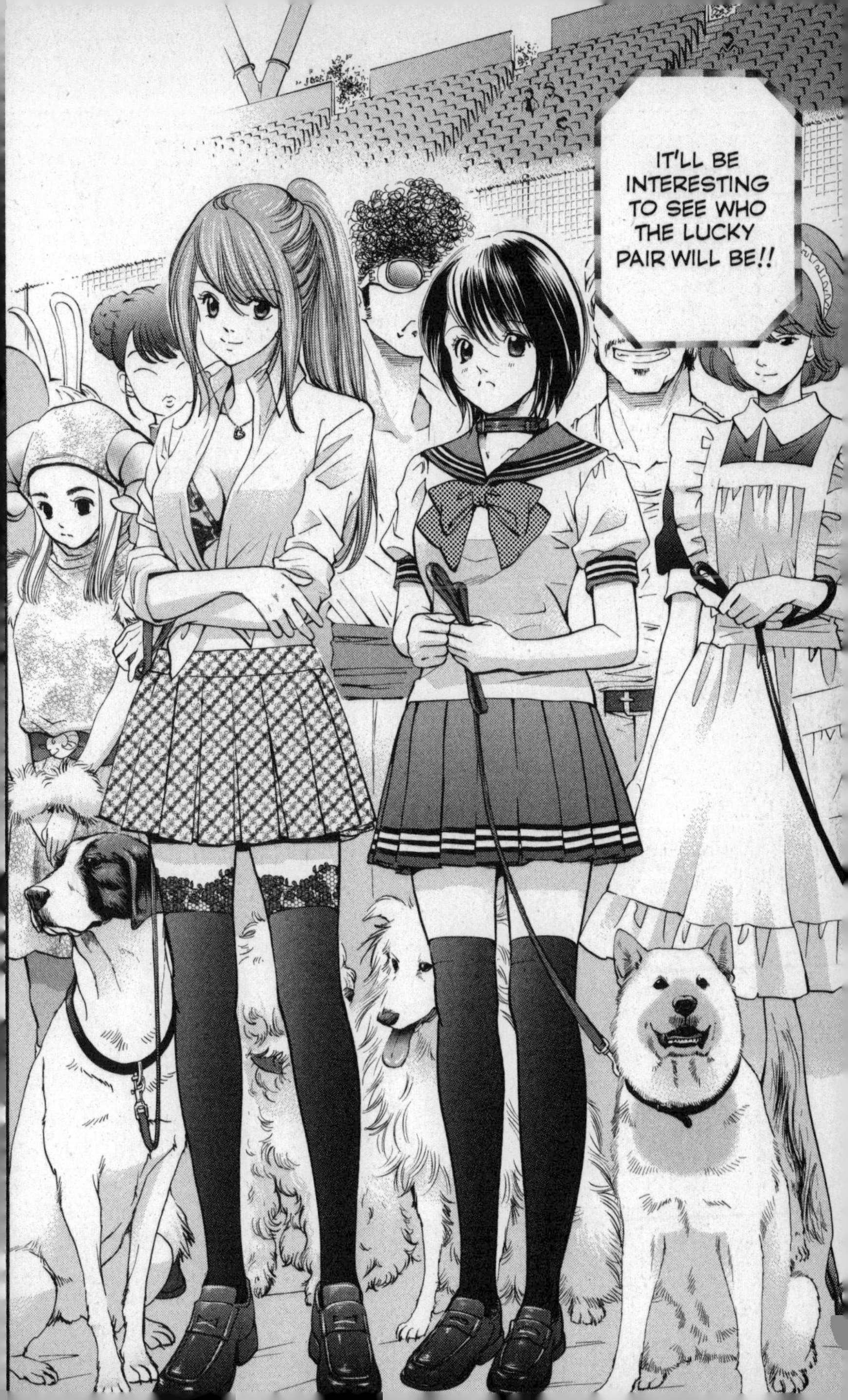
IT'LL BE INTERESTING TO SEE WHO THE LUCKY PAIR WILL BE!!

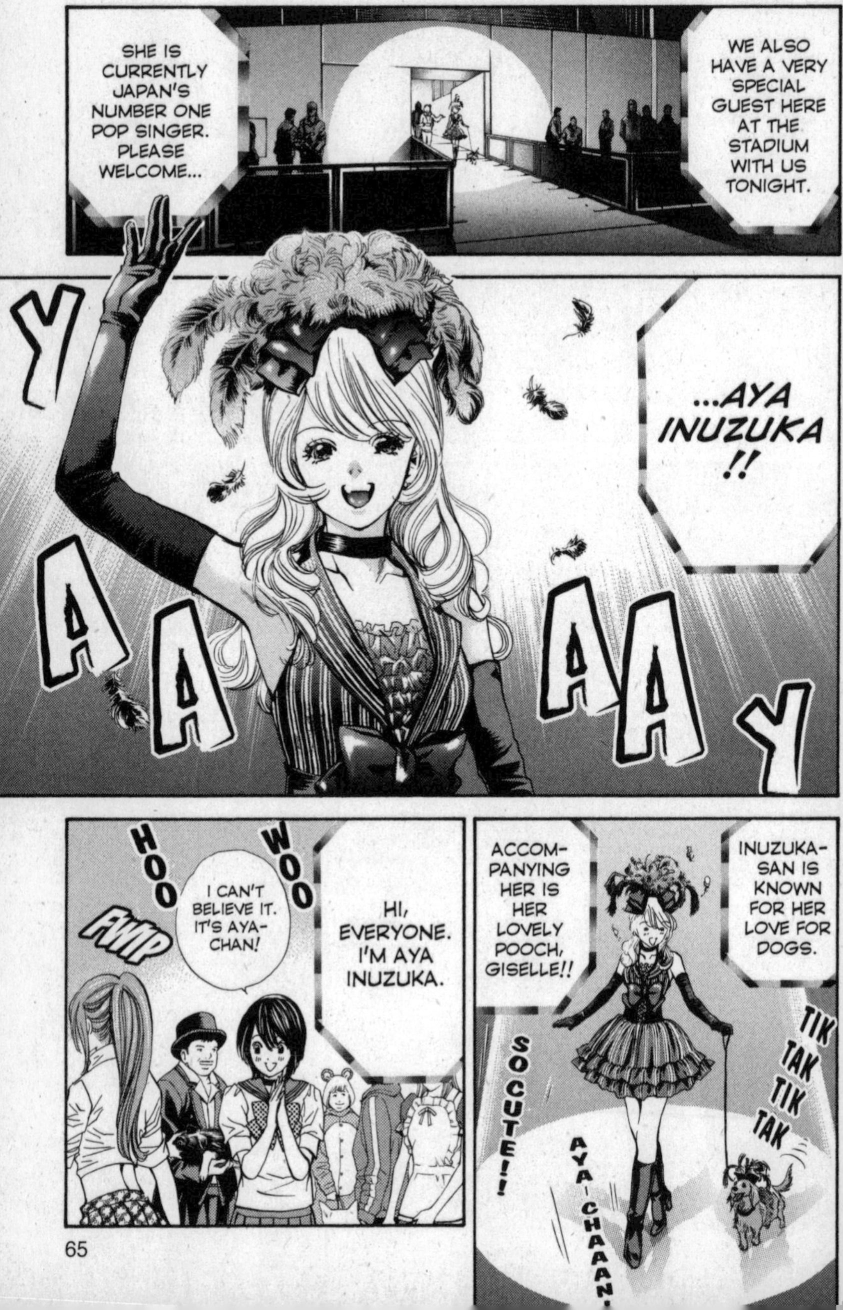
WE ALSO HAVE A VERY SPECIAL GUEST HERE AT THE STADIUM WITH US TONIGHT.
SHE IS CURRENTLY JAPAN'S NUMBER ONE POP SINGER. PLEASE WELCOME...
...AYA INUZUKA !!
YAAAAAY
INUZUKA-SAN IS KNOWN FOR HER LOVE FOR DOGS.
ACCOMPANYING HER IS HER LOVELY POOCH, GISELLE!!
TIK TAK TIK TAK
SO CUTE!!
AYA-CHAAAN!
HI, EVERYONE. I'M AYA INUZUKA.
WOO
I CAN'T BELIEVE IT. IT'S AYA-CHAN!
HOO
FWIP

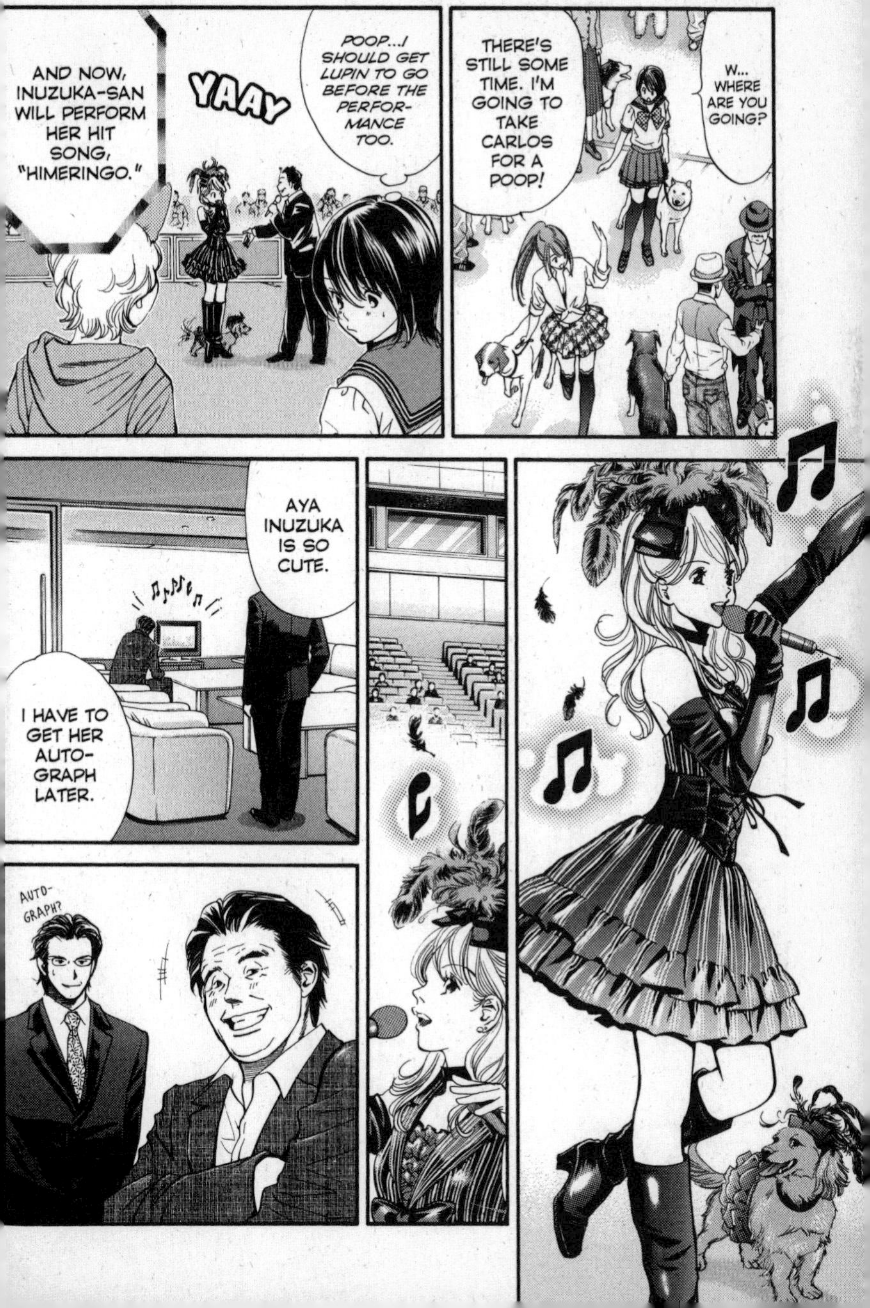
W... WHERE ARE YOU GOING?
THERE'S STILL SOME TIME. I'M GOING TO TAKE CARLOS FOR A POOP!
POOP...I SHOULD GET LUPIN TO GO BEFORE THE PERFORMANCE TOO.
YAAY
AND NOW, INUZUKA-SAN WILL PERFORM HER HIT SONG, "HIMERINGO."
AYA INUZUKA IS SO CUTE.
I HAVE TO GET HER AUTOGRAPH LATER.
AUTOGRAPH?

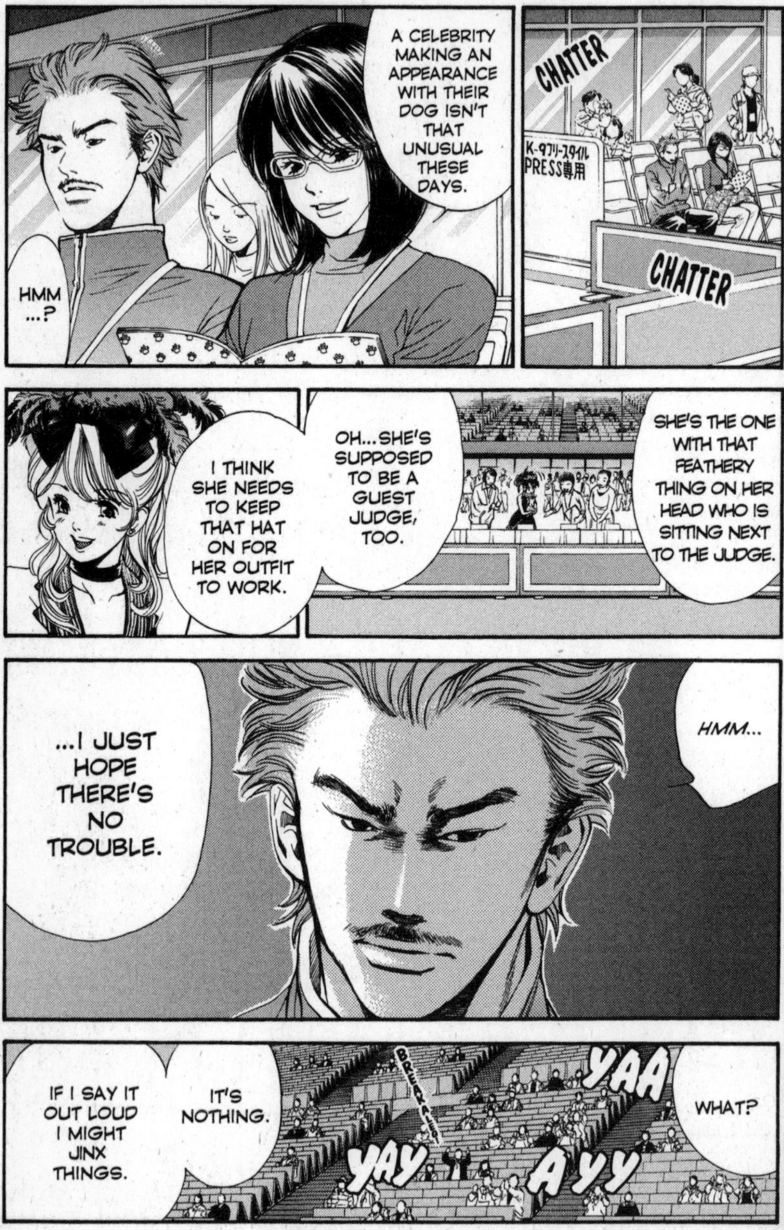
CHATTER
K-9フリースタイル
PRESS専用
CHATTER
A CELEBRITY MAKING AN APPEARANCE WITH THEIR DOG ISN'T THAT UNUSUAL THESE DAYS.
HMM ...?
SHE'S THE ONE WITH THAT FEATHERY THING ON HER HEAD WHO IS SITTING NEXT TO THE JUDGE.
OH...SHE'S SUPPOSED TO BE A GUEST JUDGE, TOO.
I THINK SHE NEEDS TO KEEP THAT HAT ON FOR HER OUTFIT TO WORK.
HMM...
...I JUST HOPE THERE'S NO TROUBLE.
WHAT?
YAA
BREAK A LEG!
YAY
AYY
IT'S NOTHING.
IF I SAY IT OUT LOUD I MIGHT JINX THINGS.

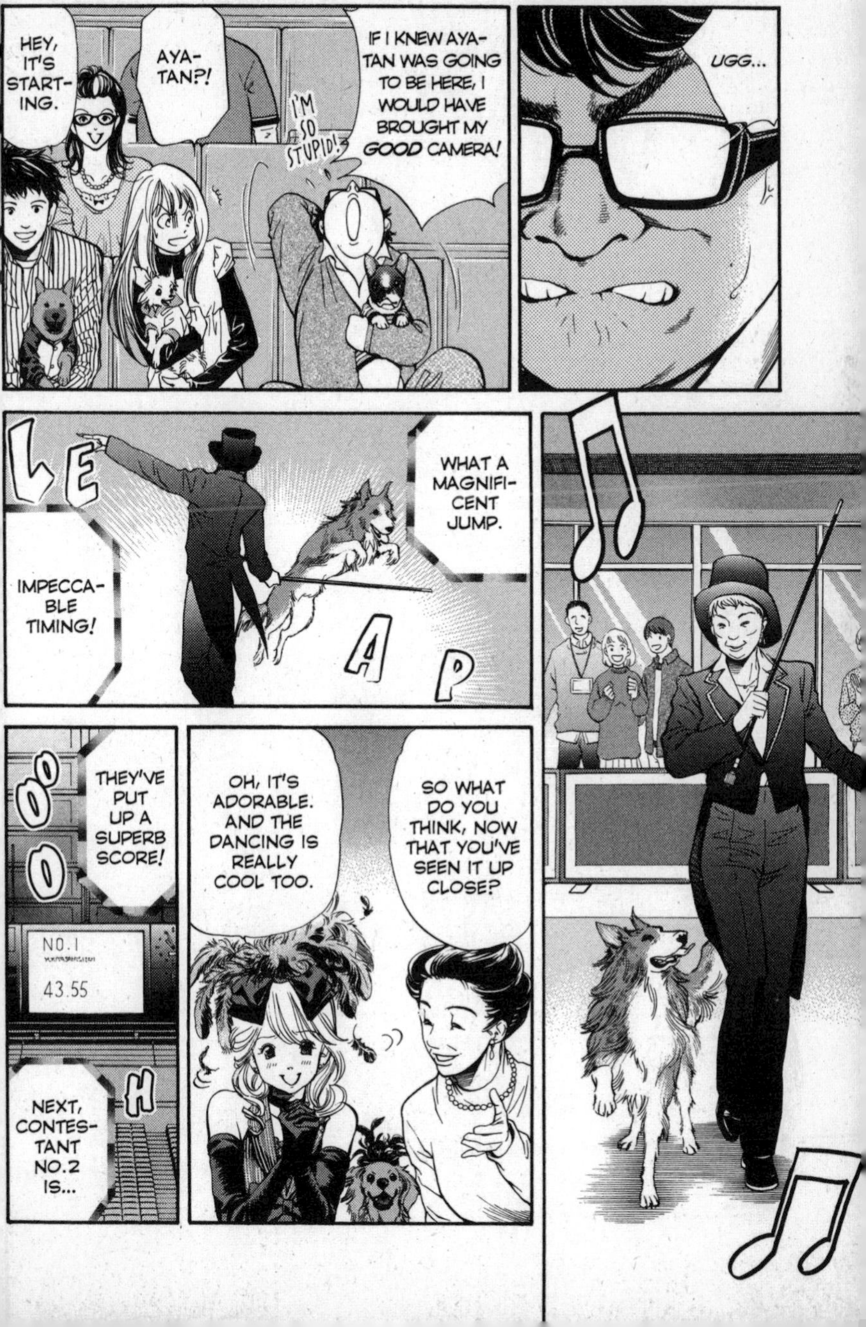

UGG...
IF I KNEW AYA-TAN WAS GOING TO BE HERE, I WOULD HAVE BROUGHT MY *GOOD* CAMERA!
I'M SO STUPID!
AYA-TAN?!
HEY, IT'S STARTING.
WHAT A MAGNIFICENT JUMP.
LE AP
IMPECCABLE TIMING!
SO WHAT DO YOU THINK, NOW THAT YOU'VE SEEN IT UP CLOSE?
OH, IT'S ADORABLE. AND THE DANCING IS REALLY COOL TOO.
THEY'VE PUT UP A SUPERB SCORE!
OOO
NO.1
43.55
H
NEXT, CONTESTANT NO.2 IS...

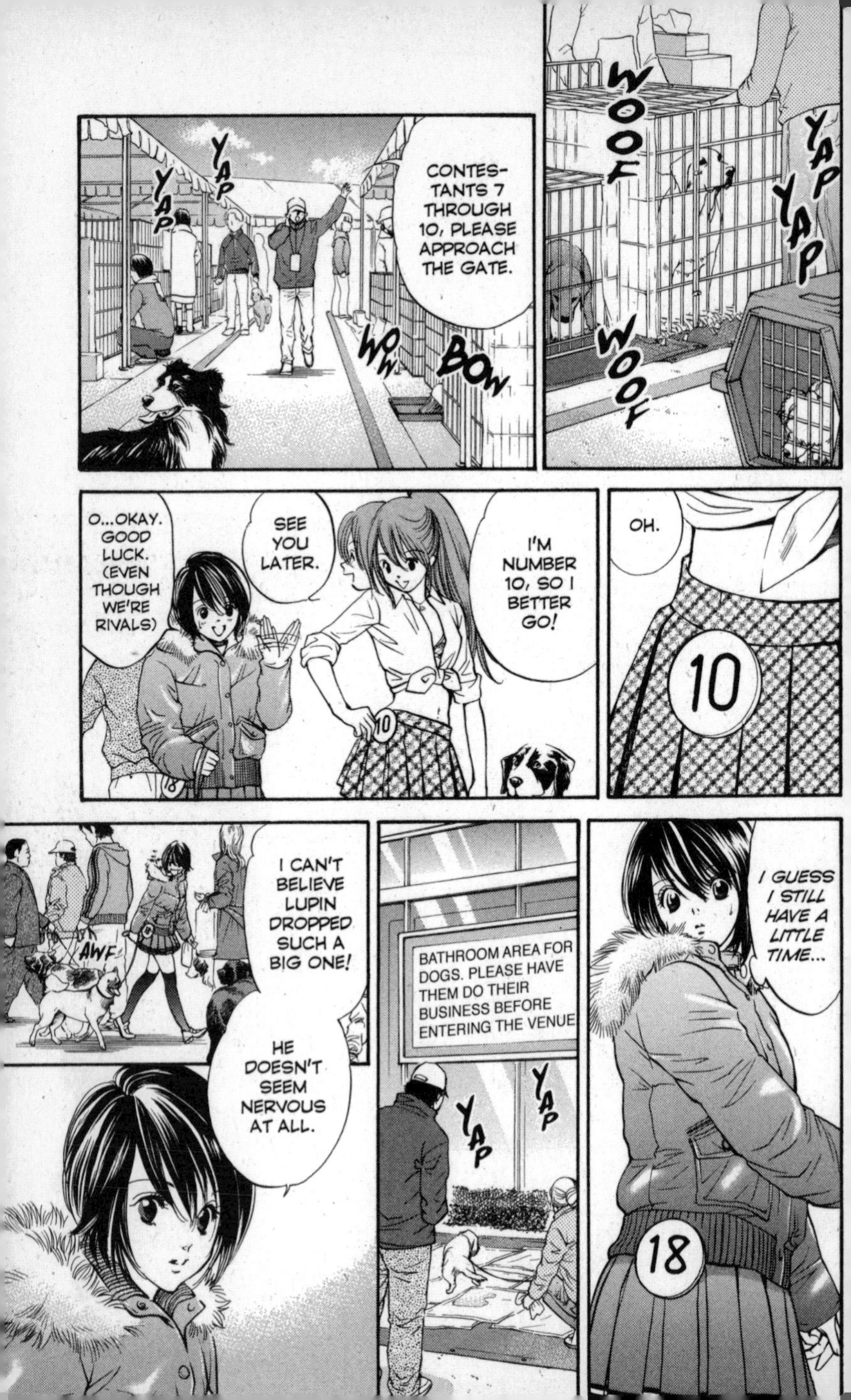
WOOF
YAP YAP
WOOF
YAP YAP
CONTESTANTS 7 THROUGH 10, PLEASE APPROACH THE GATE.
WOW
BOW
OH.
10
I'M NUMBER 10, SO I BETTER GO!
SEE YOU LATER.
O...OKAY. GOOD LUCK. (EVEN THOUGH WE'RE RIVALS)
I GUESS I STILL HAVE A LITTLE TIME...
18
BATHROOM AREA FOR DOGS. PLEASE HAVE THEM DO THEIR BUSINESS BEFORE ENTERING THE VENUE
YAP YAP
AWF
I CAN'T BELIEVE LUPIN DROPPED SUCH A BIG ONE!
HE DOESN'T SEEM NERVOUS AT ALL.

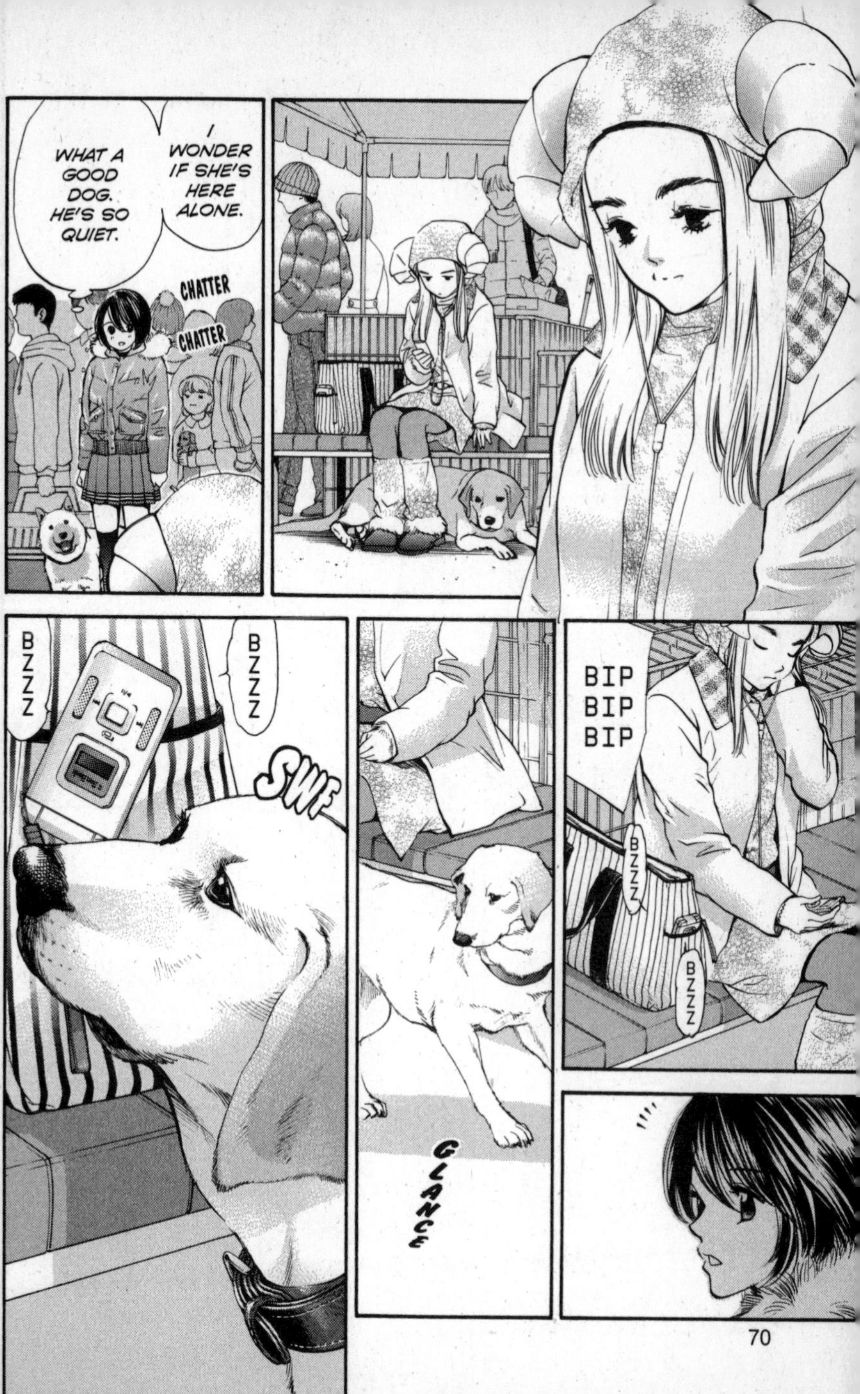
I WONDER IF SHE'S HERE ALONE.
WHAT A GOOD DOG. HE'S SO QUIET.
CHATTER
CHATTER
BIP BIP BIP
BZZZ
BZZZ
GLANCE
BZZZ
BZZZ
SNIF

JOLT
BZZZ
BZZZ
HE'S LETTING HER KNOW HER PHONE IS BUZZ-ING!
THAT DOGGY IS SO SMART.
... HELLO?
... YEAH. I'M FINE.
HA HA HA HA.
NO, IT'S NOT LIKE THAT!!
SHE SEEMS SO RELAXED ...
ISN'T SHE NER-VOUS AT ALL?!
HARF

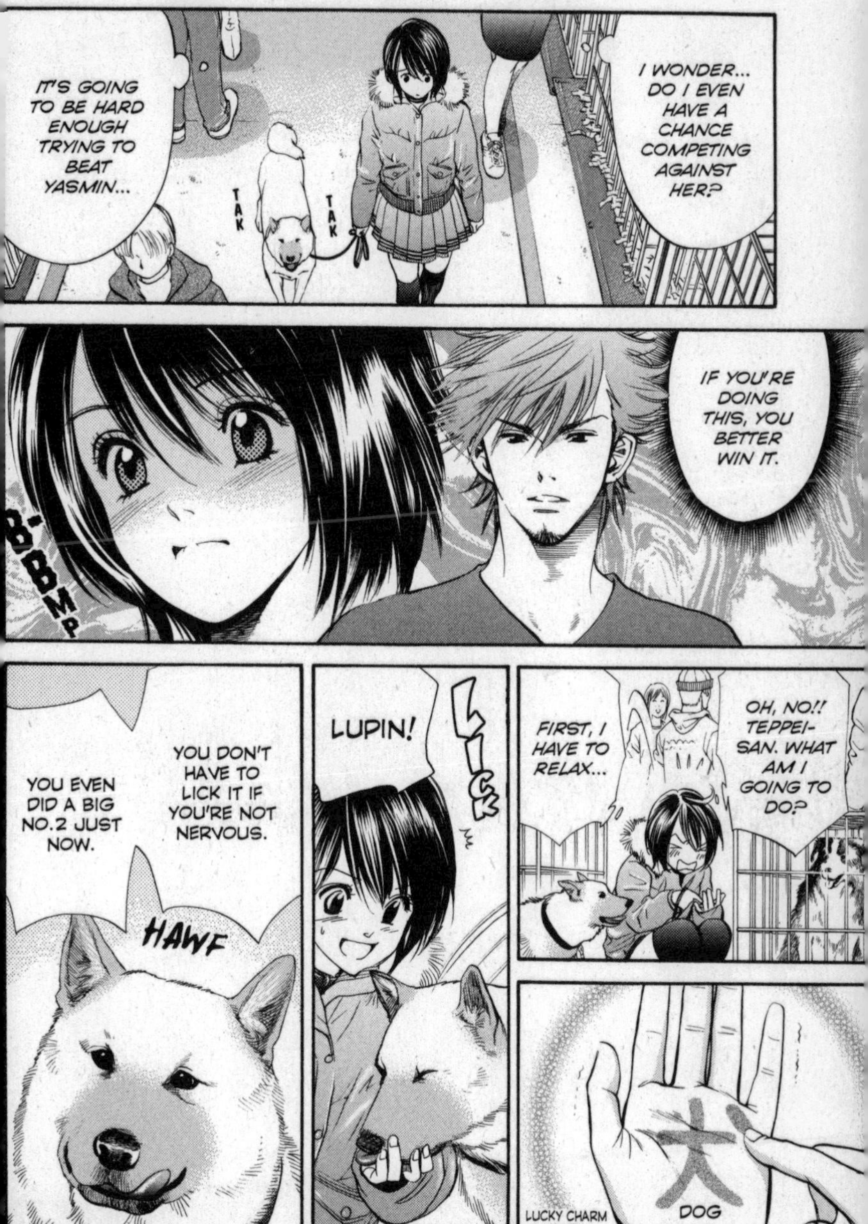
I WONDER... DO I EVEN HAVE A CHANCE COMPETING AGAINST HER?
TAK
TAK
IT'S GOING TO BE HARD ENOUGH TRYING TO BEAT YASMIN...
IF YOU'RE DOING THIS, YOU BETTER WIN IT.
B-BBMP
OH, NO!! TEPPEI-SAN. WHAT AM I GOING TO DO?
FIRST, I HAVE TO RELAX...
大
DOG
LUCKY CHARM
LICK
LUPIN!
YOU DON'T HAVE TO LICK IT IF YOU'RE NOT NERVOUS.
YOU EVEN DID A BIG NO.2 JUST NOW.
HAWF

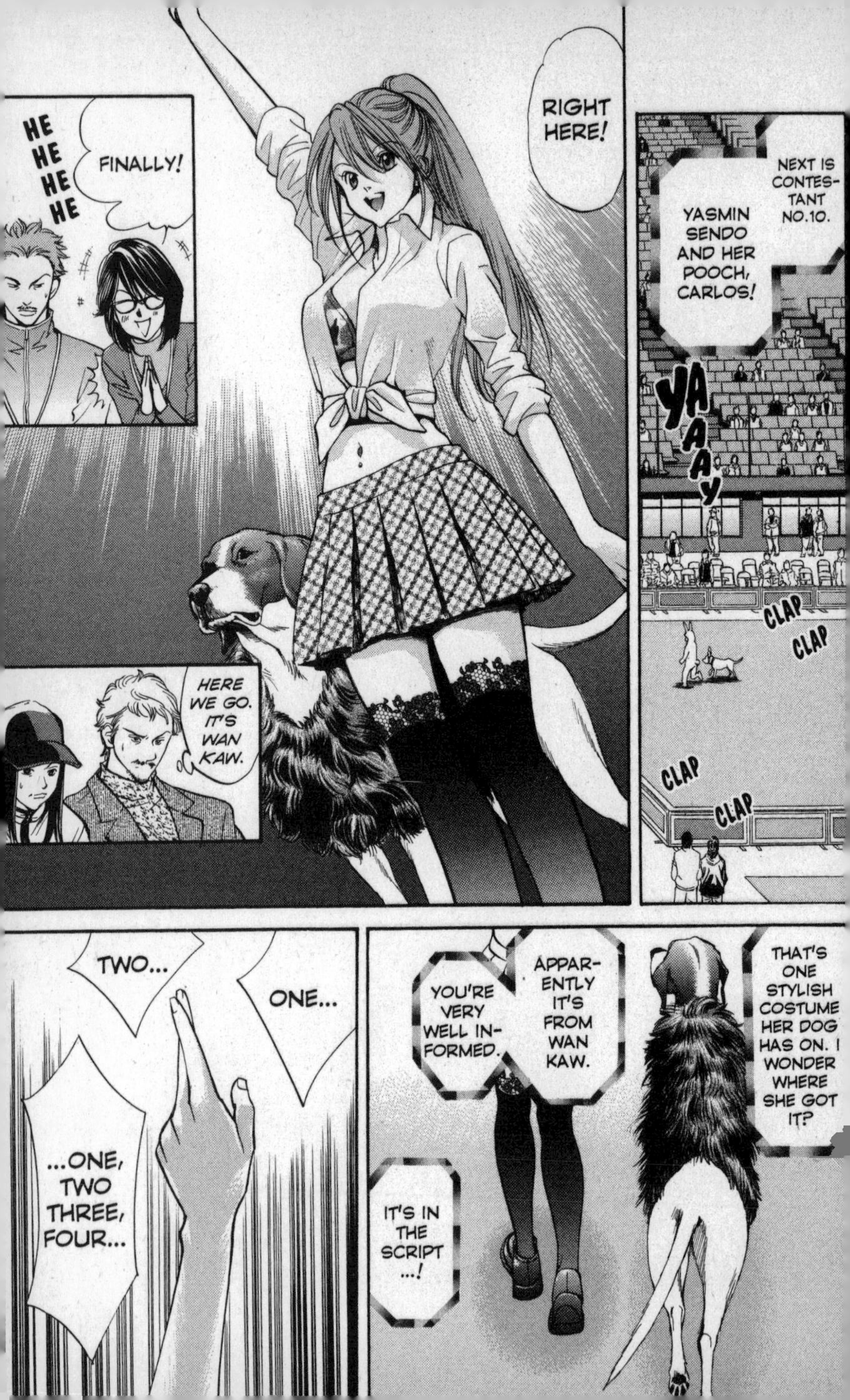
NEXT IS CONTESTANT NO.10.
YASMIN SENDO AND HER POOCH, CARLOS!
YAAAAY
CLAP
CLAP
CLAP
CLAP
RIGHT HERE!
FINALLY!
HE HE HE HE
HERE WE GO. IT'S WAN KAW.
THAT'S ONE STYLISH COSTUME HER DOG HAS ON. I WONDER WHERE SHE GOT IT?
APPARENTLY IT'S FROM WAN KAW.
YOU'RE VERY WELL INFORMED.
IT'S IN THE SCRIPT ...!
ONE...
TWO...
...ONE, TWO THREE, FOUR...

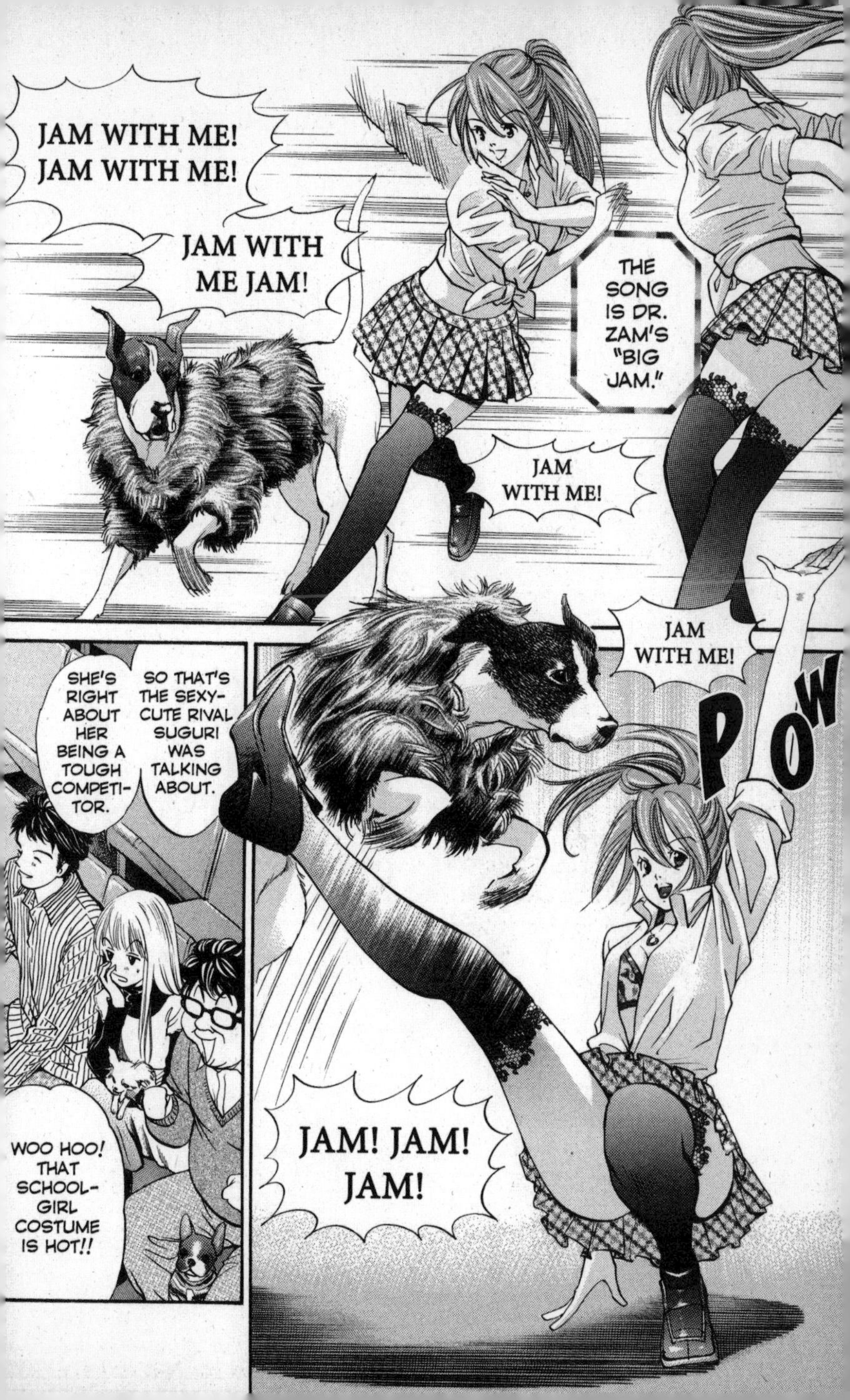
THE SONG IS DR. ZAM'S "BIG JAM."
JAM WITH ME! JAM WITH ME!
JAM WITH ME JAM!
JAM WITH ME!
JAM WITH ME!
POW
JAM! JAM! JAM!
SO THAT'S THE SEXY-CUTE RIVAL SUGURI WAS TALKING ABOUT.
SHE'S RIGHT ABOUT HER BEING A TOUGH COMPETITOR.
WOO HOO! THAT SCHOOLGIRL COSTUME IS HOT!!

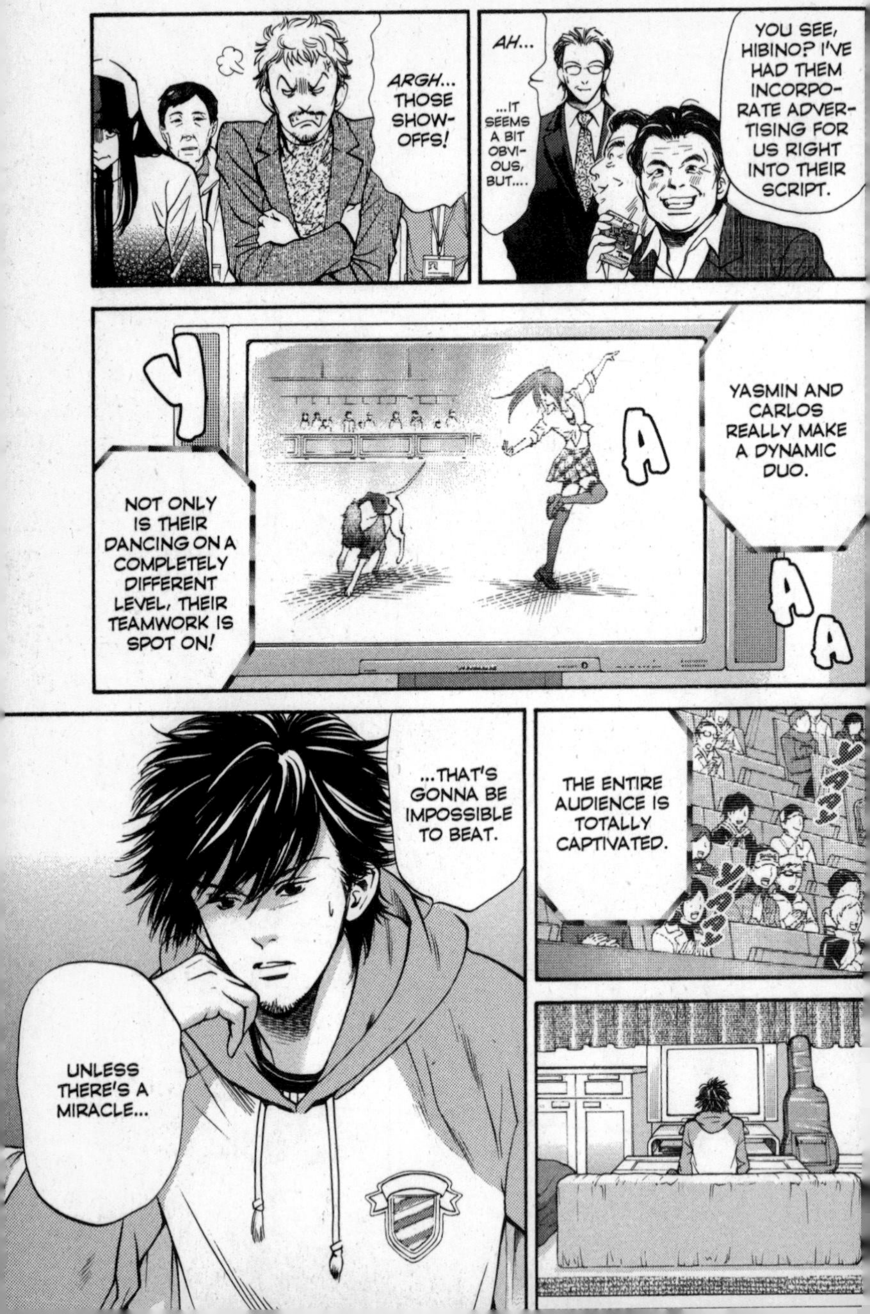
YOU SEE, HIBINO? I'VE HAD THEM INCORPORATE ADVERTISING FOR US RIGHT INTO THEIR SCRIPT.
AH...
...IT SEEMS A BIT OBVIOUS, BUT....
ARGH... THOSE SHOW-OFFS!
YASMIN AND CARLOS REALLY MAKE A DYNAMIC DUO.
YAAA
NOT ONLY IS THEIR DANCING ON A COMPLETELY DIFFERENT LEVEL, THEIR TEAMWORK IS SPOT ON!
THE ENTIRE AUDIENCE IS TOTALLY CAPTIVATED.
...THAT'S GONNA BE IMPOSSIBLE TO BEAT.
UNLESS THERE'S A MIRACLE...

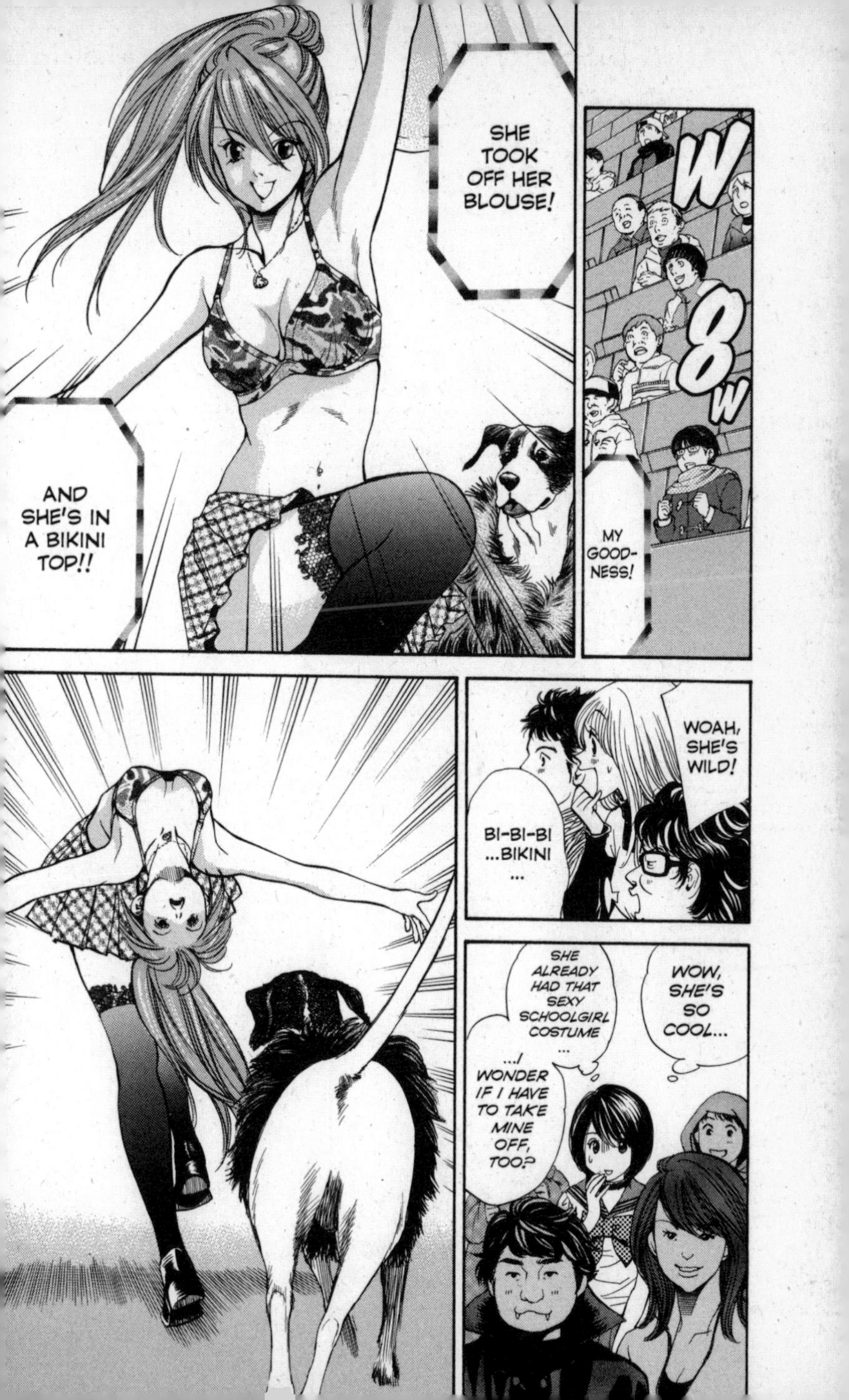
WOW
MY GOODNESS!
SHE TOOK OFF HER BLOUSE!
AND SHE'S IN A BIKINI TOP!!
WOAH, SHE'S WILD!
BI-BI-BI ...BIKINI ...
WOW, SHE'S SO COOL...
SHE ALREADY HAD THAT SEXY SCHOOLGIRL COSTUME ...
...I WONDER IF I HAVE TO TAKE MINE OFF, TOO?

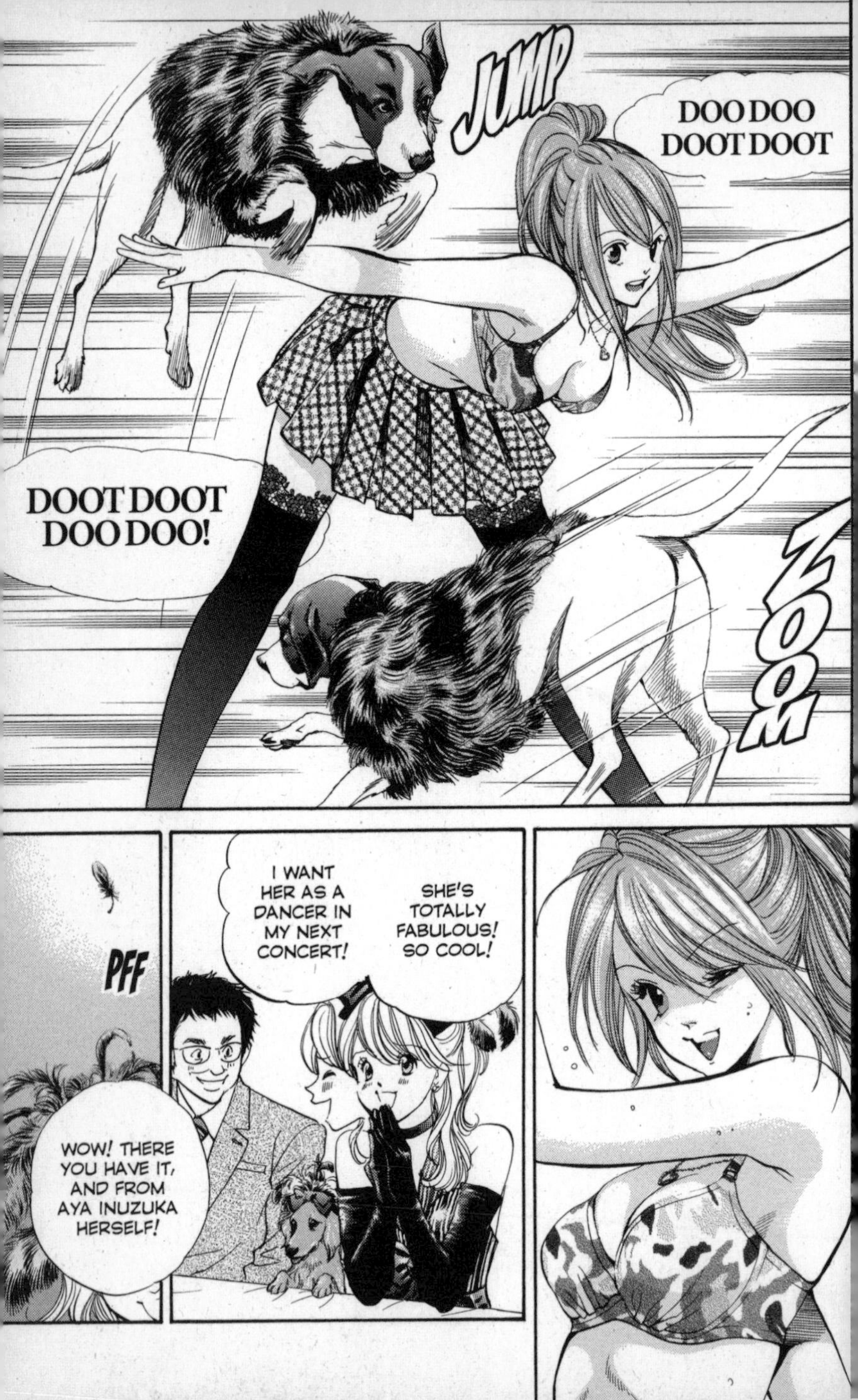
DOO DOO DOOT DOOT
JUMP
VOOM
DOOT DOOT DOO DOO!
I WANT HER AS A DANCER IN MY NEXT CONCERT! SHE'S TOTALLY FABULOUS! SO COOL!
PFF
WOW! THERE YOU HAVE IT, AND FROM AYA INUZUKA HERSELF!

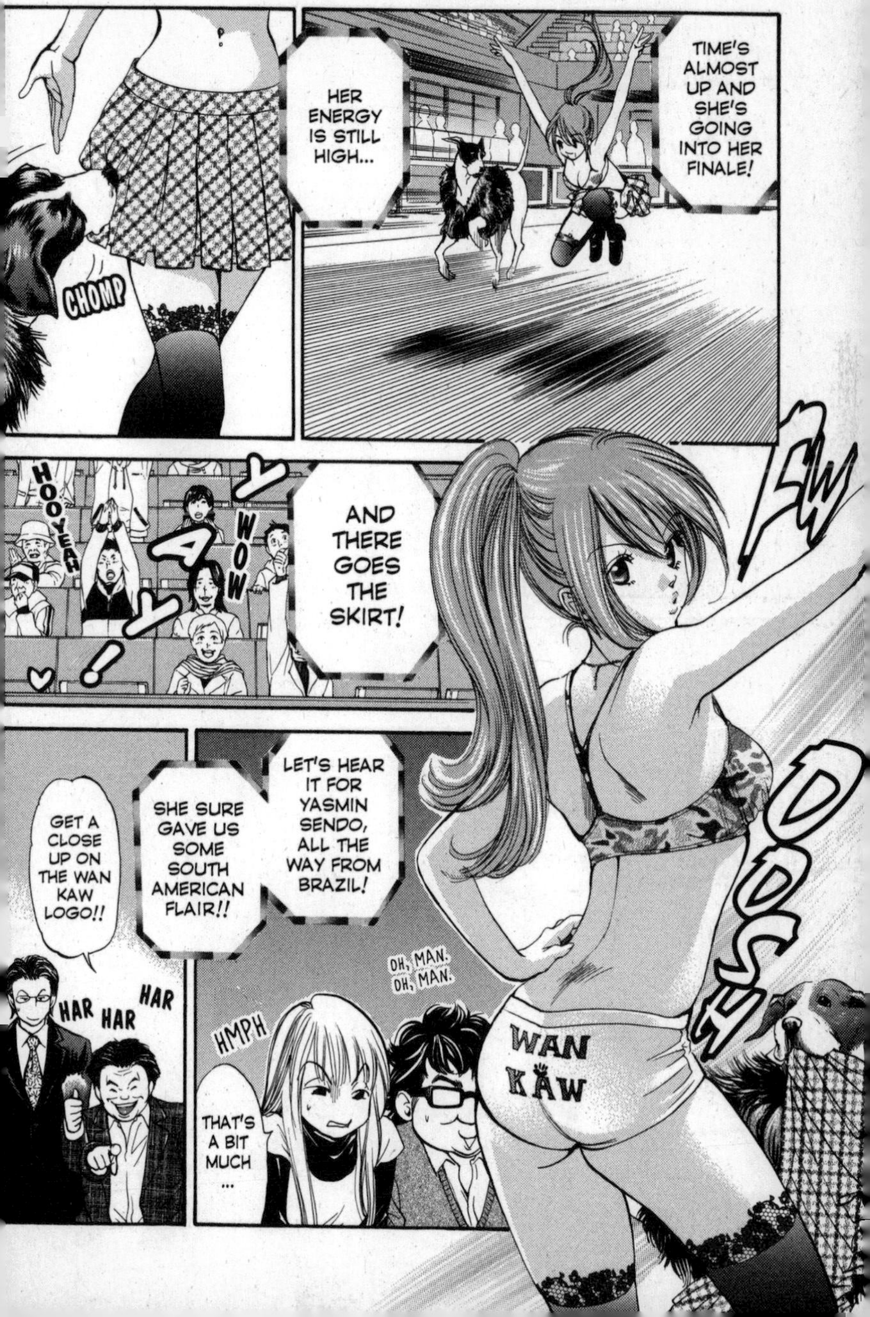
TIME'S ALMOST UP AND SHE'S GOING INTO HER FINALE!
HER ENERGY IS STILL HIGH...
CHOMP
FW
DOSH
WAN KAW
AND THERE GOES THE SKIRT!
WOW
YAY!
HOOYEAH
LET'S HEAR IT FOR YASMIN SENDO, ALL THE WAY FROM BRAZIL!
SHE SURE GAVE US SOME SOUTH AMERICAN FLAIR!!
OH, MAN. OH, MAN.
HMPH
THAT'S A BIT MUCH ...
GET A CLOSE UP ON THE WAN KAW LOGO!!
HAR HAR HAR

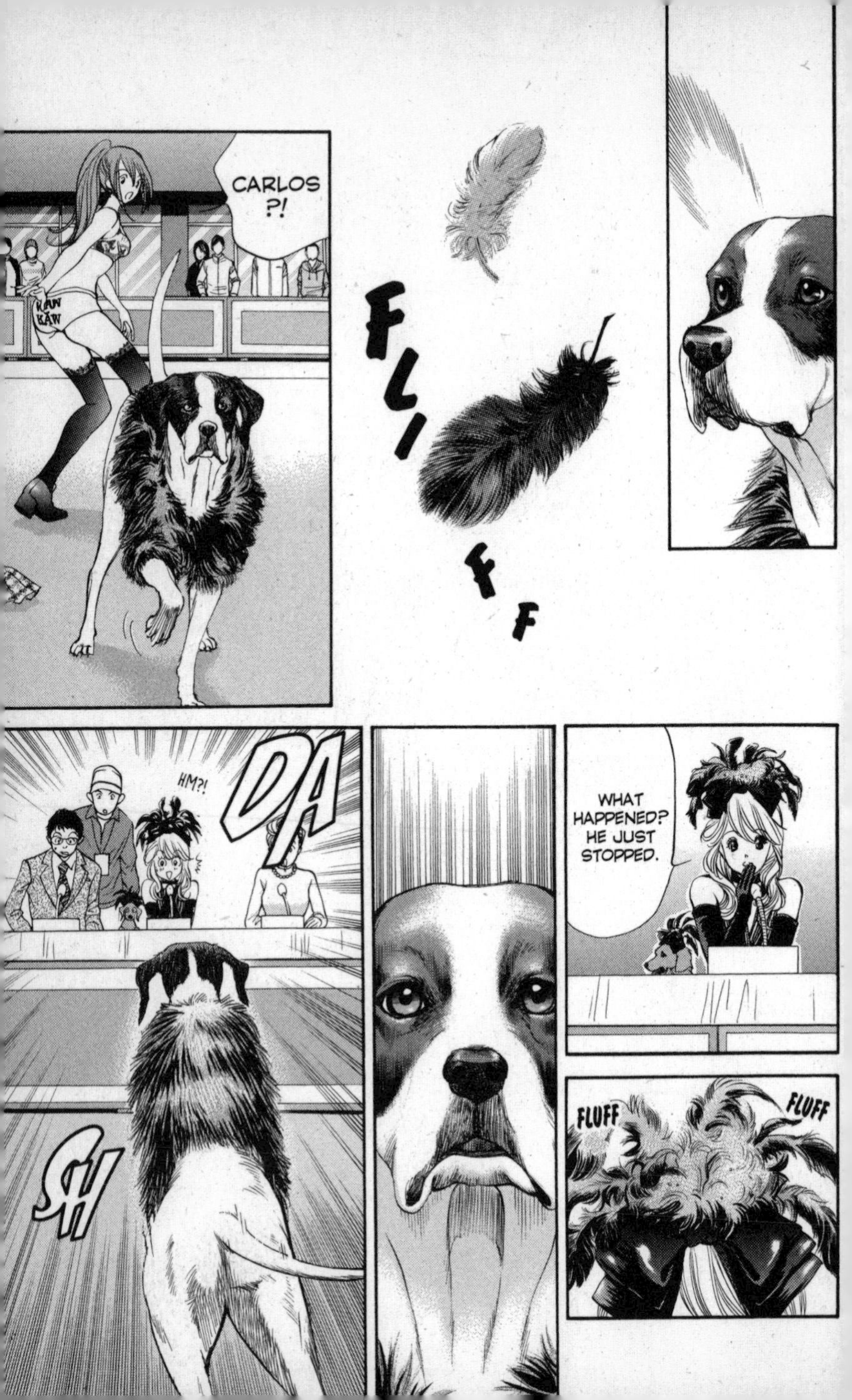
FLIFF
CARLOS ?!
WHAT HAPPENED? HE JUST STOPPED.
FLUFF
FLUFF
DA
HM?!
SH

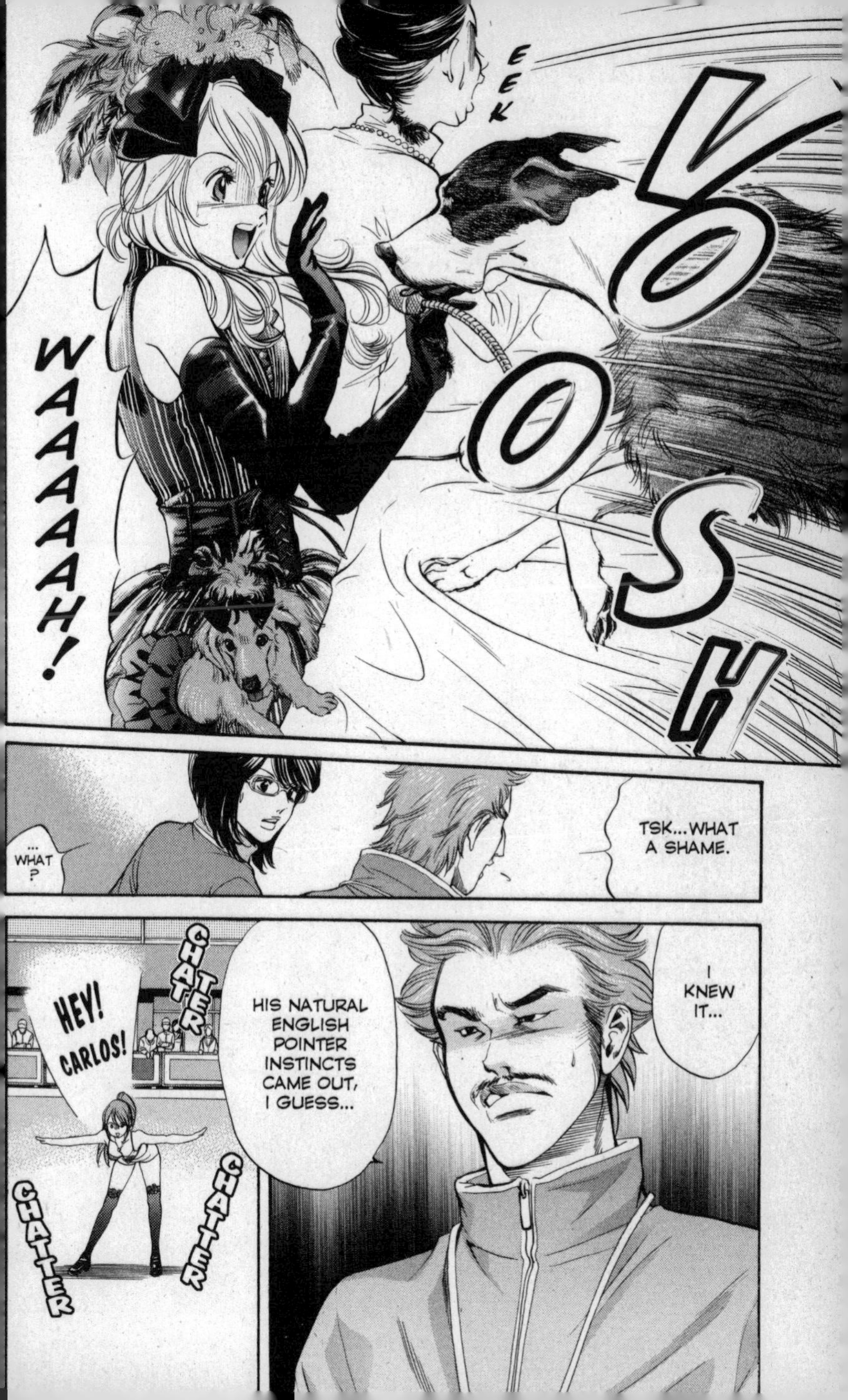
EEK
VOOOSH
WAAAAAH!
TSK...WHAT A SHAME.
...WHAT?
I KNEW IT...
HIS NATURAL ENGLISH POINTER INSTINCTS CAME OUT, I GUESS...
CHATTER
HEY! CARLOS!
CHATTER
CHATTER

# CHAPTER 124: SUGURI'S DANCE

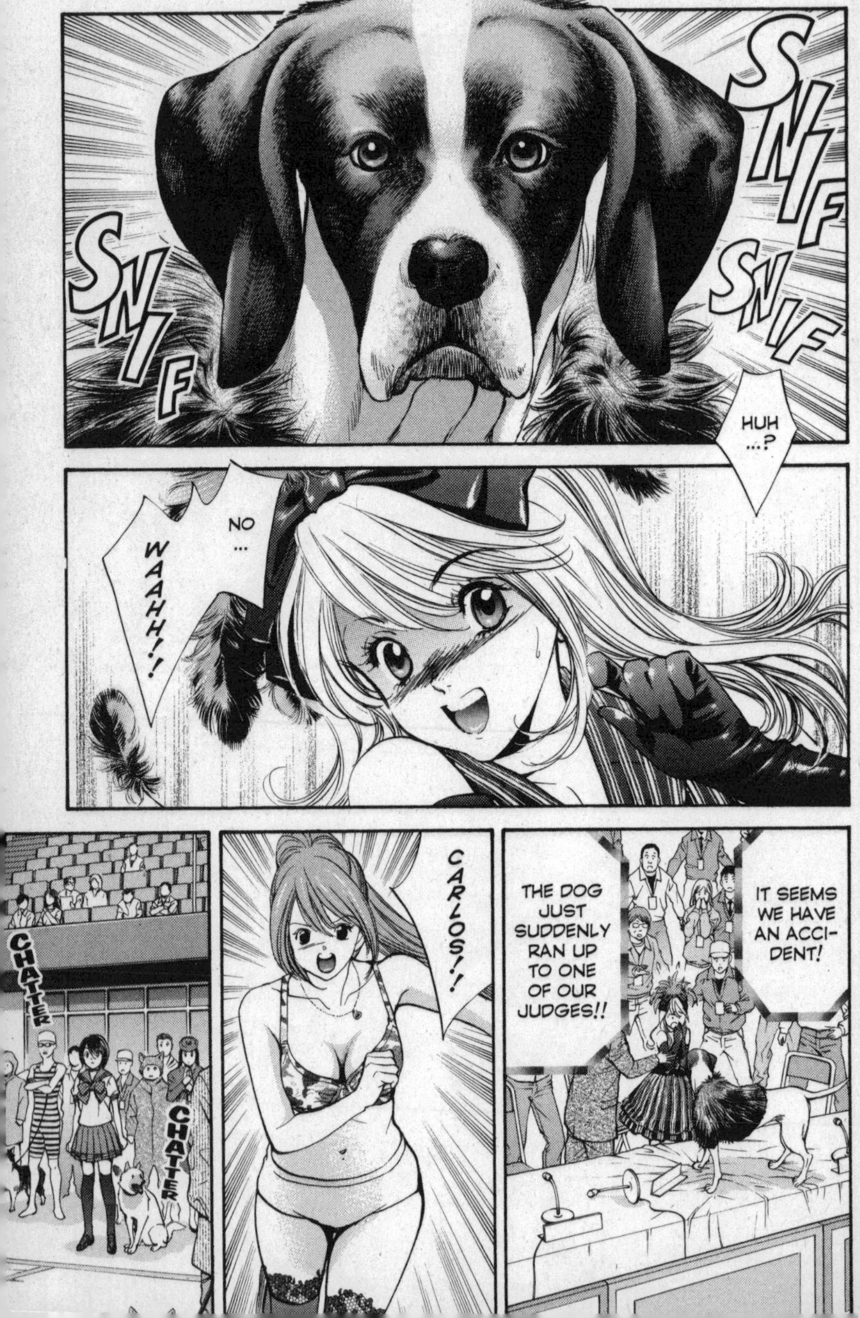
SNIF SNIF
SNIF
HUH ...?
NO ...
WAAHH!!
IT SEEMS WE HAVE AN ACCI-DENT!
THE DOG JUST SUDDENLY RAN UP TO ONE OF OUR JUDGES!!
CARLOS!!
CHATTER
CHATTER

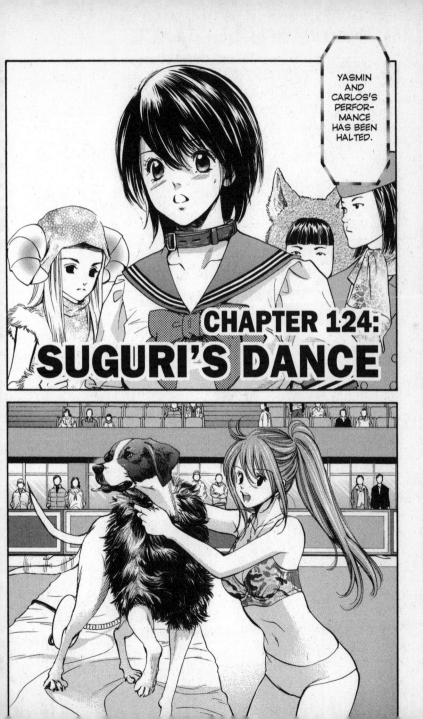

YASMIN AND CARLOS'S PERFORMANCE HAS BEEN HALTED.

CHAPTER 124:
SUGURI'S DANCE

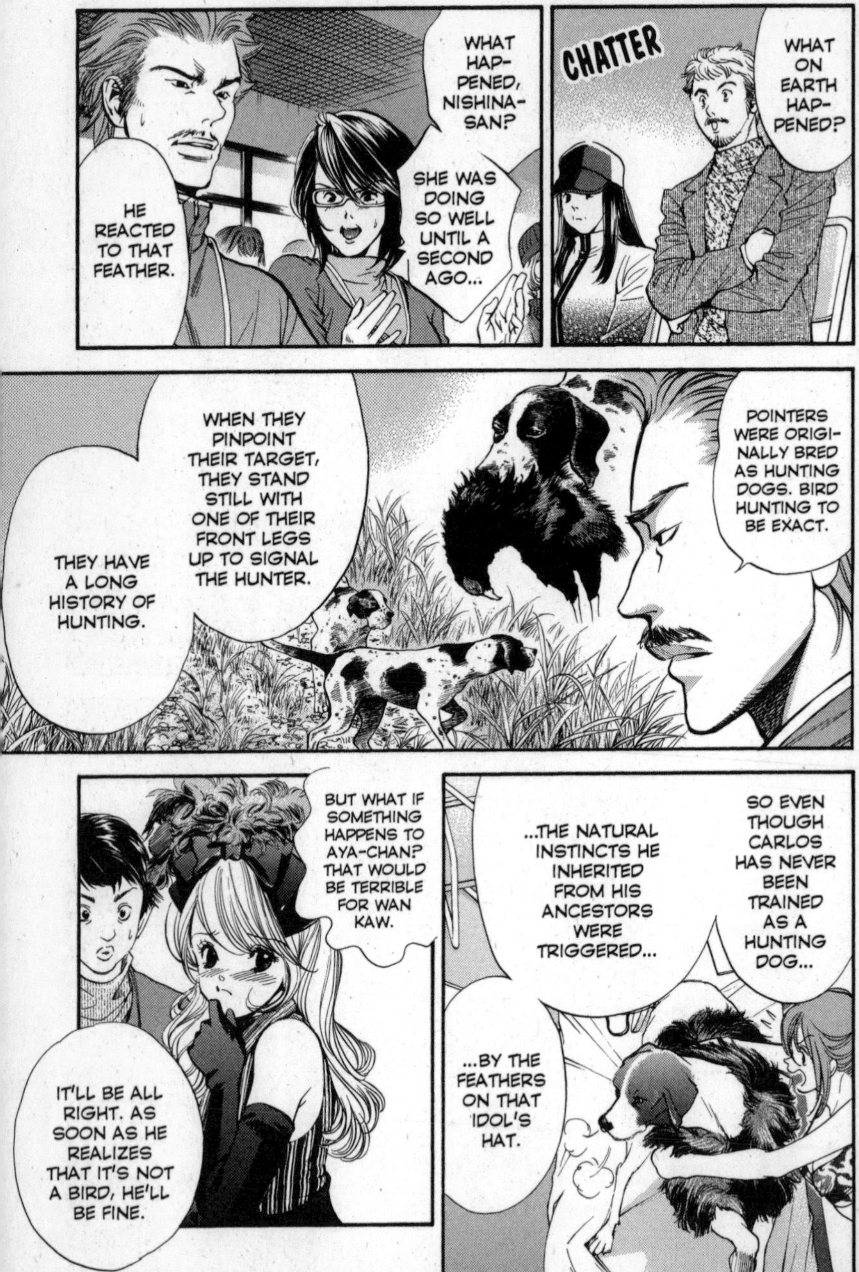
CHATTER
WHAT ON EARTH HAP-PENED?
WHAT HAP-PENED, NISHINA-SAN?
SHE WAS DOING SO WELL UNTIL A SECOND AGO...
HE REACTED TO THAT FEATHER.
POINTERS WERE ORIGI-NALLY BRED AS HUNTING DOGS. BIRD HUNTING TO BE EXACT.
WHEN THEY PINPOINT THEIR TARGET, THEY STAND STILL WITH ONE OF THEIR FRONT LEGS UP TO SIGNAL THE HUNTER.
THEY HAVE A LONG HISTORY OF HUNTING.
SO EVEN THOUGH CARLOS HAS NEVER BEEN TRAINED AS A HUNTING DOG...
...THE NATURAL INSTINCTS HE INHERITED FROM HIS ANCESTORS WERE TRIGGERED...
...BY THE FEATHERS ON THAT IDOL'S HAT.
BUT WHAT IF SOMETHING HAPPENS TO AYA-CHAN? THAT WOULD BE TERRIBLE FOR WAN KAW.
IT'LL BE ALL RIGHT. AS SOON AS HE REALIZES THAT IT'S NOT A BIRD, HE'LL BE FINE.

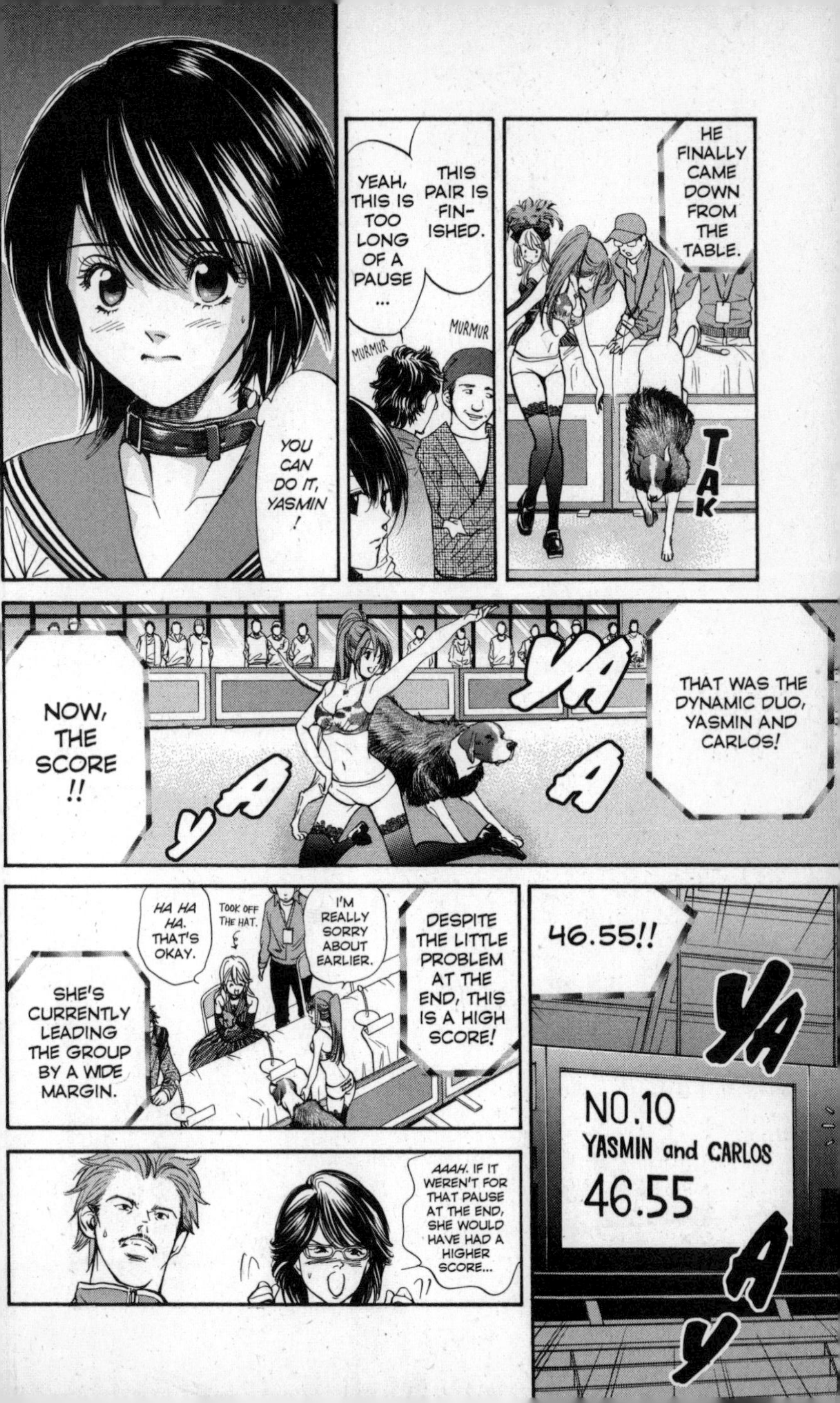
HE FINALLY CAME DOWN FROM THE TABLE.
TAK
THIS PAIR IS FIN-ISHED.
YEAH, THIS IS TOO LONG OF A PAUSE ...
MURMUR
MURMUR
YOU CAN DO IT, YASMIN!
THAT WAS THE DYNAMIC DUO, YASMIN AND CARLOS!
YA
A
YA
NOW, THE SCORE!!
46.55!!
YA
NO.10
YASMIN and CARLOS
46.55
A
Y
DESPITE THE LITTLE PROBLEM AT THE END, THIS IS A HIGH SCORE!
I'M REALLY SORRY ABOUT EARLIER.
TOOK OFF THE HAT.
HA HA HA. THAT'S OKAY.
SHE'S CURRENTLY LEADING THE GROUP BY A WIDE MARGIN.
AAAH. IF IT WEREN'T FOR THAT PAUSE AT THE END, SHE WOULD HAVE HAD A HIGHER SCORE...

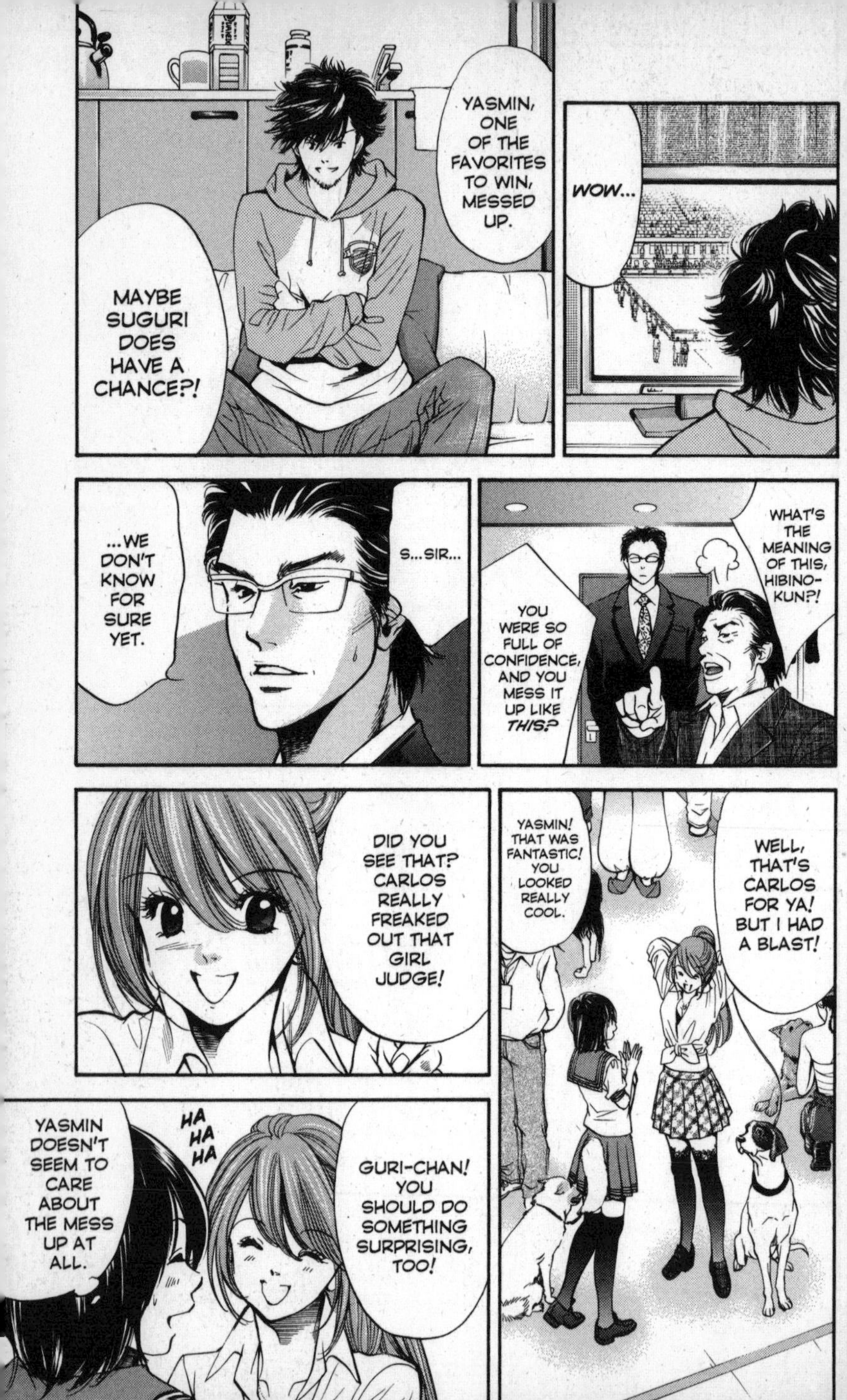
WOW...
YASMIN, ONE OF THE FAVORITES TO WIN, MESSED UP.
MAYBE SUGURI DOES HAVE A CHANCE?!
WHAT'S THE MEANING OF THIS, HIBINO-KUN?!
YOU WERE SO FULL OF CONFIDENCE, AND YOU MESS IT UP LIKE *THIS?*
S...SIR...
...WE DON'T KNOW FOR SURE YET.
WELL, THAT'S CARLOS FOR YA! BUT I HAD A BLAST!
YASMIN! THAT WAS FANTASTIC! YOU LOOKED REALLY COOL.
DID YOU SEE THAT? CARLOS REALLY FREAKED OUT THAT GIRL JUDGE!
GURI-CHAN! YOU SHOULD DO SOMETHING SURPRISING, TOO!
HA HA HA
YASMIN DOESN'T SEEM TO CARE ABOUT THE MESS UP AT ALL.

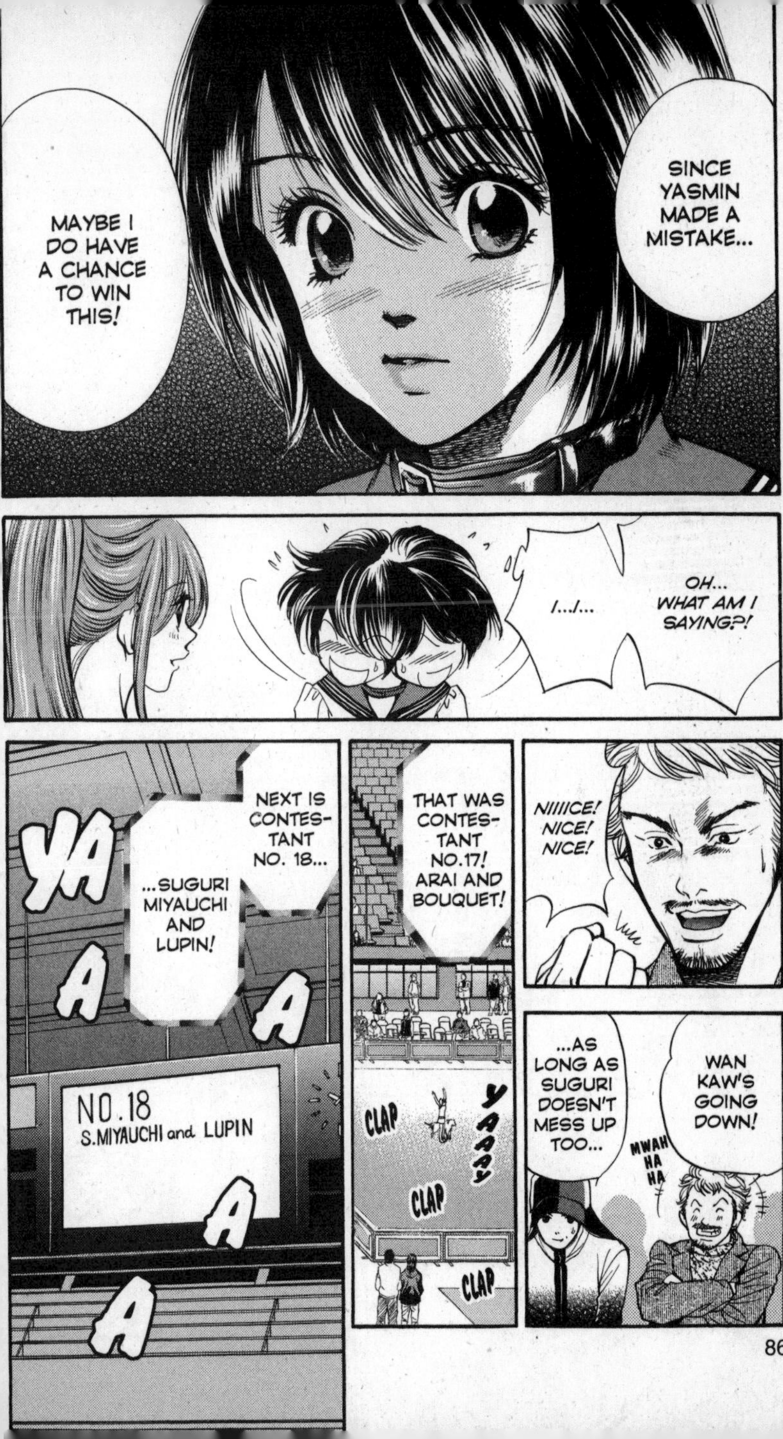
SINCE YASMIN MADE A MISTAKE...
MAYBE I DO HAVE A CHANCE TO WIN THIS!
OH... WHAT AM I SAYING?!
I...I...
NIIIICE! NICE! NICE!
WAN KAW'S GOING DOWN!
MWAH HA HA
...AS LONG AS SUGURI DOESN'T MESS UP TOO...
THAT WAS CONTESTANT NO.17! ARAI AND BOUQUET!
YAAAAY
CLAP
CLAP
CLAP
NEXT IS CONTESTANT NO. 18...
...SUGURI MIYAUCHI AND LUPIN!
YAAAAA
NO.18
S.MIYAUCHI and LUPIN

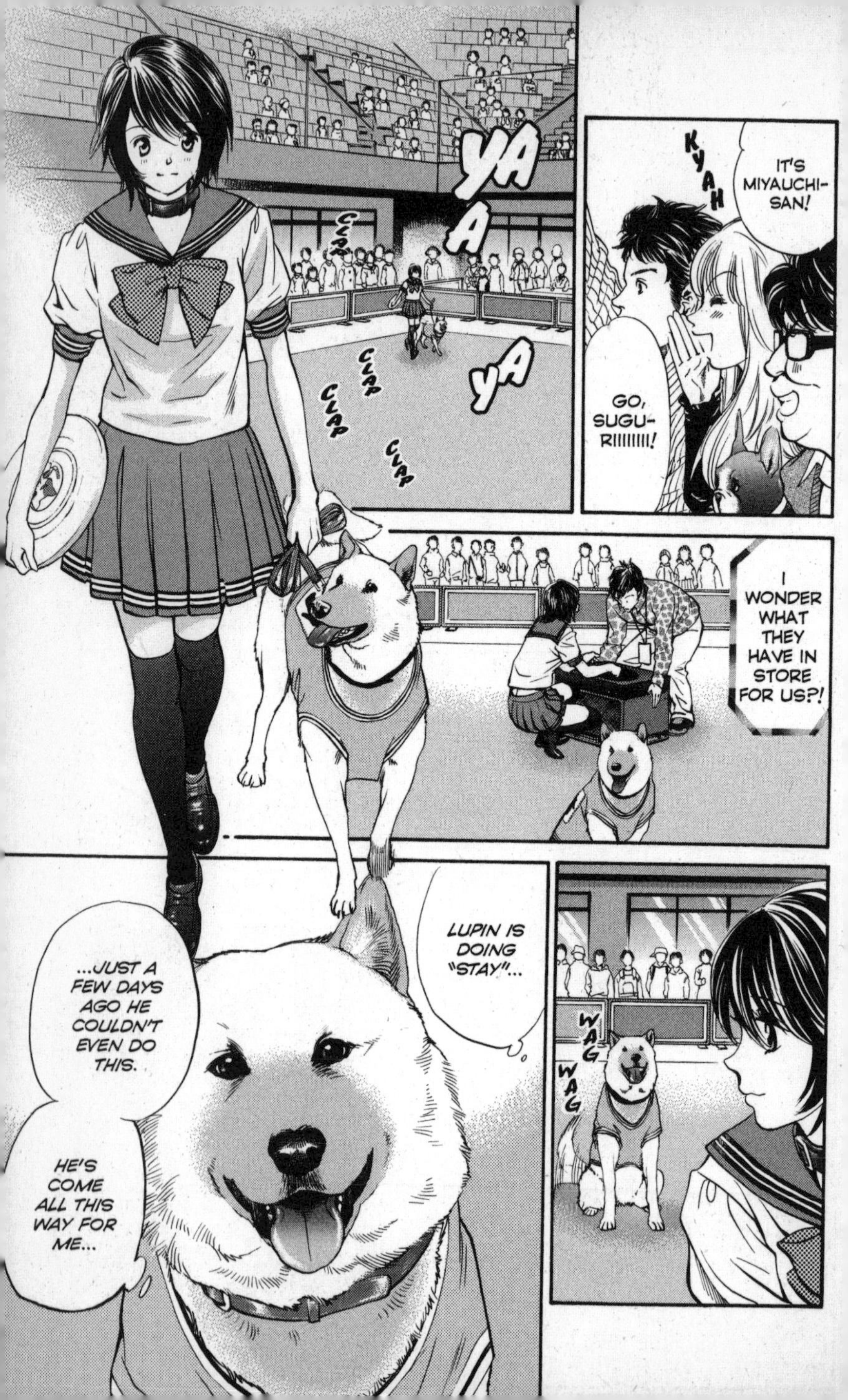
IT'S MIYAUCHI-SAN!
KYAH
GO, SUGURIIIIIIII!
YA A YA
CLAP CLAP
CLAP CLAP
CLAP
I WONDER WHAT THEY HAVE IN STORE FOR US?!
WAG WAG
LUPIN IS DOING "STAY"...
...JUST A FEW DAYS AGO HE COULDN'T EVEN DO THIS.
HE'S COME ALL THIS WAY FOR ME...

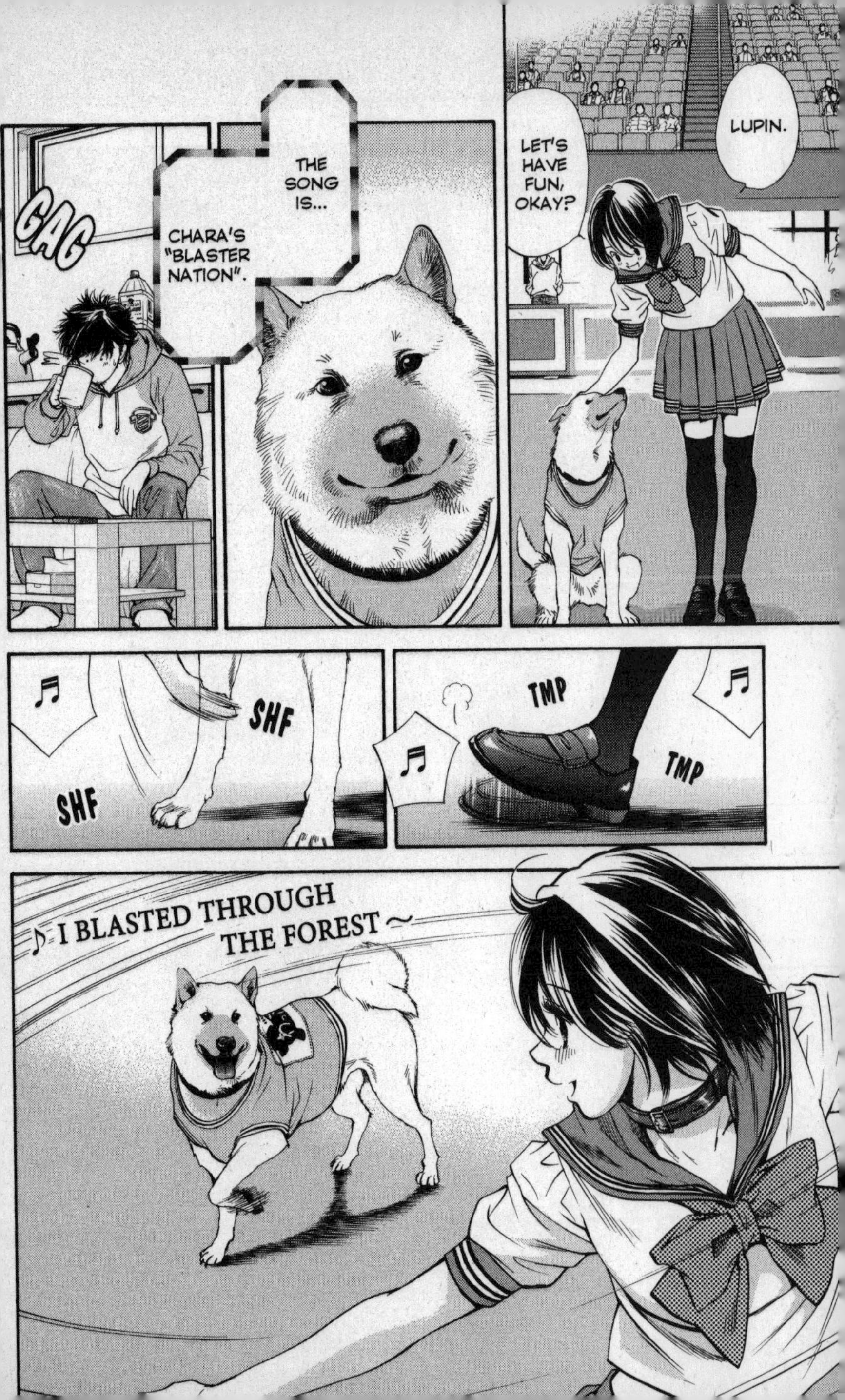
LUPIN.
LET'S HAVE FUN, OKAY?
THE SONG IS...
CHARA'S "BLASTER NATION".
GAG
♬
TMP
♬
TMP
♬
SHF
SHF
♪ I BLASTED THROUGH THE FOREST ~

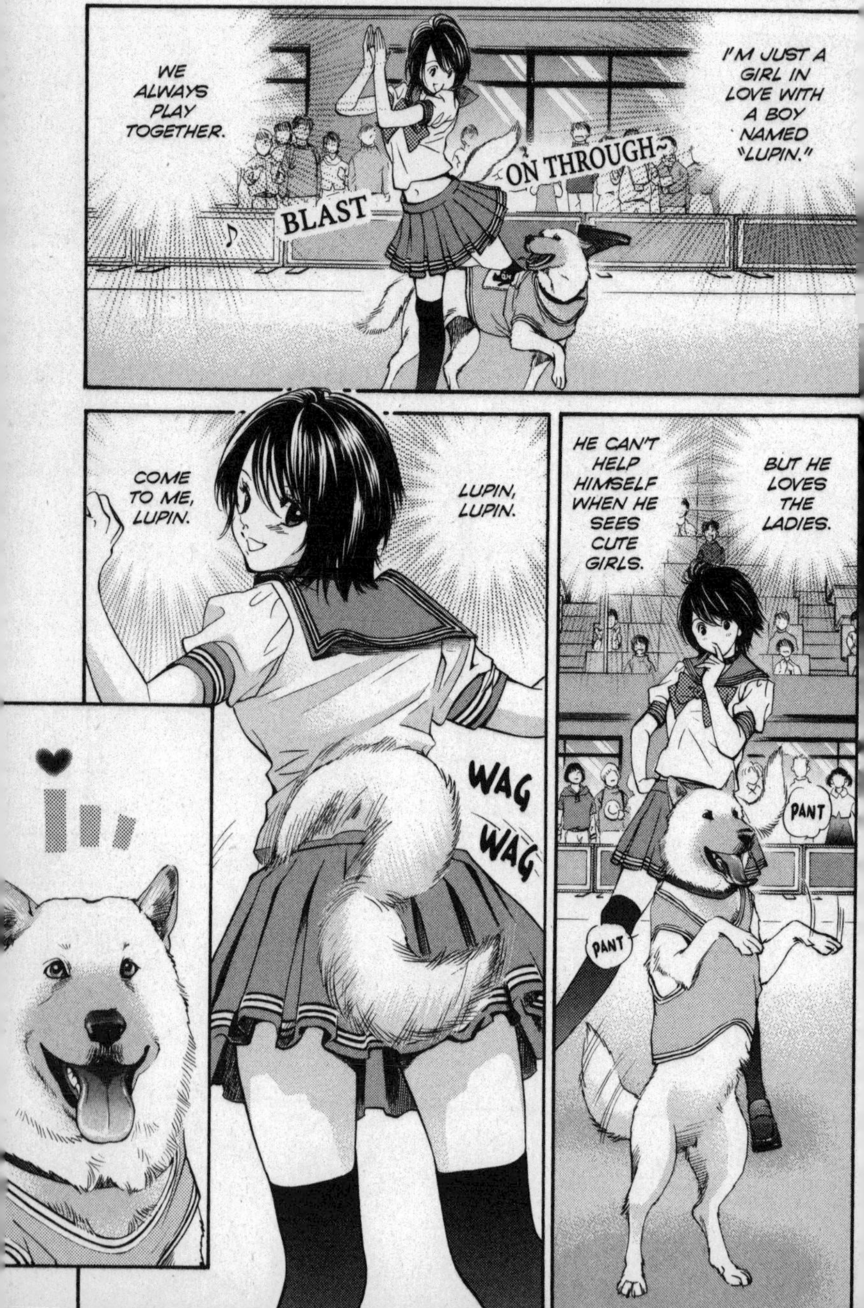
I'M JUST A GIRL IN LOVE WITH A BOY NAMED "LUPIN."
WE ALWAYS PLAY TOGETHER.
BLAST
ON THROUGH~
BUT HE LOVES THE LADIES.
HE CAN'T HELP HIMSELF WHEN HE SEES CUTE GIRLS.
PANT
PANT
LUPIN, LUPIN.
COME TO ME, LUPIN.
WAG
WAG

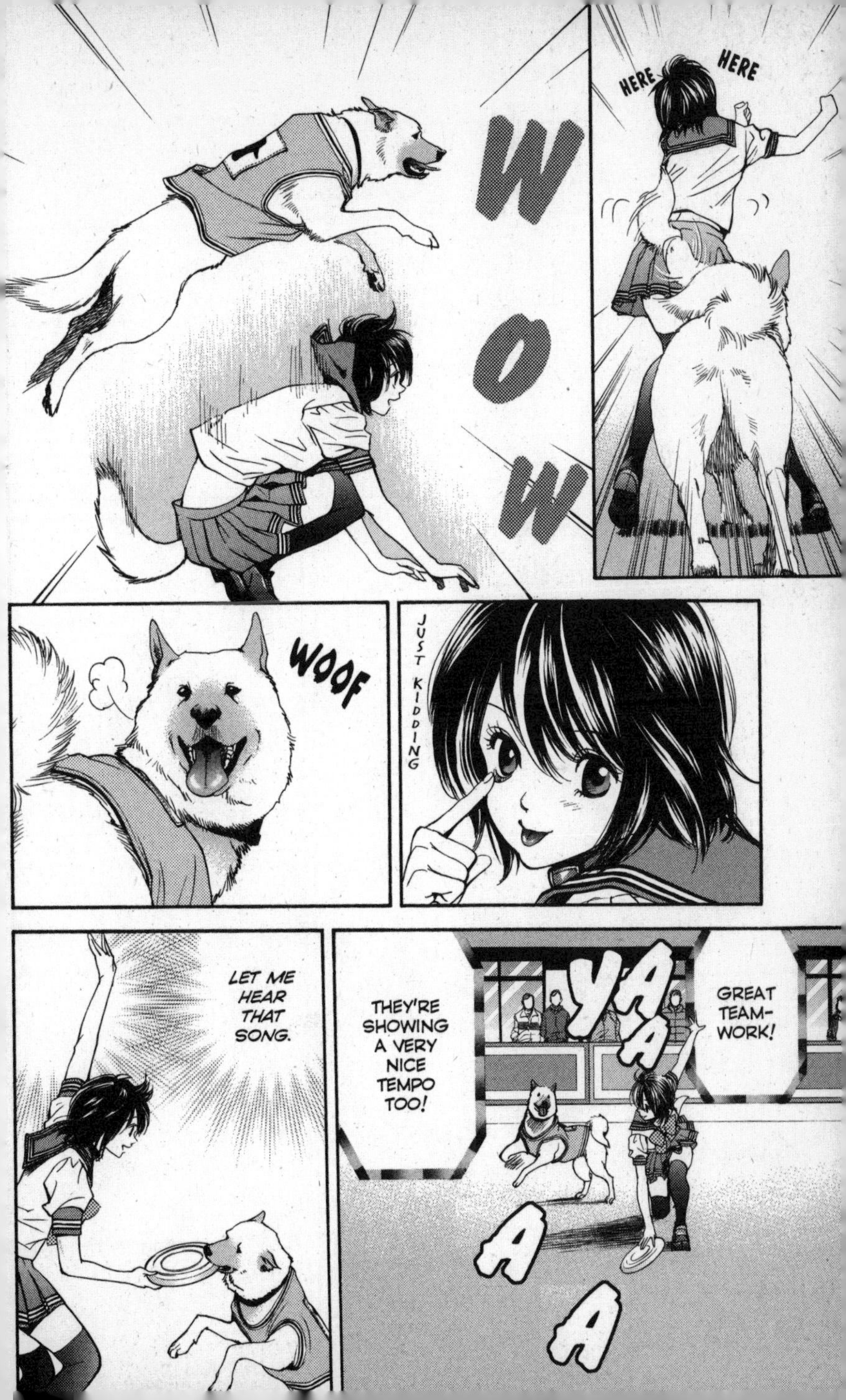
HERE
HERE
WOW
JUST KIDDING
WOOF
YAAAAA
GREAT TEAM-WORK!
THEY'RE SHOWING A VERY NICE TEMPO TOO!
LET ME HEAR THAT SONG.

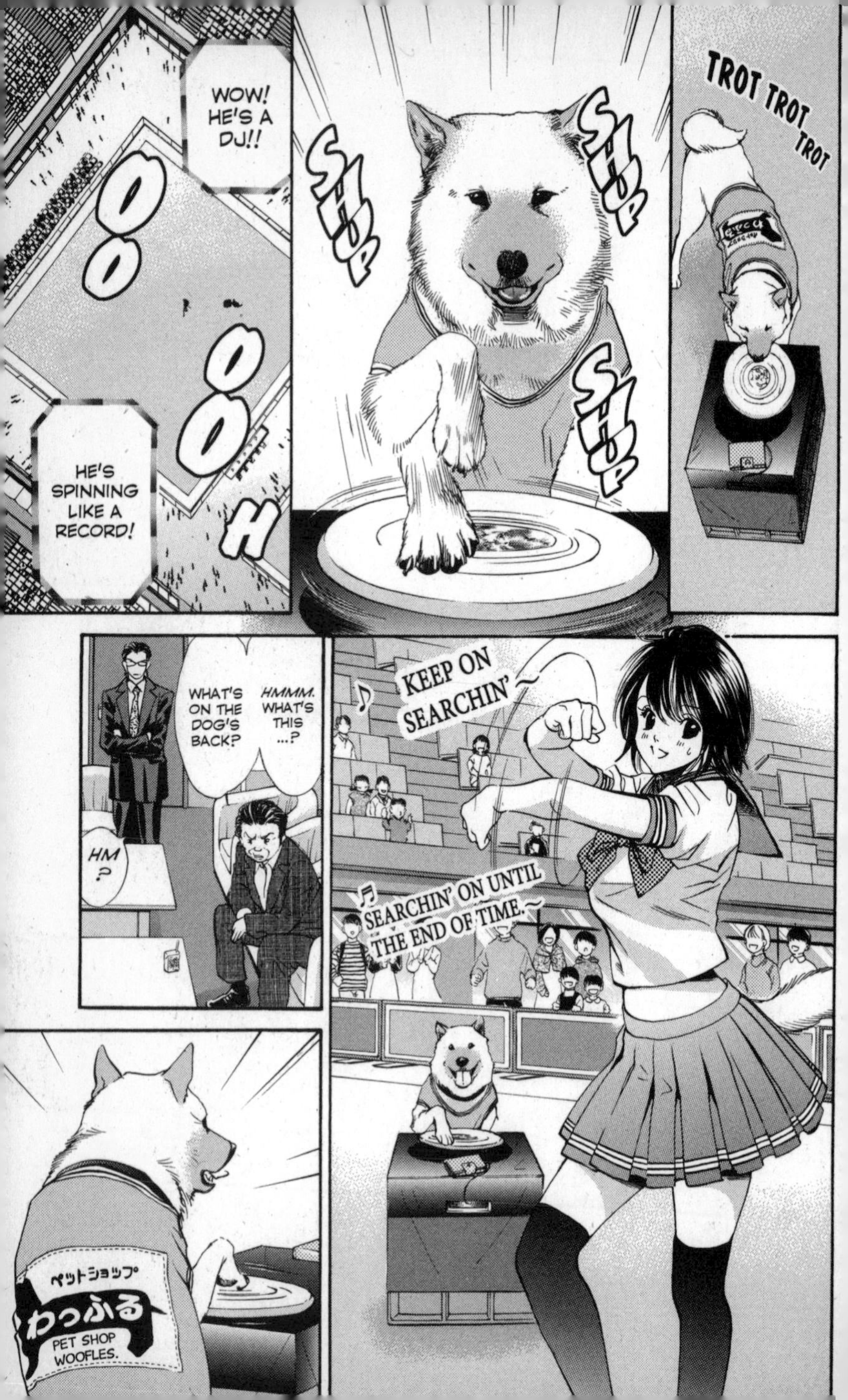
TROT TROT TROT TROT
SHOP SHOP
SHOP SHOP
WOW! HE'S A DJ!!
OOOOH
HE'S SPINNING LIKE A RECORD!
KEEP ON SEARCHIN'~
SEARCHIN' ON UNTIL THE END OF TIME.~
HMMM. WHAT'S THIS ...?
WHAT'S ON THE DOG'S BACK?
HM ?
ペットショップ
わっふる
PET SHOP WOOFLES.

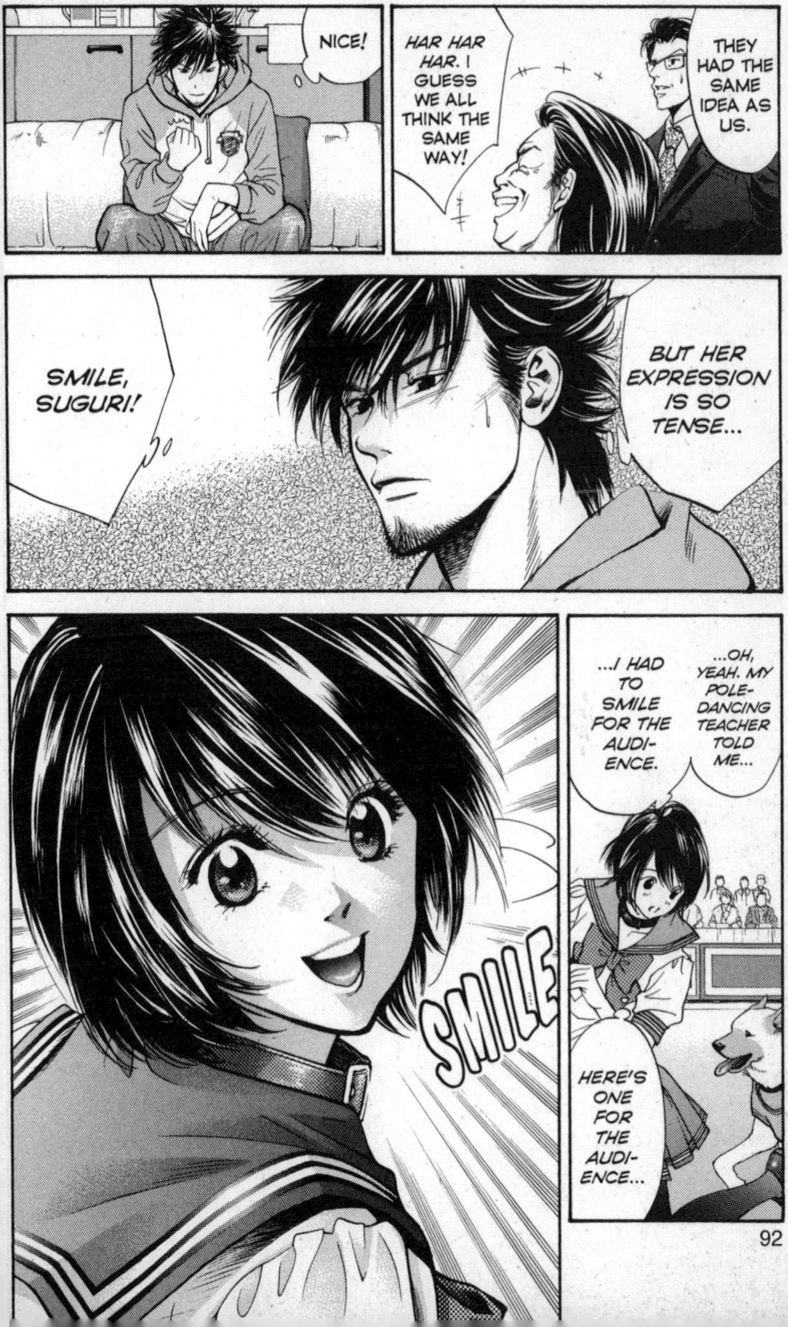
THEY HAD THE SAME IDEA AS US.
HAR HAR HAR. I GUESS WE ALL THINK THE SAME WAY!
NICE!
BUT HER EXPRESSION IS SO TENSE...
SMILE, SUGURI!
...OH, YEAH. MY POLE-DANCING TEACHER TOLD ME...
...I HAD TO SMILE FOR THE AUDI-ENCE.
HERE'S ONE FOR THE AUDI-ENCE...
SMILE

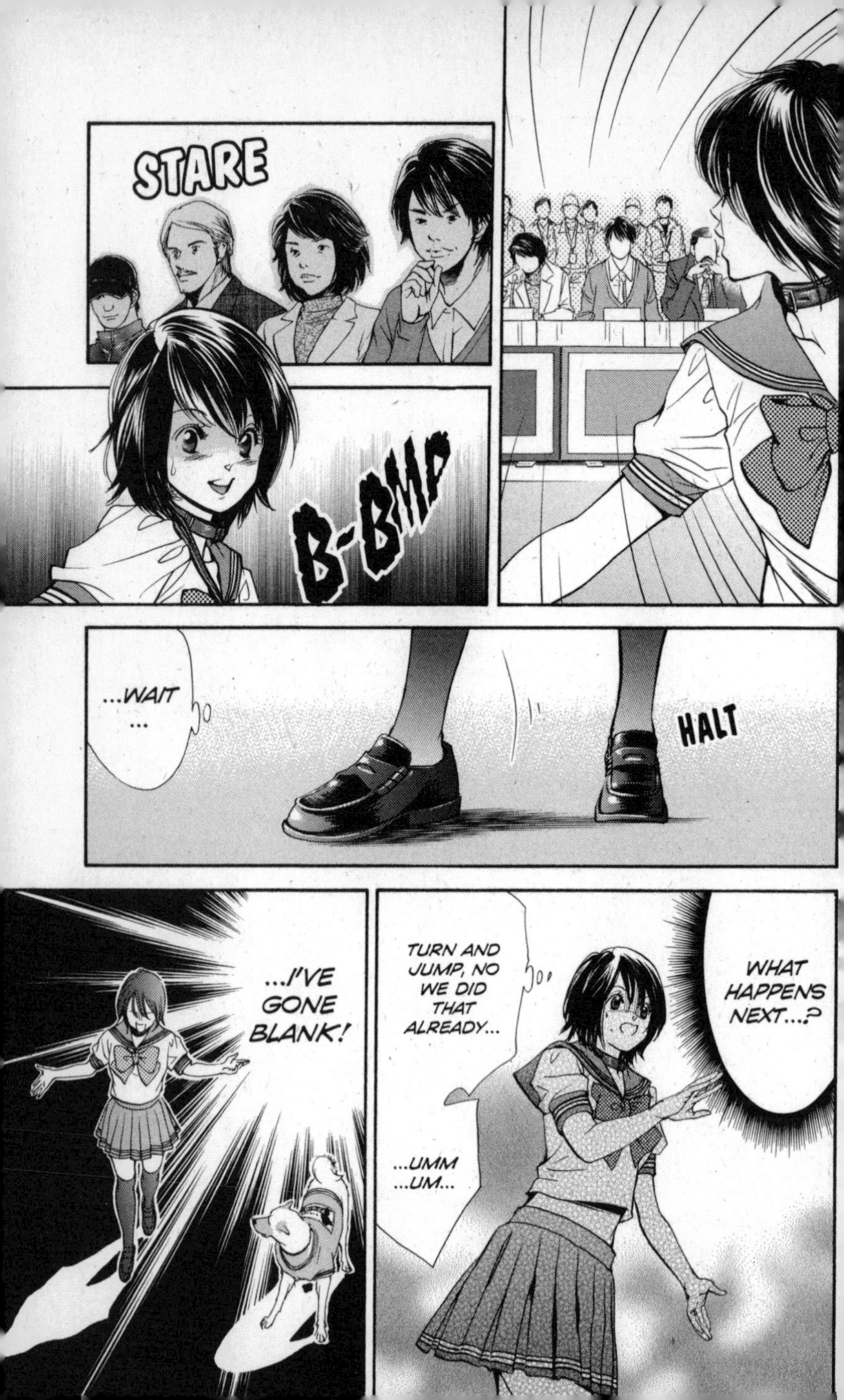
STARE
B-BMP
HALT
...WAIT ...
WHAT HAPPENS NEXT...?
TURN AND JUMP, NO WE DID THAT ALREADY...
...UMM ...UM...
...I'VE GONE BLANK!

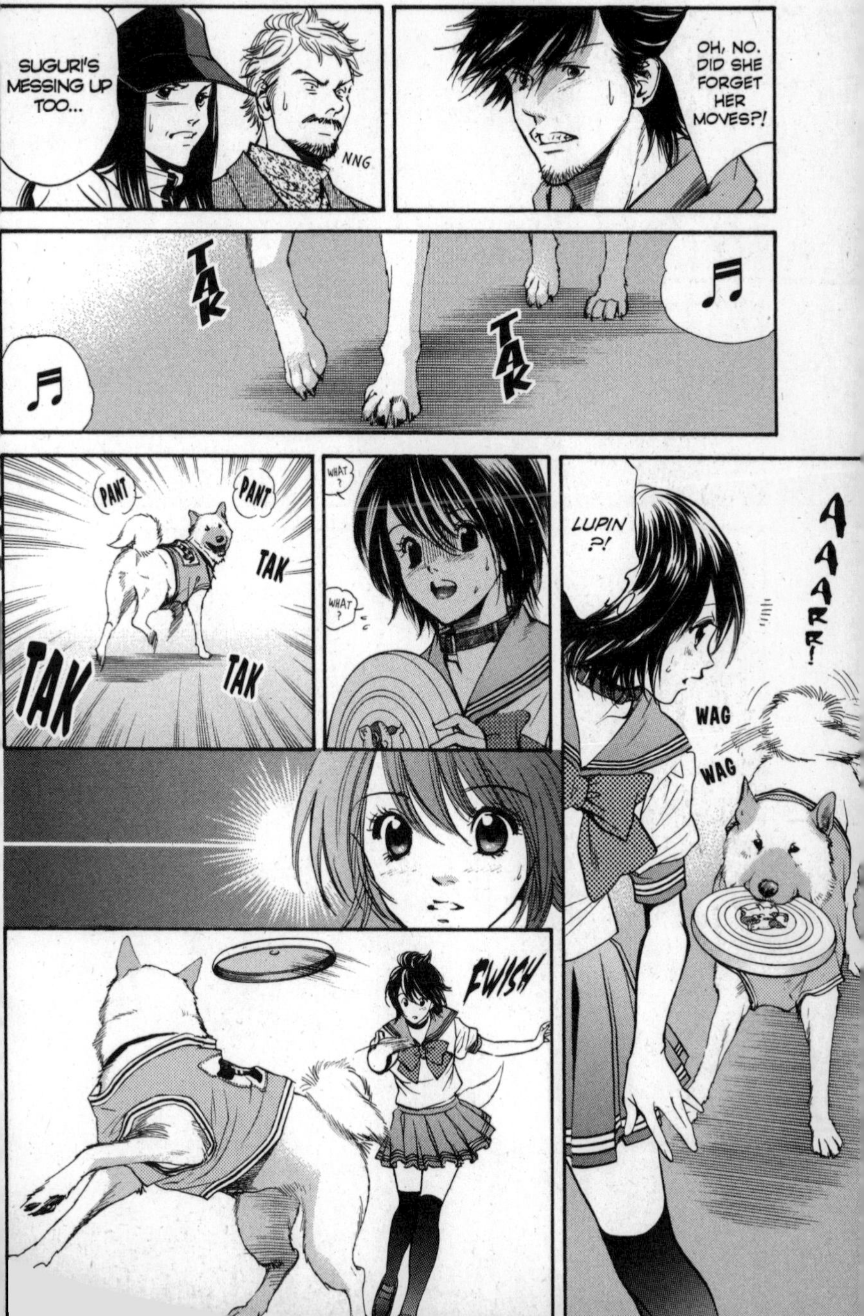
OH, NO. DID SHE FORGET HER MOVES?!
SUGURI'S MESSING UP TOO...
NNG
♫
TAK
TAK
♫
LUPIN?!
AAAARR!
WAG
WAG
WHAT?
WHAT?
PANT
PANT
TAK
TAK
TAK
FWISH

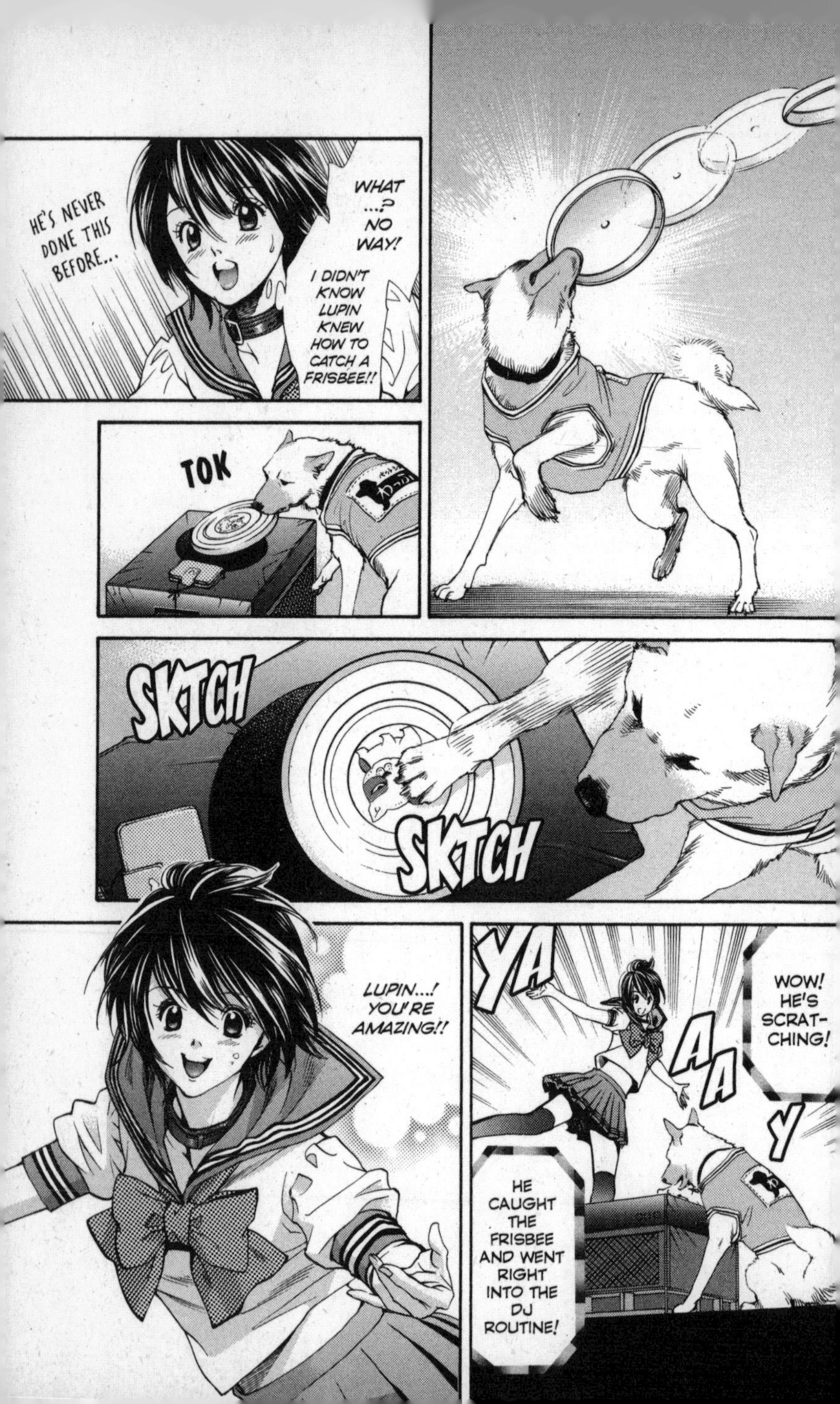
WHAT ...? NO WAY!
I DIDN'T KNOW LUPIN KNEW HOW TO CATCH A FRISBEE!!
HE'S NEVER DONE THIS BEFORE...
TOK
SKTCH
SKTCH
WOW! HE'S SCRAT-CHING!
YAAAY
HE CAUGHT THE FRISBEE AND WENT RIGHT INTO THE DJ ROUTINE!
LUPIN...! YOU'RE AMAZING!!

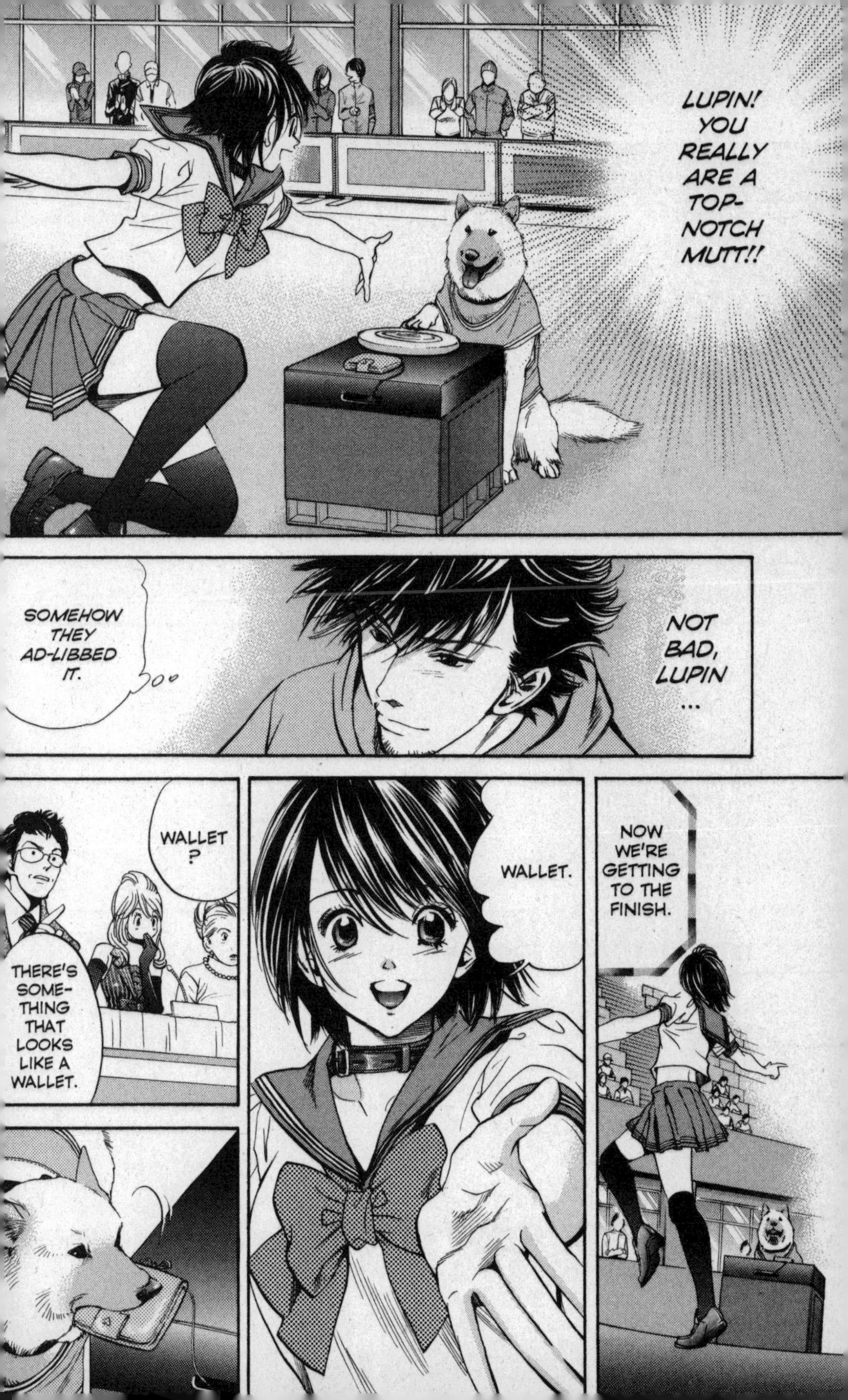

LUPIN! YOU REALLY ARE A TOP-NOTCH MUTT!!
NOT BAD, LUPIN...
SOMEHOW THEY AD-LIBBED IT.
NOW WE'RE GETTING TO THE FINISH.
WALLET.
WALLET?
THERE'S SOMETHING THAT LOOKS LIKE A WALLET.

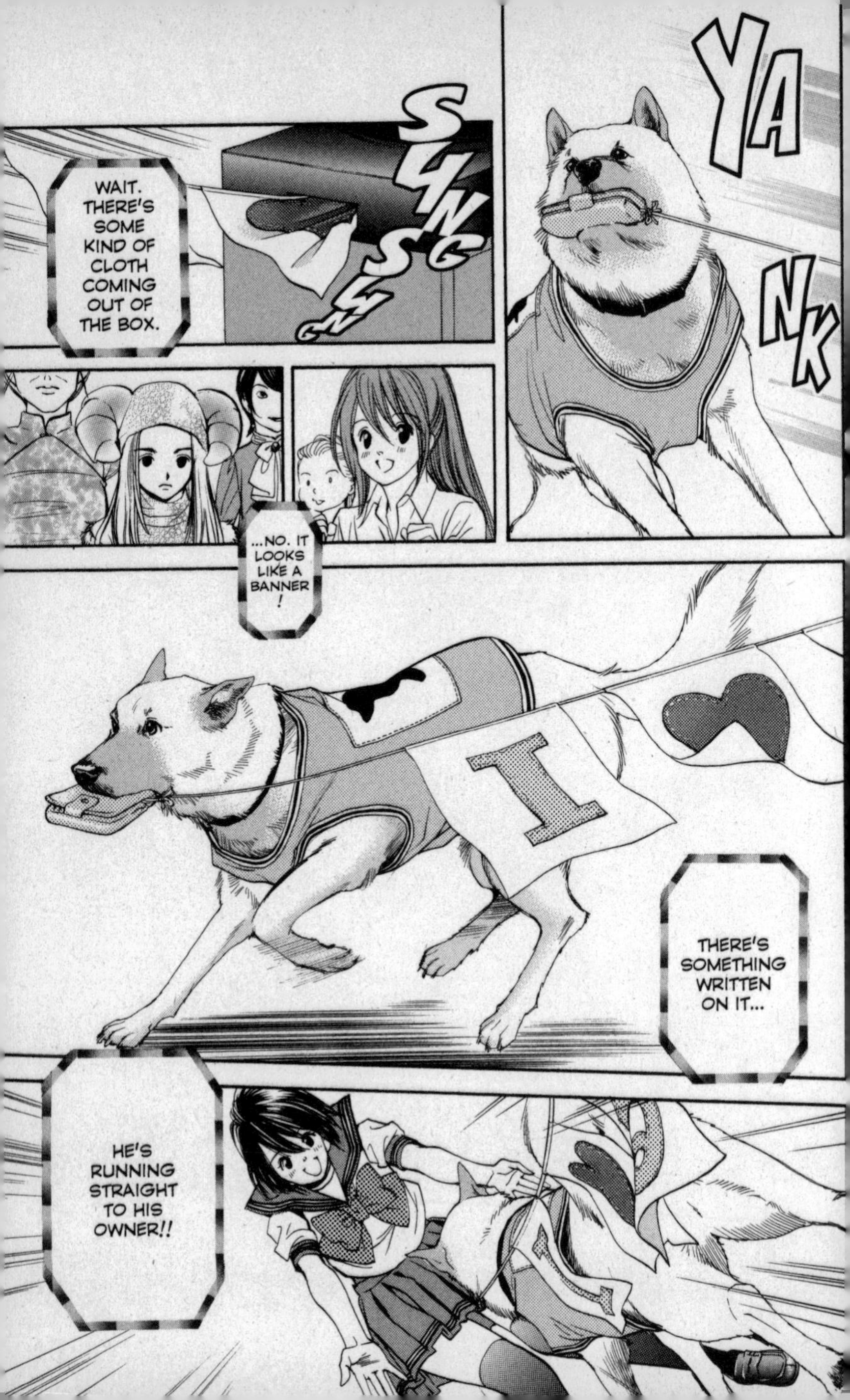
YANK
SWNG
SWNG
WAIT. THERE'S SOME KIND OF CLOTH COMING OUT OF THE BOX.
...NO. IT LOOKS LIKE A BANNER!
THERE'S SOMETHING WRITTEN ON IT...
HE'S RUNNING STRAIGHT TO HIS OWNER!!

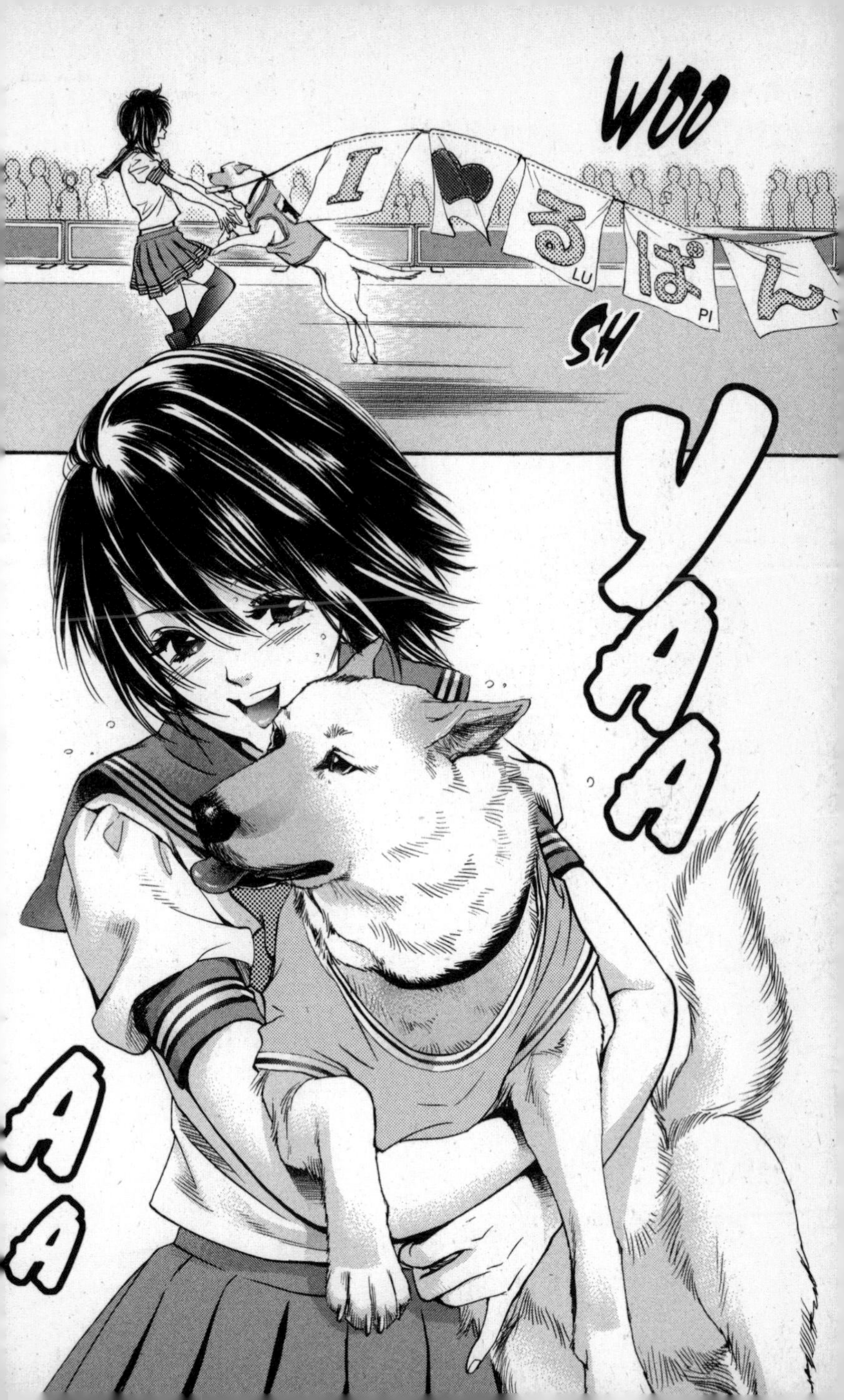
WOO
I ♥ るぱん
LU
PI
SH
YAA
AA

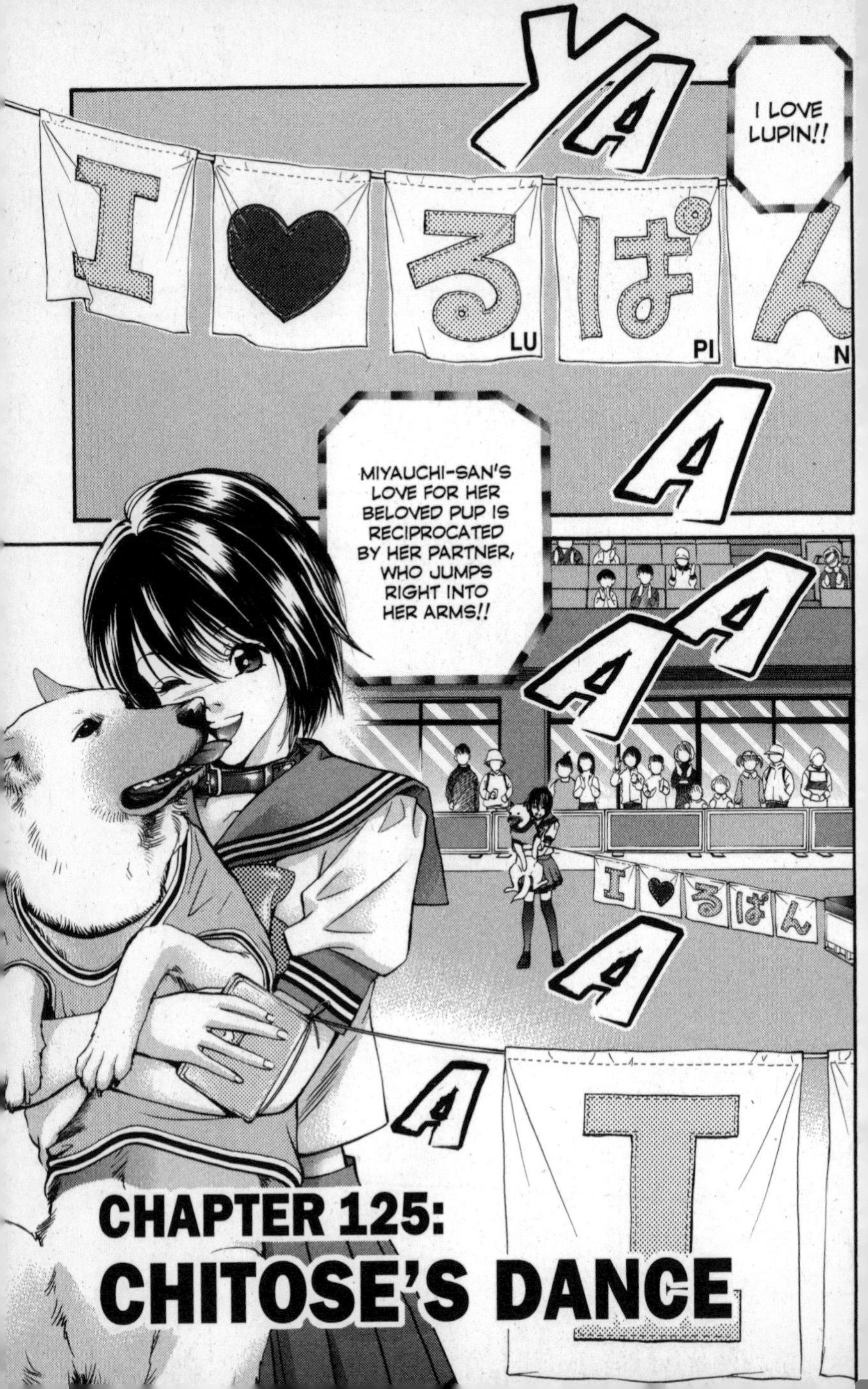
I LOVE LUPIN!!
YAAAAAAT
I ♥ るぱん
LU
PI
N
MIYAUCHI-SAN'S LOVE FOR HER BELOVED PUP IS RECIPROCATED BY HER PARTNER, WHO JUMPS RIGHT INTO HER ARMS!!
I ♥ るぱん

# CHAPTER 125: CHITOSE'S DANCE

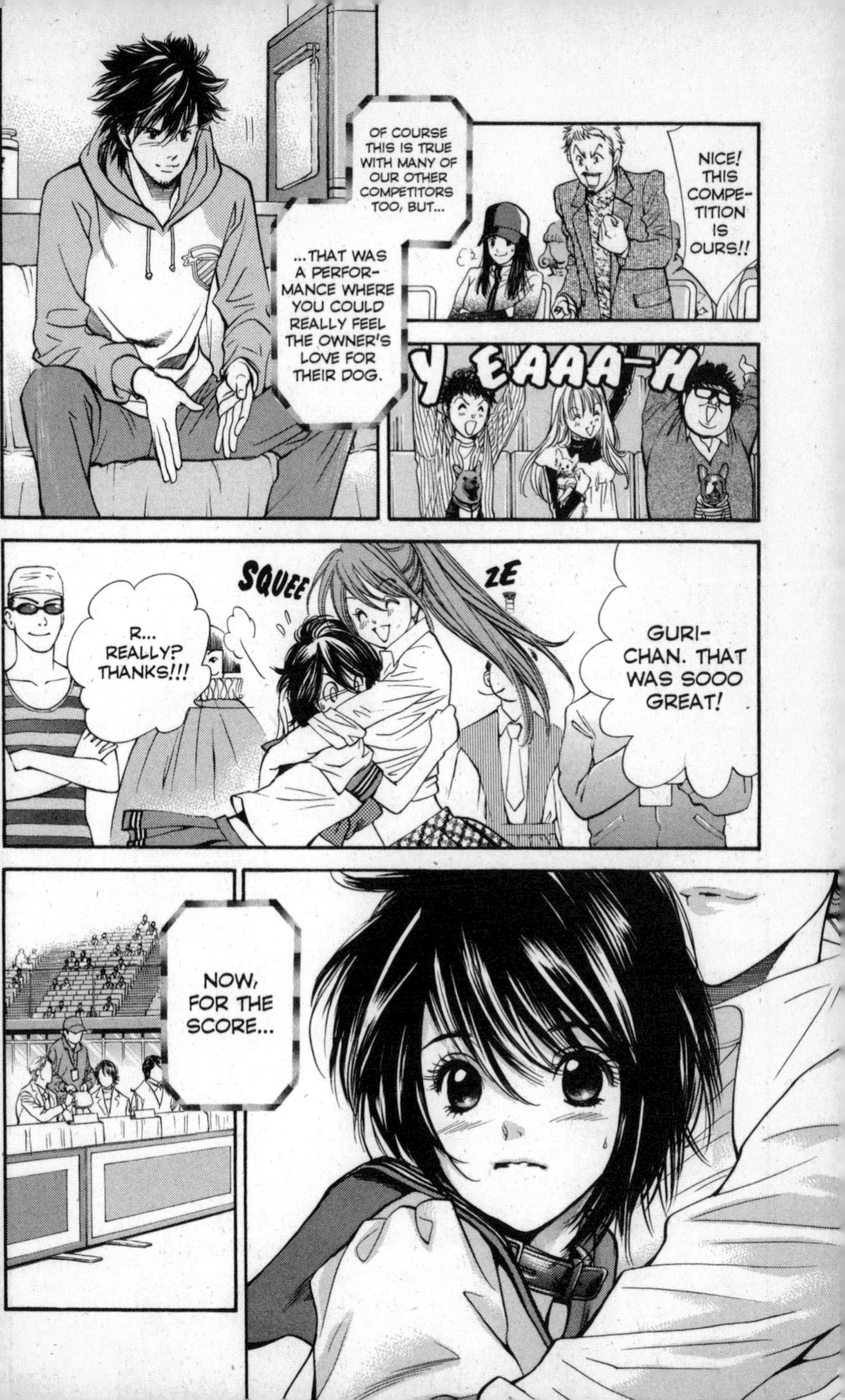
NICE! THIS COMPE-TITION IS OURS!!
YEAAA-H
OF COURSE THIS IS TRUE WITH MANY OF OUR OTHER COMPETITORS TOO, BUT...
...THAT WAS A PERFOR-MANCE WHERE YOU COULD REALLY FEEL THE OWNER'S LOVE FOR THEIR DOG.
GURI-CHAN. THAT WAS SOOO GREAT!
SQUEEZE
R... REALLY? THANKS!!!
NOW, FOR THE SCORE...

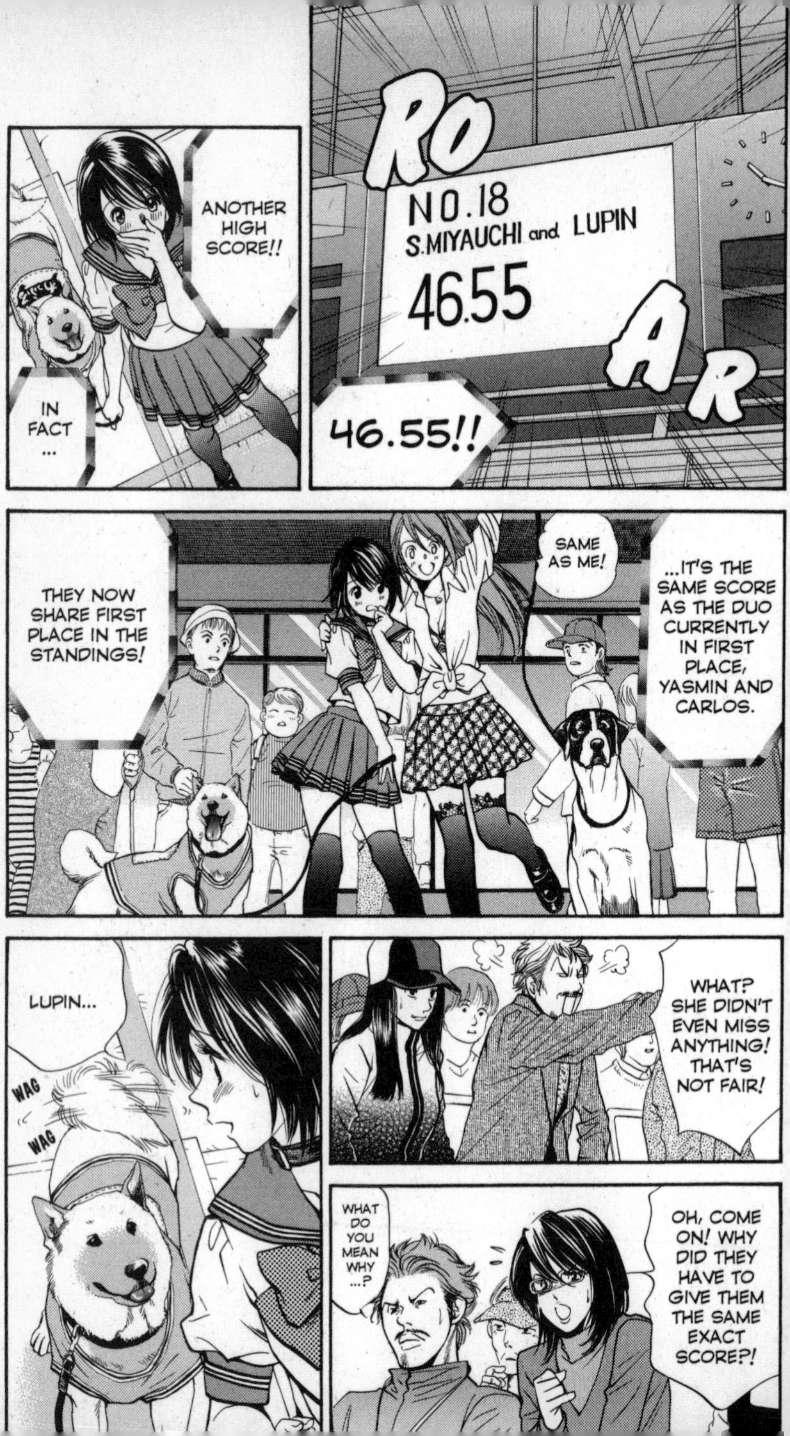
RO
NO.18
S.MIYAUCHI and LUPIN
46.55
AR
46.55!!
ANOTHER HIGH SCORE!!
IN FACT ...
...IT'S THE SAME SCORE AS THE DUO CURRENTLY IN FIRST PLACE, YASMIN AND CARLOS.
SAME AS ME!
THEY NOW SHARE FIRST PLACE IN THE STANDINGS!
WHAT? SHE DIDN'T EVEN MISS ANYTHING! THAT'S NOT FAIR!
OH, COME ON! WHY DID THEY HAVE TO GIVE THEM THE SAME EXACT SCORE?!
WHAT DO YOU MEAN WHY ...?
LUPIN...
WAG
WAG

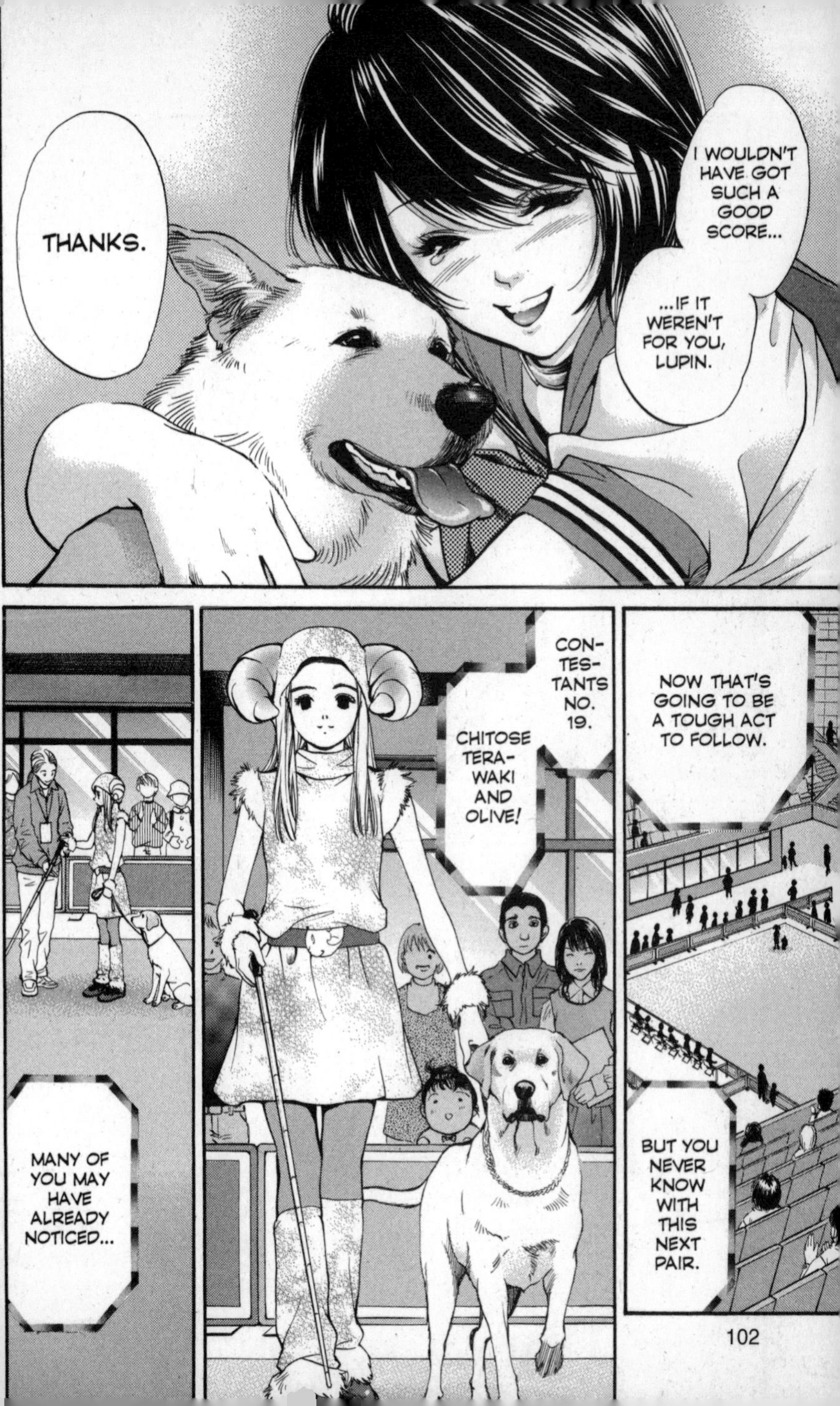
I WOULDN'T HAVE GOT SUCH A GOOD SCORE...
...IF IT WEREN'T FOR YOU, LUPIN.
THANKS.
NOW THAT'S GOING TO BE A TOUGH ACT TO FOLLOW.
BUT YOU NEVER KNOW WITH THIS NEXT PAIR.
CON-TES-TANTS NO. 19.
CHITOSE TERA-WAKI AND OLIVE!
MANY OF YOU MAY HAVE ALREADY NOTICED...

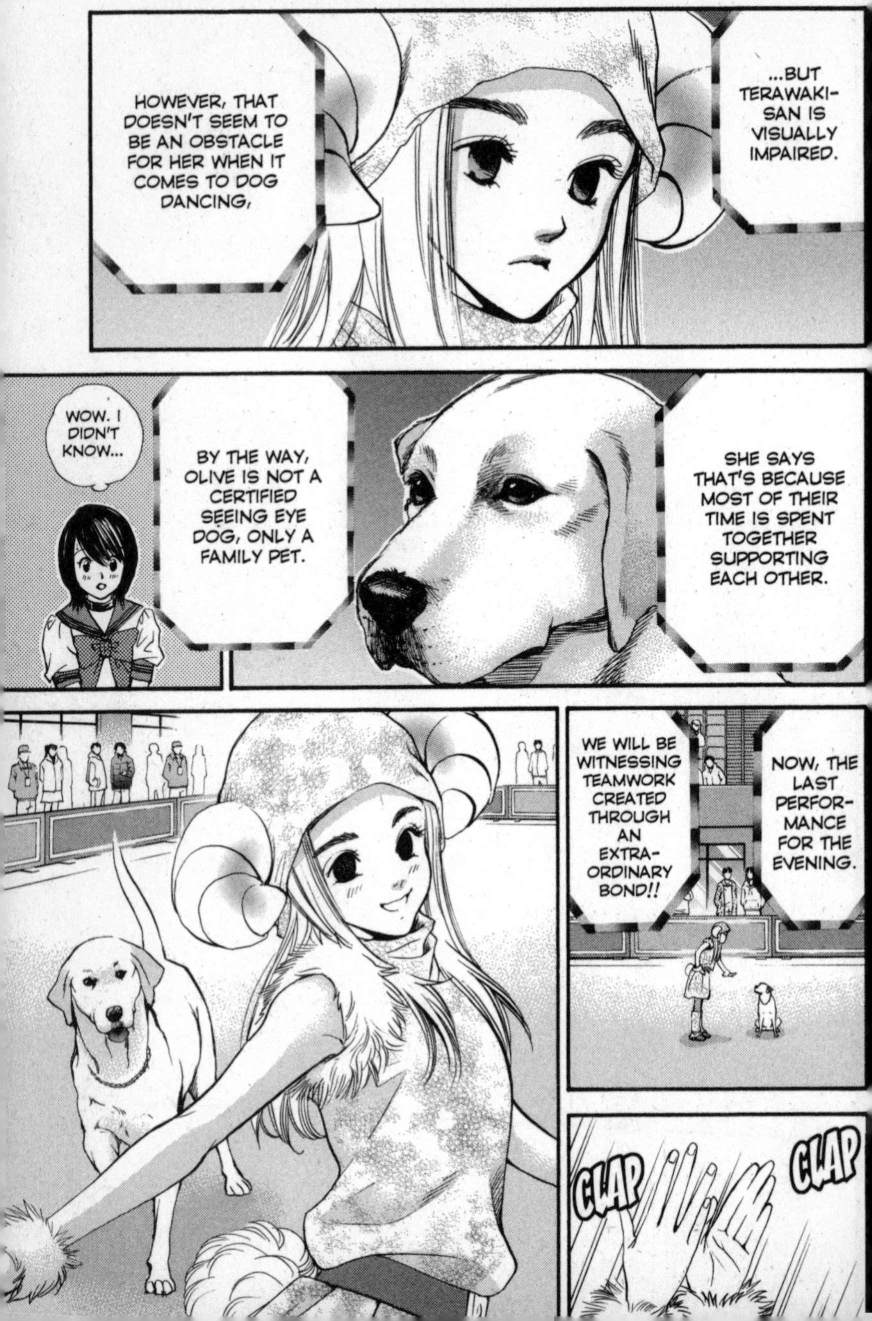
...BUT TERAWAKI-SAN IS VISUALLY IMPAIRED.
HOWEVER, THAT DOESN'T SEEM TO BE AN OBSTACLE FOR HER WHEN IT COMES TO DOG DANCING,
SHE SAYS THAT'S BECAUSE MOST OF THEIR TIME IS SPENT TOGETHER SUPPORTING EACH OTHER.
BY THE WAY, OLIVE IS NOT A CERTIFIED SEEING EYE DOG, ONLY A FAMILY PET.
WOW. I DIDN'T KNOW...
NOW, THE LAST PERFORMANCE FOR THE EVENING.
WE WILL BE WITNESSING TEAMWORK CREATED THROUGH AN EXTRAORDINARY BOND!!
CLAP
CLAP

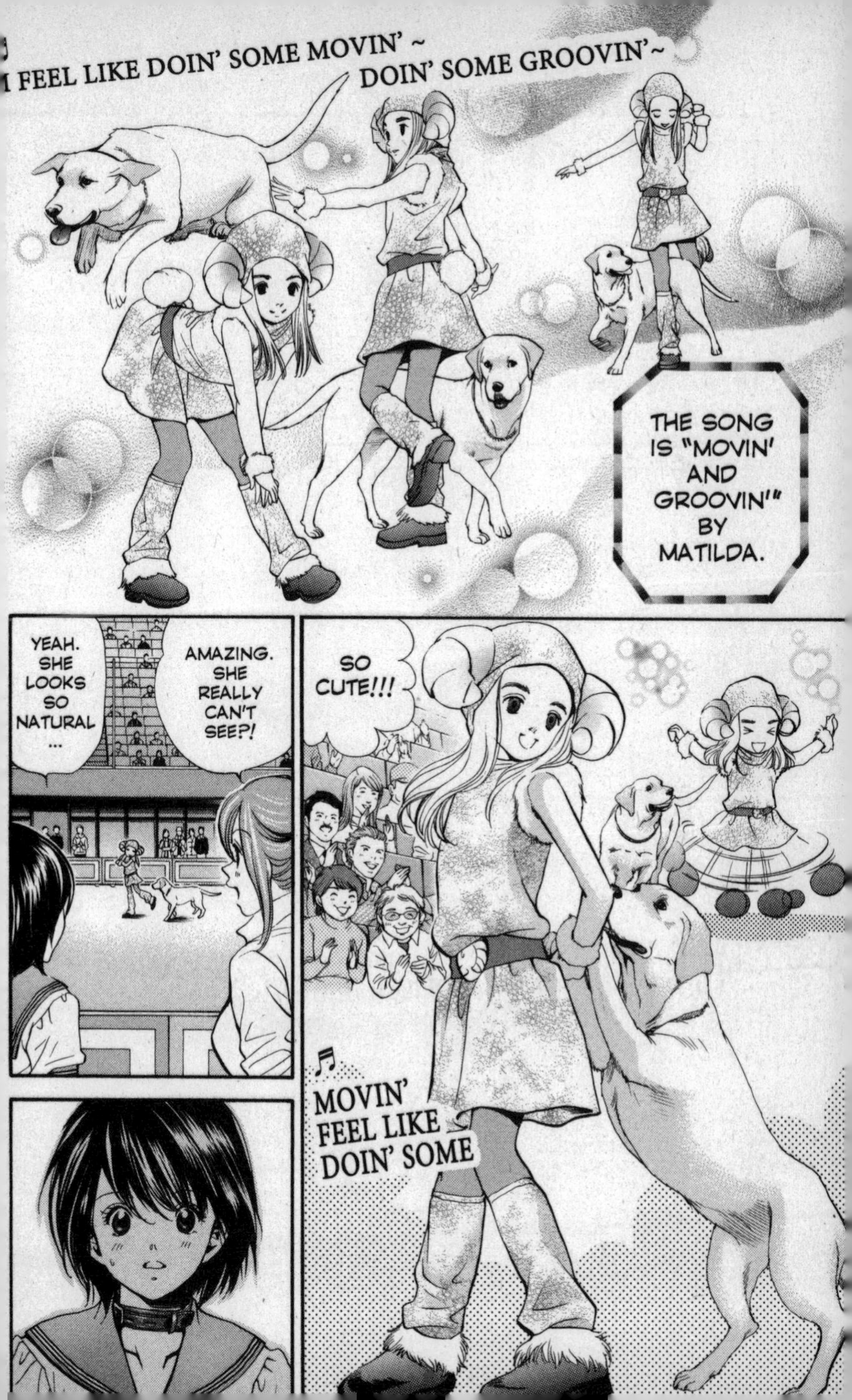

♪ I FEEL LIKE DOIN' SOME MOVIN' ~ DOIN' SOME GROOVIN'~
THE SONG IS "MOVIN' AND GROOVIN'" BY MATILDA.
SO CUTE!!!
♪ MOVIN' FEEL LIKE DOIN' SOME
AMAZING. SHE REALLY CAN'T SEE?!
YEAH. SHE LOOKS SO NATURAL ...

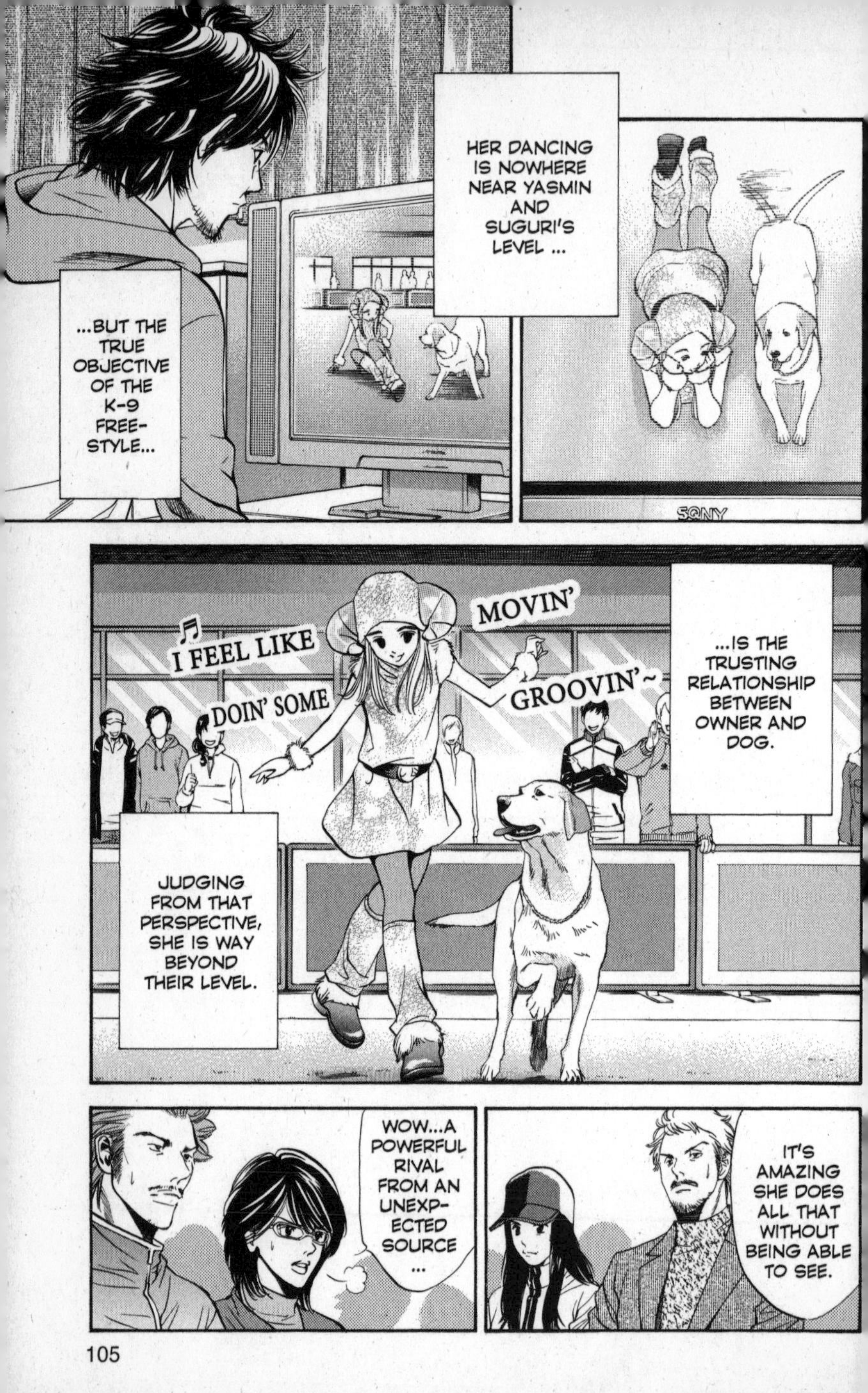
HER DANCING IS NOWHERE NEAR YASMIN AND SUGURI'S LEVEL ...
...BUT THE TRUE OBJECTIVE OF THE K-9 FREE-STYLE...
SQNY
...IS THE TRUSTING RELATIONSHIP BETWEEN OWNER AND DOG.
♫ I FEEL LIKE MOVIN'
DOIN' SOME GROOVIN'~
JUDGING FROM THAT PERSPECTIVE, SHE IS WAY BEYOND THEIR LEVEL.
IT'S AMAZING SHE DOES ALL THAT WITHOUT BEING ABLE TO SEE.
WOW...A POWERFUL RIVAL FROM AN UNEXPECTED SOURCE ...

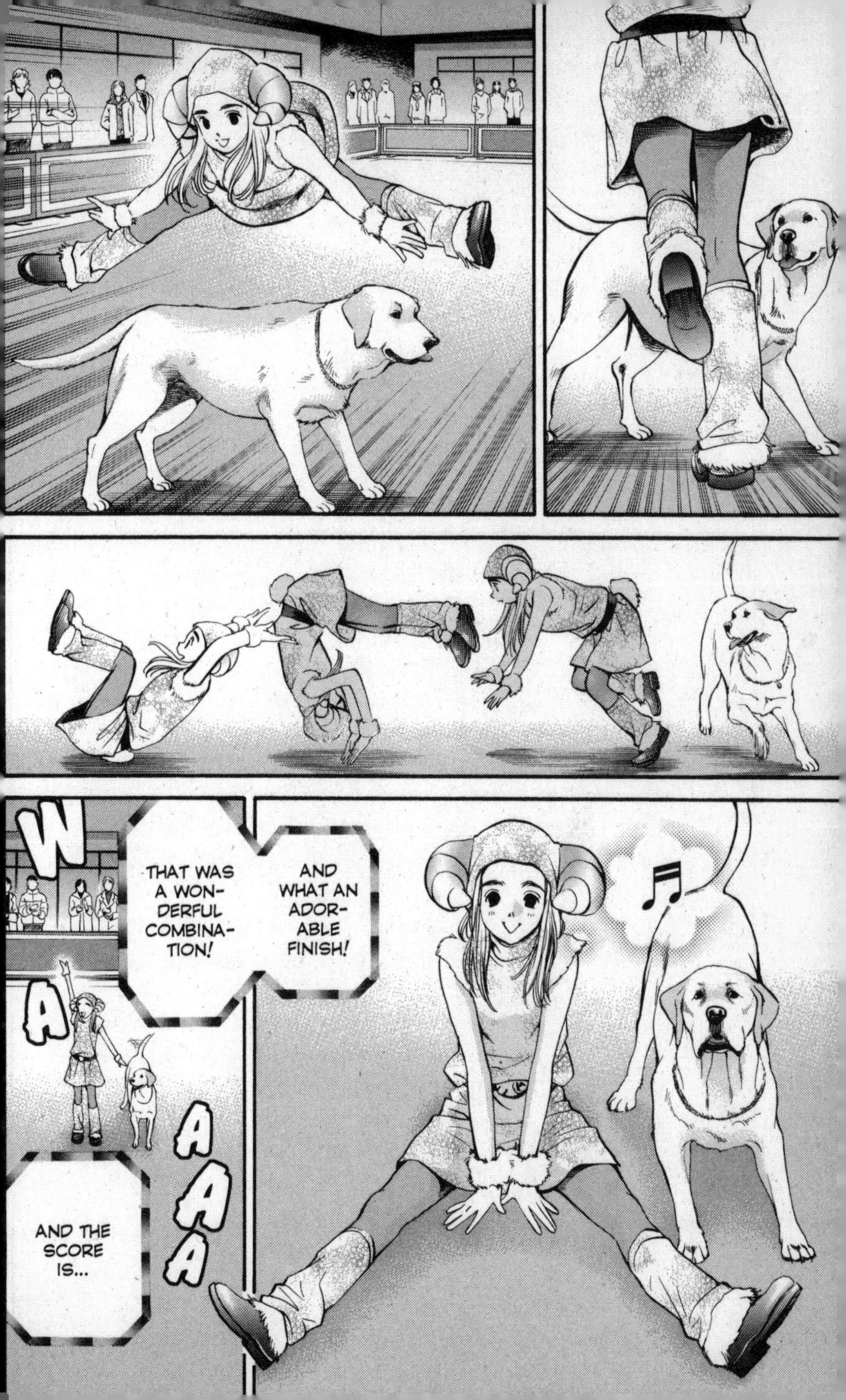
AND WHAT AN ADORABLE FINISH!
THAT WAS A WONDERFUL COMBINATION!
WAAAAA
AND THE SCORE IS...

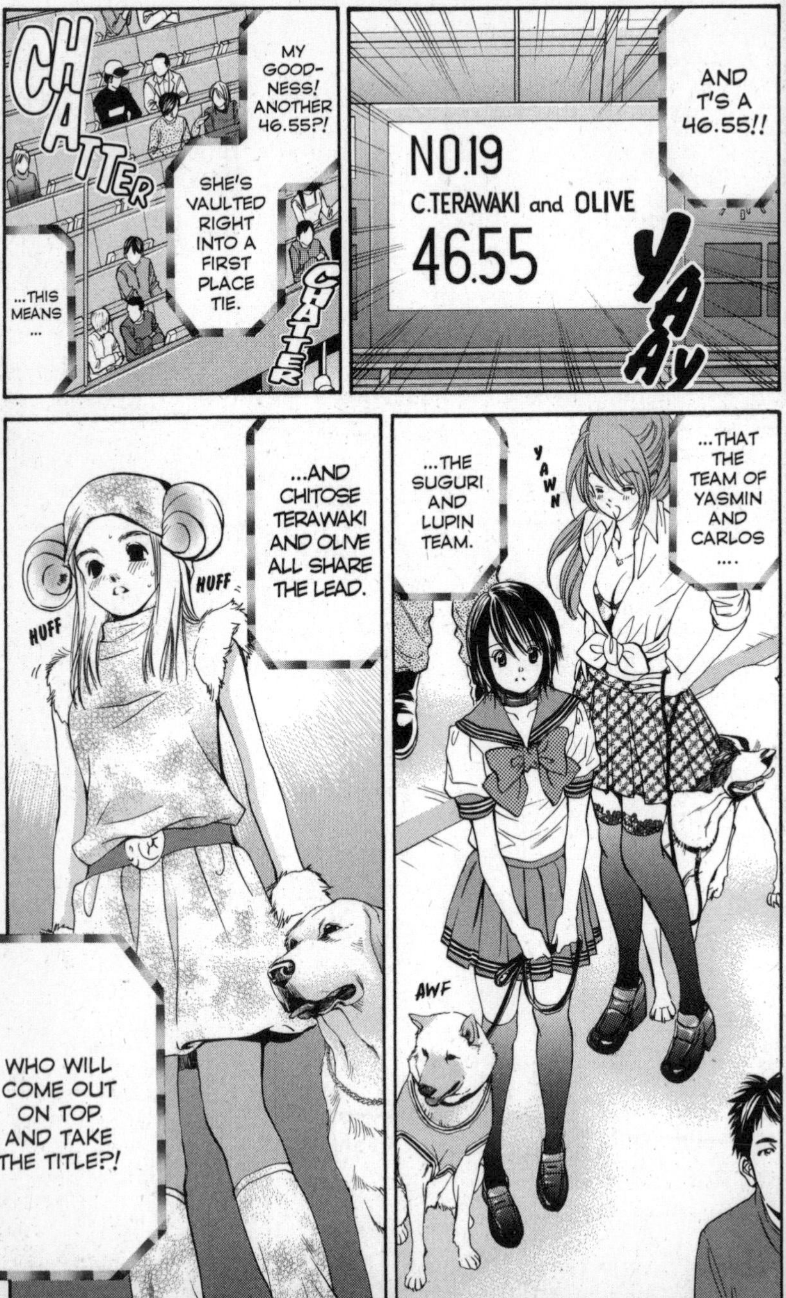
AND T'S A 46.55!!
NO.19
C.TERAWAKI and OLIVE
46.55
YAAY
MY GOODNESS! ANOTHER 46.55?!
SHE'S VAULTED RIGHT INTO A FIRST PLACE TIE.
CHATTER
CHATTER
...THIS MEANS...
...THAT THE TEAM OF YASMIN AND CARLOS....
YAWN
...THE SUGURI AND LUPIN TEAM.
AWF
...AND CHITOSE TERAWAKI AND OLIVE ALL SHARE THE LEAD.
HUFF
HUFF
WHO WILL COME OUT ON TOP AND TAKE THE TITLE?!

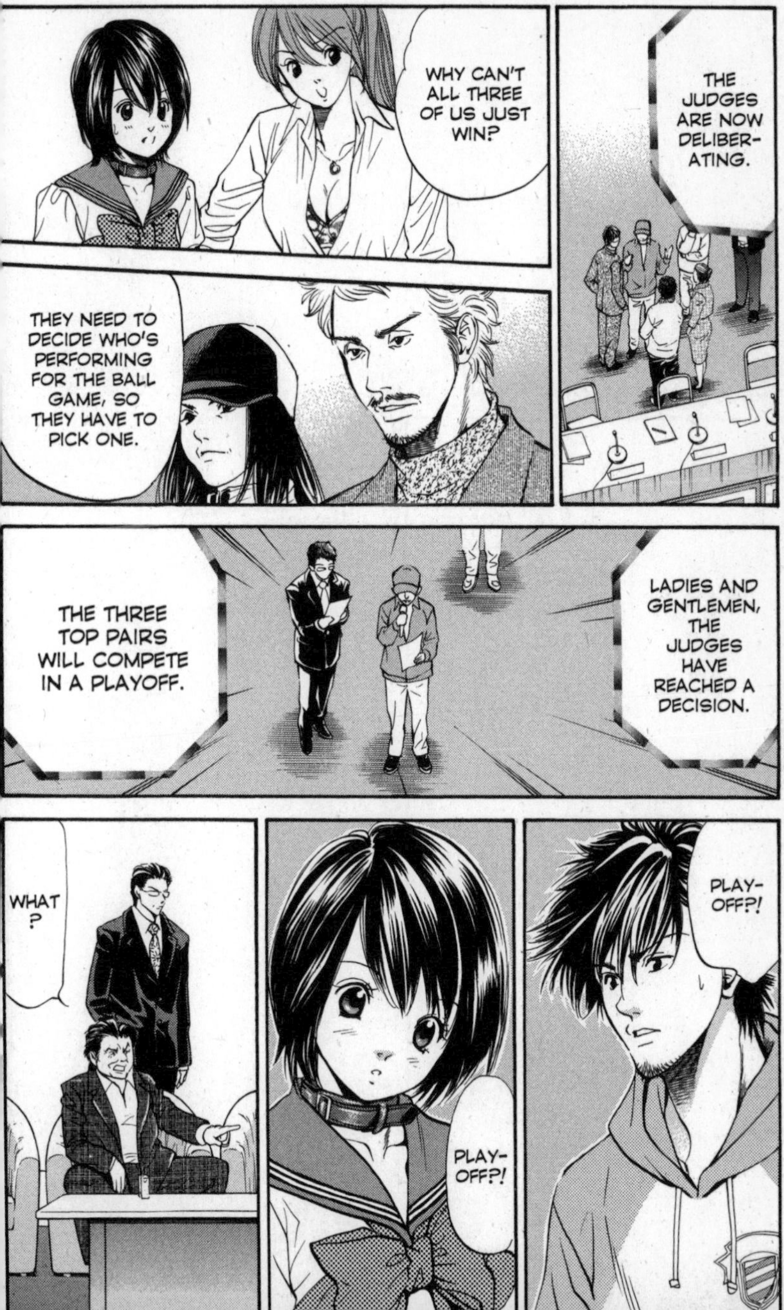
THE JUDGES ARE NOW DELIBER-ATING.
WHY CAN'T ALL THREE OF US JUST WIN?
THEY NEED TO DECIDE WHO'S PERFORMING FOR THE BALL GAME, SO THEY HAVE TO PICK ONE.
LADIES AND GENTLEMEN, THE JUDGES HAVE REACHED A DECISION.
THE THREE TOP PAIRS WILL COMPETE IN A PLAYOFF.
PLAY-OFF?!
PLAY-OFF?!
WHAT ?

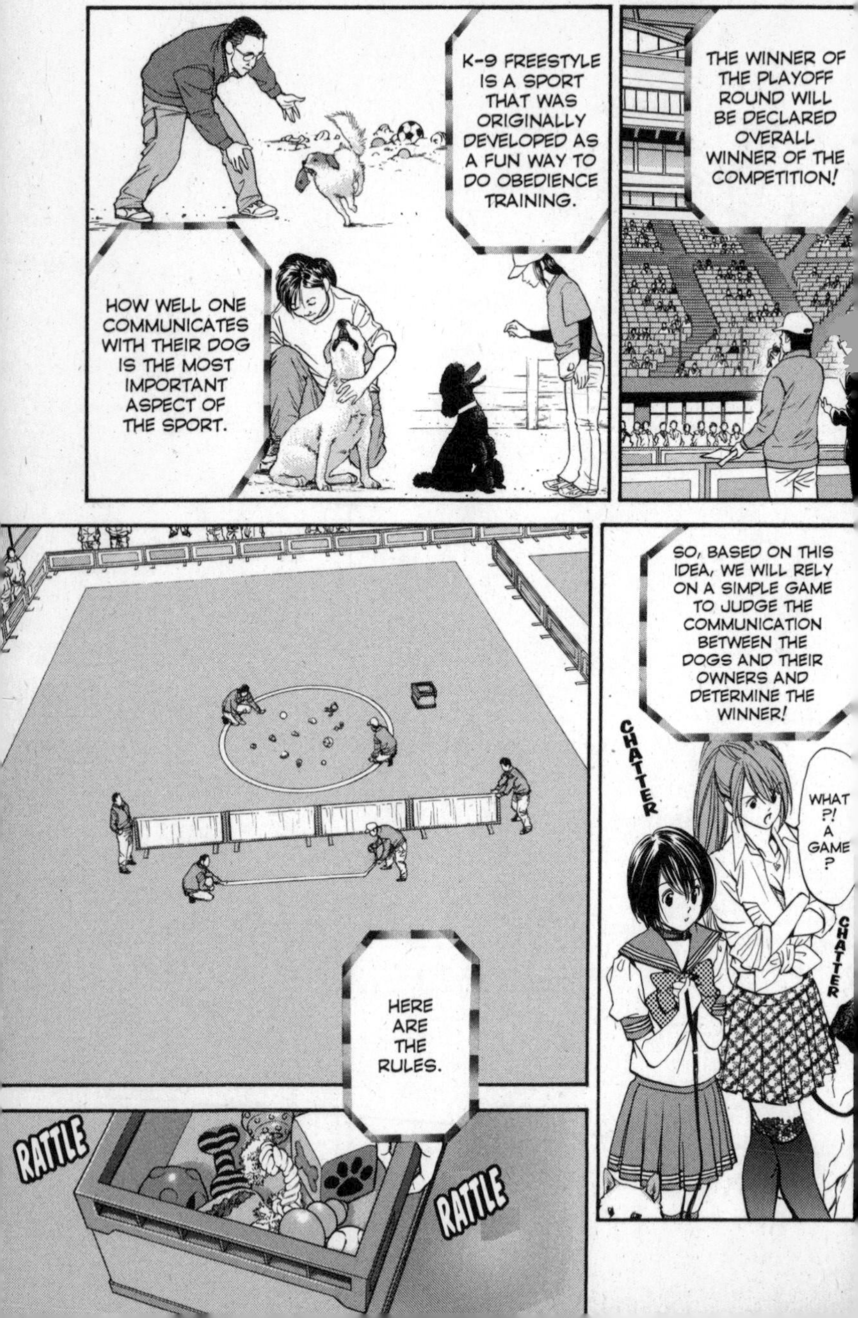
THE WINNER OF THE PLAYOFF ROUND WILL BE DECLARED OVERALL WINNER OF THE COMPETITION!
K-9 FREESTYLE IS A SPORT THAT WAS ORIGINALLY DEVELOPED AS A FUN WAY TO DO OBEDIENCE TRAINING.
HOW WELL ONE COMMUNICATES WITH THEIR DOG IS THE MOST IMPORTANT ASPECT OF THE SPORT.
SO, BASED ON THIS IDEA, WE WILL RELY ON A SIMPLE GAME TO JUDGE THE COMMUNICATION BETWEEN THE DOGS AND THEIR OWNERS AND DETERMINE THE WINNER!
CHATTER
WHAT?! A GAME?
CHATTER
HERE ARE THE RULES.
RATTLE
RATTLE

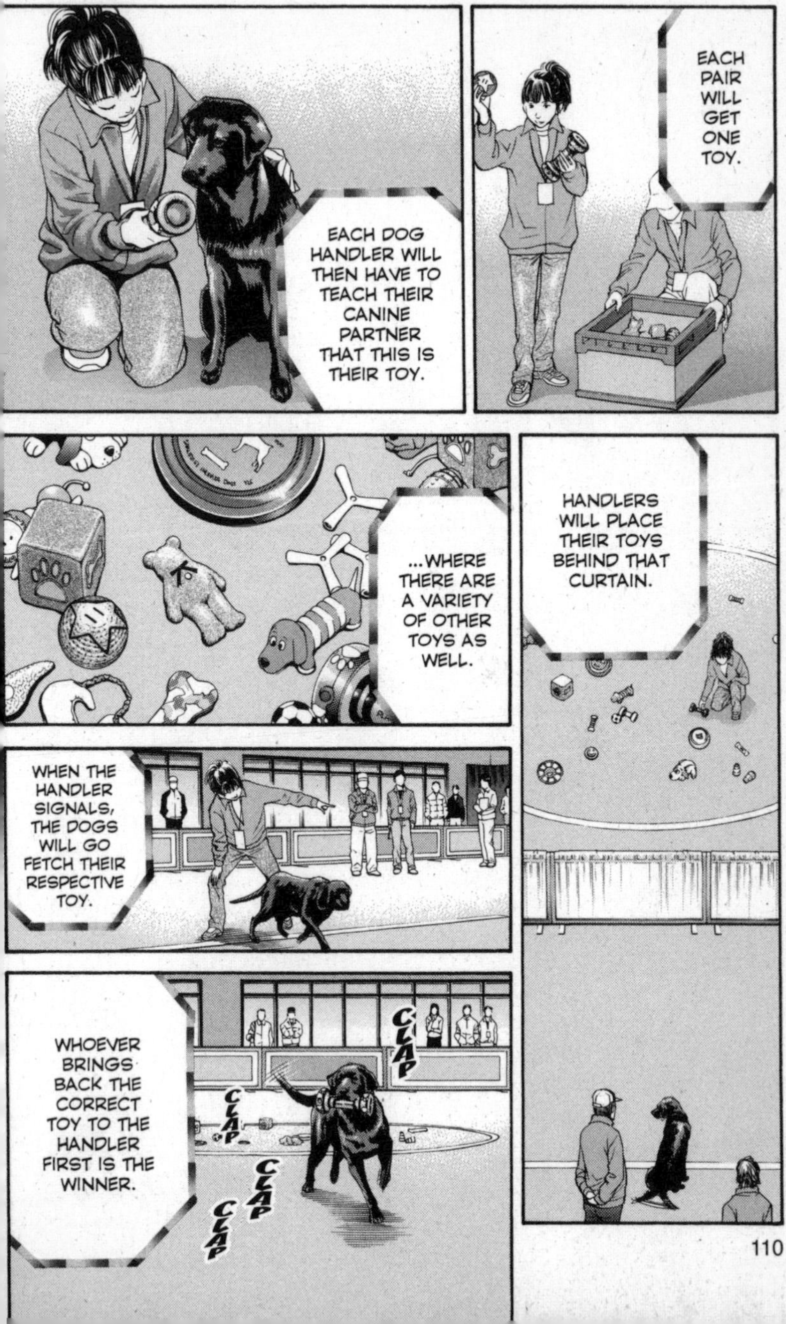
EACH PAIR WILL GET ONE TOY.
EACH DOG HANDLER WILL THEN HAVE TO TEACH THEIR CANINE PARTNER THAT THIS IS THEIR TOY.
HANDLERS WILL PLACE THEIR TOYS BEHIND THAT CURTAIN.
...WHERE THERE ARE A VARIETY OF OTHER TOYS AS WELL.
WHEN THE HANDLER SIGNALS, THE DOGS WILL GO FETCH THEIR RESPECTIVE TOY.
CLAP
CLAP
CLAP
CLAP
WHOEVER BRINGS BACK THE CORRECT TOY TO THE HANDLER FIRST IS THE WINNER.

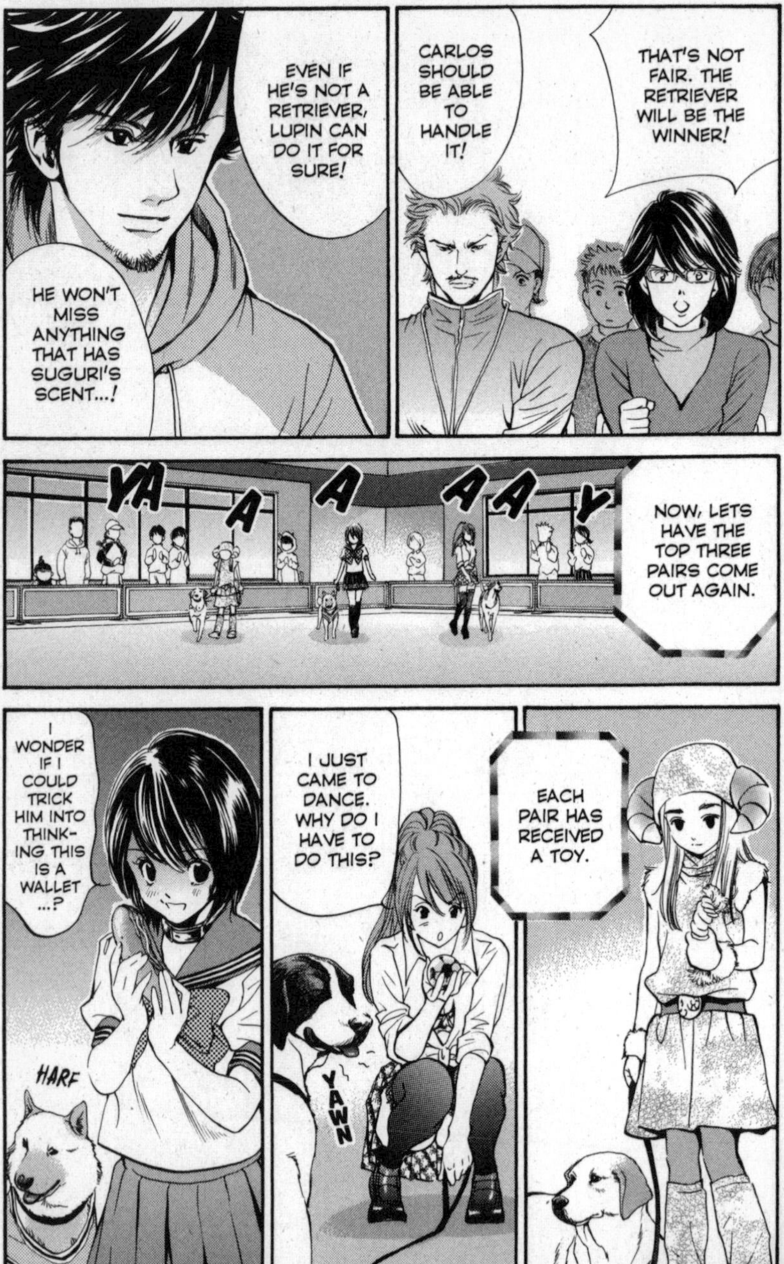
THAT'S NOT FAIR. THE RETRIEVER WILL BE THE WINNER!
CARLOS SHOULD BE ABLE TO HANDLE IT!
EVEN IF HE'S NOT A RETRIEVER, LUPIN CAN DO IT FOR SURE!
HE WON'T MISS ANYTHING THAT HAS SUGURI'S SCENT...!
NOW, LETS HAVE THE TOP THREE PAIRS COME OUT AGAIN.
YAAAAAY
EACH PAIR HAS RECEIVED A TOY.
I JUST CAME TO DANCE. WHY DO I HAVE TO DO THIS?
YAWN
I WONDER IF I COULD TRICK HIM INTO THINKING THIS IS A WALLET ...?
HARF

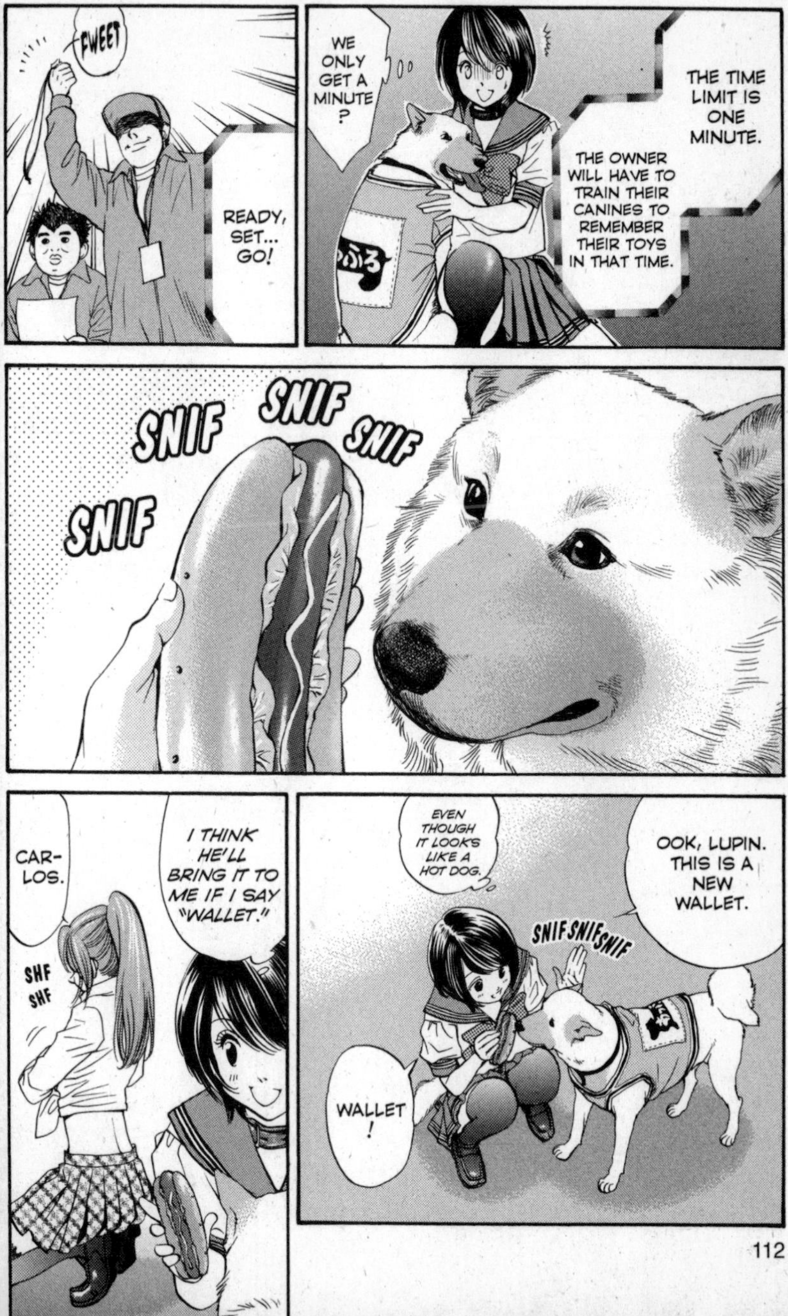
THE TIME LIMIT IS ONE MINUTE.
THE OWNER WILL HAVE TO TRAIN THEIR CANINES TO REMEMBER THEIR TOYS IN THAT TIME.
WE ONLY GET A MINUTE?
FWEET
READY, SET... GO!
SNIF
SNIF
SNIF
SNIF
OOK, LUPIN. THIS IS A NEW WALLET.
EVEN THOUGH IT LOOKS LIKE A HOT DOG.
SNIF SNIF SNIF
WALLET!
I THINK HE'LL BRING IT TO ME IF I SAY "WALLET."
CAR-LOS.
SHF SHF

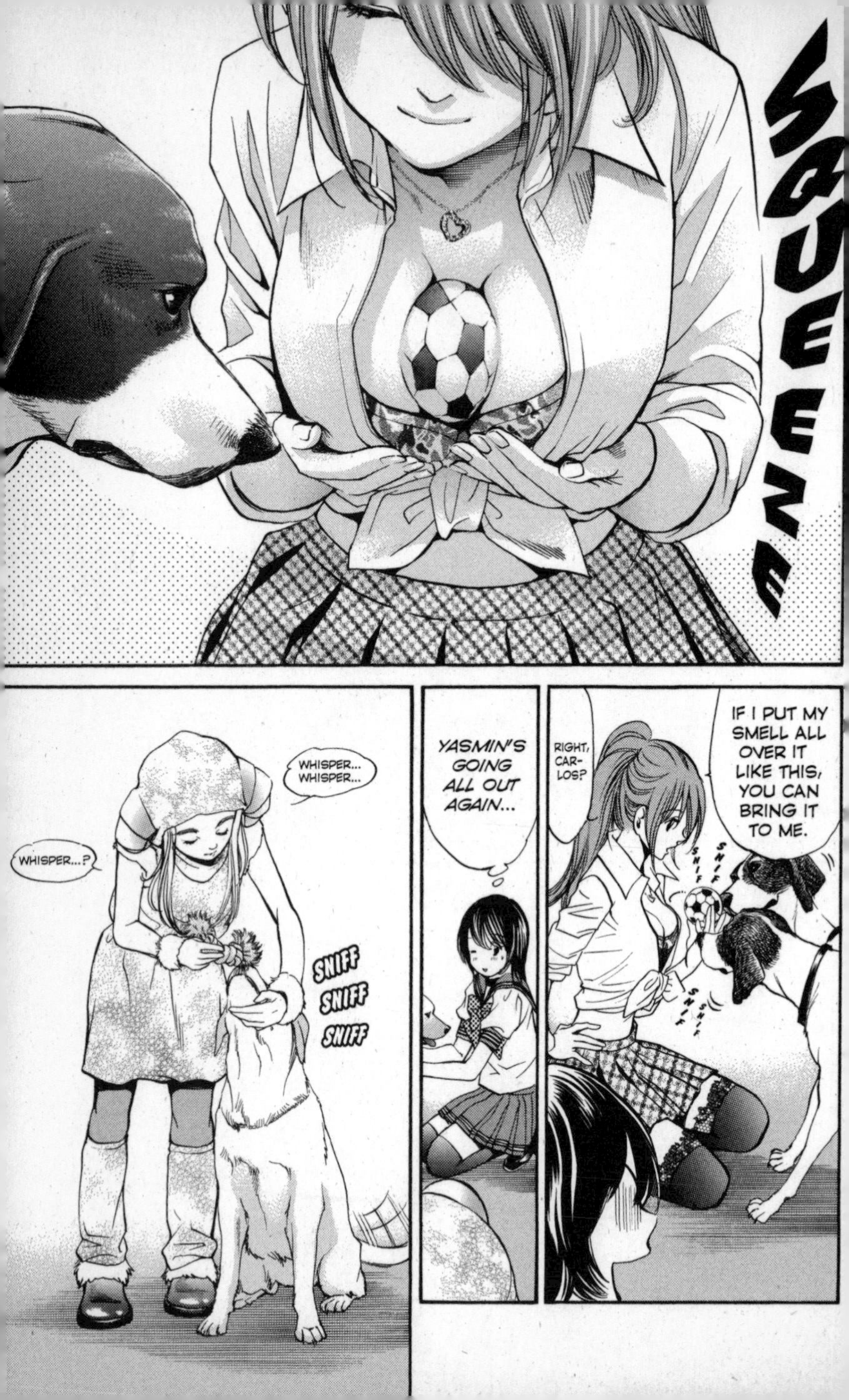
SQUEEZE
IF I PUT MY SMELL ALL OVER IT LIKE THIS, YOU CAN BRING IT TO ME.
RIGHT, CARLOS?
SNIF SNIF
SNIF SNIF
YASMIN'S GOING ALL OUT AGAIN...
WHISPER... WHISPER...
WHISPER...?
SNIFF SNIFF SNIFF

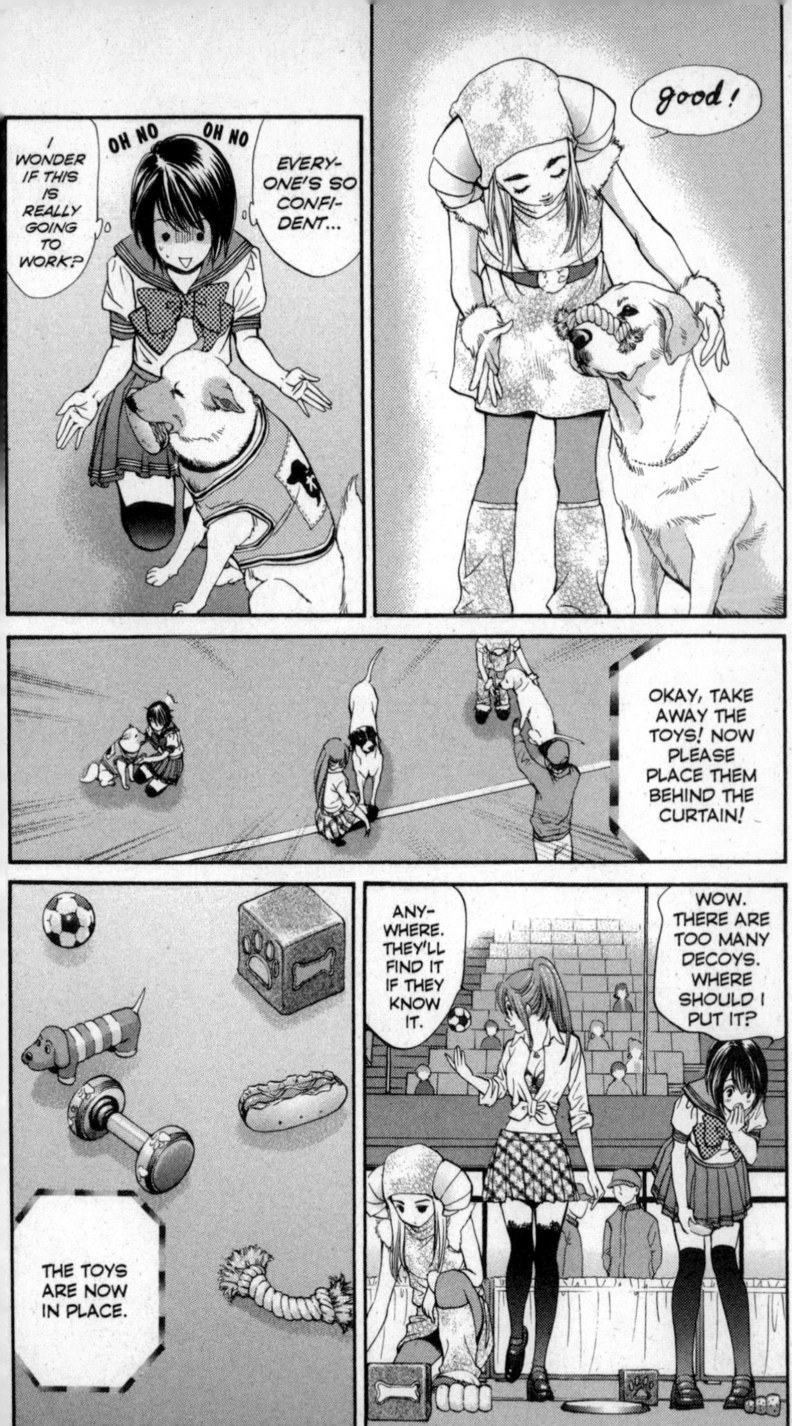
good!
EVERY-ONE'S SO CONFI-DENT...
OH NO
OH NO
I WONDER IF THIS IS REALLY GOING TO WORK?
OKAY, TAKE AWAY THE TOYS! NOW PLEASE PLACE THEM BEHIND THE CURTAIN!
WOW. THERE ARE TOO MANY DECOYS. WHERE SHOULD I PUT IT?
ANY-WHERE. THEY'LL FIND IT IF THEY KNOW IT.
THE TOYS ARE NOW IN PLACE.

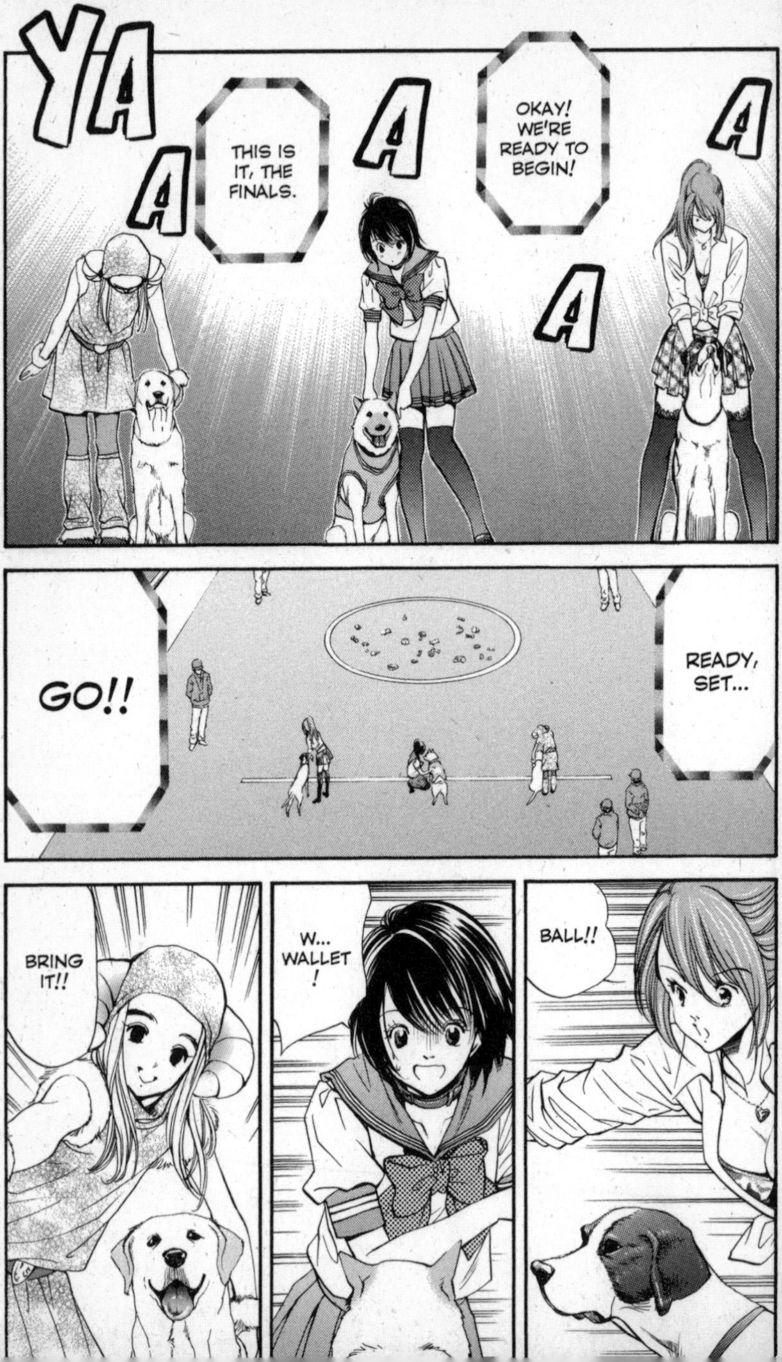
YAAAAA
OKAY! WE'RE READY TO BEGIN!
THIS IS IT, THE FINALS.
READY, SET...
GO!!
BALL!!
W... WALLET!
BRING IT!!

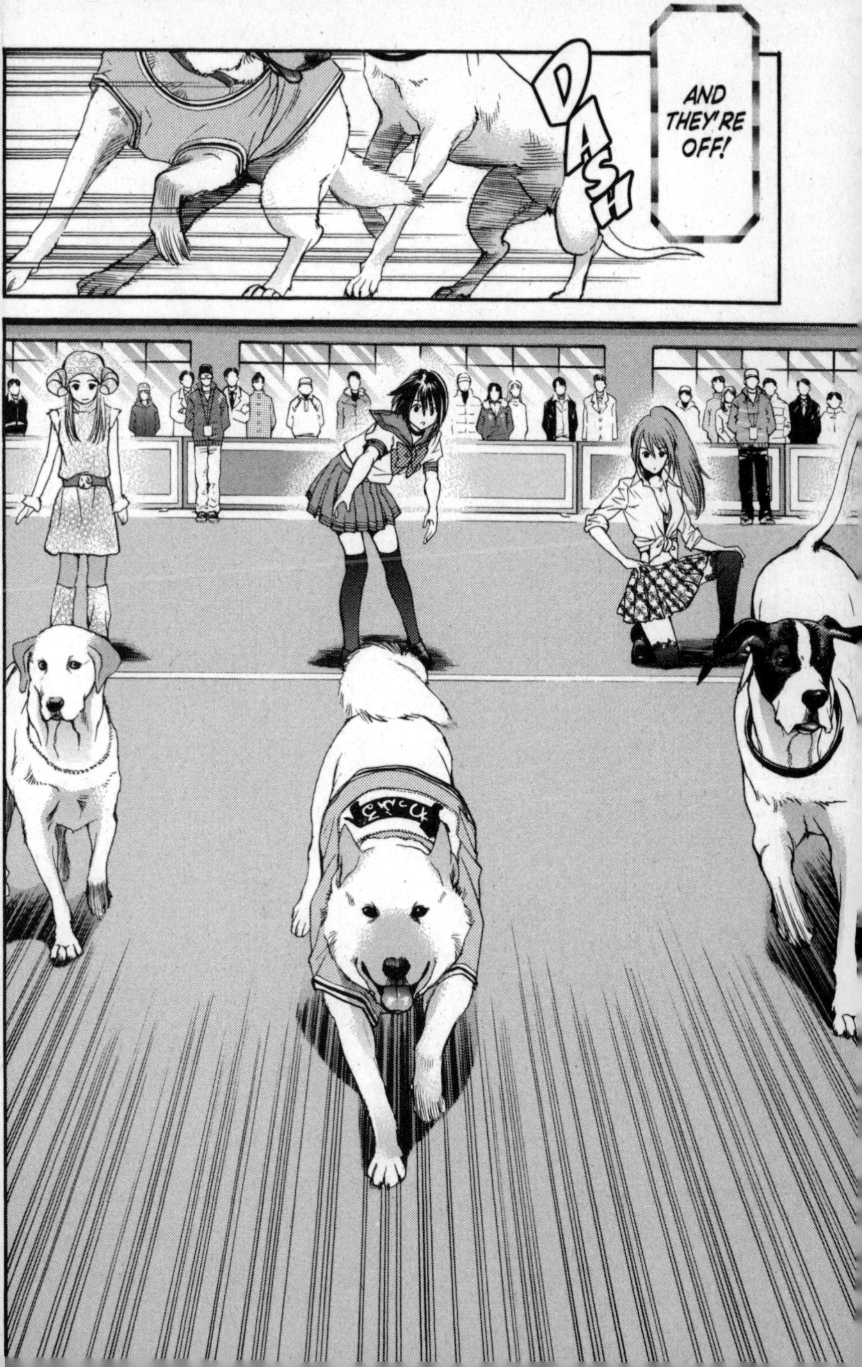
AND THEY'RE OFF!
DASH

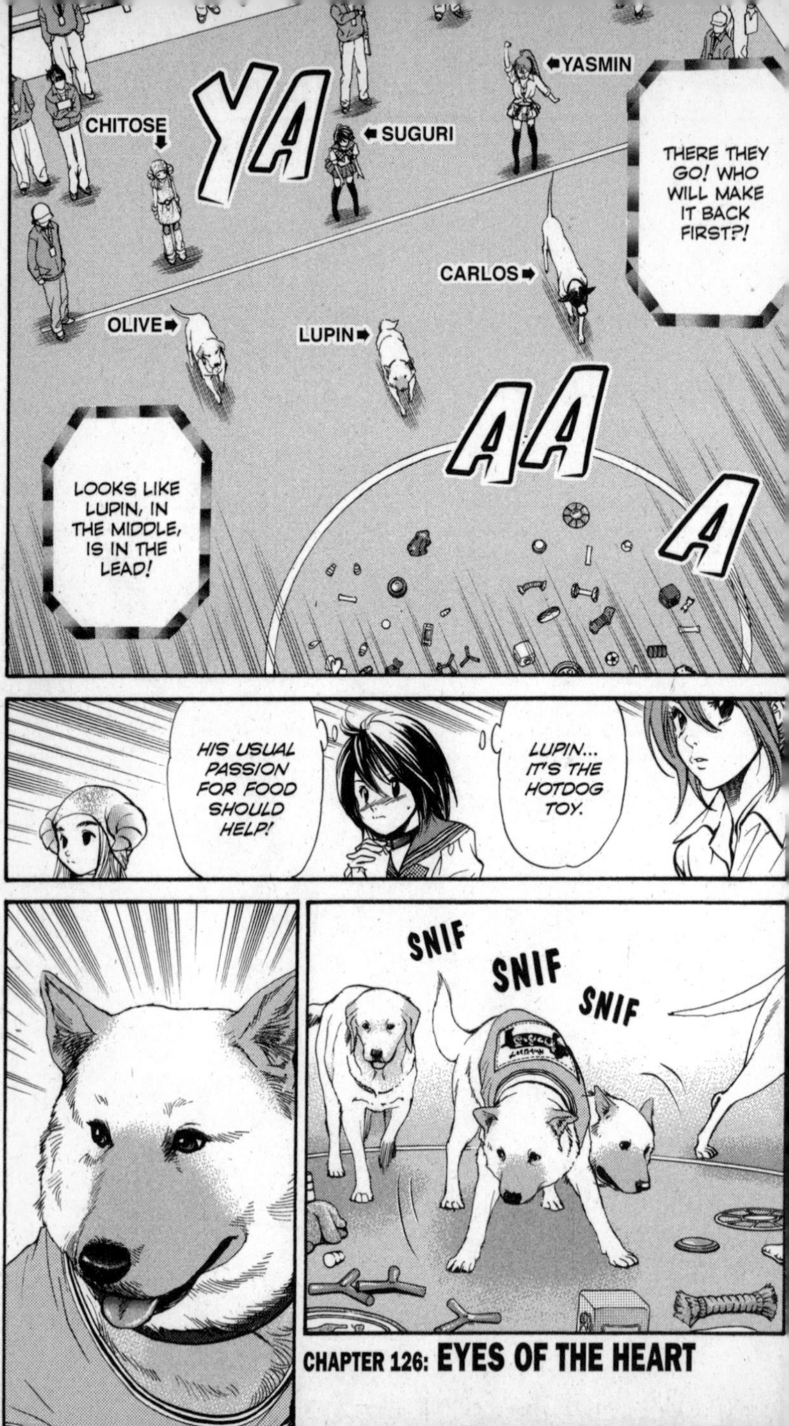
THERE THEY GO! WHO WILL MAKE IT BACK FIRST?!
YASMIN
YA
SUGURI
CHITOSE
CARLOS
LUPIN
OLIVE
AA
A
LOOKS LIKE LUPIN, IN THE MIDDLE, IS IN THE LEAD!
LUPIN... IT'S THE HOTDOG TOY.
HIS USUAL PASSION FOR FOOD SHOULD HELP!
SNIF
SNIF
SNIF

## CHAPTER 126: EYES OF THE HEART

# CHAPTER 126: EYES OF THE HEART

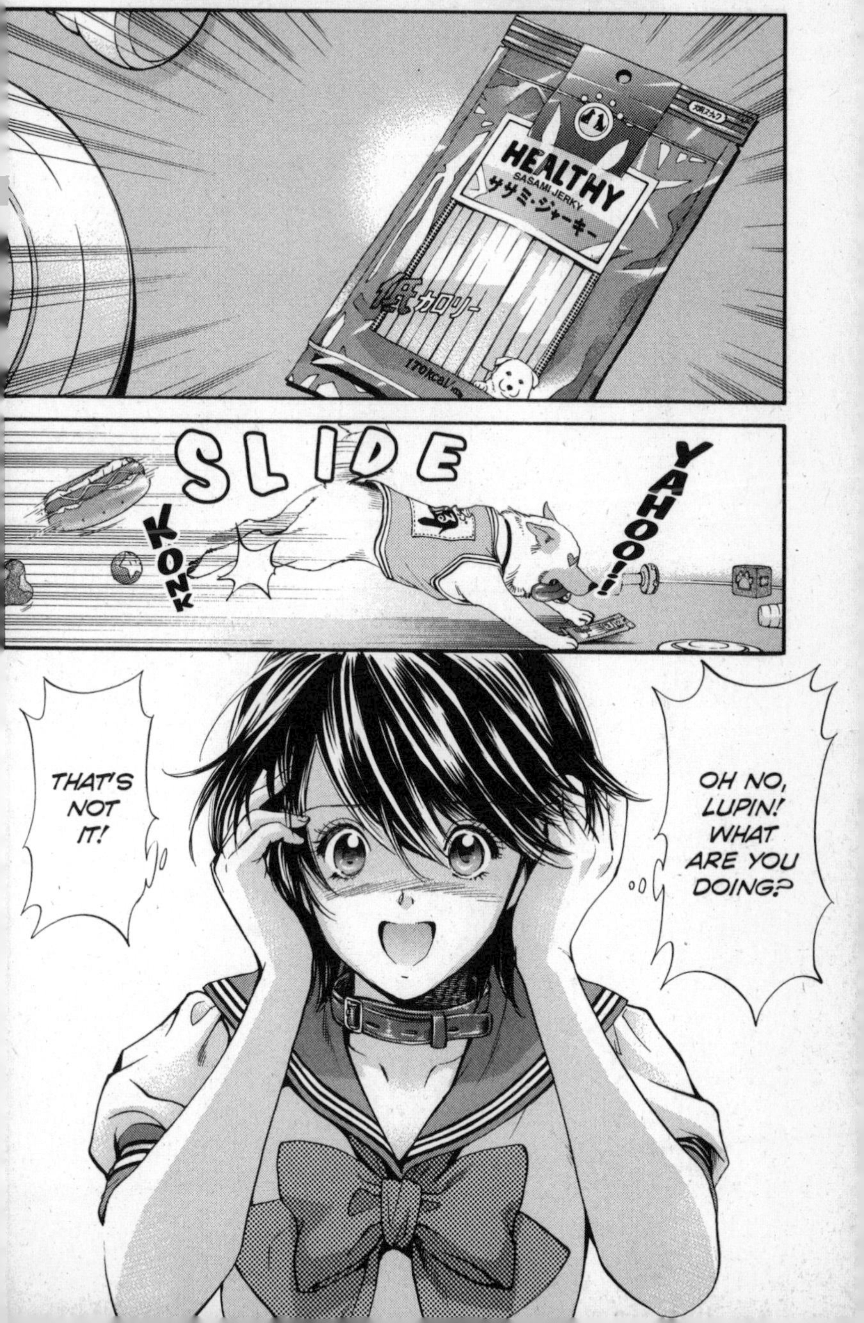
HEALTHY
SASAMI JERKY
ササミ・ジャーキー
低カロリー
170kcal
YAHOO!!
SLIDE
KONK
OH NO, LUPIN! WHAT ARE YOU DOING?
THAT'S NOT IT!

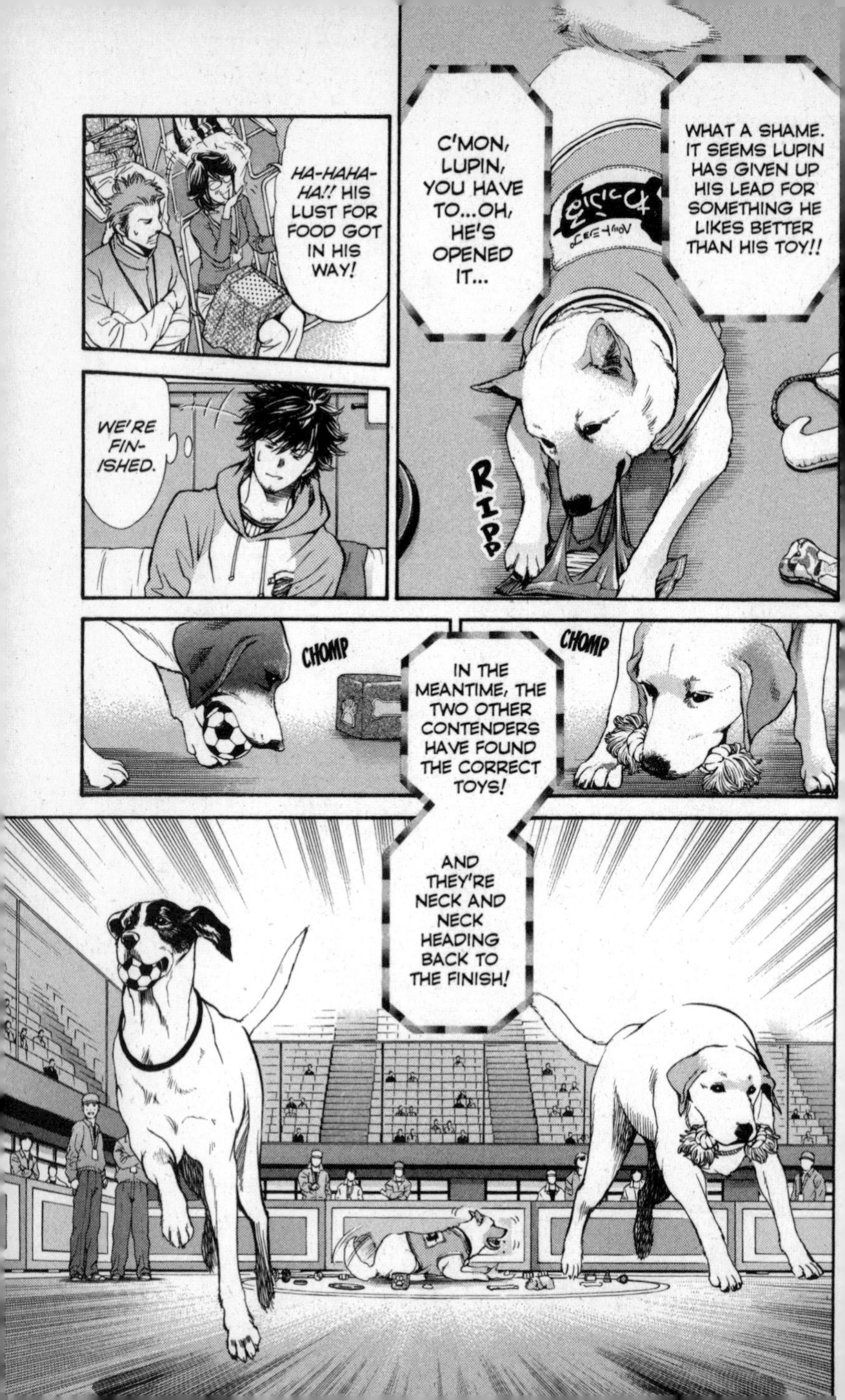
WHAT A SHAME. IT SEEMS LUPIN HAS GIVEN UP HIS LEAD FOR SOMETHING HE LIKES BETTER THAN HIS TOY!!
C'MON, LUPIN, YOU HAVE TO...OH, HE'S OPENED IT...
RIPP
HA-HAHA-HA!! HIS LUST FOR FOOD GOT IN HIS WAY!
WE'RE FIN-ISHED.
CHOMP
IN THE MEANTIME, THE TWO OTHER CONTENDERS HAVE FOUND THE CORRECT TOYS!
CHOMP
AND THEY'RE NECK AND NECK HEADING BACK TO THE FINISH!

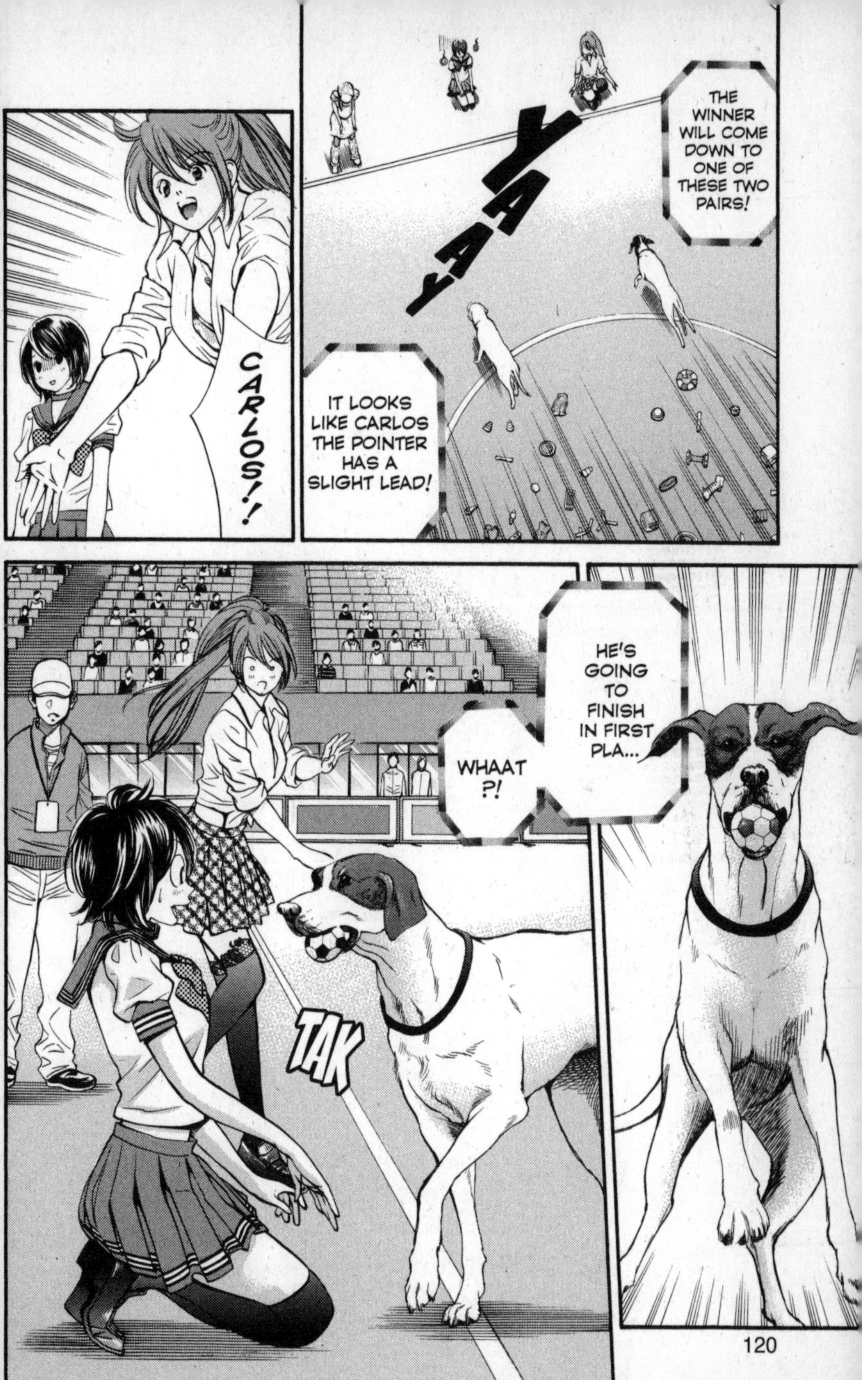
THE WINNER WILL COME DOWN TO ONE OF THESE TWO PAIRS!
YAAY
IT LOOKS LIKE CARLOS THE POINTER HAS A SLIGHT LEAD!
CARLOS!!
HE'S GOING TO FINISH IN FIRST PLA...
WHAAT?!
TAK

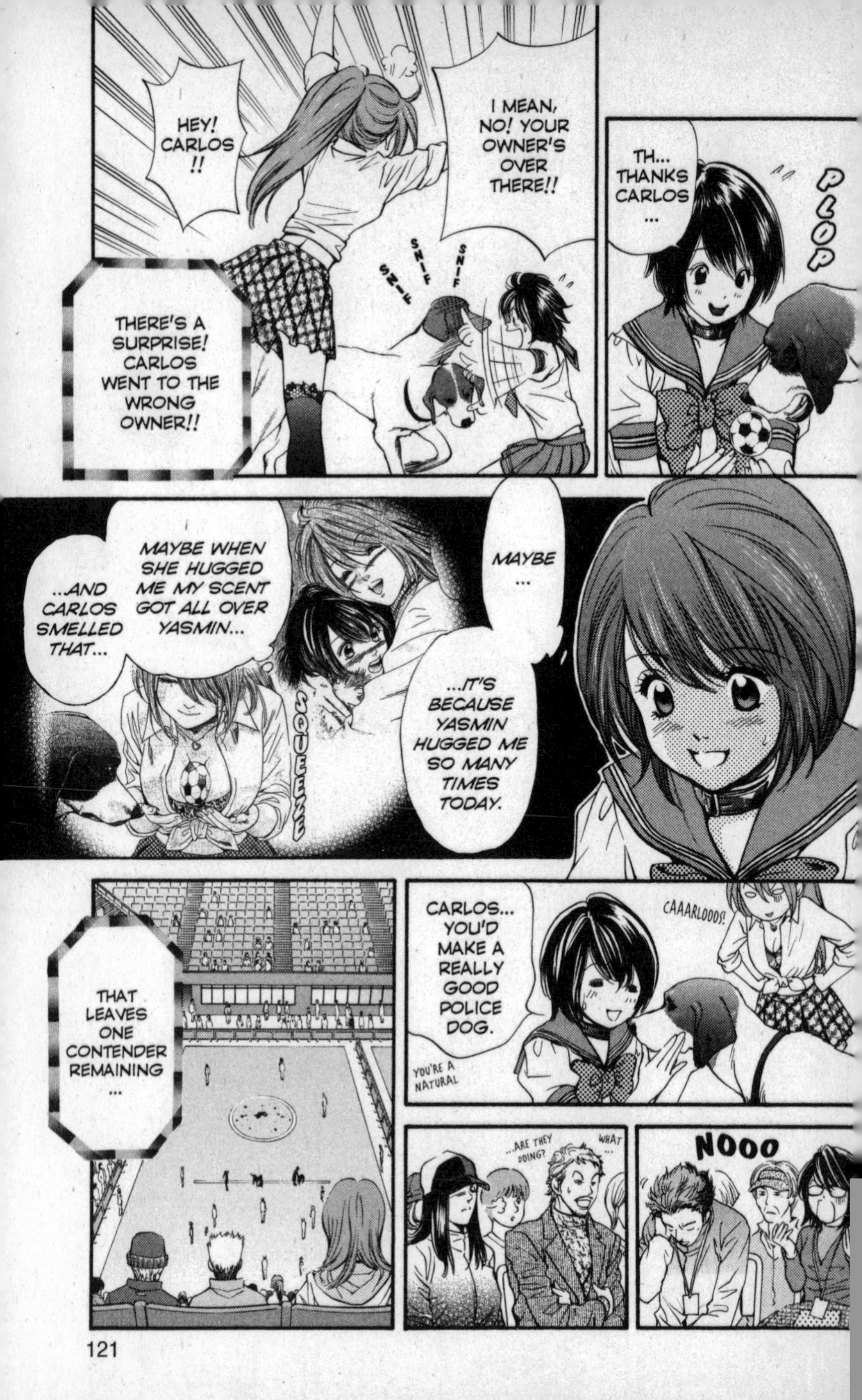
TH... THANKS CARLOS ...
PLOP
HEY! CARLOS !!
I MEAN, NO! YOUR OWNER'S OVER THERE!!
SNIF SNIF SNIF
THERE'S A SURPRISE! CARLOS WENT TO THE WRONG OWNER!!
MAYBE ...
...IT'S BECAUSE YASMIN HUGGED ME SO MANY TIMES TODAY.
MAYBE WHEN SHE HUGGED ME MY SCENT GOT ALL OVER YASMIN...
...AND CARLOS SMELLED THAT...
SQUEEEZE
CARLOS... YOU'D MAKE A REALLY GOOD POLICE DOG.
CAAARLOOOS!
YOU'RE A NATURAL
NOOO
WHAT ...
...ARE THEY DOING?
THAT LEAVES ONE CONTENDER REMAINING ...

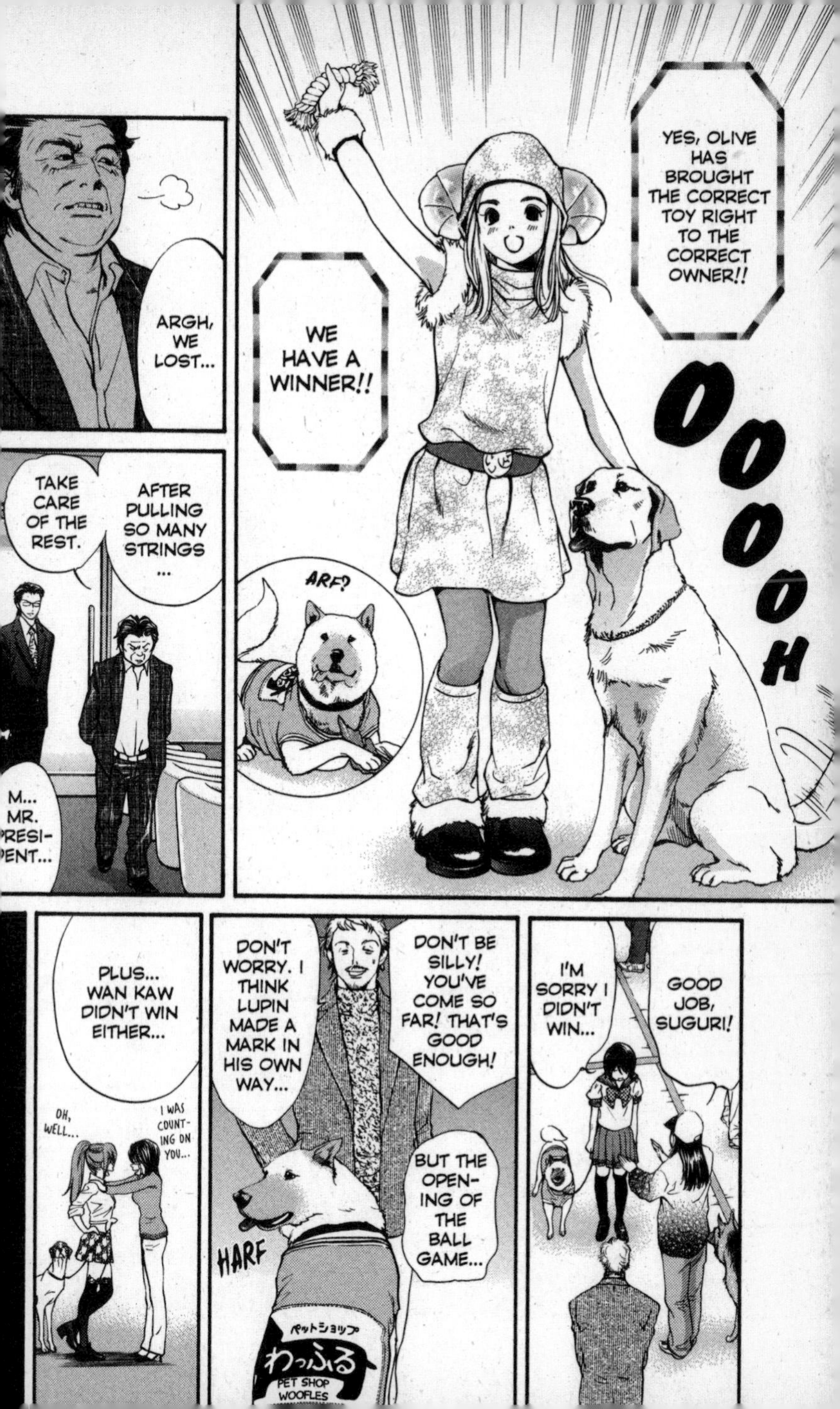
YES, OLIVE HAS BROUGHT THE CORRECT TOY RIGHT TO THE CORRECT OWNER!!
OOOOOH
WE HAVE A WINNER!!
ARF?
ARGH, WE LOST...
AFTER PULLING SO MANY STRINGS ...
TAKE CARE OF THE REST.
M... MR. PRESI- DENT...
GOOD JOB, SUGURI!
I'M SORRY I DIDN'T WIN...
DON'T BE SILLY! YOU'VE COME SO FAR! THAT'S GOOD ENOUGH!
DON'T WORRY. I THINK LUPIN MADE A MARK IN HIS OWN WAY...
BUT THE OPEN- ING OF THE BALL GAME...
HARF
ペットショップ
わっふる
PET SHOP WOOFLES
PLUS... WAN KAW DIDN'T WIN EITHER...
I WAS COUNT- ING ON YOU...
OH, WELL...

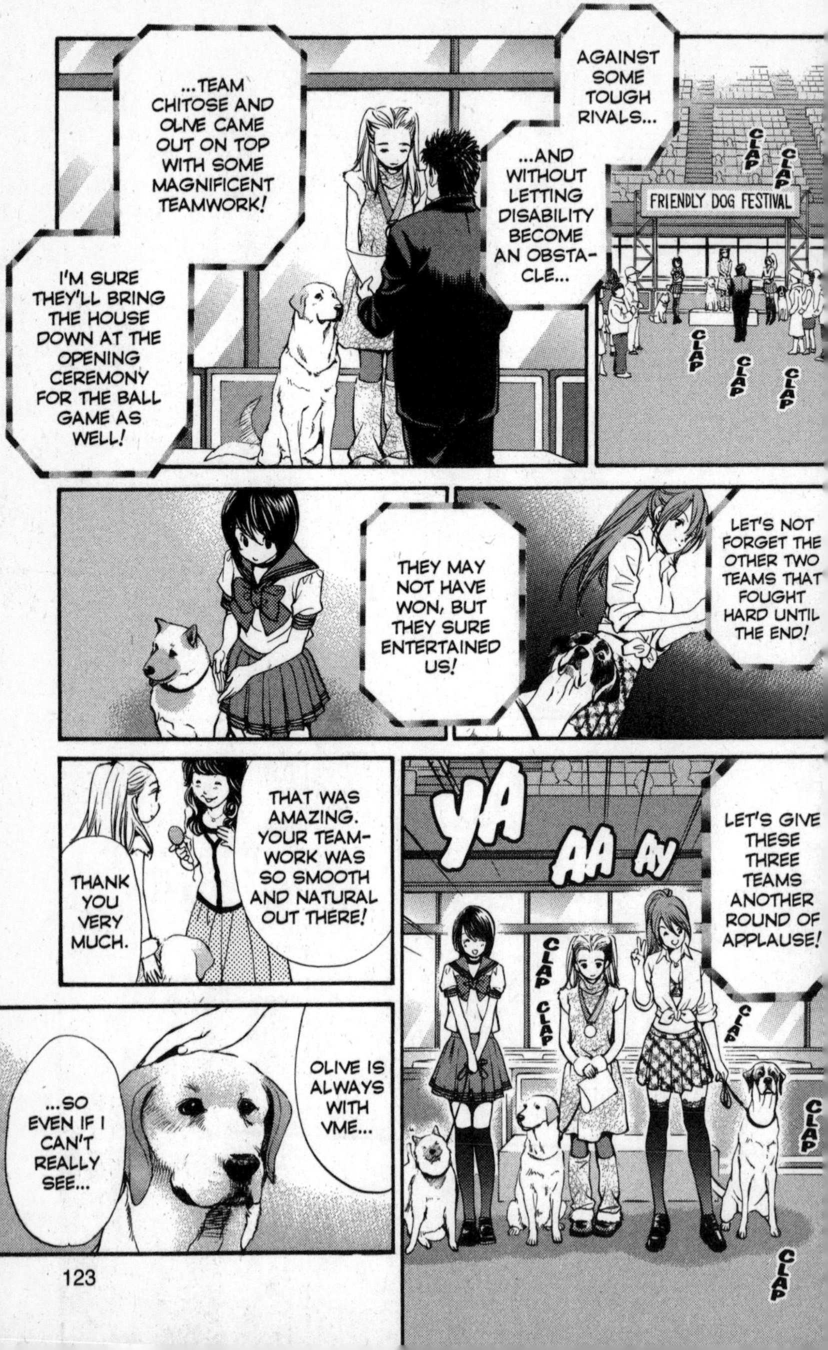
AGAINST SOME TOUGH RIVALS...
...AND WITHOUT LETTING DISABILITY BECOME AN OBSTACLE...
FRIENDLY DOG FESTIVAL
CLAP CLAP
CLAP CLAP CLAP
...TEAM CHITOSE AND OLIVE CAME OUT ON TOP WITH SOME MAGNIFICENT TEAMWORK!
I'M SURE THEY'LL BRING THE HOUSE DOWN AT THE OPENING CEREMONY FOR THE BALL GAME AS WELL!
LET'S NOT FORGET THE OTHER TWO TEAMS THAT FOUGHT HARD UNTIL THE END!
THEY MAY NOT HAVE WON, BUT THEY SURE ENTERTAINED US!
LET'S GIVE THESE THREE TEAMS ANOTHER ROUND OF APPLAUSE!
YA AA AY
CLAP CLAP
CLAP CLAP
CLAP
THAT WAS AMAZING. YOUR TEAM-WORK WAS SO SMOOTH AND NATURAL OUT THERE!
THANK YOU VERY MUCH.
OLIVE IS ALWAYS WITH VME...
...SO EVEN IF I CAN'T REALLY SEE...

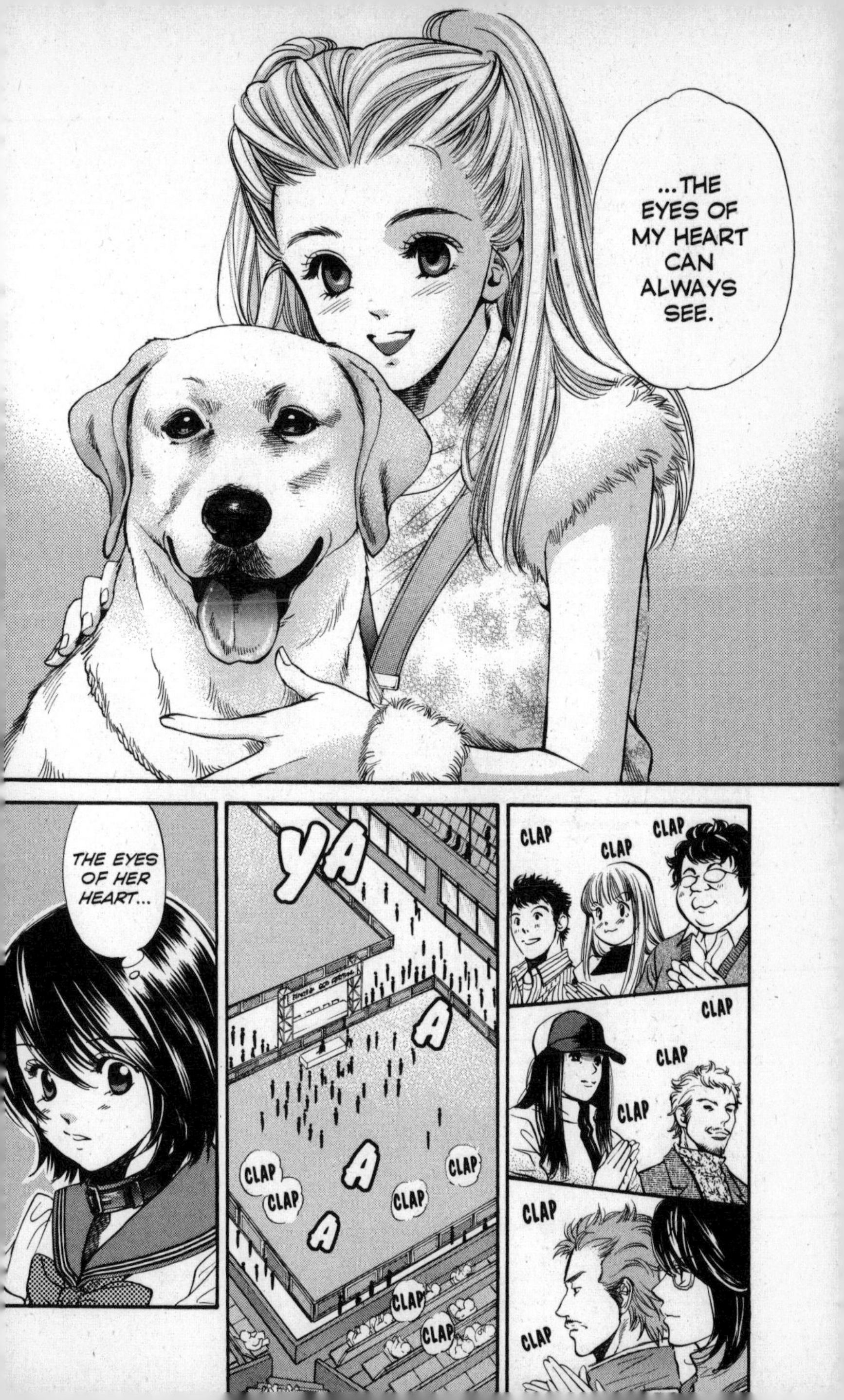

...THE EYES OF MY HEART CAN ALWAYS SEE.
CLAP
CLAP
CLAP
CLAP
CLAP
CLAP
CLAP
CLAP
YAAAAA
CLAP
CLAP
CLAP
CLAP
CLAP
CLAP
THE EYES OF HER HEART...

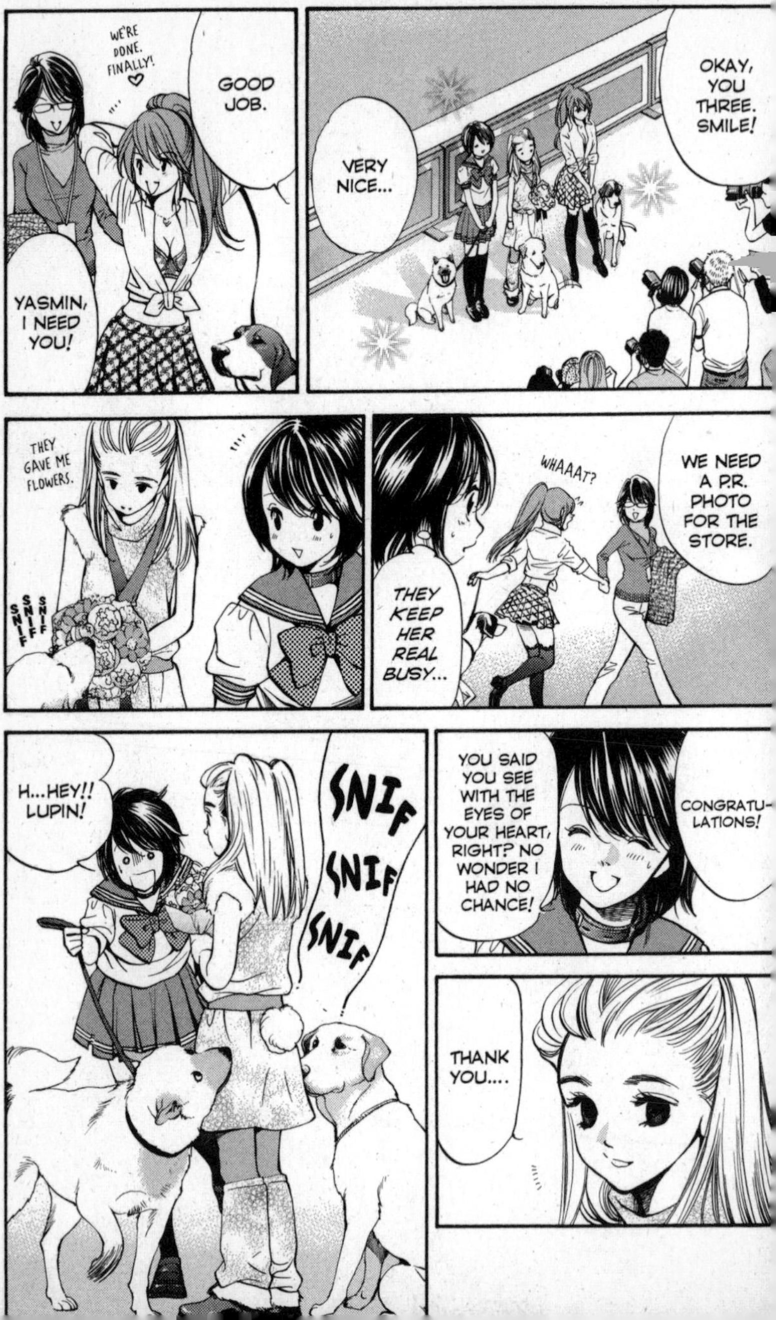
OKAY, YOU THREE. SMILE!
VERY NICE...
GOOD JOB.
WE'RE DONE. FINALLY! ♡
YASMIN, I NEED YOU!
WE NEED A P.R. PHOTO FOR THE STORE.
WHAAAT?
THEY KEEP HER REAL BUSY...
THEY GAVE ME FLOWERS.
SNIF SNIF SNIF
CONGRATU-LATIONS!
YOU SAID YOU SEE WITH THE EYES OF YOUR HEART, RIGHT? NO WONDER I HAD NO CHANCE!
THANK YOU....
SNIF SNIF SNIF
H...HEY!! LUPIN!

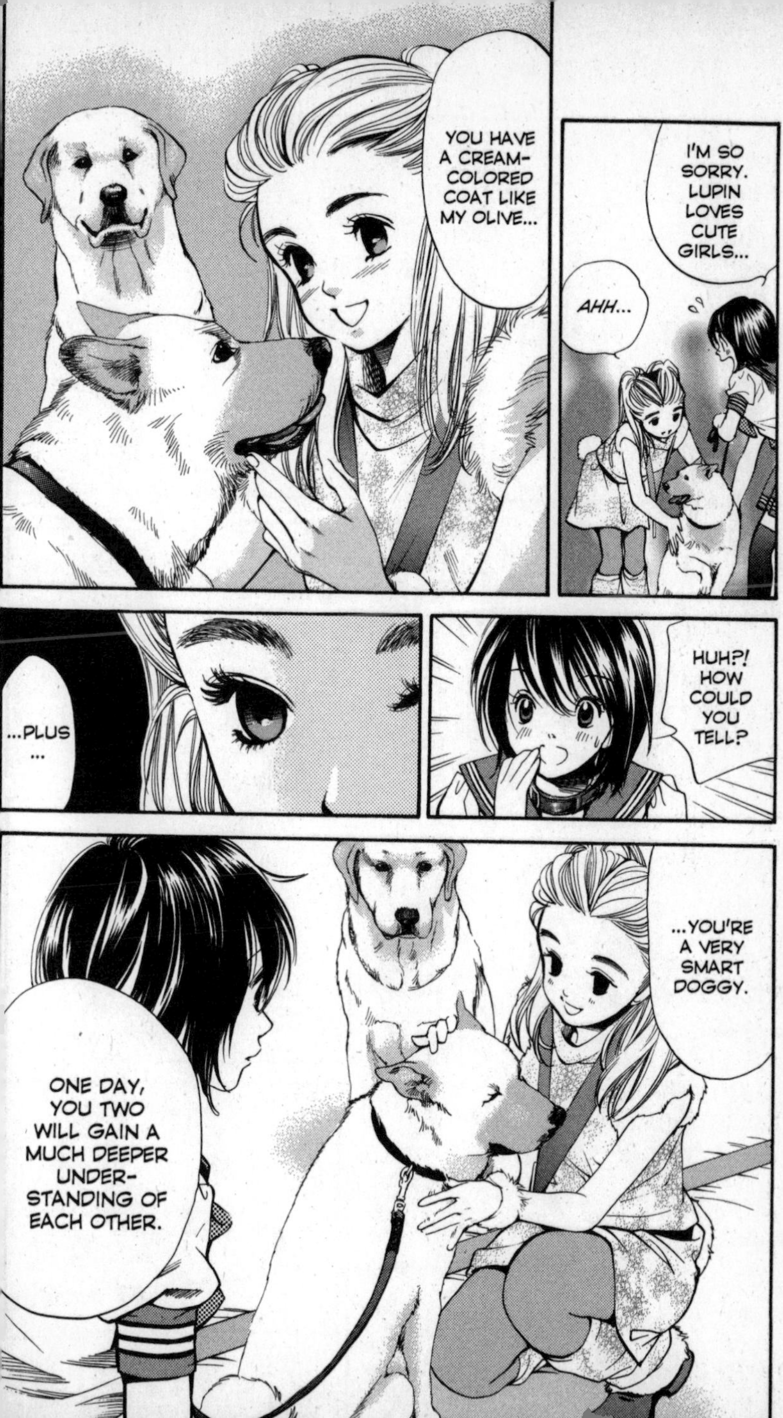
I'M SO SORRY. LUPIN LOVES CUTE GIRLS...
AHH...
YOU HAVE A CREAM-COLORED COAT LIKE MY OLIVE...
HUH?! HOW COULD YOU TELL?
...PLUS ...
...YOU'RE A VERY SMART DOGGY.
ONE DAY, YOU TWO WILL GAIN A MUCH DEEPER UNDER-STANDING OF EACH OTHER.

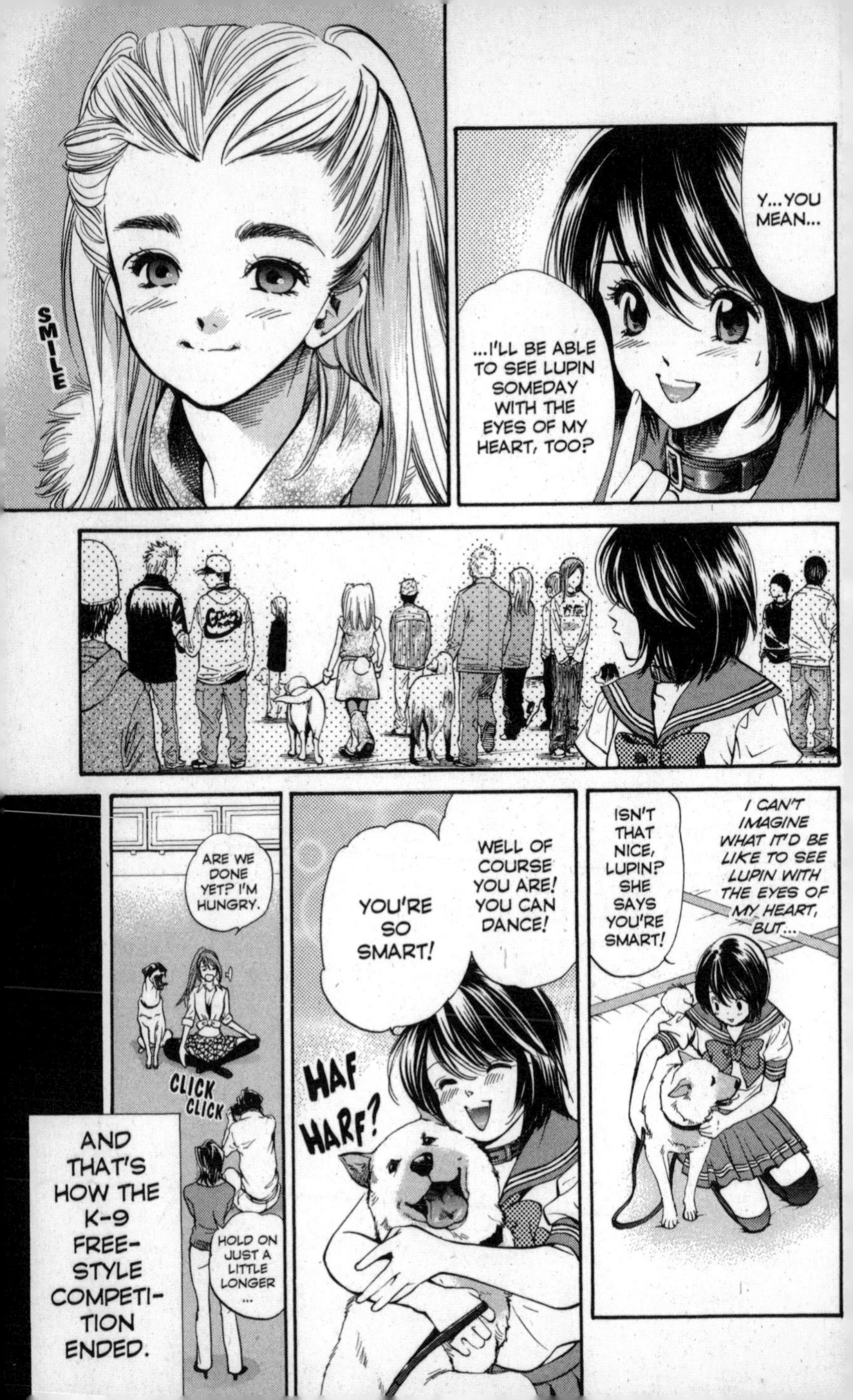
Y...YOU MEAN...
...I'LL BE ABLE TO SEE LUPIN SOMEDAY WITH THE EYES OF MY HEART, TOO?
SMILE
I CAN'T IMAGINE WHAT IT'D BE LIKE TO SEE LUPIN WITH THE EYES OF MY HEART, BUT...
ISN'T THAT NICE, LUPIN? SHE SAYS YOU'RE SMART!
WELL OF COURSE YOU ARE! YOU CAN DANCE!
YOU'RE SO SMART!
HAF HARF?
ARE WE DONE YET? I'M HUNGRY.
CLICK CLICK
HOLD ON JUST A LITTLE LONGER ...
AND THAT'S HOW THE K-9 FREE-STYLE COMPETITION ENDED.

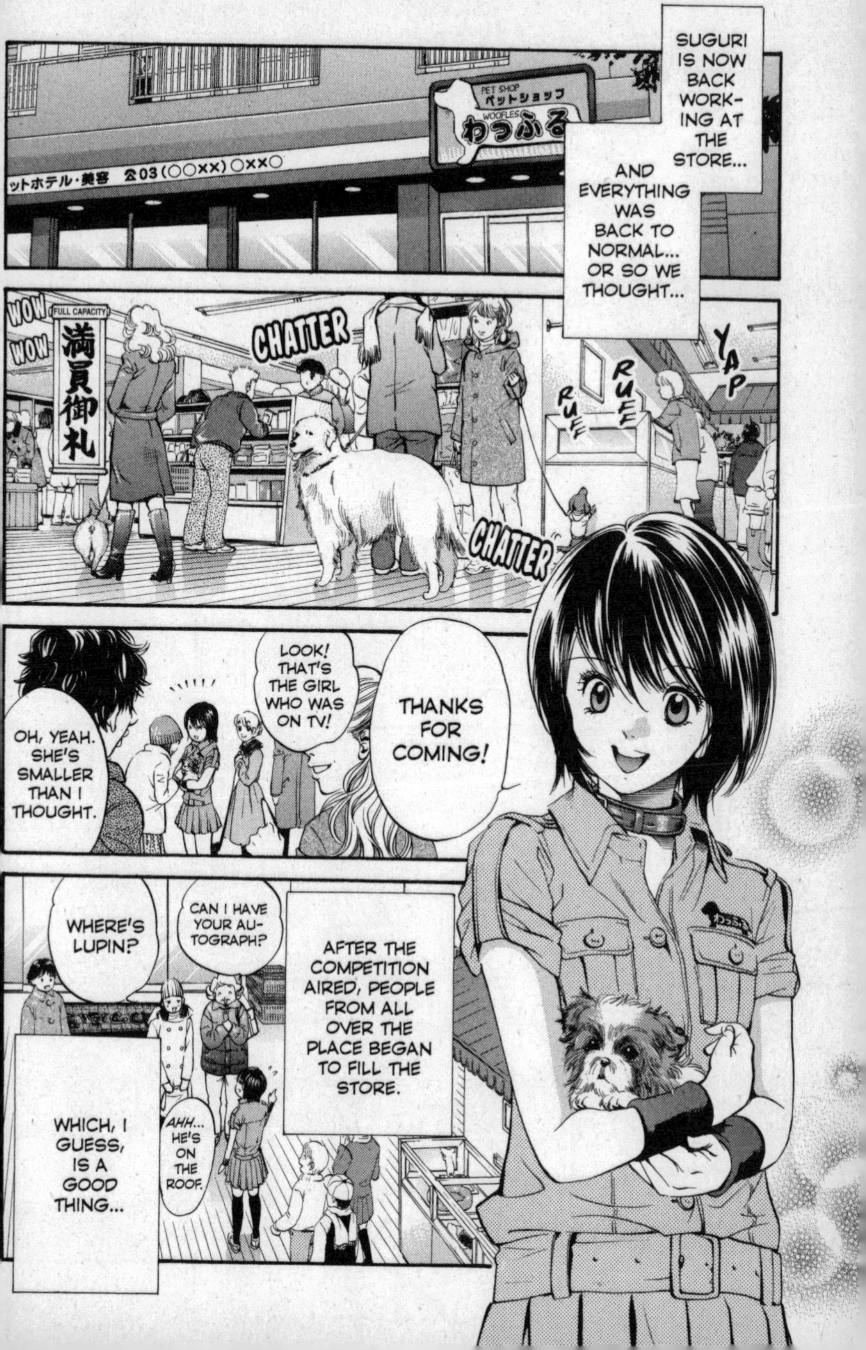
PET SHOP
ペットショップ
WOOFLES
わっふる
ットホテル・美容 ☎03(○○××)○××○
SUGURI IS NOW BACK WORKING AT THE STORE...
AND EVERYTHING WAS BACK TO NORMAL... OR SO WE THOUGHT...
YAP
RUFF
RUFF
CHATTER
CHATTER
FULL CAPACITY
満員御礼
WOW
WOW
THANKS FOR COMING!
LOOK! THAT'S THE GIRL WHO WAS ON TV!
OH, YEAH. SHE'S SMALLER THAN I THOUGHT.
AFTER THE COMPETITION AIRED, PEOPLE FROM ALL OVER THE PLACE BEGAN TO FILL THE STORE.
CAN I HAVE YOUR AUTOGRAPH?
WHERE'S LUPIN?
AHH... HE'S ON THE ROOF.
WHICH, I GUESS, IS A GOOD THING...

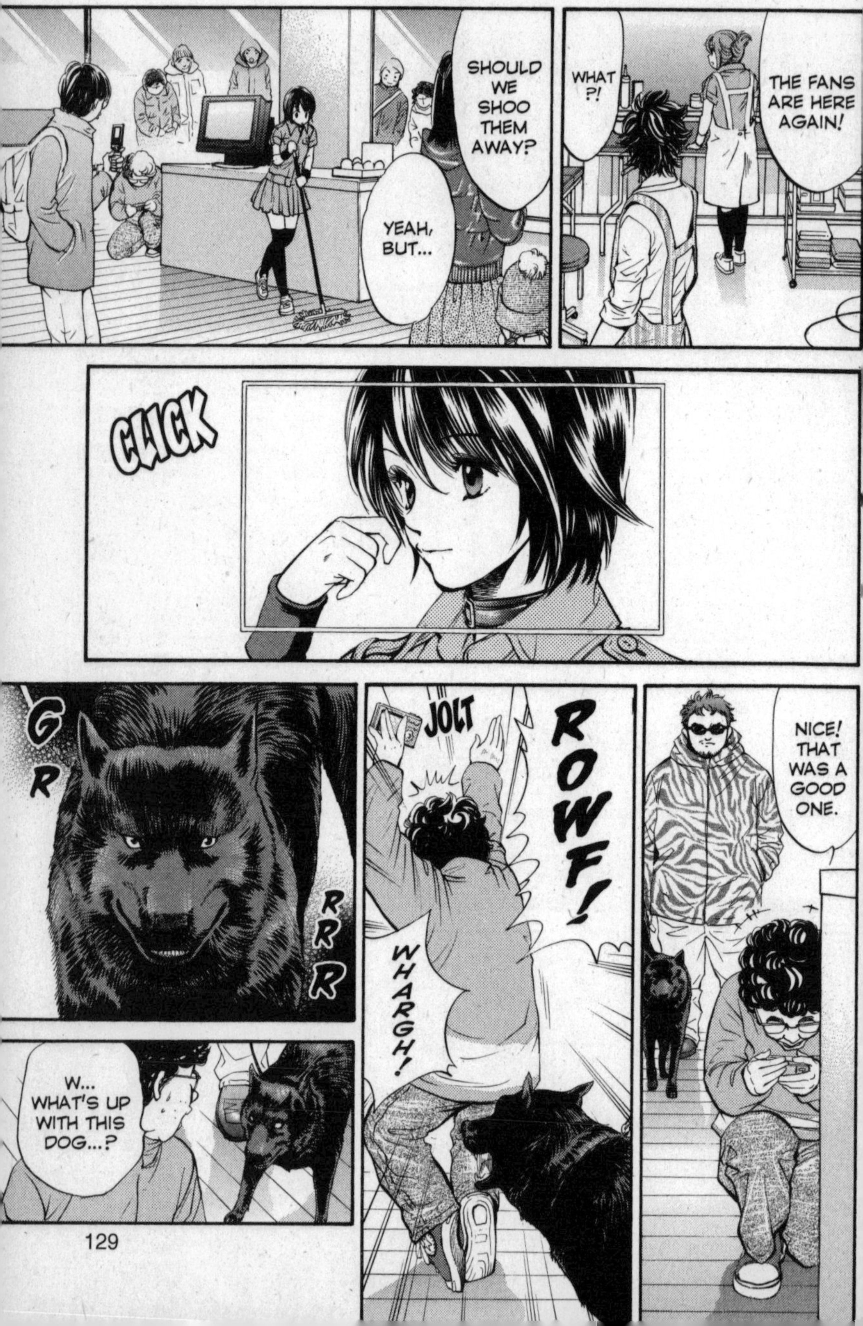
THE FANS ARE HERE AGAIN!
WHAT?!
SHOULD WE SHOO THEM AWAY?
YEAH, BUT...
CLICK
NICE! THAT WAS A GOOD ONE.
ROWF!
JOLT
WHARGH!
G R
R R R
W... WHAT'S UP WITH THIS DOG...?

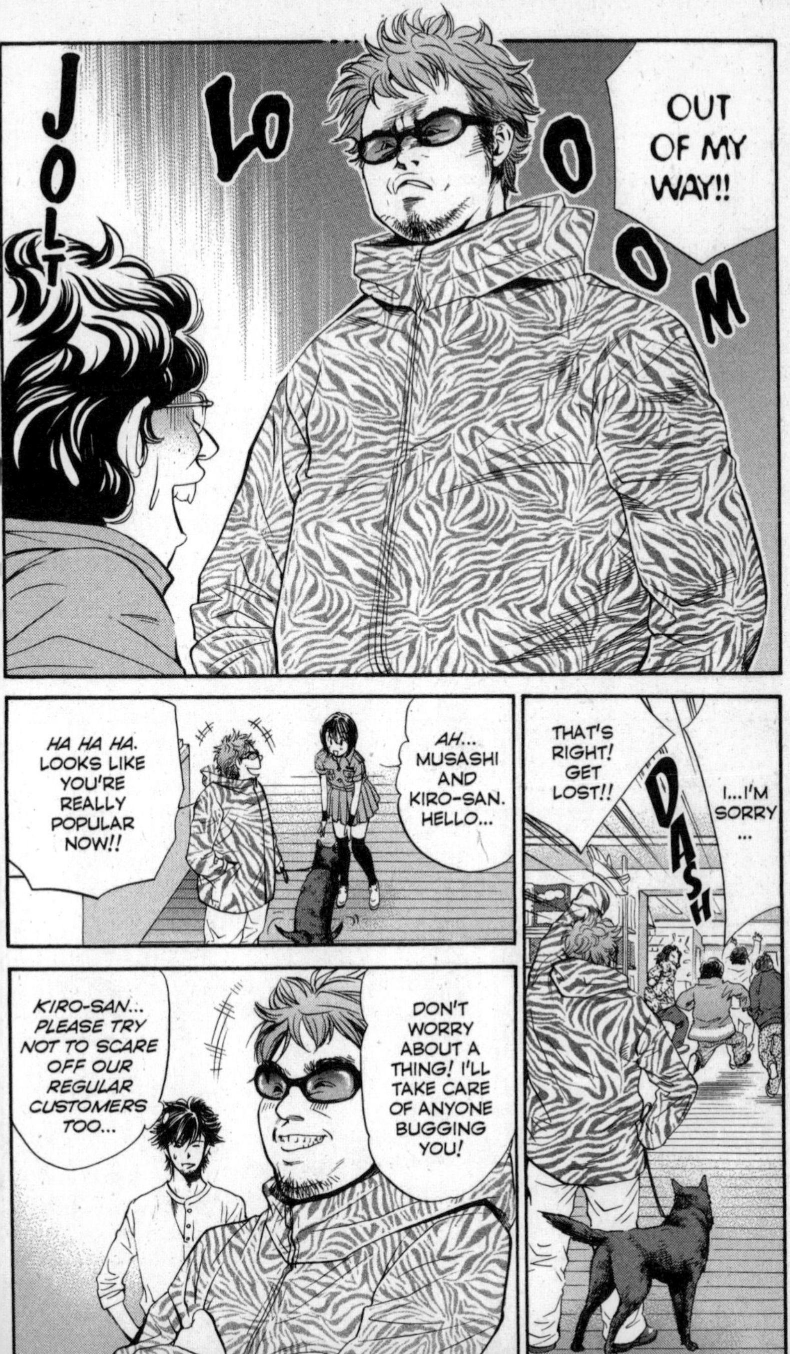
OUT OF MY WAY!!
LOOOOM
JOLT
THAT'S RIGHT! GET LOST!!
DASH
I...I'M SORRY...
AH... MUSASHI AND KIRO-SAN. HELLO...
HA HA HA. LOOKS LIKE YOU'RE REALLY POPULAR NOW!!
DON'T WORRY ABOUT A THING! I'LL TAKE CARE OF ANYONE BUGGING YOU!
KIRO-SAN... PLEASE TRY NOT TO SCARE OFF OUR REGULAR CUSTOMERS TOO...

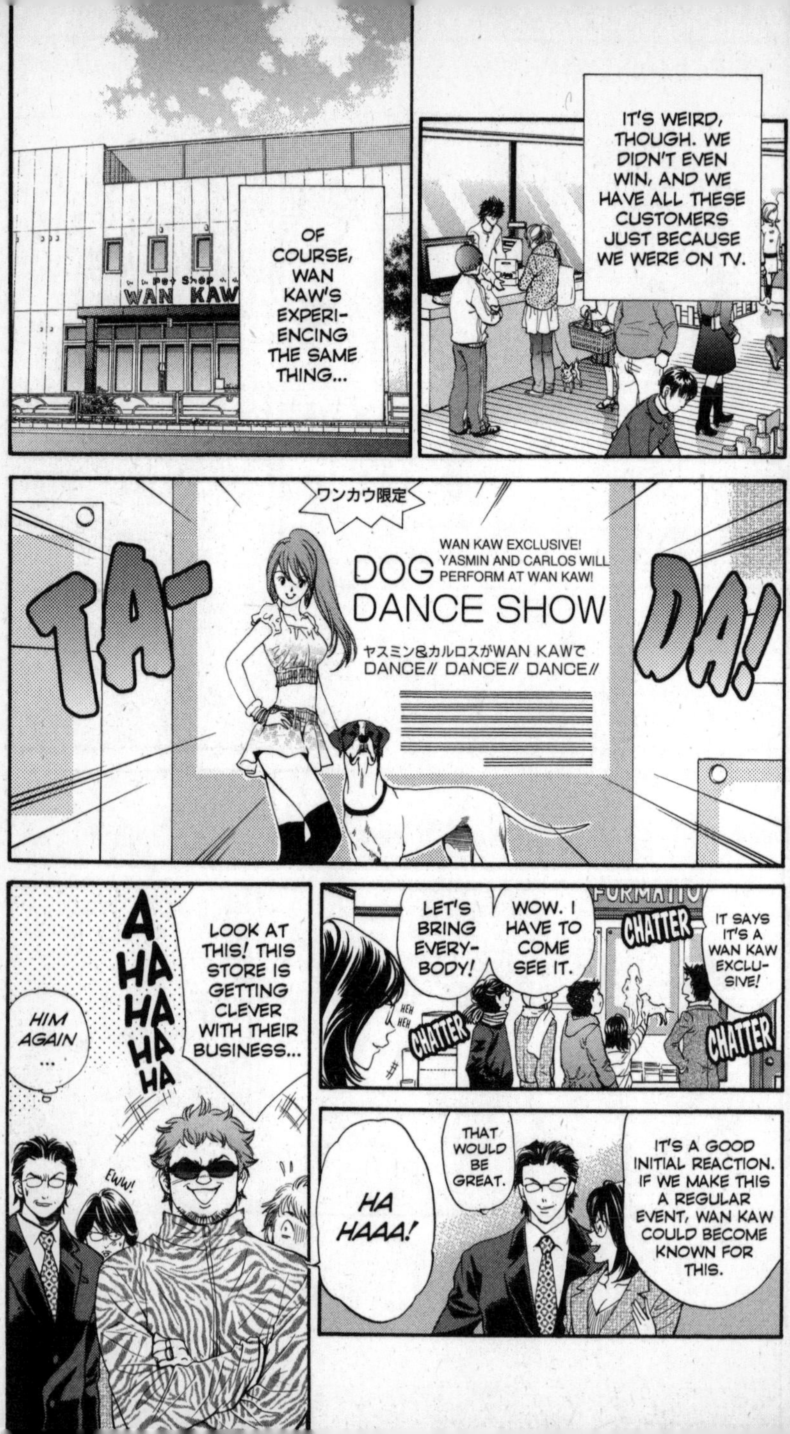
IT'S WEIRD, THOUGH. WE DIDN'T EVEN WIN, AND WE HAVE ALL THESE CUSTOMERS JUST BECAUSE WE WERE ON TV.
Pet Shop WAN KAW
OF COURSE, WAN KAW'S EXPERIENCING THE SAME THING...
ワンカウ限定
WAN KAW EXCLUSIVE! YASMIN AND CARLOS WILL PERFORM AT WAN KAW!
DOG DANCE SHOW
ヤスミン&カルロスがWAN KAWで
DANCE// DANCE// DANCE//
TA-
DA!
IT SAYS IT'S A WAN KAW EXCLUSIVE!
CHATTER
CHATTER
WOW. I HAVE TO COME SEE IT.
LET'S BRING EVERYBODY!
HEH HEH
CHATTER
IT'S A GOOD INITIAL REACTION. IF WE MAKE THIS A REGULAR EVENT, WAN KAW COULD BECOME KNOWN FOR THIS.
THAT WOULD BE GREAT.
HA HAAA!
LOOK AT THIS! THIS STORE IS GETTING CLEVER WITH THEIR BUSINESS...
AHAHAHAHAHA
HIM AGAIN...
EWW!

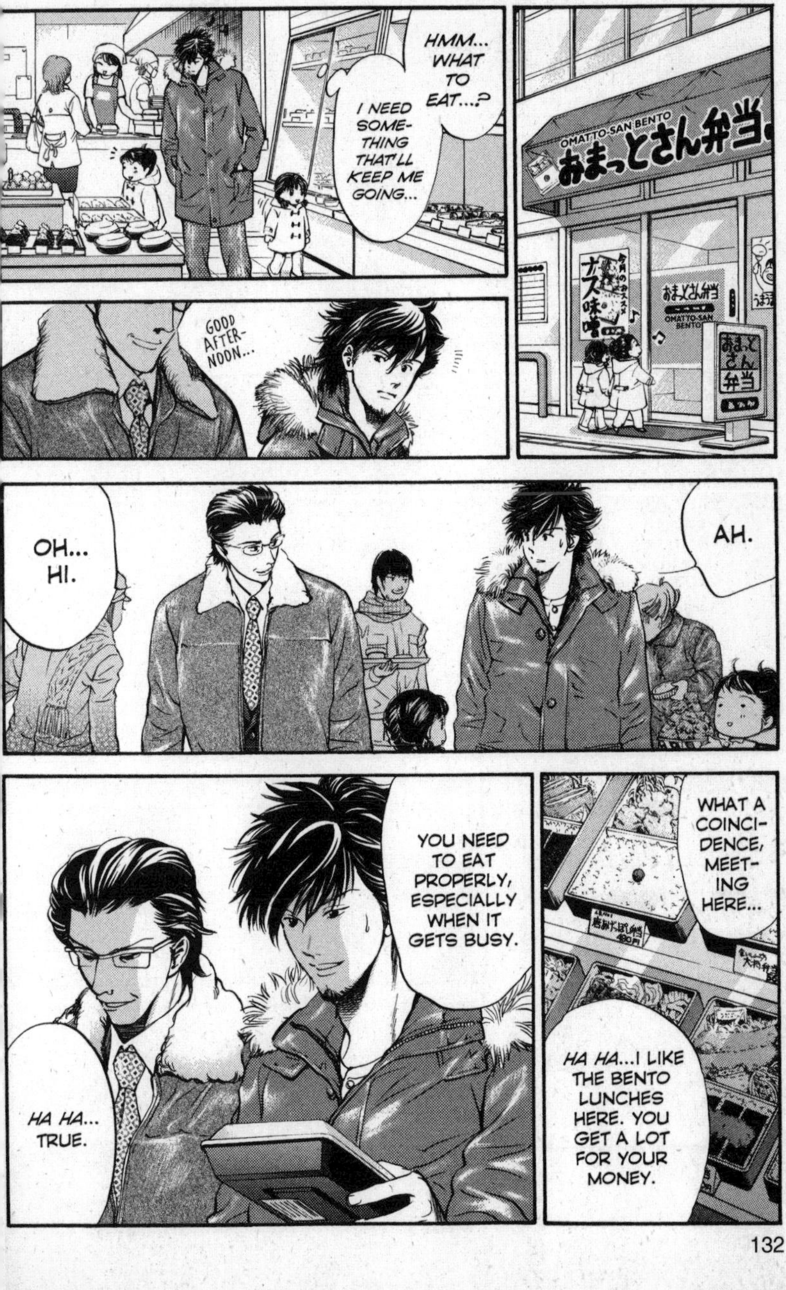
OMATTO-SAN BENTO
おまっとさん弁当
OMATTO-SAN BENTO
おまっとさん弁当
HMM... WHAT TO EAT...?
I NEED SOMETHING THAT'LL KEEP ME GOING...
GOOD AFTERNOON...
AH.
OH... HI.
WHAT A COINCIDENCE, MEETING HERE...
HA HA...I LIKE THE BENTO LUNCHES HERE. YOU GET A LOT FOR YOUR MONEY.
YOU NEED TO EAT PROPERLY, ESPECIALLY WHEN IT GETS BUSY.
HA HA... TRUE.

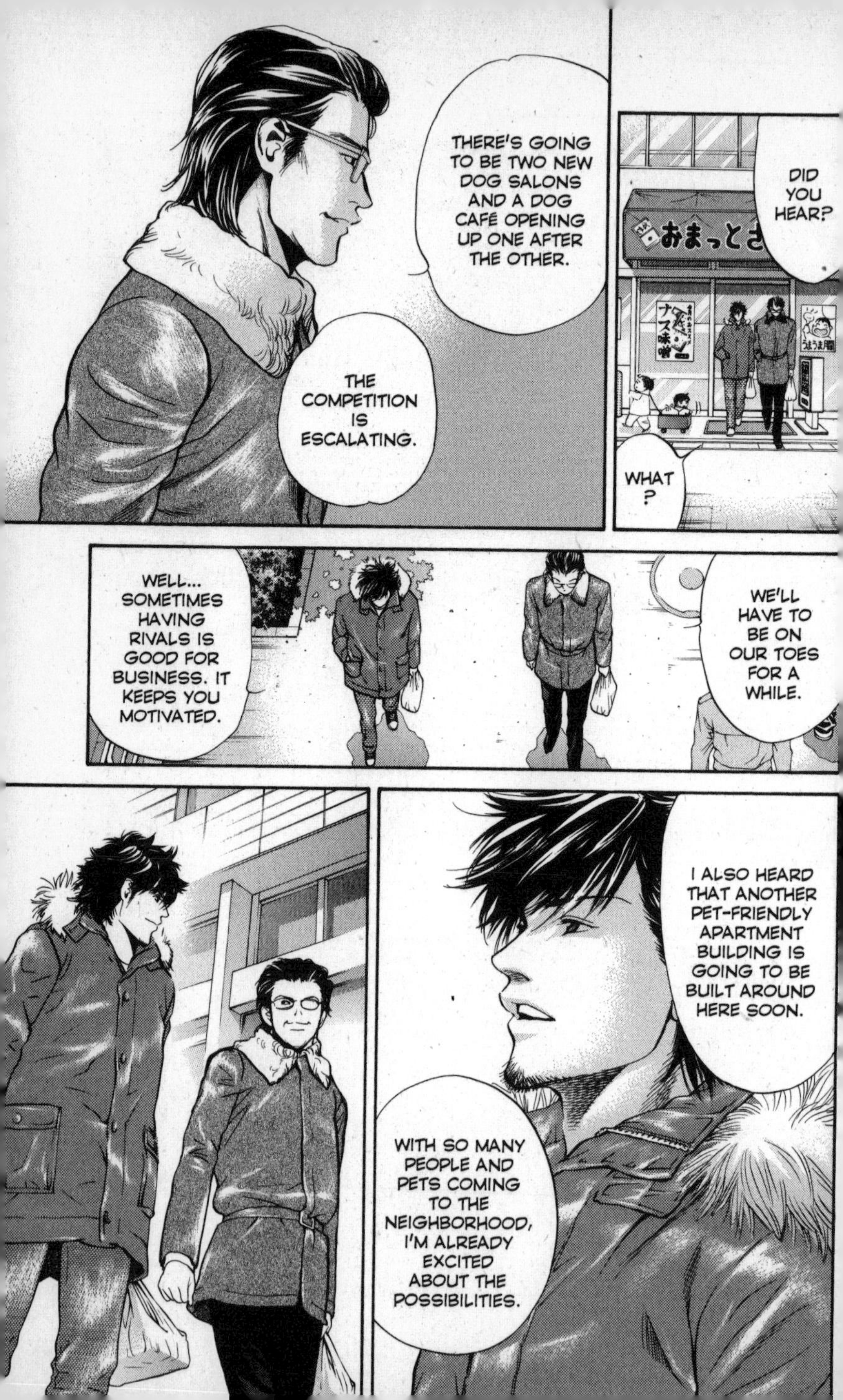
DID YOU HEAR?
WHAT?
THERE'S GOING TO BE TWO NEW DOG SALONS AND A DOG CAFÉ OPENING UP ONE AFTER THE OTHER.
THE COMPETITION IS ESCALATING.
WE'LL HAVE TO BE ON OUR TOES FOR A WHILE.
WELL... SOMETIMES HAVING RIVALS IS GOOD FOR BUSINESS. IT KEEPS YOU MOTIVATED.
I ALSO HEARD THAT ANOTHER PET-FRIENDLY APARTMENT BUILDING IS GOING TO BE BUILT AROUND HERE SOON.
WITH SO MANY PEOPLE AND PETS COMING TO THE NEIGHBORHOOD, I'M ALREADY EXCITED ABOUT THE POSSIBILITIES.

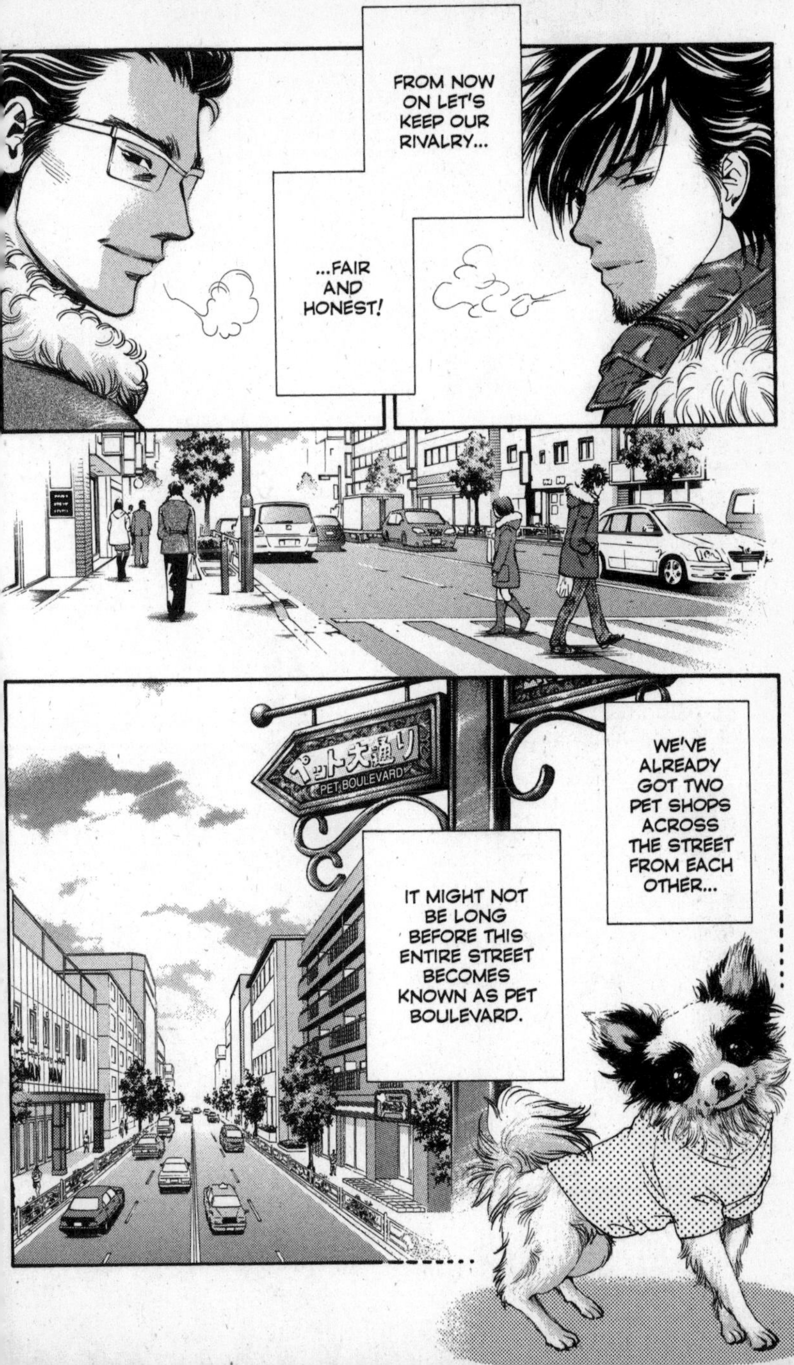
FROM NOW ON LET'S KEEP OUR RIVALRY...
...FAIR AND HONEST!
WE'VE ALREADY GOT TWO PET SHOPS ACROSS THE STREET FROM EACH OTHER...
ペット大通り
PET BOULEVARD
IT MIGHT NOT BE LONG BEFORE THIS ENTIRE STREET BECOMES KNOWN AS PET BOULEVARD.

# CHAPTER127: FLY BALL CHALLENGE!

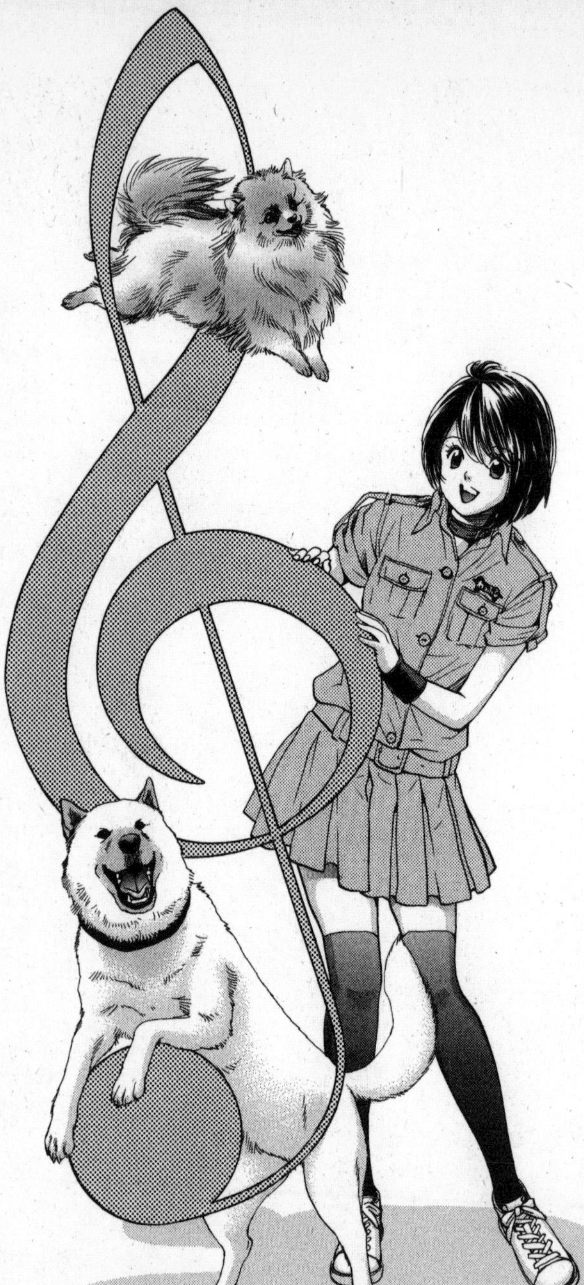

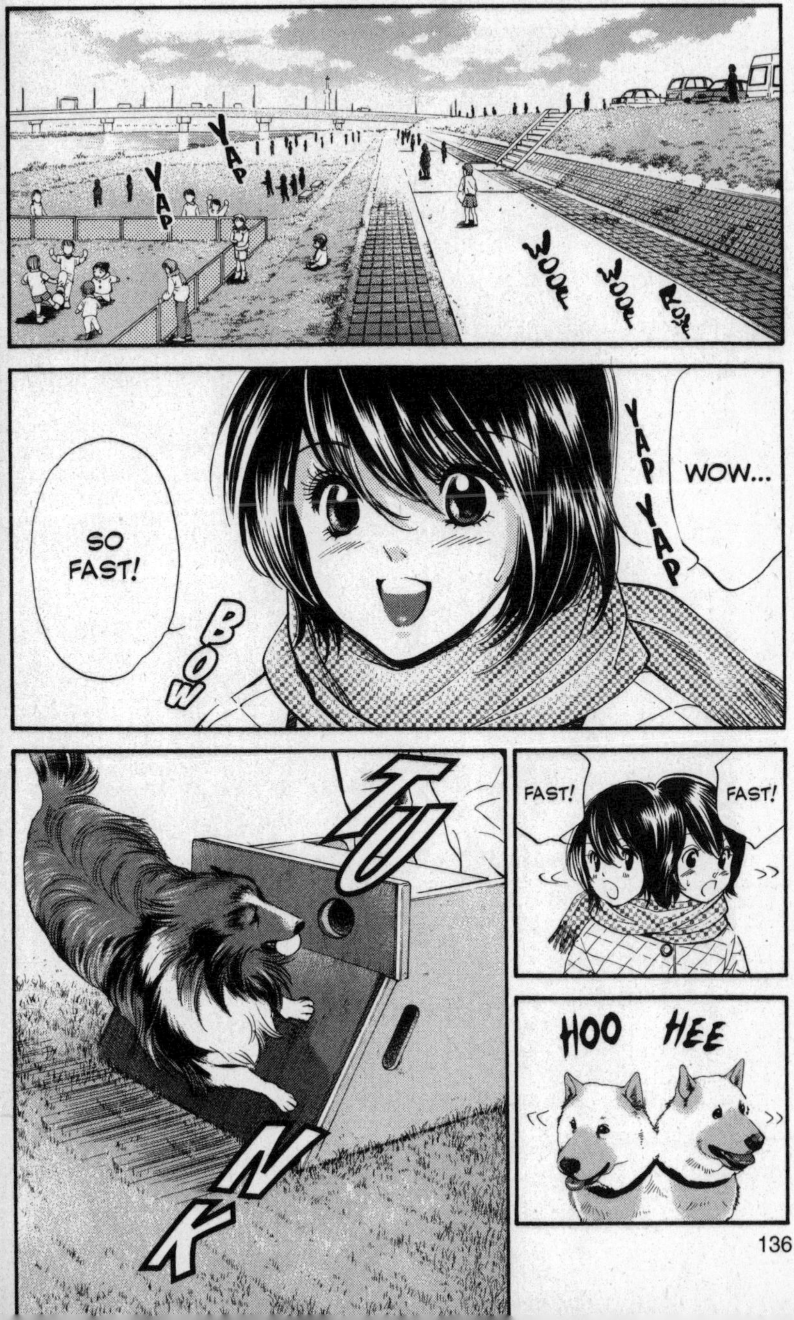
YAP
YAP
YAP
WOOF
WOOF
WOOF
WOW...
YAP YAP YAP
SO FAST!
BOW
FAST!
FAST!
HOO HEE
TUNK

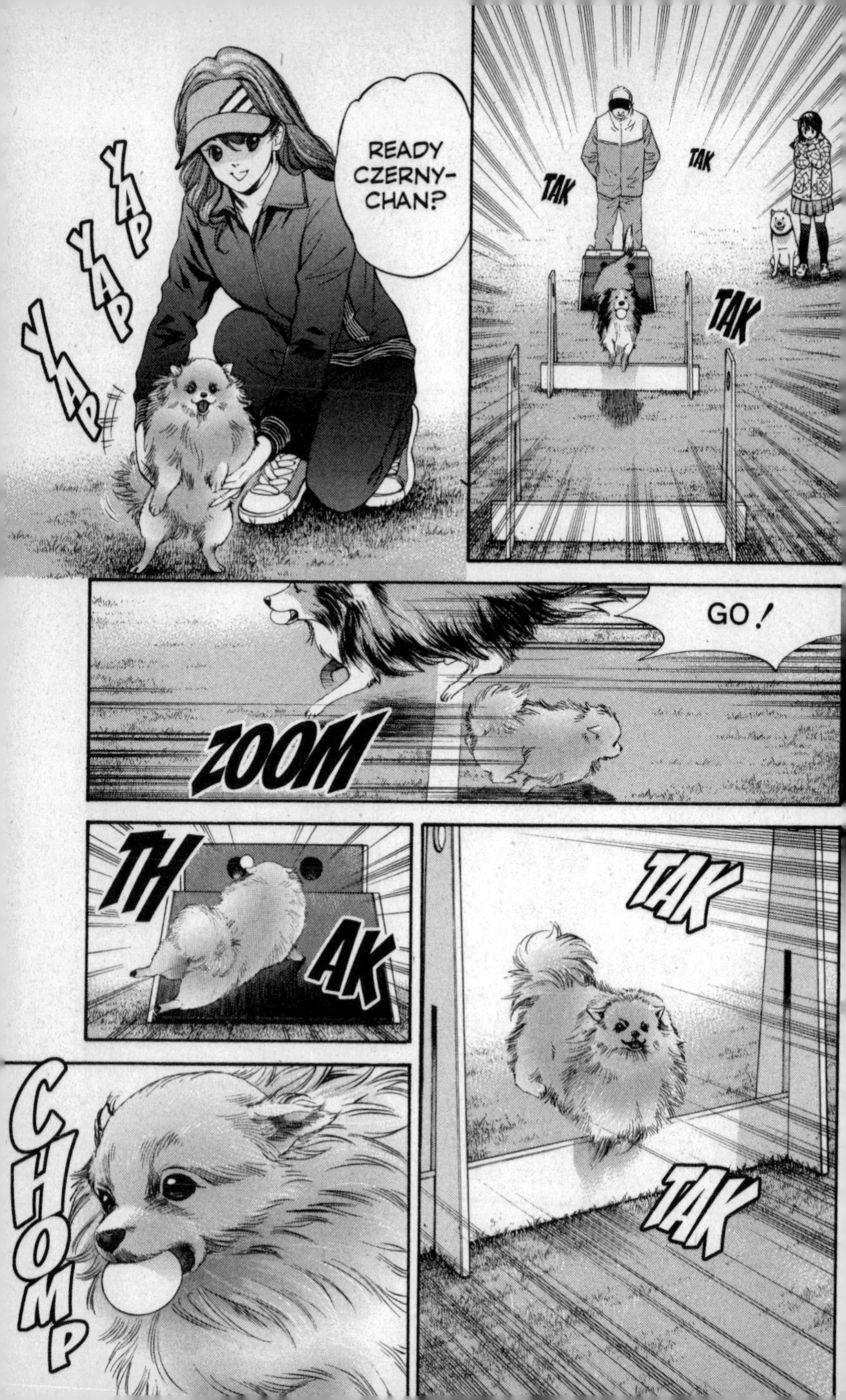
TAK
TAK
TAK
READY CZERNY-CHAN?
YAP
YAP
YAP
GO!
ZOOM
TAK
TAK
THAK
CHOMP

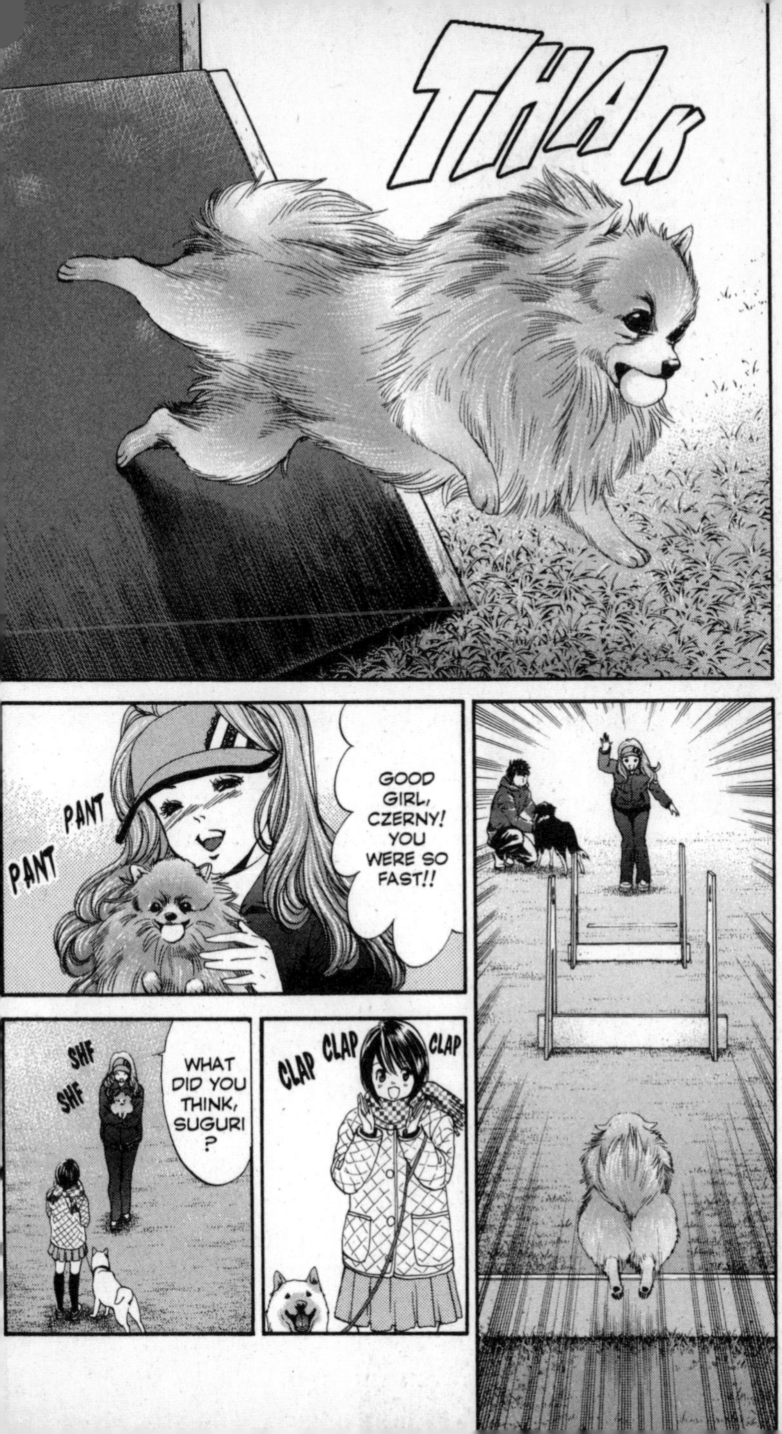
THAK
GOOD GIRL, CZERNY! YOU WERE SO FAST!!
PANT
PANT
CLAP
CLAP
CLAP
SHF
SHF
WHAT DID YOU THINK, SUGURI?

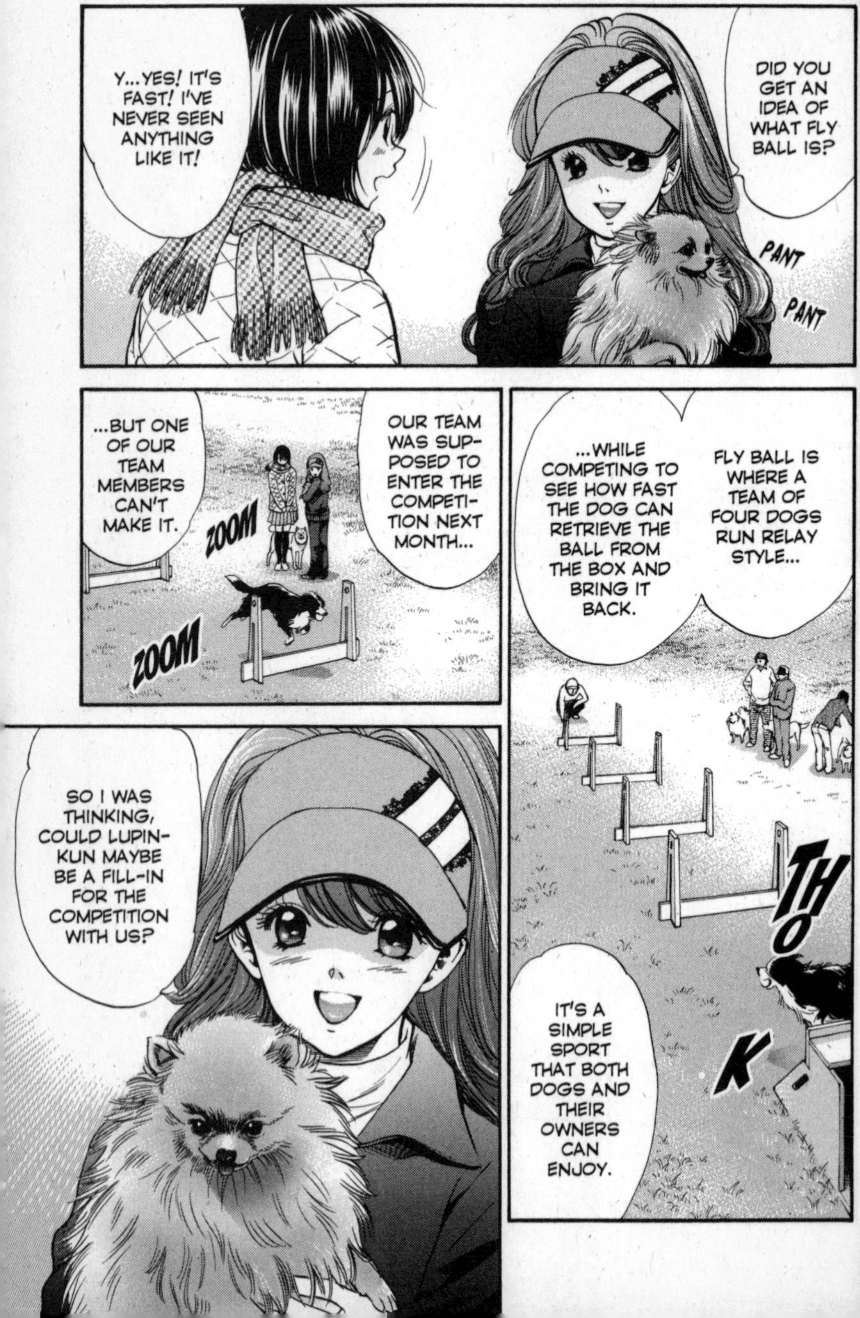

DID YOU GET AN IDEA OF WHAT FLY BALL IS?
PANT
PANT
Y...YES! IT'S FAST! I'VE NEVER SEEN ANYTHING LIKE IT!
FLY BALL IS WHERE A TEAM OF FOUR DOGS RUN RELAY STYLE...
...WHILE COMPETING TO SEE HOW FAST THE DOG CAN RETRIEVE THE BALL FROM THE BOX AND BRING IT BACK.
THOOK
IT'S A SIMPLE SPORT THAT BOTH DOGS AND THEIR OWNERS CAN ENJOY.
OUR TEAM WAS SUP-POSED TO ENTER THE COMPETI-TION NEXT MONTH...
...BUT ONE OF OUR TEAM MEMBERS CAN'T MAKE IT.
ZOOM
ZOOM
SO I WAS THINKING, COULD LUPIN-KUN MAYBE BE A FILL-IN FOR THE COMPETITION WITH US?

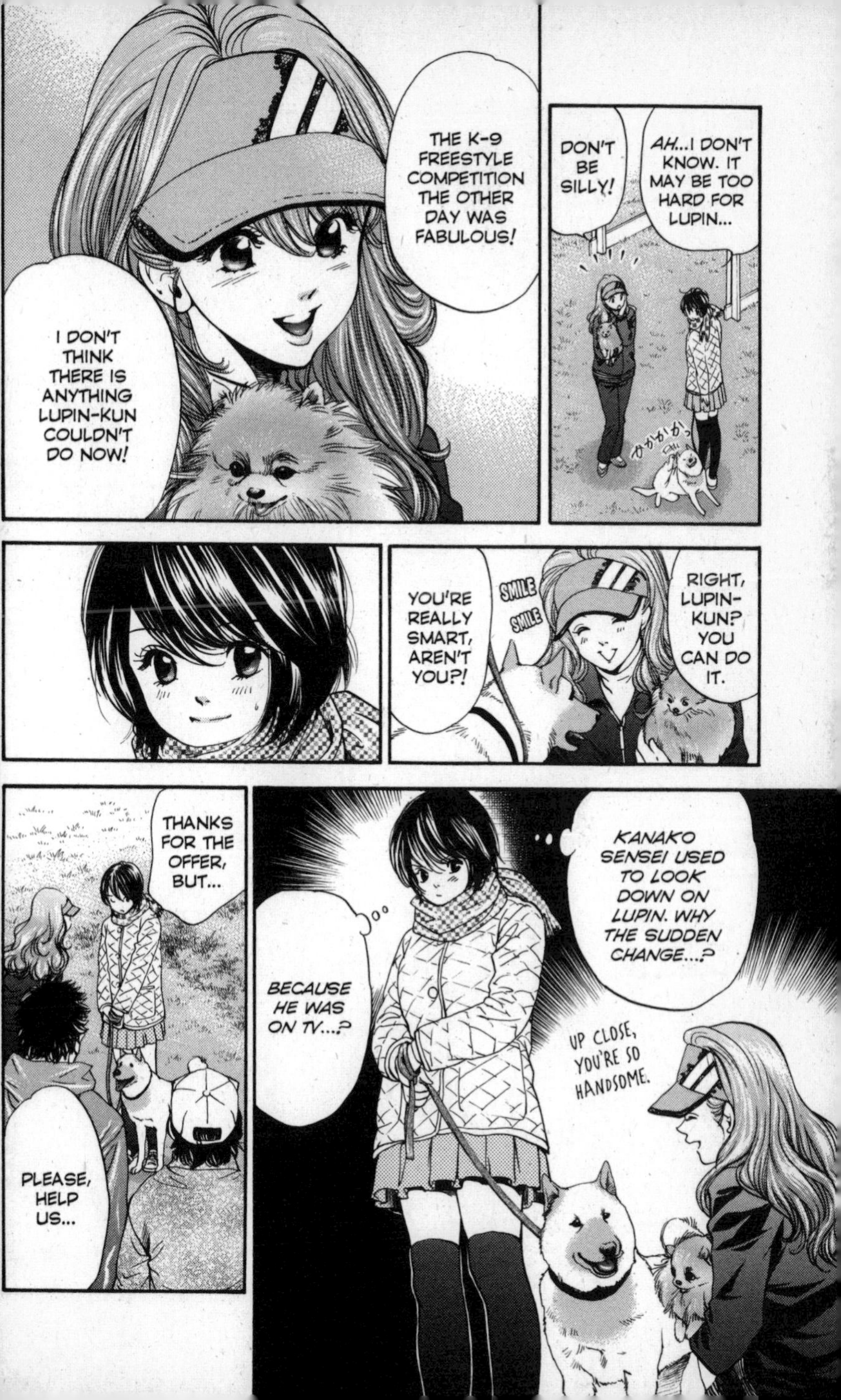
AH...I DON'T KNOW. IT MAY BE TOO HARD FOR LUPIN...
DON'T BE SILLY!
かかかっ
THE K-9 FREESTYLE COMPETITION THE OTHER DAY WAS FABULOUS!
I DON'T THINK THERE IS ANYTHING LUPIN-KUN COULDN'T DO NOW!
RIGHT, LUPIN-KUN? YOU CAN DO IT.
SMILE
SMILE
YOU'RE REALLY SMART, AREN'T YOU?!
KANAKO SENSEI USED TO LOOK DOWN ON LUPIN. WHY THE SUDDEN CHANGE...?
BECAUSE HE WAS ON TV...?
UP CLOSE, YOU'RE SO HANDSOME.
THANKS FOR THE OFFER, BUT...
PLEASE, HELP US...

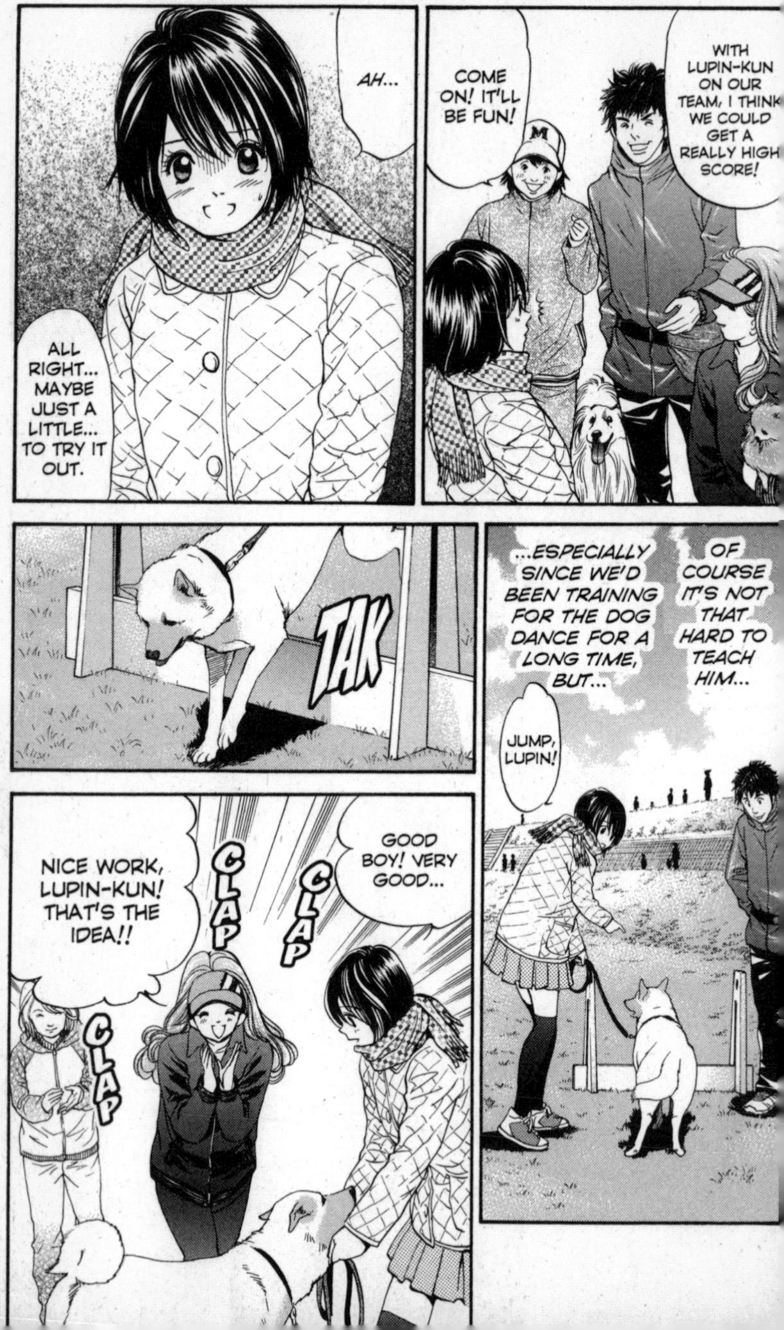
WITH LUPIN-KUN ON OUR TEAM, I THINK WE COULD GET A REALLY HIGH SCORE!
COME ON! IT'LL BE FUN!
AH...
ALL RIGHT... MAYBE JUST A LITTLE... TO TRY IT OUT.
OF COURSE IT'S NOT THAT HARD TO TEACH HIM...
...ESPECIALLY SINCE WE'D BEEN TRAINING FOR THE DOG DANCE FOR A LONG TIME, BUT...
JUMP, LUPIN!
TAK
GOOD BOY! VERY GOOD...
CLAP
CLAP
NICE WORK, LUPIN-KUN! THAT'S THE IDEA!!
CLAP

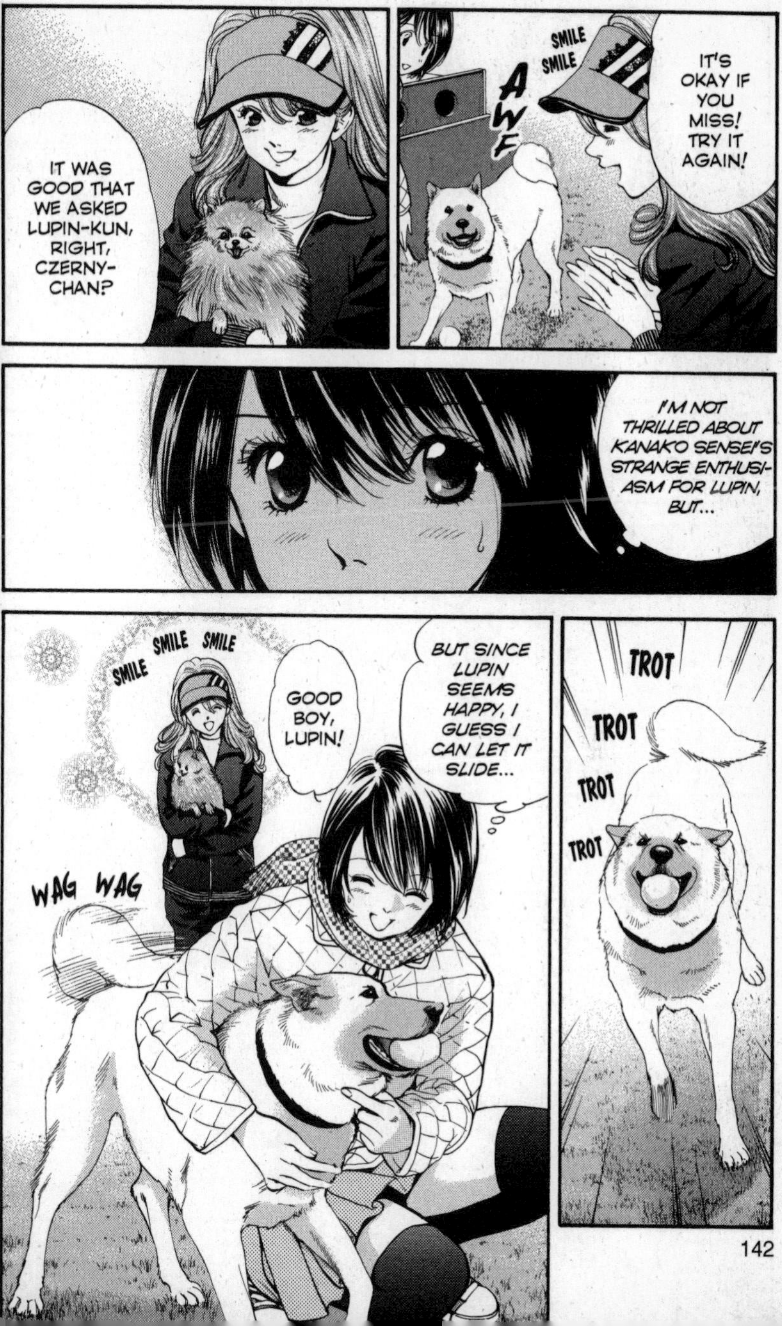
IT'S OKAY IF YOU MISS! TRY IT AGAIN!
SMILE SMILE
AWF
IT WAS GOOD THAT WE ASKED LUPIN-KUN, RIGHT, CZERNY-CHAN?
I'M NOT THRILLED ABOUT KANAKO SENSEI'S STRANGE ENTHUSI-ASM FOR LUPIN, BUT...
TROT
TROT
TROT
TROT
BUT SINCE LUPIN SEEMS HAPPY, I GUESS I CAN LET IT SLIDE...
GOOD BOY, LUPIN!
SMILE SMILE SMILE
WAG WAG

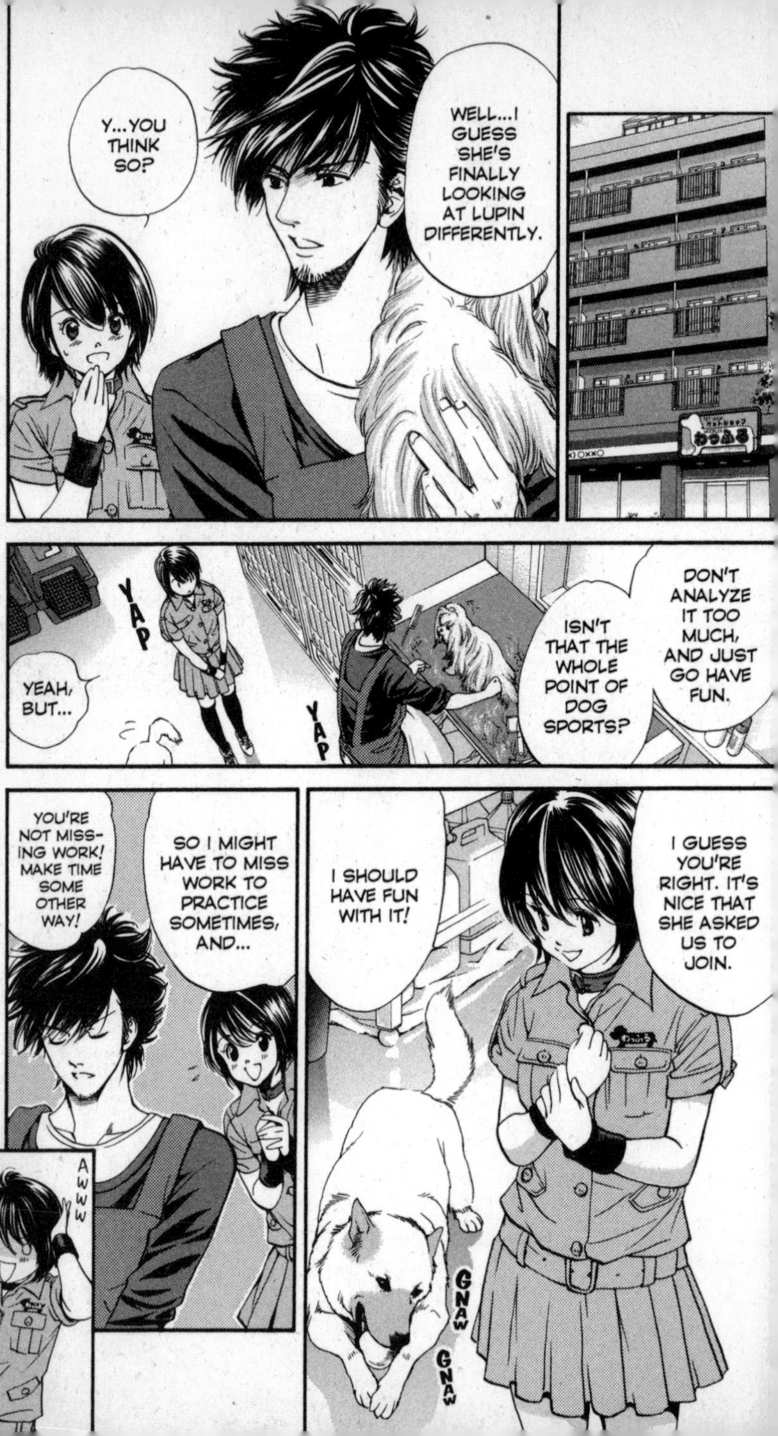
WELL...I GUESS SHE'S FINALLY LOOKING AT LUPIN DIFFERENTLY.
Y...YOU THINK SO?
DON'T ANALYZE IT TOO MUCH, AND JUST GO HAVE FUN.
ISN'T THAT THE WHOLE POINT OF DOG SPORTS?
YAP
YAP
YEAH, BUT...
I GUESS YOU'RE RIGHT. IT'S NICE THAT SHE ASKED US TO JOIN.
I SHOULD HAVE FUN WITH IT!
GNAW
GNAW
SO I MIGHT HAVE TO MISS WORK TO PRACTICE SOMETIMES, AND...
YOU'RE NOT MISSING WORK! MAKE TIME SOME OTHER WAY!
AWWW
THAT'S HARSH...

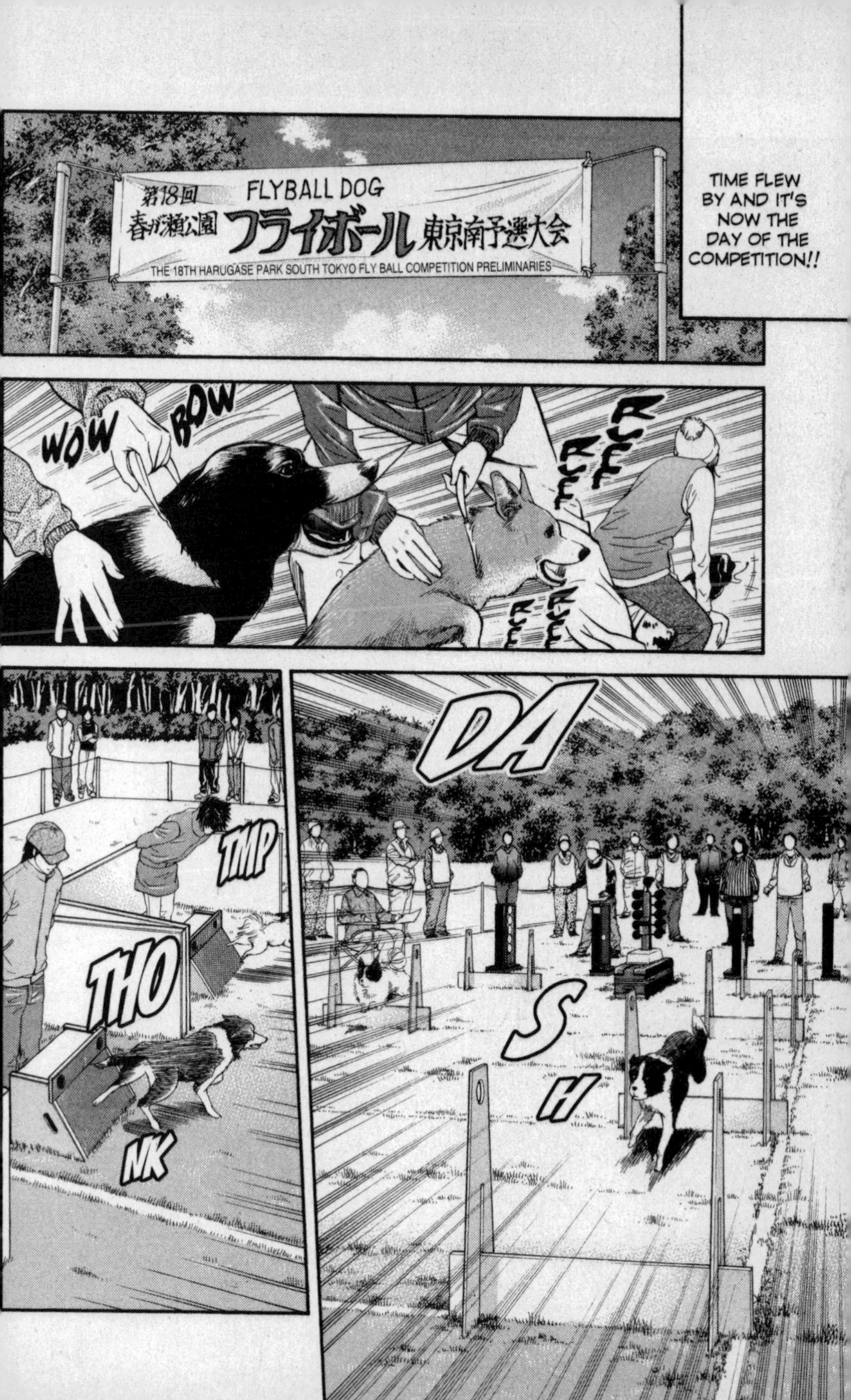
TIME FLEW BY AND IT'S NOW THE DAY OF THE COMPETITION!!
第18回
春ガ瀬公園
FLYBALL DOG
フライボール
東京南予選大会
THE 18TH HARUGASE PARK SOUTH TOKYO FLY BALL COMPETITION PRELIMINARIES
RUFF RUFF
RUFF RUFF
WOW BOW
DA S H
TMP
THO NK

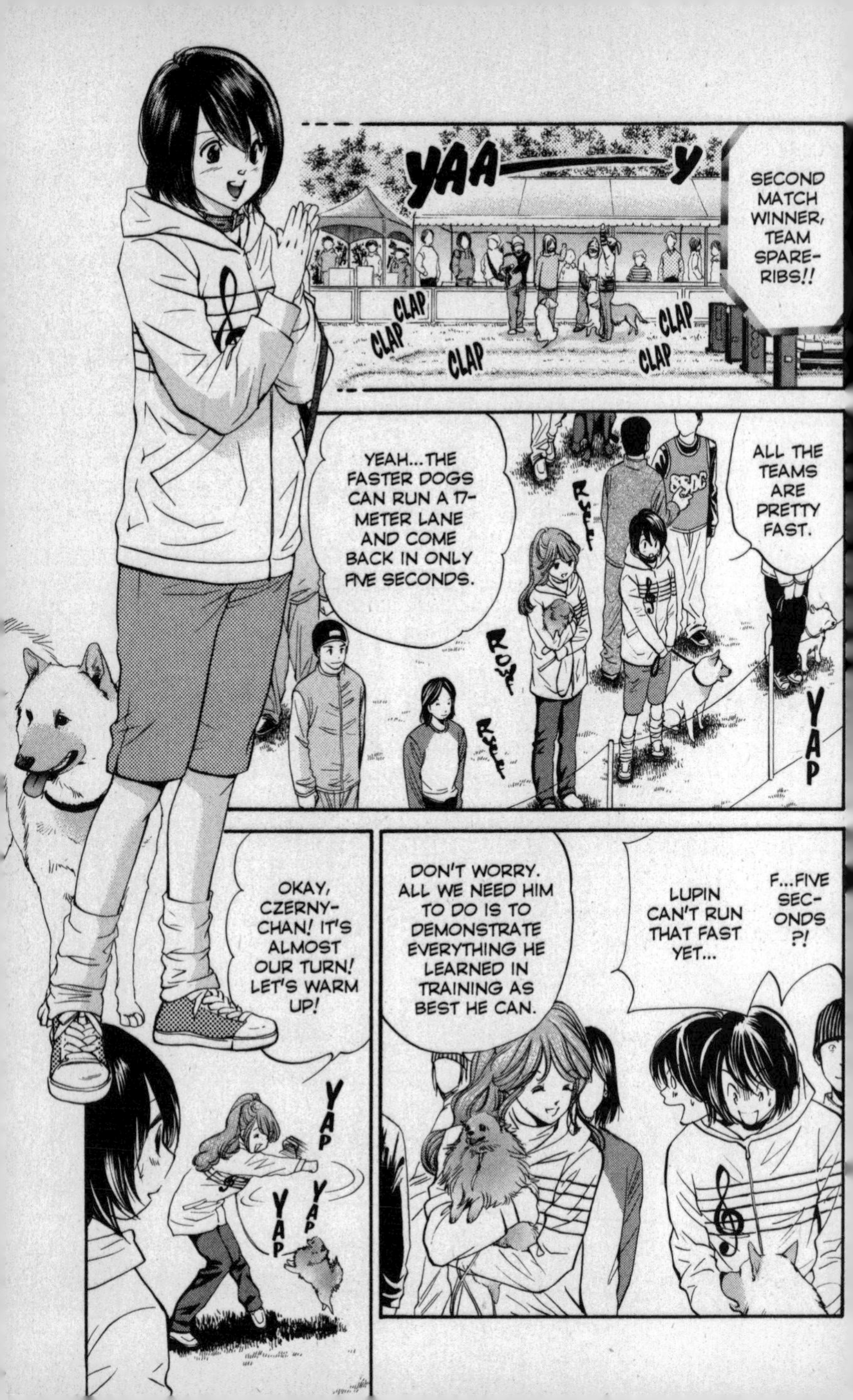
YAA—Y
SECOND MATCH WINNER, TEAM SPARE-RIBS!!
CLAP CLAP
CLAP CLAP
CLAP CLAP
ALL THE TEAMS ARE PRETTY FAST.
YAP
YEAH...THE FASTER DOGS CAN RUN A 17-METER LANE AND COME BACK IN ONLY FIVE SECONDS.
F...FIVE SECONDS?!
LUPIN CAN'T RUN THAT FAST YET...
DON'T WORRY. ALL WE NEED HIM TO DO IS TO DEMONSTRATE EVERYTHING HE LEARNED IN TRAINING AS BEST HE CAN.
OKAY, CZERNY-CHAN! IT'S ALMOST OUR TURN! LET'S WARM UP!
YAP
YAP
YAP

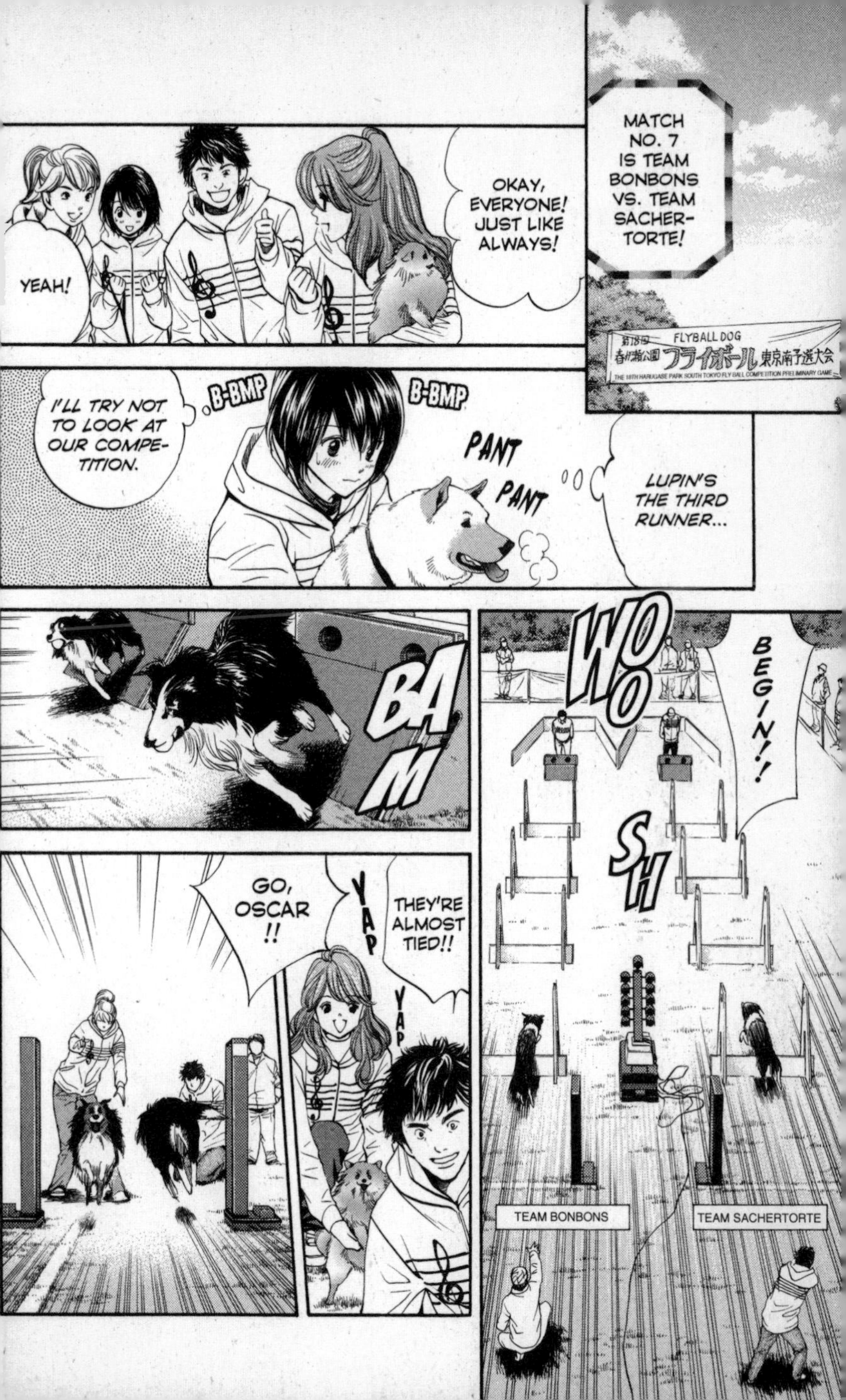
MATCH NO. 7 IS TEAM BONBONS VS. TEAM SACHER-TORTE!
FLYBALL DOG
フライボール 東京南予選大会
THE 18TH HARUGASE PARK SOUTH TOKYO FLY BALL COMPETITION PRELIMINARY GAME
OKAY, EVERYONE! JUST LIKE ALWAYS!
YEAH!
LUPIN'S THE THIRD RUNNER...
PANT PANT
B-BMP B-BMP
I'LL TRY NOT TO LOOK AT OUR COMPE-TITION.
WOOSH
BEGIN!!
TEAM SACHERTORTE
TEAM BONBONS
BAM
THEY'RE ALMOST TIED!!
YAP YAP
GO, OSCAR!!

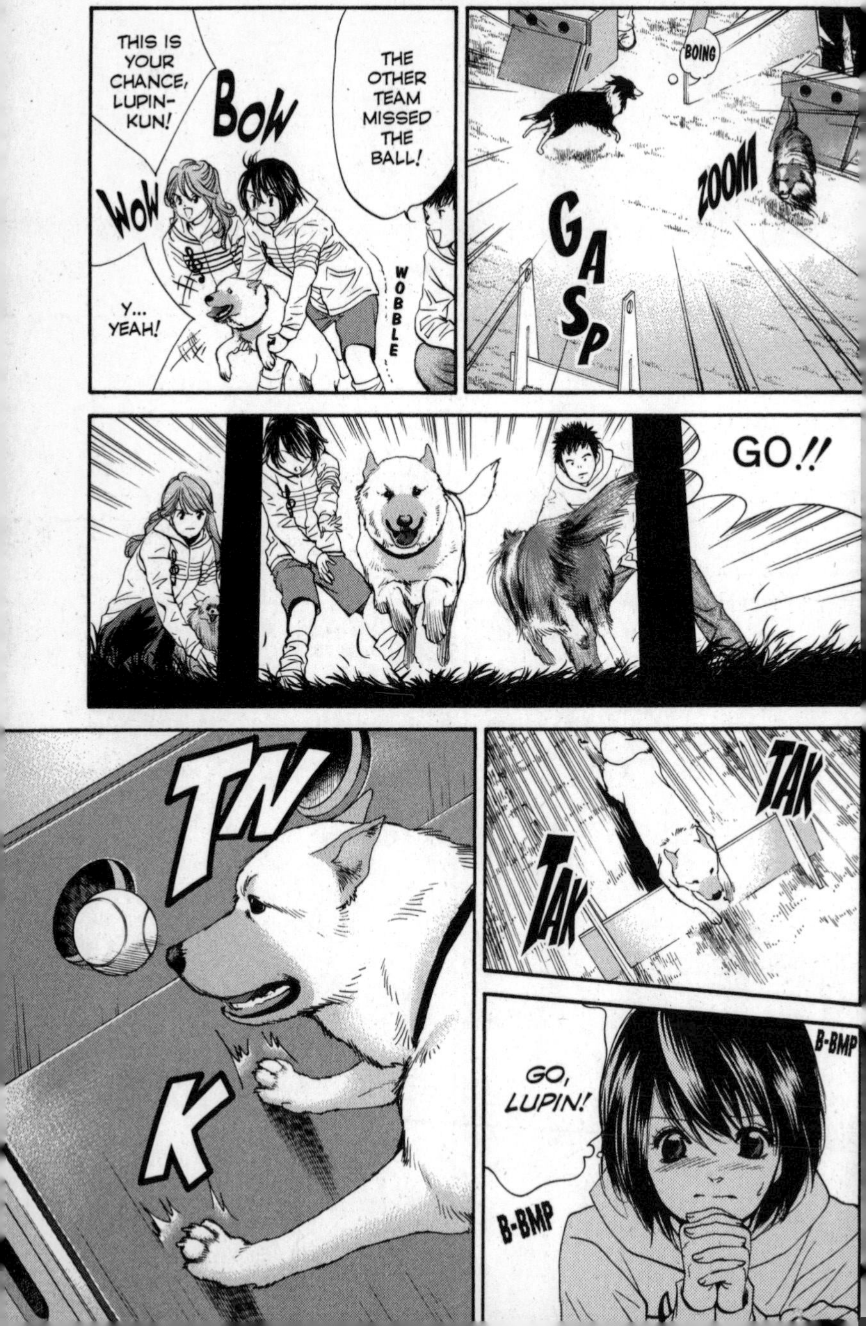
BOING
ZOOM
GASP
THE OTHER TEAM MISSED THE BALL!
THIS IS YOUR CHANCE, LUPIN-KUN!
BOW
WOW
WOBBLE
Y... YEAH!
GO!!
TAK
TAK
B-BMP
GO, LUPIN!
B-BMP
TNK

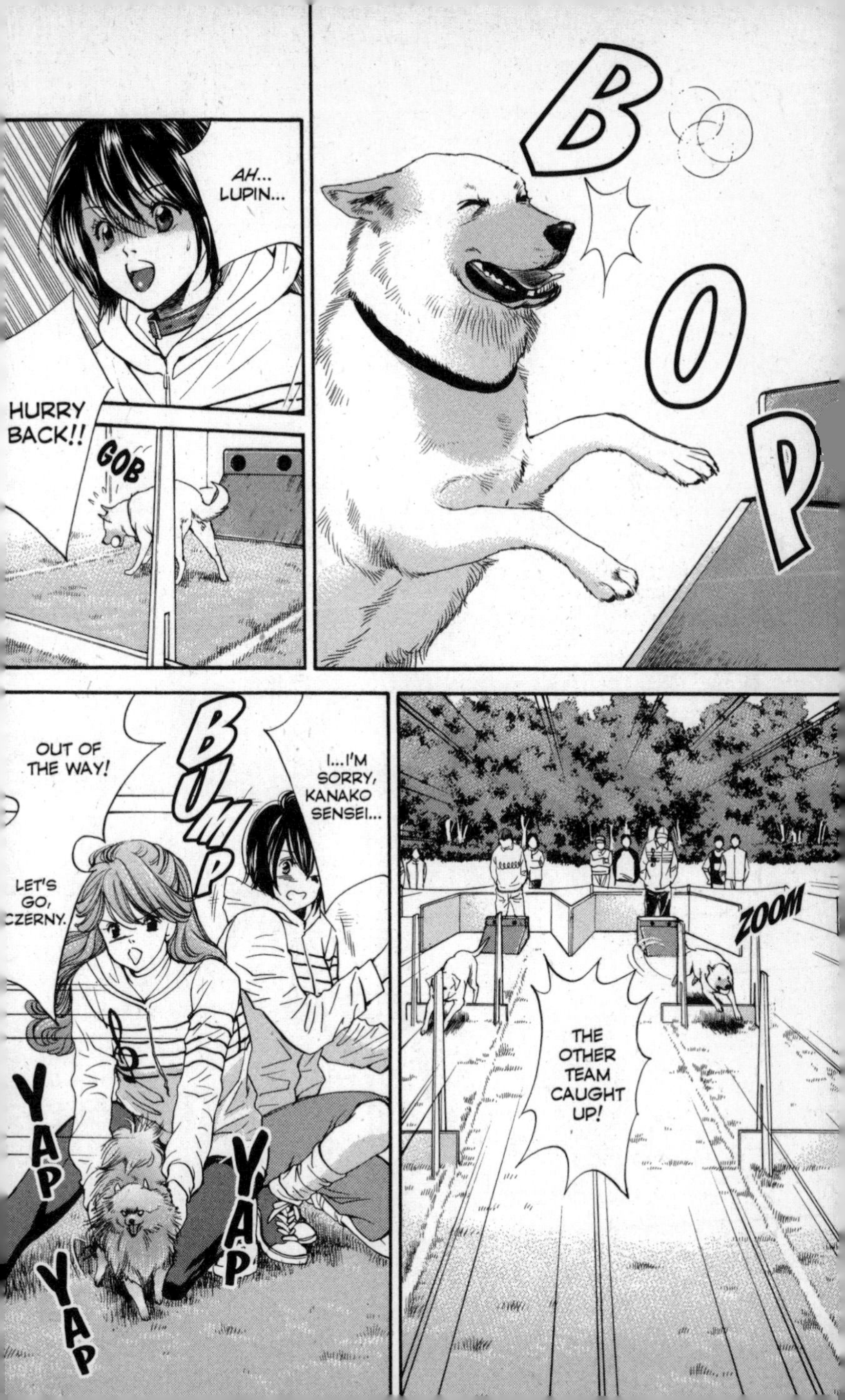
BOP
AH... LUPIN...
HURRY BACK!!
GOB
ZOOM
THE OTHER TEAM CAUGHT UP!
I...I'M SORRY, KANAKO SENSEI...
BUMP
OUT OF THE WAY!
LET'S GO, CZERNY.
YAP YAP
YAP YAP
YAP YAP

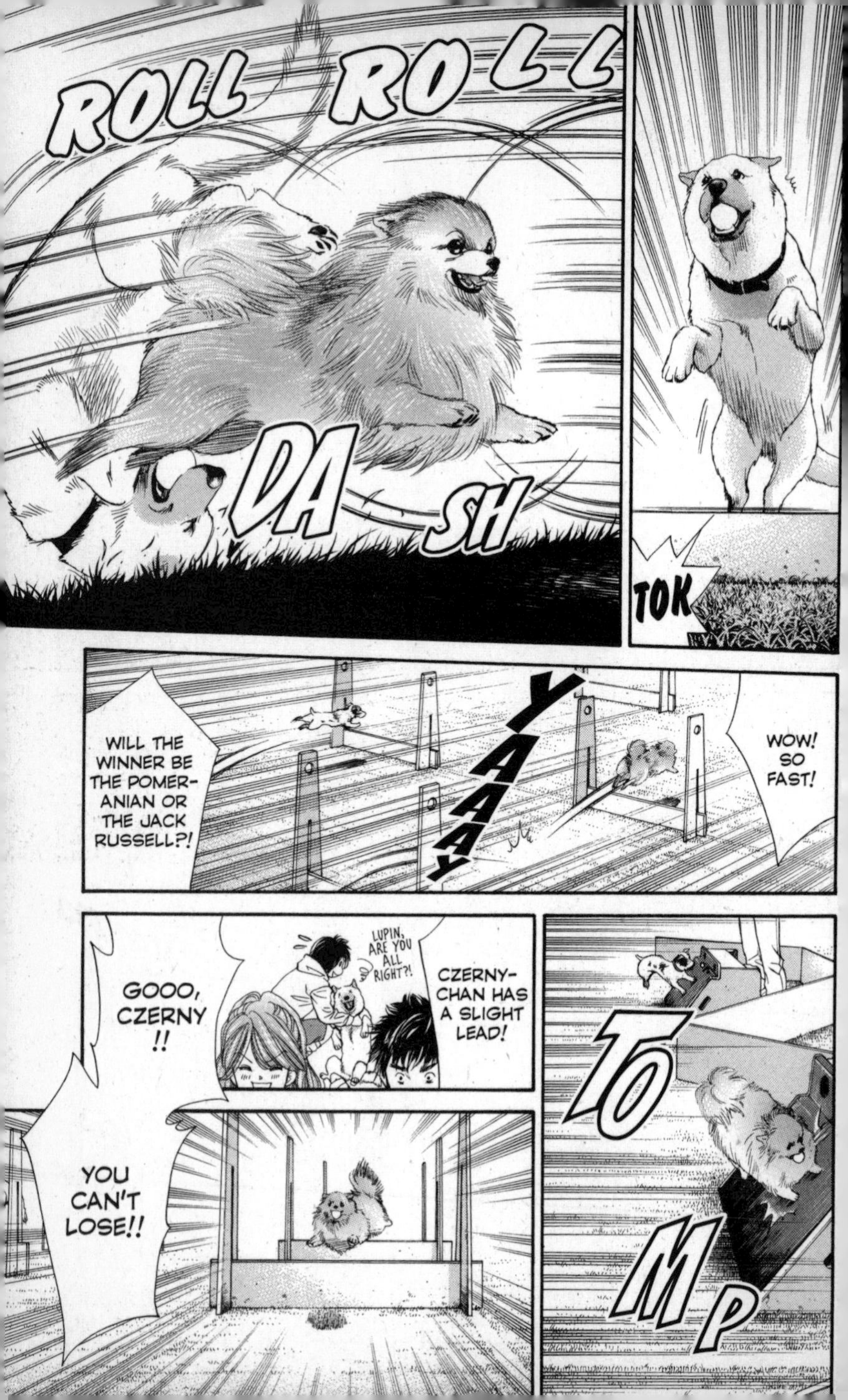
TOK
ROLL ROLL
DASH
WOW! SO FAST!
YAAAAY
WILL THE WINNER BE THE POMERANIAN OR THE JACK RUSSELL?!
TOMP
CZERNY-CHAN HAS A SLIGHT LEAD!
LUPIN, ARE YOU ALL RIGHT?!
GOOO, CZERNY!!
YOU CAN'T LOSE!!

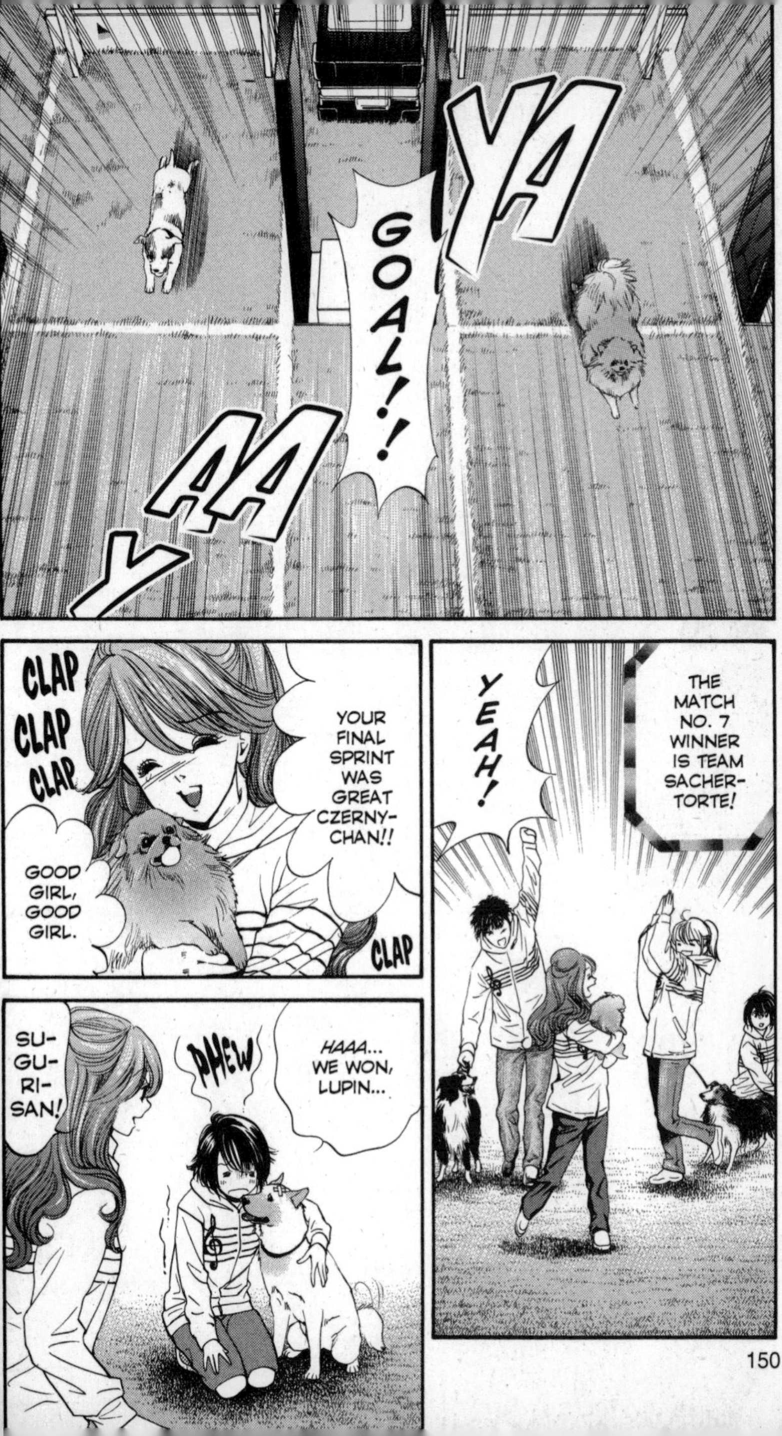
YAAAAY
GOAL!!
THE MATCH NO. 7 WINNER IS TEAM SACHER-TORTE!
YEAH!
YOUR FINAL SPRINT WAS GREAT CZERNY-CHAN!!
CLAP CLAP CLAP
GOOD GIRL, GOOD GIRL.
CLAP
*HAAA*... WE WON, LUPIN...
PHEW
SU-GU-RI-SAN!

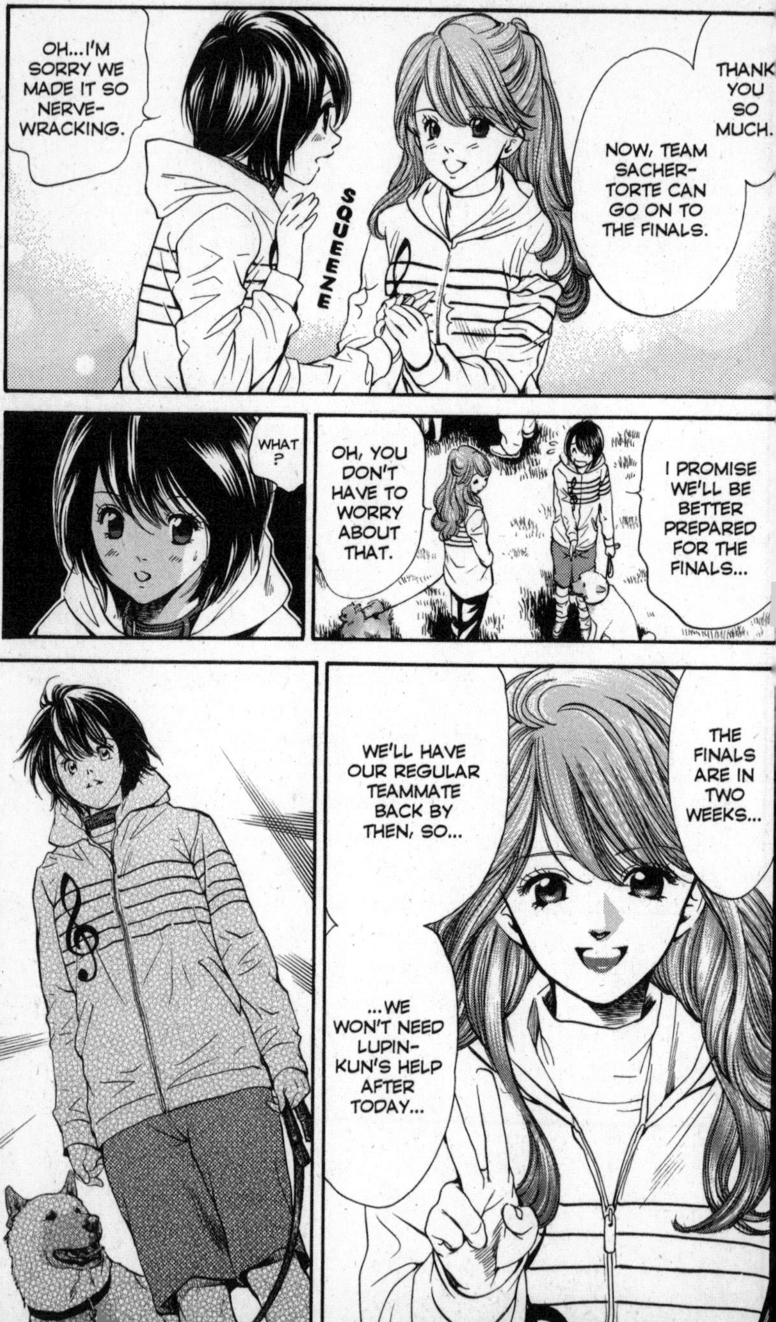
THANK YOU SO MUCH.
NOW, TEAM SACHER-TORTE CAN GO ON TO THE FINALS.
SQUEEZE
OH...I'M SORRY WE MADE IT SO NERVE-WRACKING.
I PROMISE WE'LL BE BETTER PREPARED FOR THE FINALS...
OH, YOU DON'T HAVE TO WORRY ABOUT THAT.
WHAT?
THE FINALS ARE IN TWO WEEKS...
WE'LL HAVE OUR REGULAR TEAMMATE BACK BY THEN, SO...
...WE WON'T NEED LUPIN-KUN'S HELP AFTER TODAY...

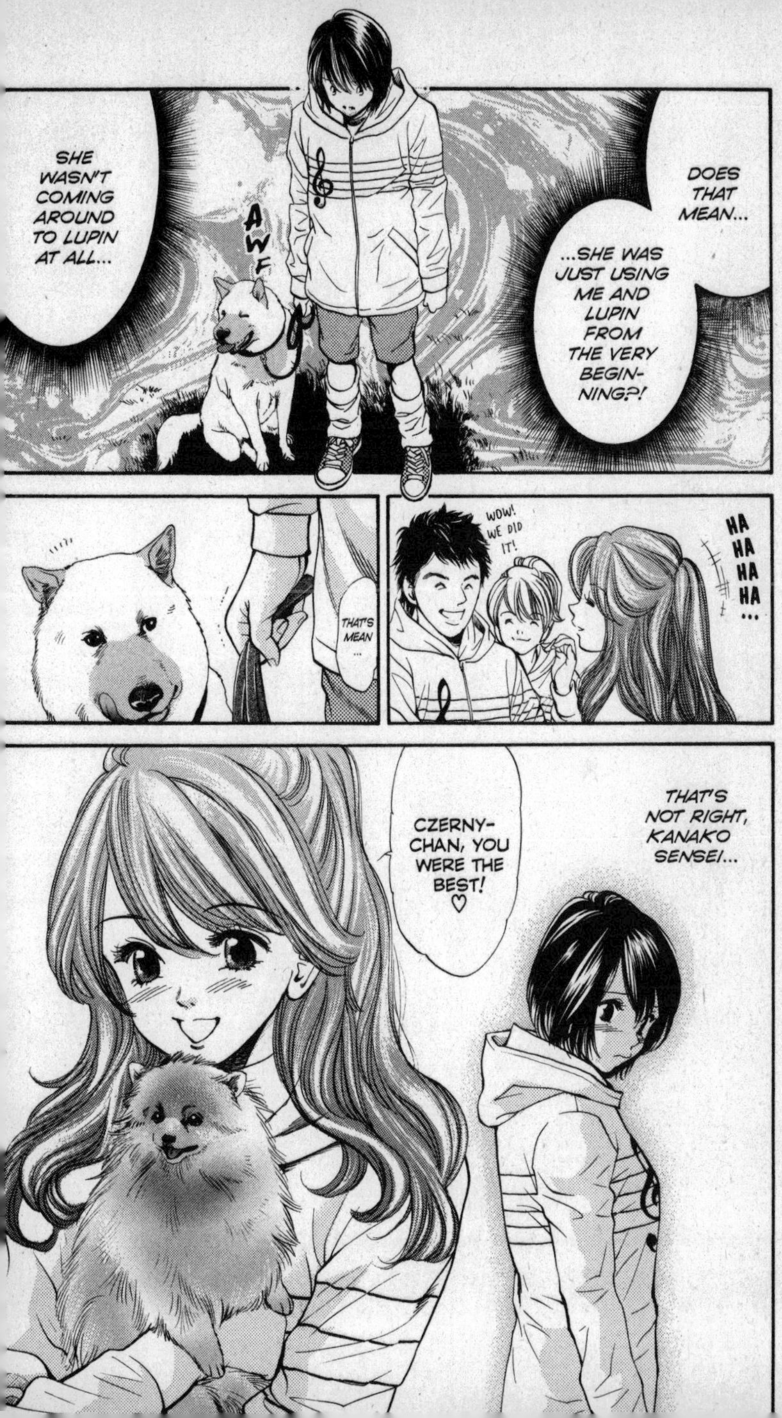
DOES THAT MEAN...
...SHE WAS JUST USING ME AND LUPIN FROM THE VERY BEGIN-NING?!
SHE WASN'T COMING AROUND TO LUPIN AT ALL...
AWF
HA HA HA HA...
WOW! WE DID IT!
THAT'S MEAN...
THAT'S NOT RIGHT, KANAKO SENSEI...
CZERNY-CHAN, YOU WERE THE BEST! ♡

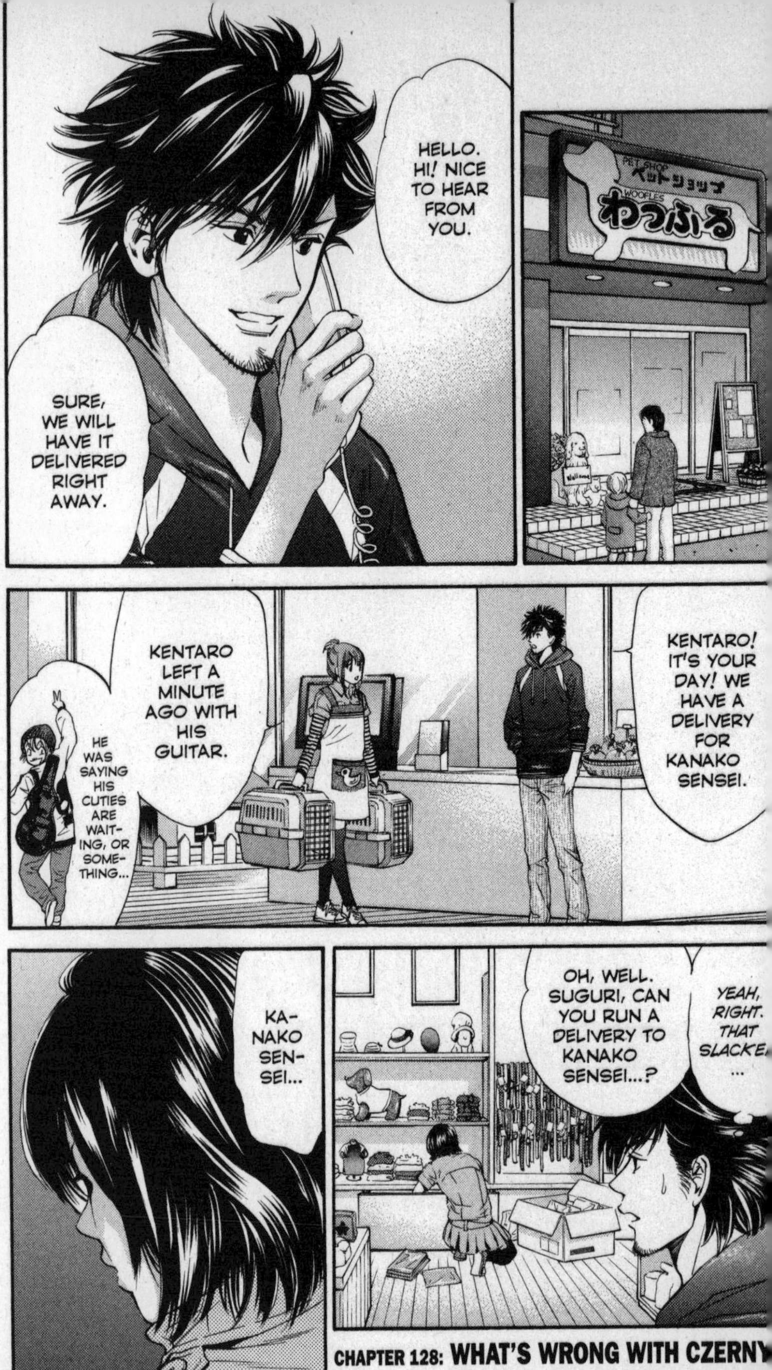
PET SHOP
ペットショップ
WOOFLES
わっふる
HELLO. HI! NICE TO HEAR FROM YOU.
SURE, WE WILL HAVE IT DELIVERED RIGHT AWAY.
KENTARO! IT'S YOUR DAY! WE HAVE A DELIVERY FOR KANAKO SENSEI.
KENTARO LEFT A MINUTE AGO WITH HIS GUITAR.
HE WAS SAYING HIS CUTIES ARE WAITING, OR SOMETHING...
OH, WELL. SUGURI, CAN YOU RUN A DELIVERY TO KANAKO SENSEI...?
YEAH, RIGHT. THAT SLACKE...
KA-NAKO SEN-SEI...

## CHAPTER 128: WHAT'S WRONG WITH CZERNY

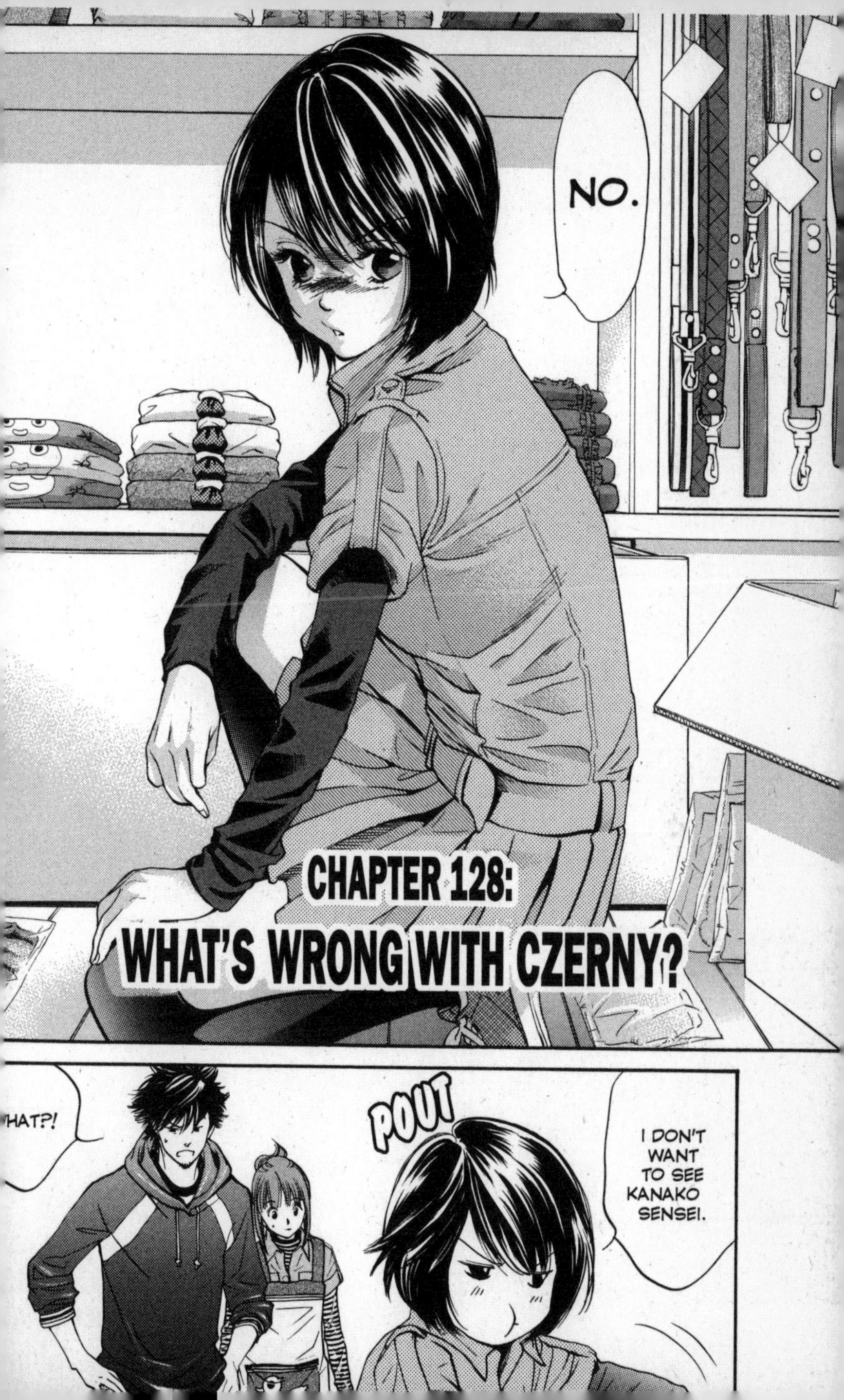
NO.
CHAPTER 128:
WHAT'S WRONG WITH CZERNY?
I DON'T WANT TO SEE KANAKO SENSEI.
POUT
HAT?!

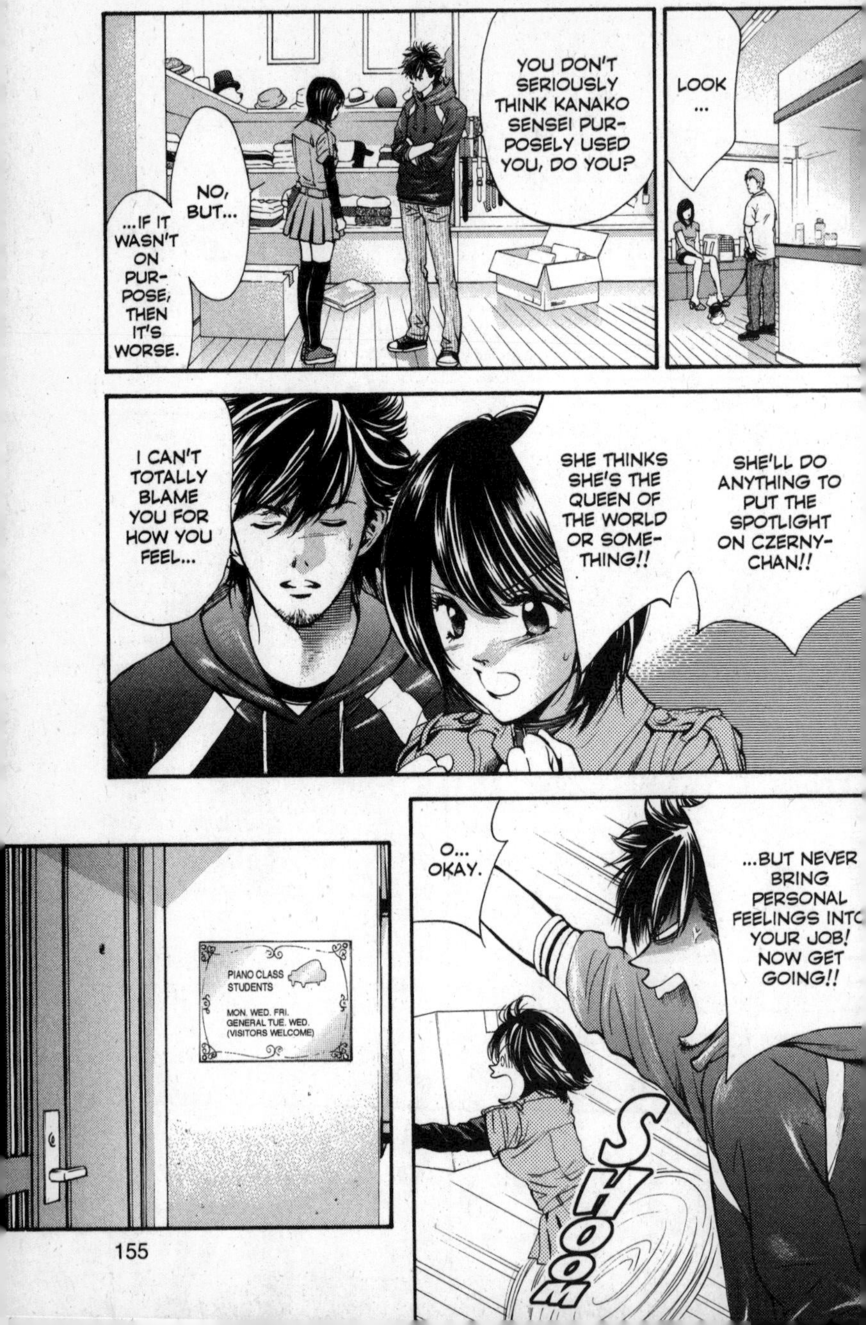
LOOK ...
YOU DON'T SERIOUSLY THINK KANAKO SENSEI PURPOSELY USED YOU, DO YOU?
NO, BUT...
...IF IT WASN'T ON PURPOSE, THEN IT'S WORSE.
SHE'LL DO ANYTHING TO PUT THE SPOTLIGHT ON CZERNY-CHAN!!
SHE THINKS SHE'S THE QUEEN OF THE WORLD OR SOMETHING!!
I CAN'T TOTALLY BLAME YOU FOR HOW YOU FEEL...
...BUT NEVER BRING PERSONAL FEELINGS INTO YOUR JOB! NOW GET GOING!!
O... OKAY.
SHOOM
PIANO CLASS STUDENTS
MON. WED. FRI.
GENERAL TUE. WED.
(VISITORS WELCOME)

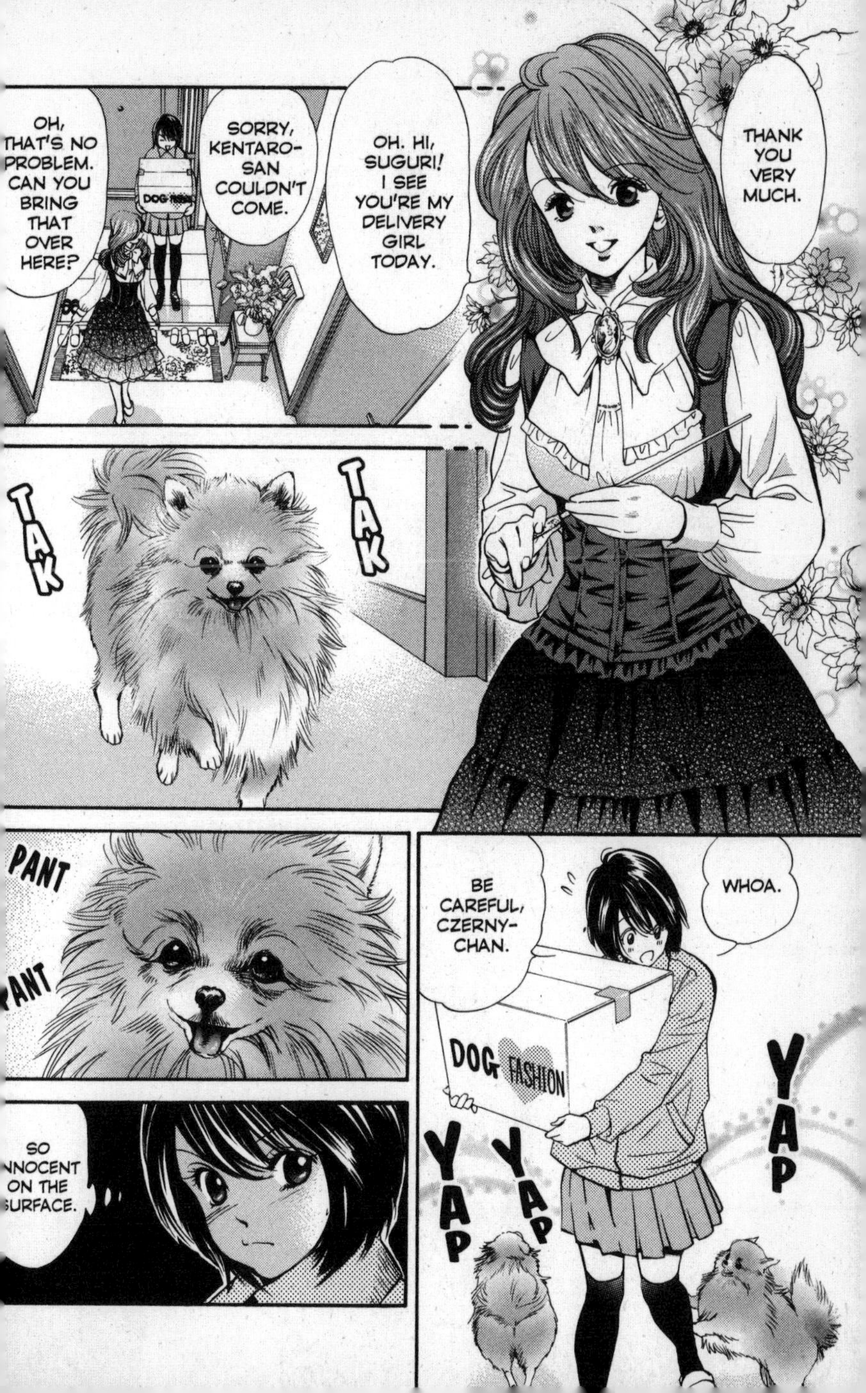
THANK YOU VERY MUCH.
OH. HI, SUGURI! I SEE YOU'RE MY DELIVERY GIRL TODAY.
SORRY, KENTARO-SAN COULDN'T COME.
OH, THAT'S NO PROBLEM. CAN YOU BRING THAT OVER HERE?
DOG
TAK
TAK
WHOA.
BE CAREFUL, CZERNY-CHAN.
DOG FASHION
YAP
YAP
YAP
PANT
ANT
SO
NNOCENT ON THE
URFACE.

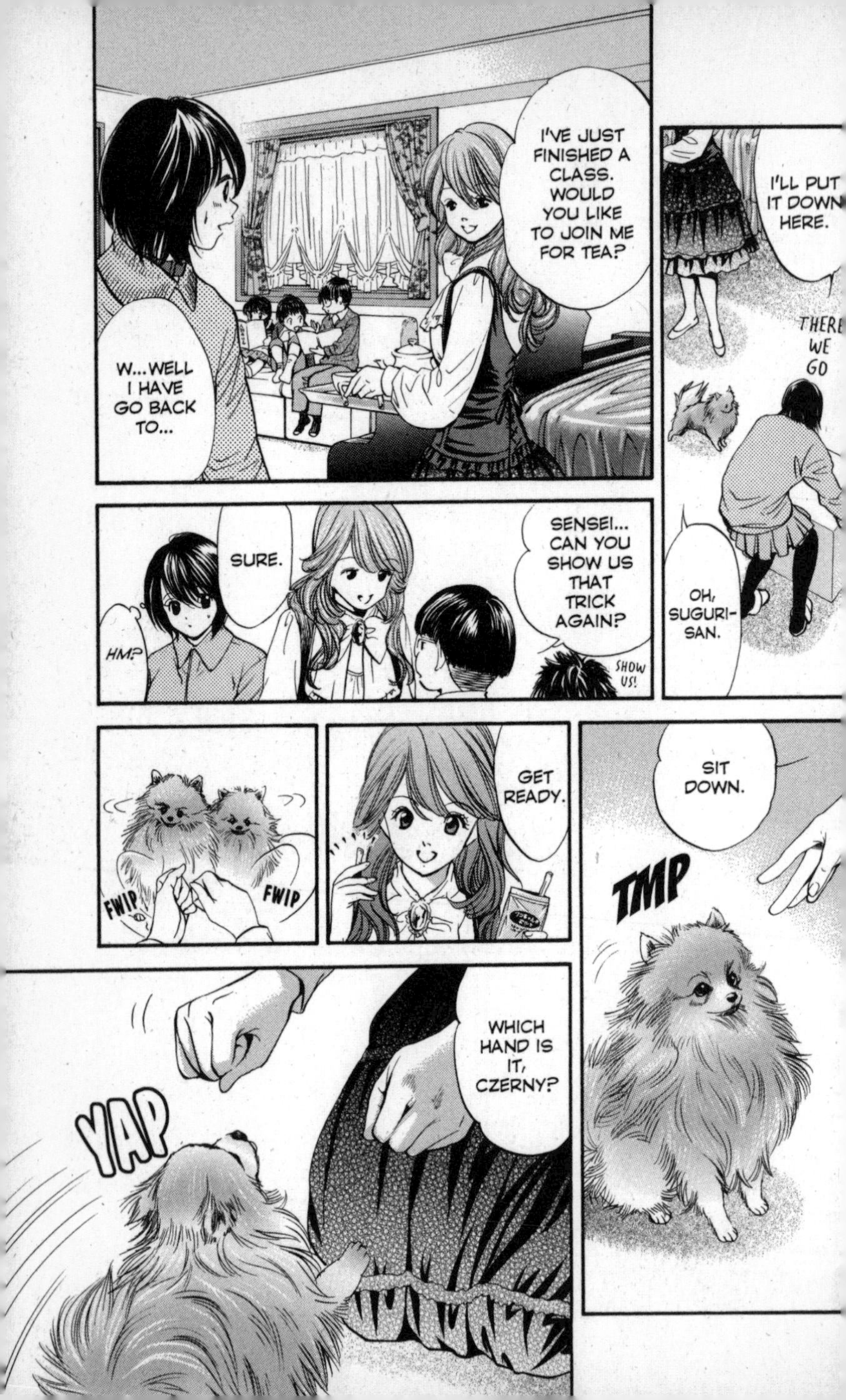
I'LL PUT IT DOWN HERE.
THERE WE GO
OH, SUGURI-SAN.
I'VE JUST FINISHED A CLASS. WOULD YOU LIKE TO JOIN ME FOR TEA?
W...WELL I HAVE GO BACK TO...
SENSEI... CAN YOU SHOW US THAT TRICK AGAIN?
SHOW US!
SURE.
HM?
SIT DOWN.
TMP
GET READY.
FWIP
FWIP
WHICH HAND IS IT, CZERNY?
YAP

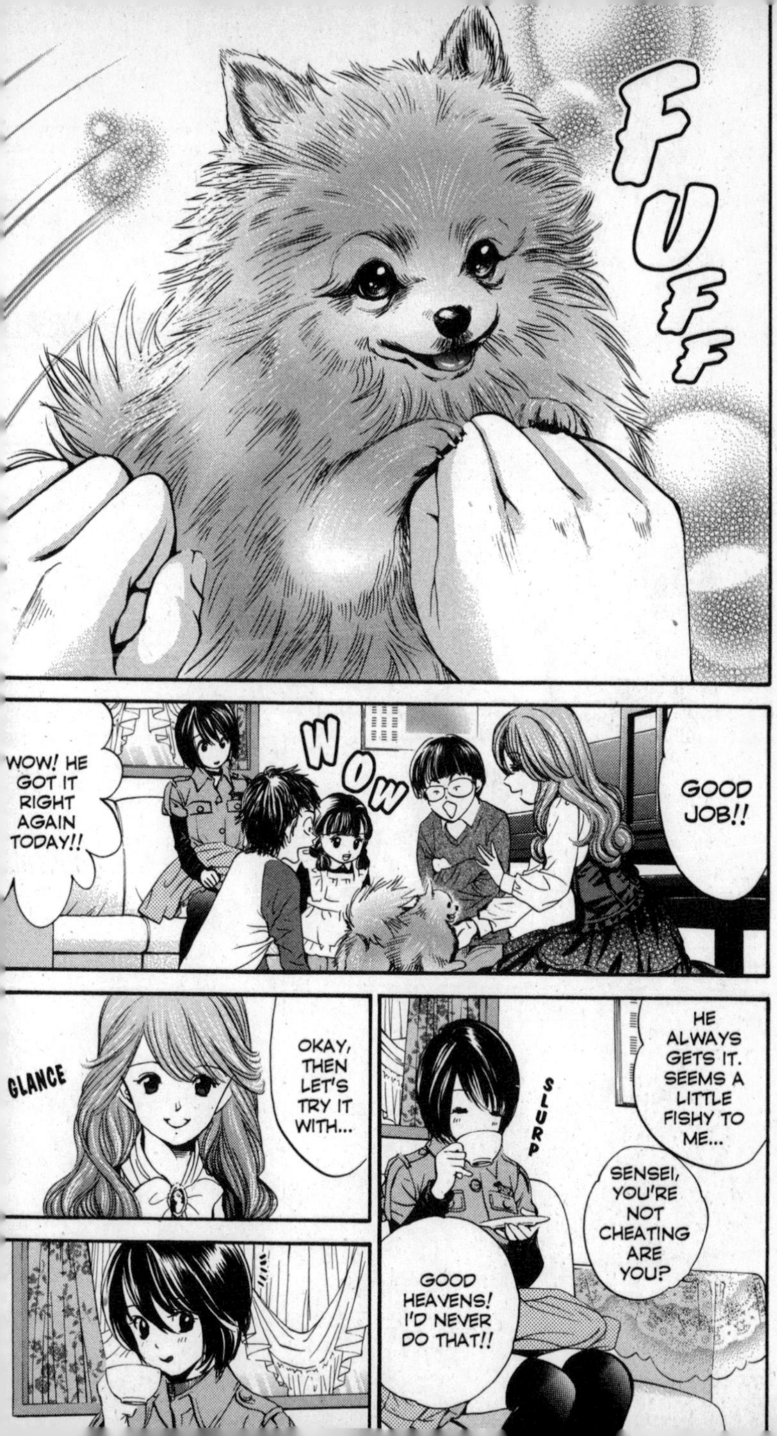
FUFFF
GOOD JOB!!
WOW
WOW! HE GOT IT RIGHT AGAIN TODAY!!
HE ALWAYS GETS IT. SEEMS A LITTLE FISHY TO ME...
SLURP
OKAY, THEN LET'S TRY IT WITH...
GLANCE
SENSEI, YOU'RE NOT CHEATING ARE YOU?
GOOD HEAVENS! I'D NEVER DO THAT!!

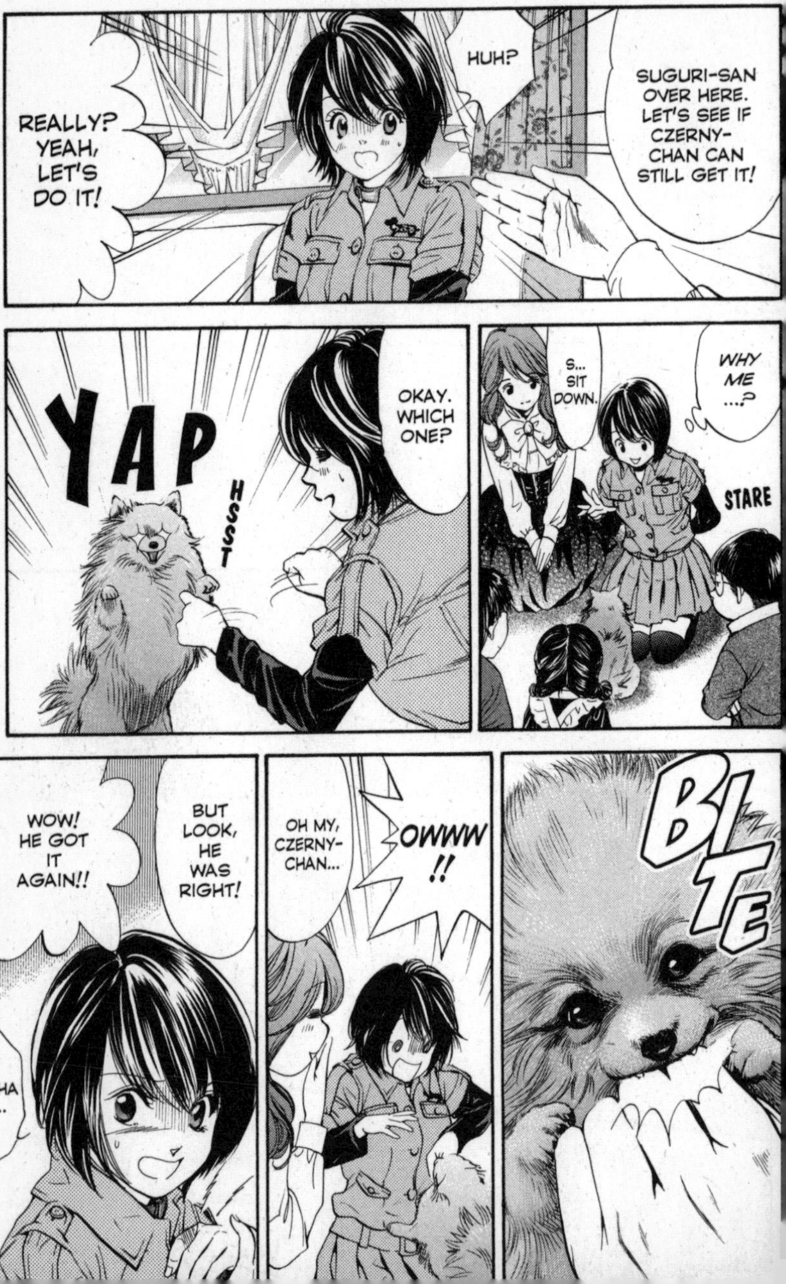
SUGURI-SAN OVER HERE. LET'S SEE IF CZERNY-CHAN CAN STILL GET IT!
HUH?
REALLY? YEAH, LET'S DO IT!
WHY ME ...?
S... SIT DOWN.
STARE
OKAY. WHICH ONE?
YAP
HSSST
BITE
OWWW!!
OH MY, CZERNY-CHAN...
BUT LOOK, HE WAS RIGHT!
WOW! HE GOT IT AGAIN!!
WHA ...

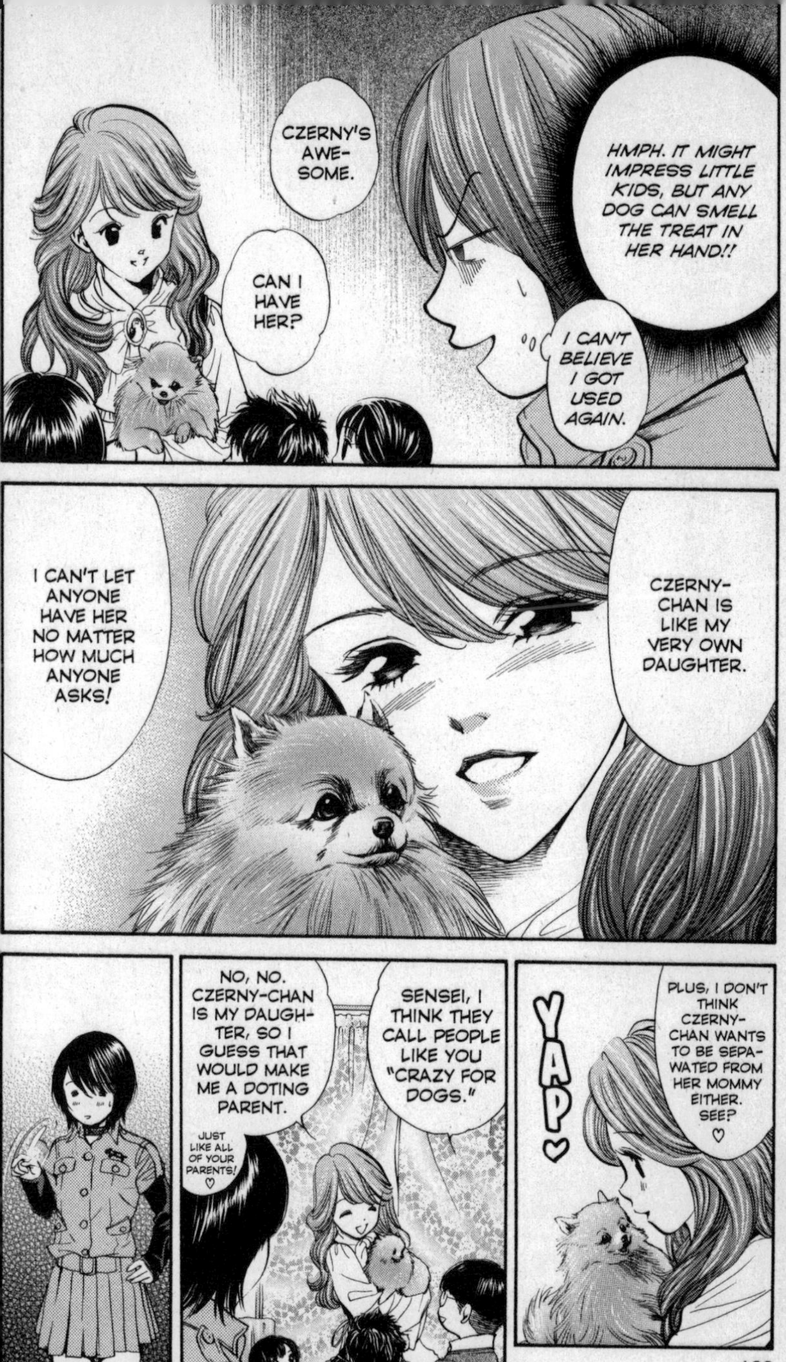
HMPH. IT MIGHT IMPRESS LITTLE KIDS, BUT ANY DOG CAN SMELL THE TREAT IN HER HAND!!
CZERNY'S AWE-SOME.
CAN I HAVE HER?
I CAN'T BELIEVE I GOT USED AGAIN.
CZERNY-CHAN IS LIKE MY VERY OWN DAUGHTER.
I CAN'T LET ANYONE HAVE HER NO MATTER HOW MUCH ANYONE ASKS!
PLUS, I DON'T THINK CZERNY-CHAN WANTS TO BE SEPA-WATED FROM HER MOMMY EITHER. SEE? ♡
YAP♥
SENSEI, I THINK THEY CALL PEOPLE LIKE YOU "CRAZY FOR DOGS."
NO, NO. CZERNY-CHAN IS MY DAUGH-TER, SO I GUESS THAT WOULD MAKE ME A DOTING PARENT.
JUST LIKE ALL OF YOUR PARENTS! ♡

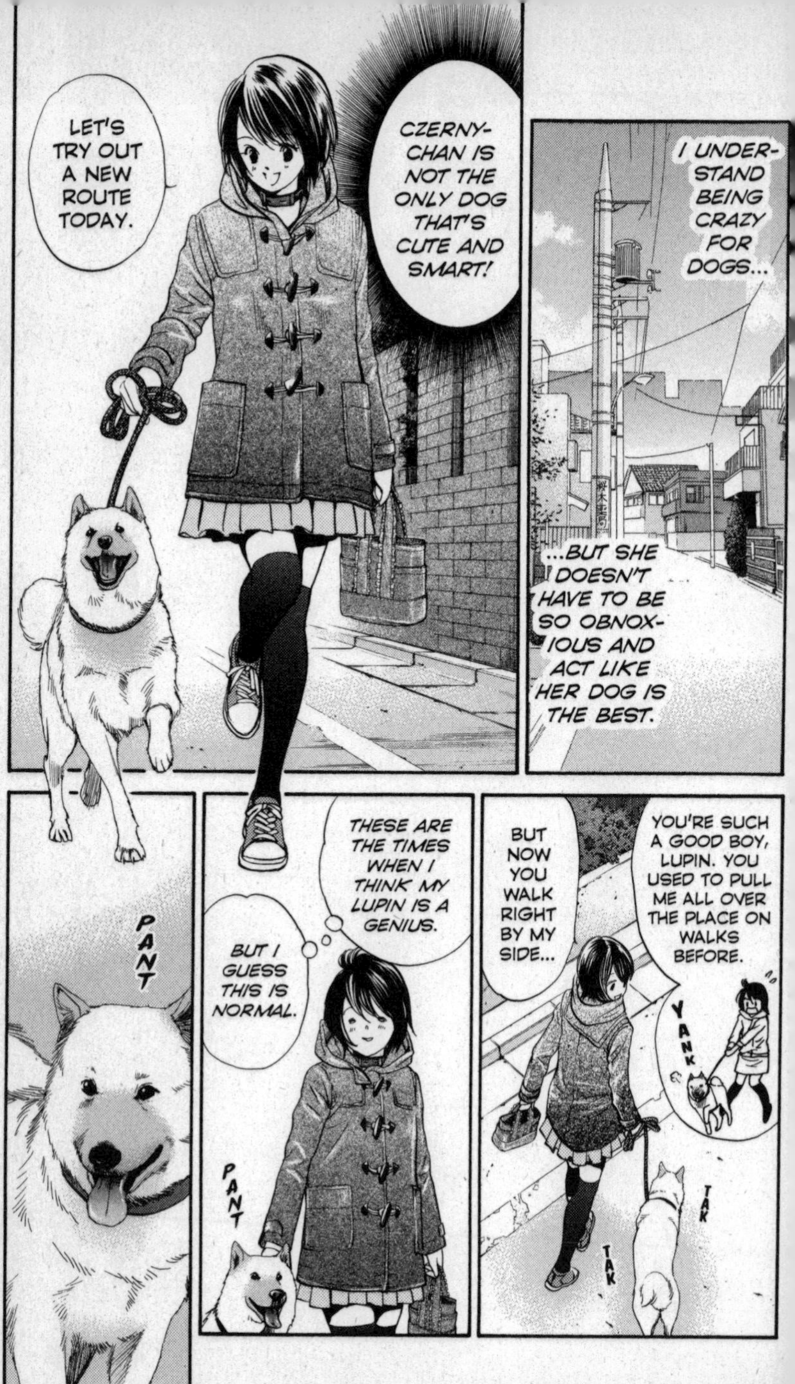

I UNDERSTAND BEING CRAZY FOR DOGS...
...BUT SHE DOESN'T HAVE TO BE SO OBNOXIOUS AND ACT LIKE HER DOG IS THE BEST.
CZERNY-CHAN IS NOT THE ONLY DOG THAT'S CUTE AND SMART!
LET'S TRY OUT A NEW ROUTE TODAY.
YOU'RE SUCH A GOOD BOY, LUPIN. YOU USED TO PULL ME ALL OVER THE PLACE ON WALKS BEFORE.
YANK
BUT NOW YOU WALK RIGHT BY MY SIDE...
TAK
TAK
THESE ARE THE TIMES WHEN I THINK MY LUPIN IS A GENIUS.
BUT I GUESS THIS IS NORMAL.
PANT
PANT

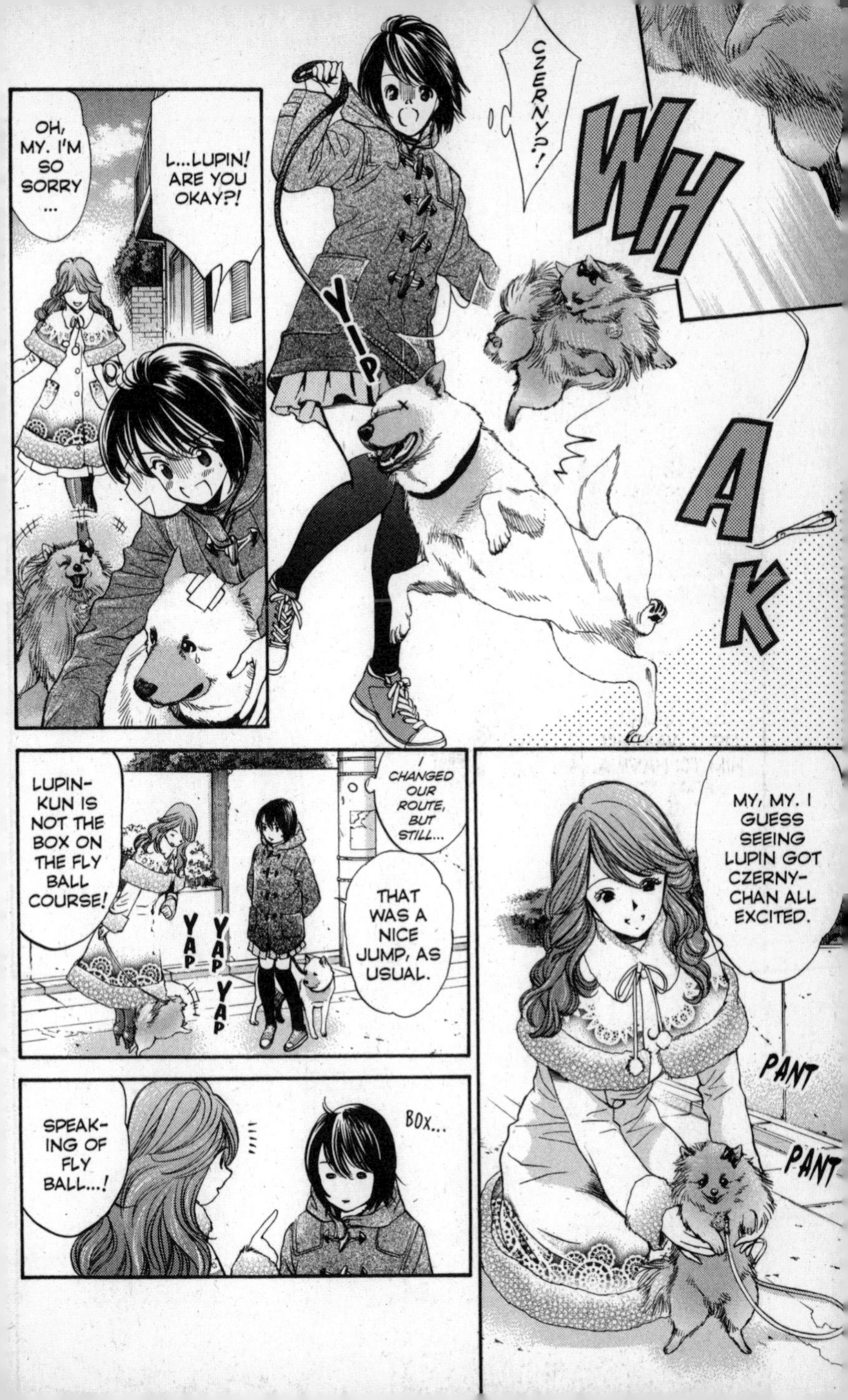
CZERNY?!
WHAK
YIP
L...LUPIN! ARE YOU OKAY?!
OH, MY. I'M SO SORRY...
MY, MY. I GUESS SEEING LUPIN GOT CZERNY-CHAN ALL EXCITED.
PANT
PANT
I CHANGED OUR ROUTE, BUT STILL...
THAT WAS A NICE JUMP, AS USUAL.
LUPIN-KUN IS NOT THE BOX ON THE FLY BALL COURSE!
YAP
YAP YAP YAP
BOX...
SPEAK-ING OF FLY BALL...!

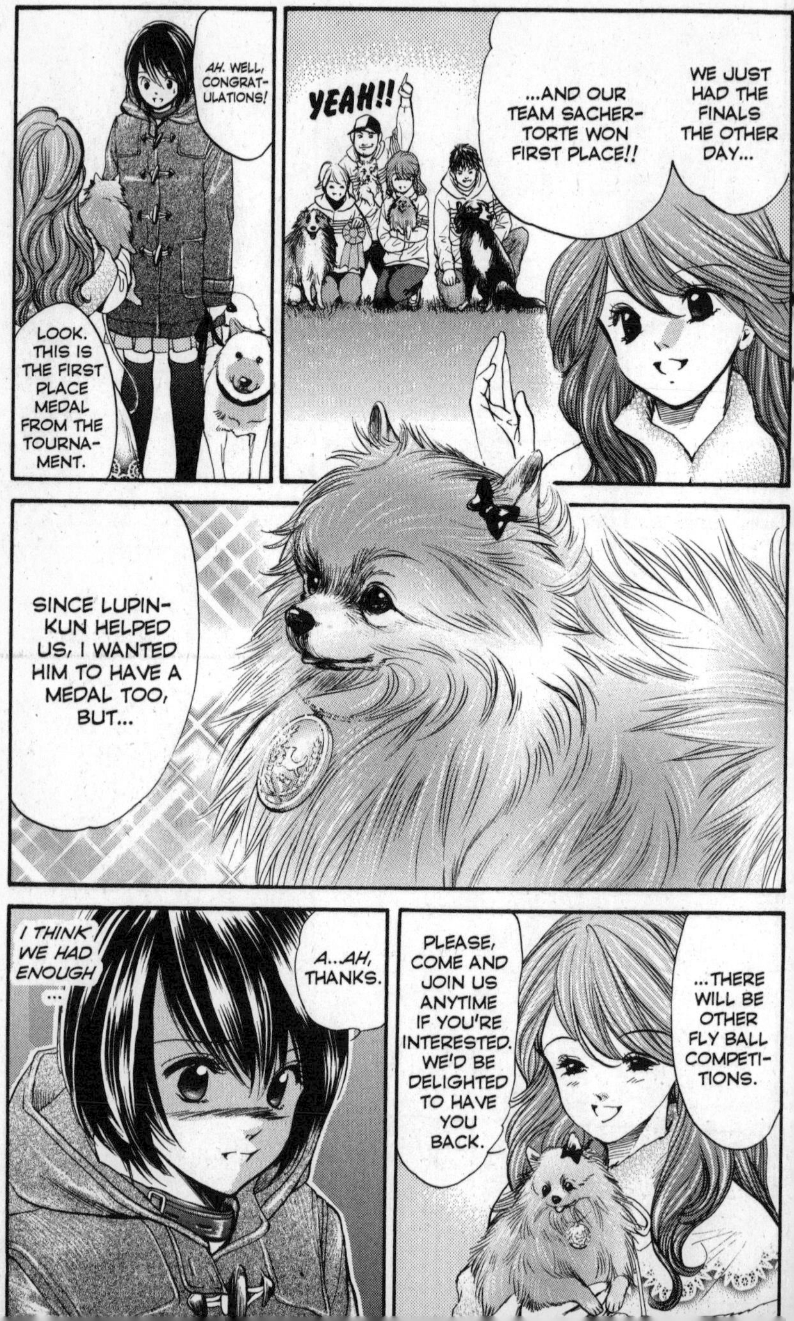
WE JUST HAD THE FINALS THE OTHER DAY...
...AND OUR TEAM SACHER-TORTE WON FIRST PLACE!!
YEAH!!
AH. WELL, CONGRATULATIONS!
LOOK. THIS IS THE FIRST PLACE MEDAL FROM THE TOURNAMENT.
SINCE LUPIN-KUN HELPED US, I WANTED HIM TO HAVE A MEDAL TOO, BUT...
...THERE WILL BE OTHER FLY BALL COMPETITIONS.
PLEASE, COME AND JOIN US ANYTIME IF YOU'RE INTERESTED. WE'D BE DELIGHTED TO HAVE YOU BACK.
A...AH, THANKS.
I THINK WE HAD ENOUGH ...

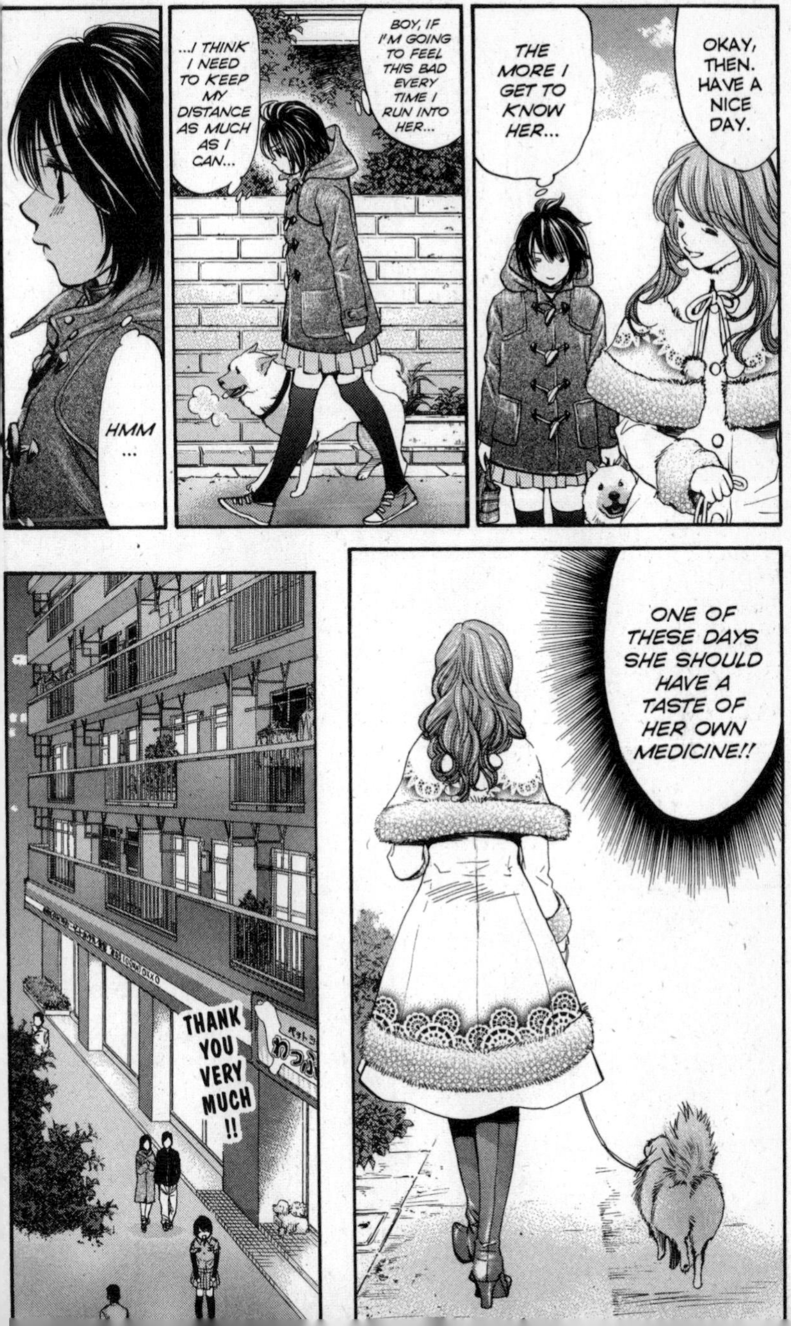
OKAY, THEN. HAVE A NICE DAY.
THE MORE I GET TO KNOW HER...
BOY, IF I'M GOING TO FEEL THIS BAD EVERY TIME I RUN INTO HER...
...I THINK I NEED TO KEEP MY DISTANCE AS MUCH AS I CAN...
HMM ...
ONE OF THESE DAYS SHE SHOULD HAVE A TASTE OF HER OWN MEDICINE!!
THANK YOU VERY MUCH !!

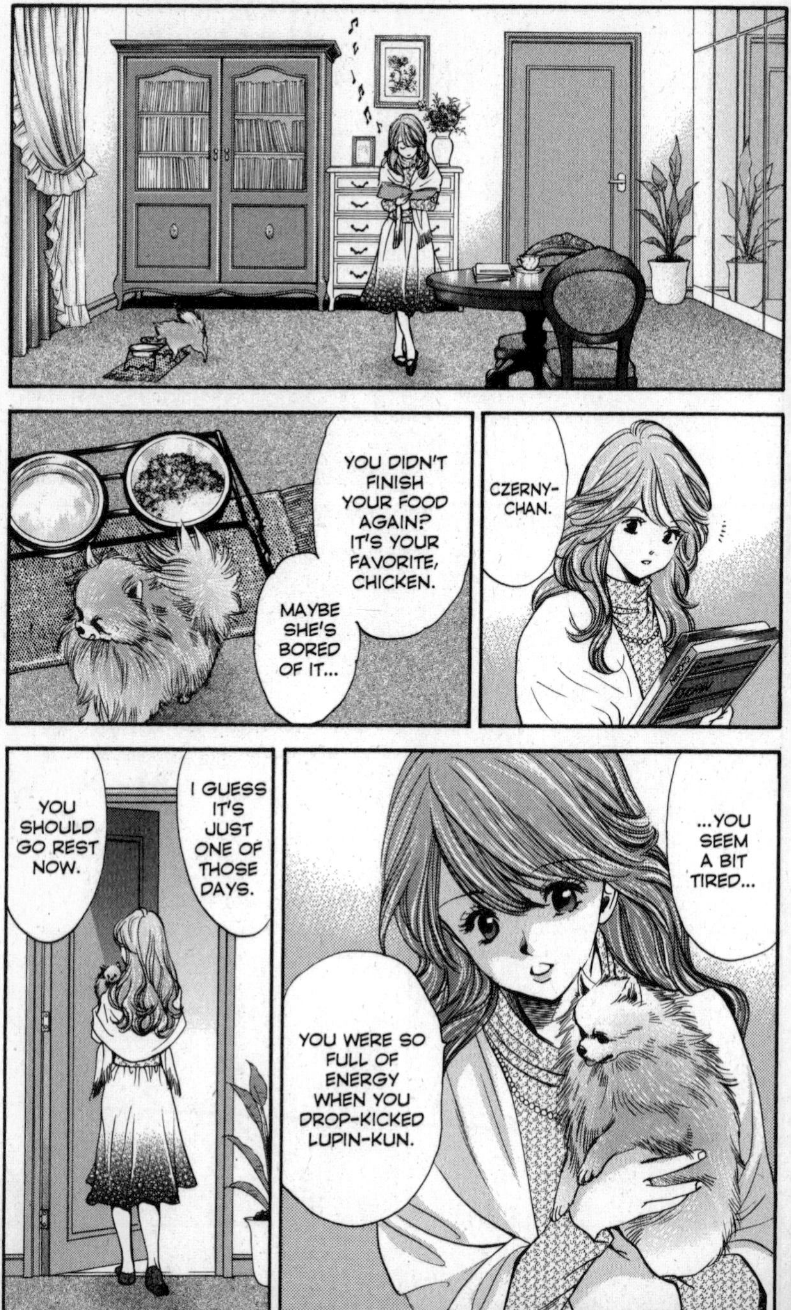
CZERNY-CHAN.
YOU DIDN'T FINISH YOUR FOOD AGAIN? IT'S YOUR FAVORITE, CHICKEN.
MAYBE SHE'S BORED OF IT...
...YOU SEEM A BIT TIRED...
YOU WERE SO FULL OF ENERGY WHEN YOU DROP-KICKED LUPIN-KUN.
I GUESS IT'S JUST ONE OF THOSE DAYS.
YOU SHOULD GO REST NOW.

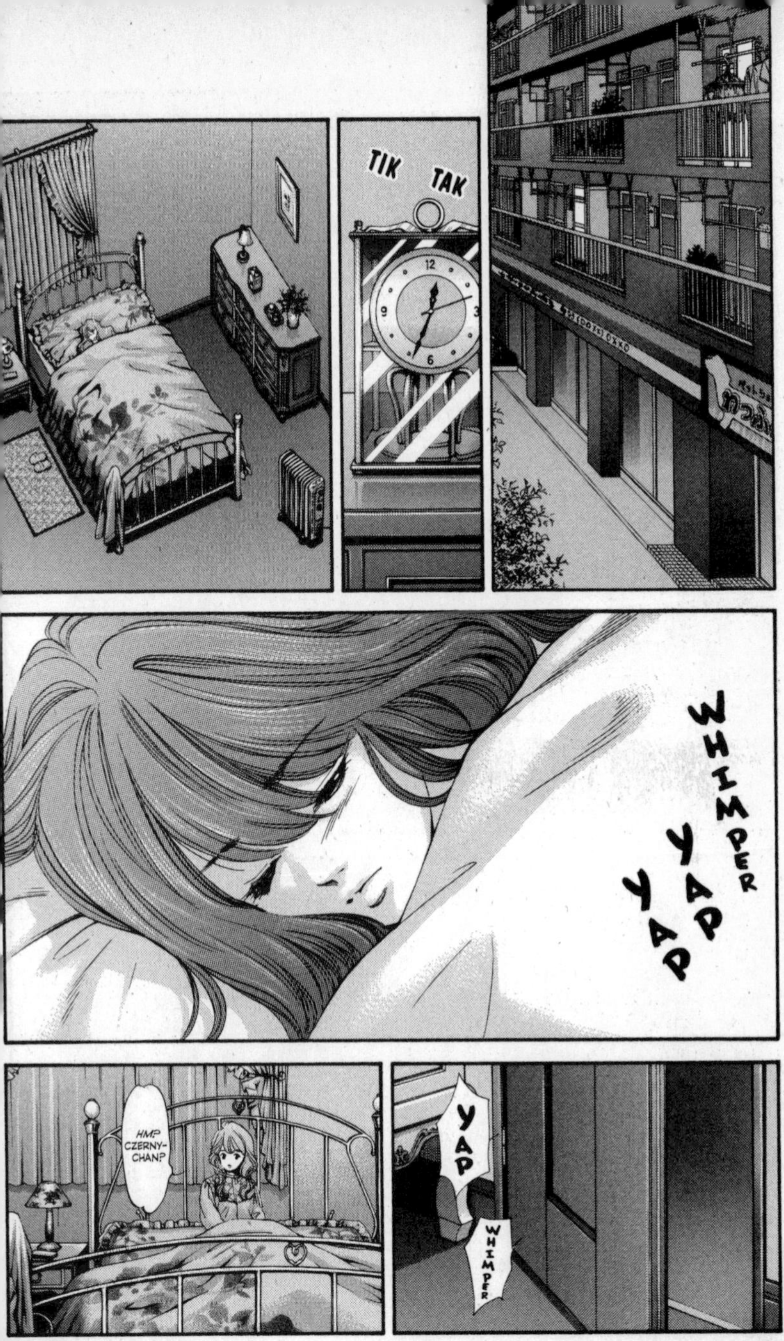
TIK
TAK
WHIMPER
YAP
YAP
YAP
YAP
WHIMPER
HMP? CZERNY-CHAN?

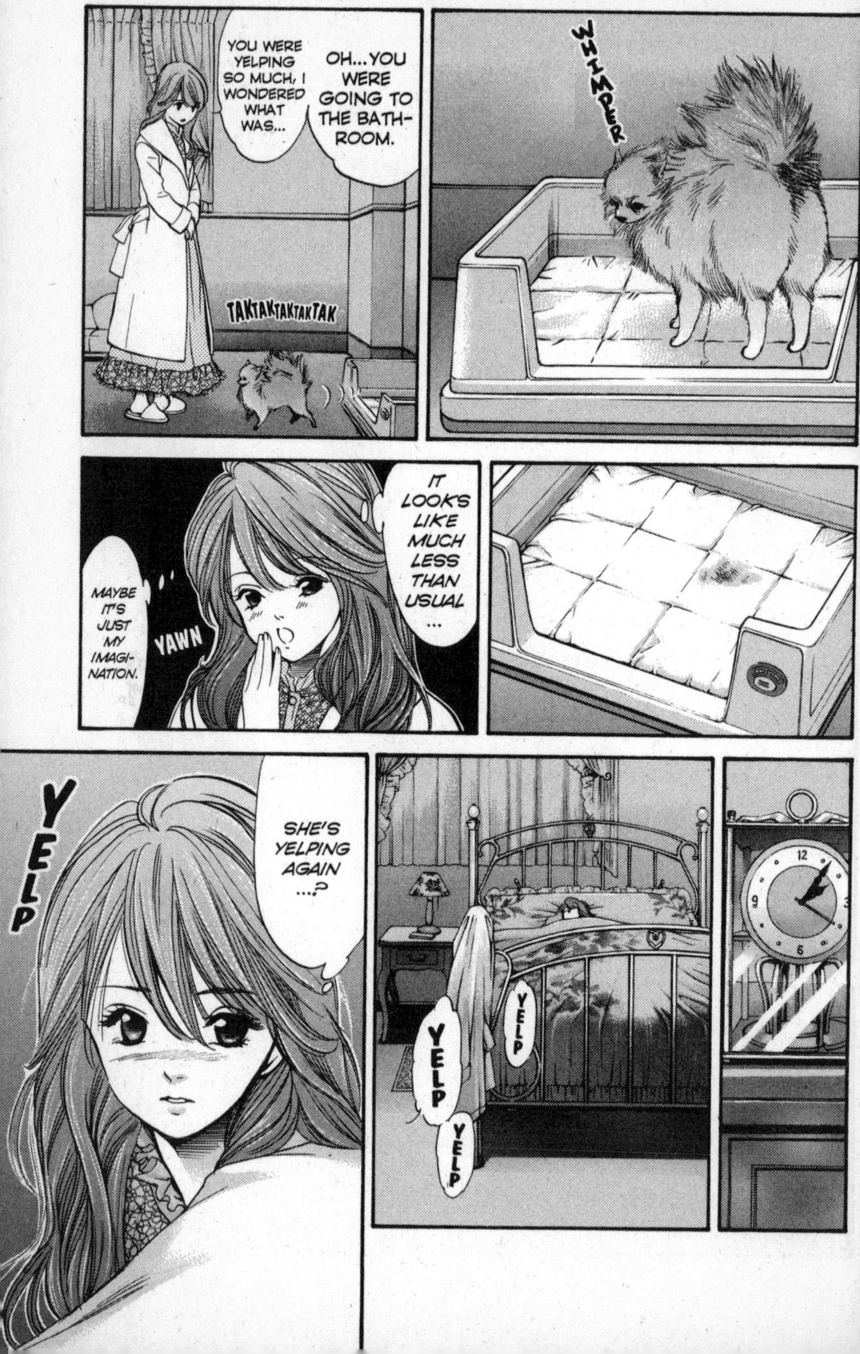
WHIMPER
YOU WERE YELPING SO MUCH, I WONDERED WHAT WAS...
OH...YOU WERE GOING TO THE BATH-ROOM.
TAKTAKTAKTAKTAK
IT LOOKS LIKE MUCH LESS THAN USUAL...
YAWN
MAYBE IT'S JUST MY IMAGI-NATION.
YELP
YELP
YELP
YELP
SHE'S YELPING AGAIN...?

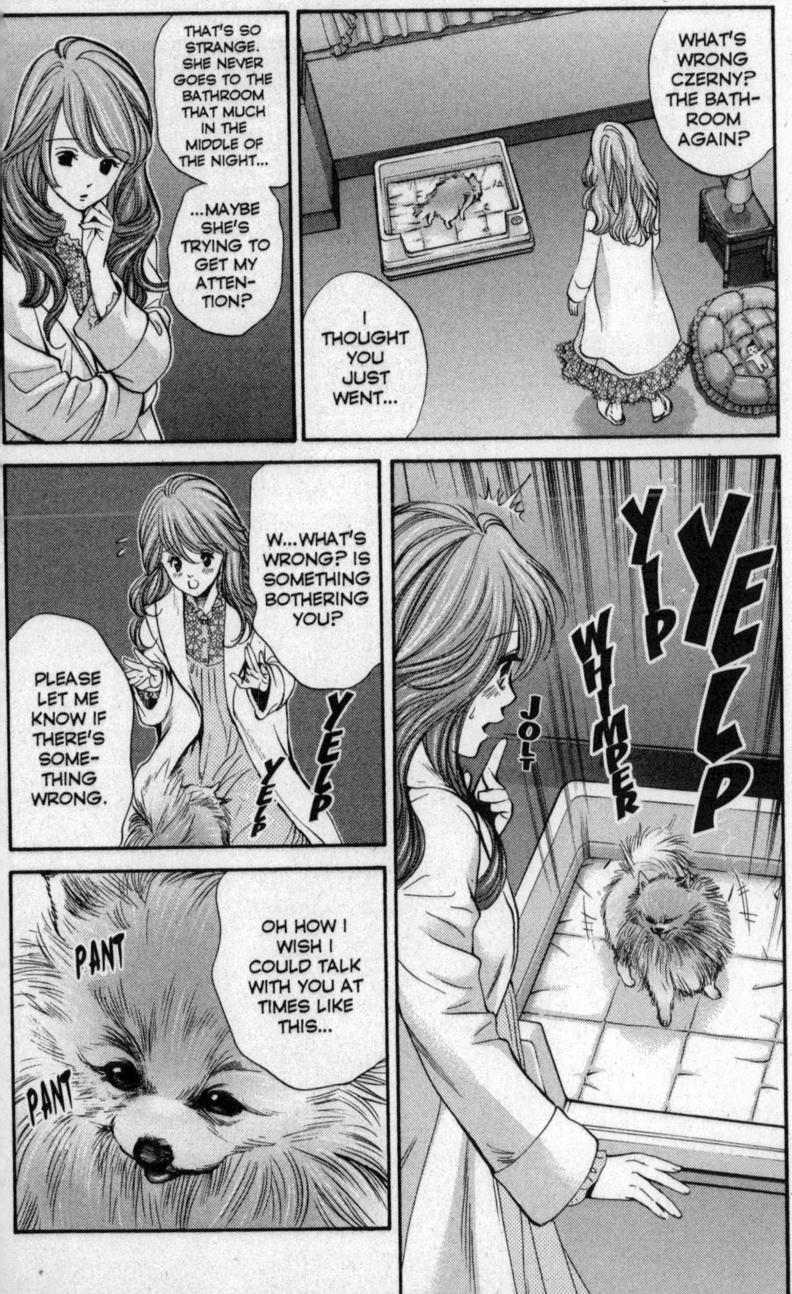
WHAT'S WRONG CZERNY? THE BATHROOM AGAIN?
I THOUGHT YOU JUST WENT...
THAT'S SO STRANGE. SHE NEVER GOES TO THE BATHROOM THAT MUCH IN THE MIDDLE OF THE NIGHT...
...MAYBE SHE'S TRYING TO GET MY ATTENTION?
YELP
YIP
WHIMPER
JOLT
W...WHAT'S WRONG? IS SOMETHING BOTHERING YOU?
PLEASE LET ME KNOW IF THERE'S SOMETHING WRONG.
YELP
YELP
OH HOW I WISH I COULD TALK WITH YOU AT TIMES LIKE THIS...
PANT
PANT

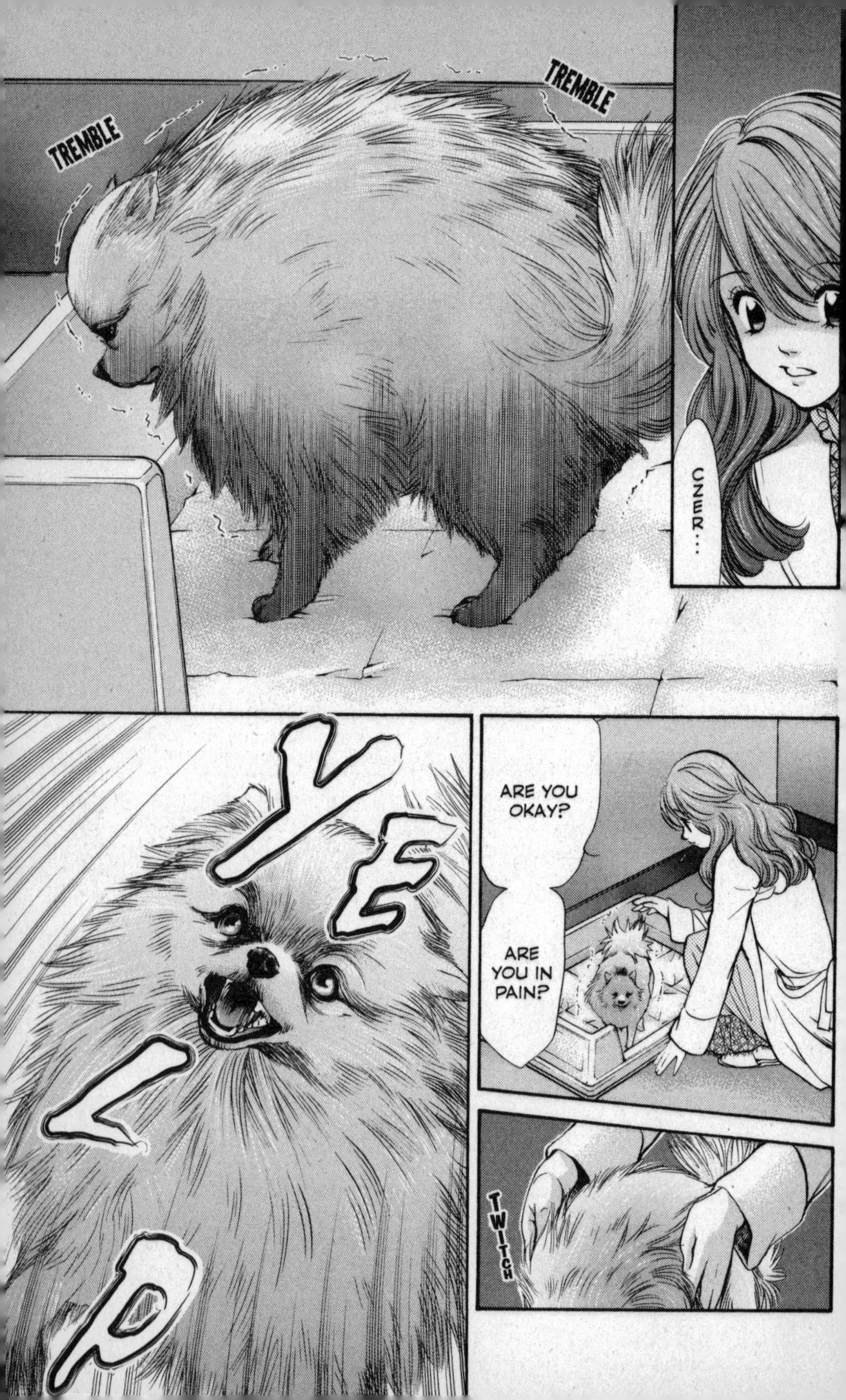
CZER...
TREMBLE
TREMBLE
ARE YOU OKAY?
ARE YOU IN PAIN?
TWITCH
YELP

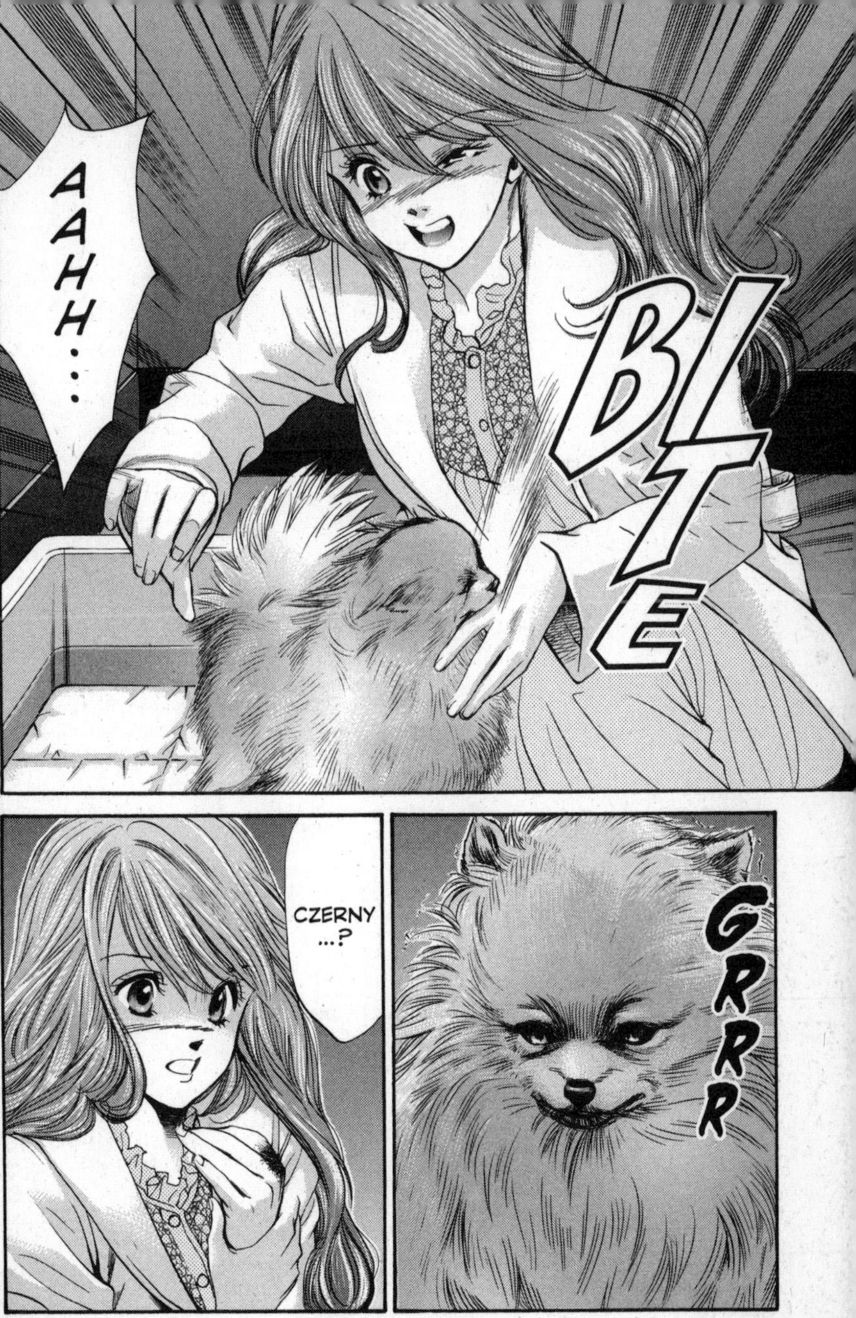
AAHH...
BITE
GRRR
CZERNY ...?

# CHAPTER 129: HOSPITALIZATION

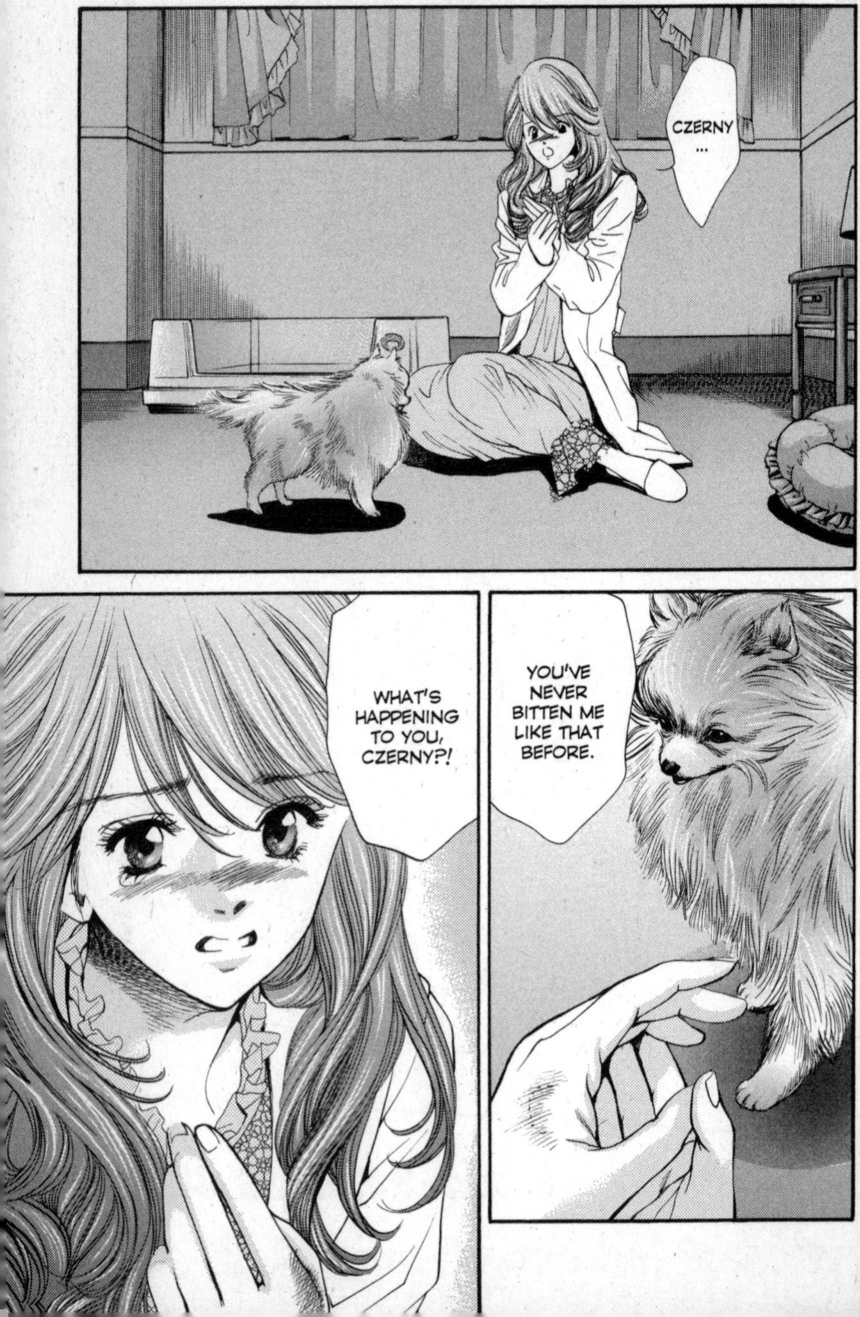

CZERNY ...
YOU'VE NEVER BITTEN ME LIKE THAT BEFORE.
WHAT'S HAPPENING TO YOU, CZERNY?!

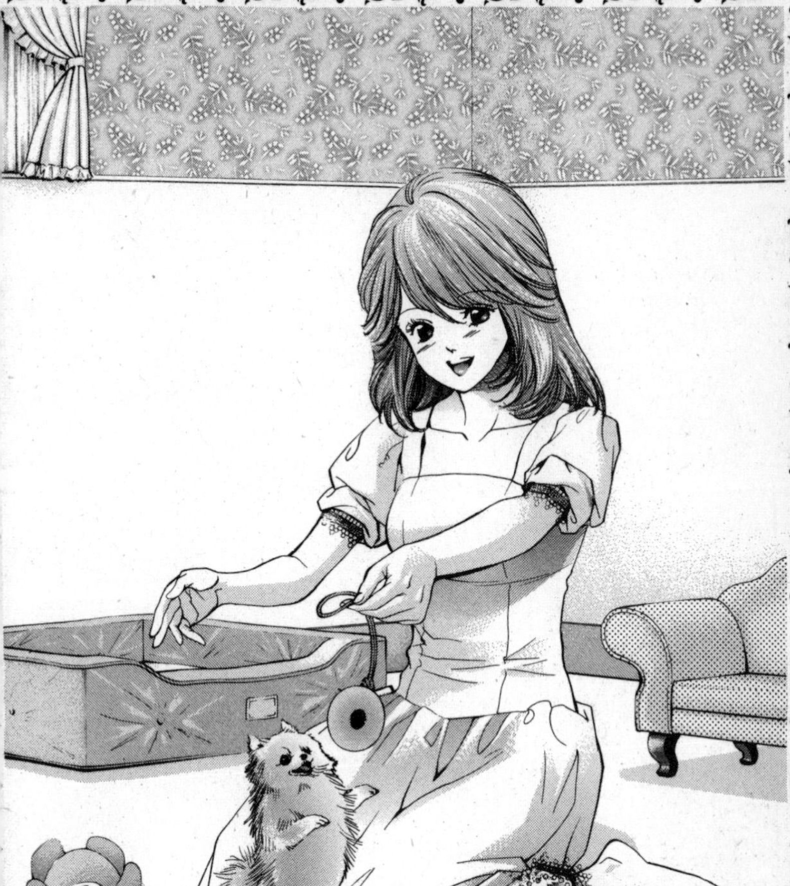

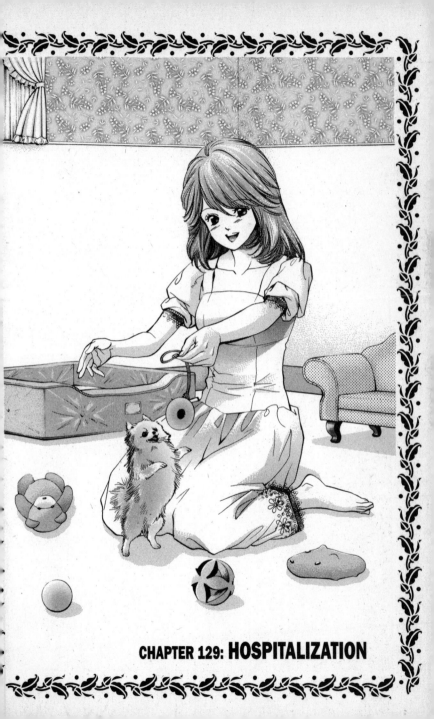

# CHAPTER 129: HOSPITALIZATION

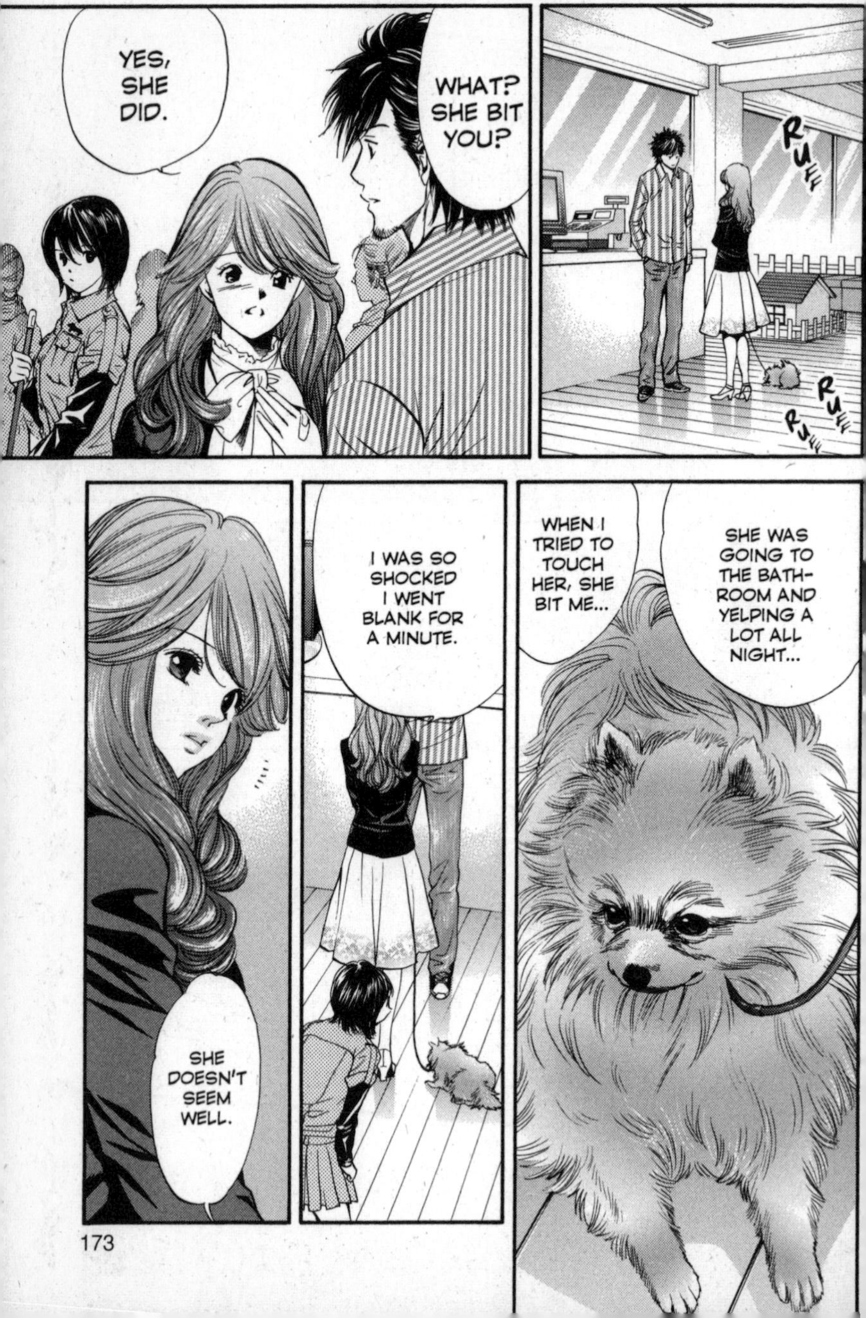
RUFF
RUFF
RUFF
WHAT? SHE BIT YOU?
YES, SHE DID.
SHE WAS GOING TO THE BATHROOM AND YELPING A LOT ALL NIGHT...
WHEN I TRIED TO TOUCH HER, SHE BIT ME...
I WAS SO SHOCKED I WENT BLANK FOR A MINUTE.
SHE DOESN'T SEEM WELL.

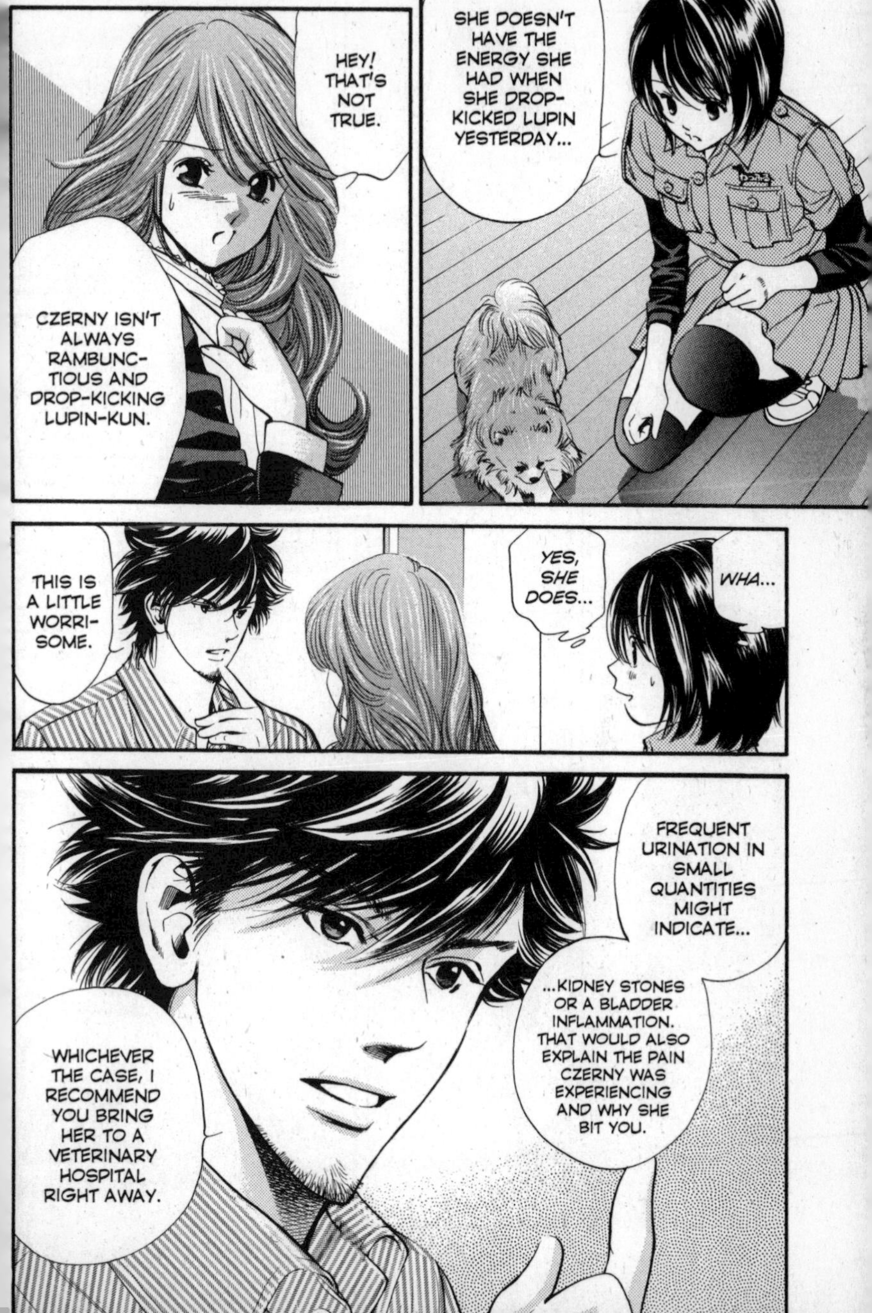
SHE DOESN'T HAVE THE ENERGY SHE HAD WHEN SHE DROP-KICKED LUPIN YESTERDAY...
HEY! THAT'S NOT TRUE.
CZERNY ISN'T ALWAYS RAMBUNC-TIOUS AND DROP-KICKING LUPIN-KUN.
WHA...
YES, SHE DOES...
THIS IS A LITTLE WORRI-SOME.
FREQUENT URINATION IN SMALL QUANTITIES MIGHT INDICATE...
...KIDNEY STONES OR A BLADDER INFLAMMATION. THAT WOULD ALSO EXPLAIN THE PAIN CZERNY WAS EXPERIENCING AND WHY SHE BIT YOU.
WHICHEVER THE CASE, I RECOMMEND YOU BRING HER TO A VETERINARY HOSPITAL RIGHT AWAY.

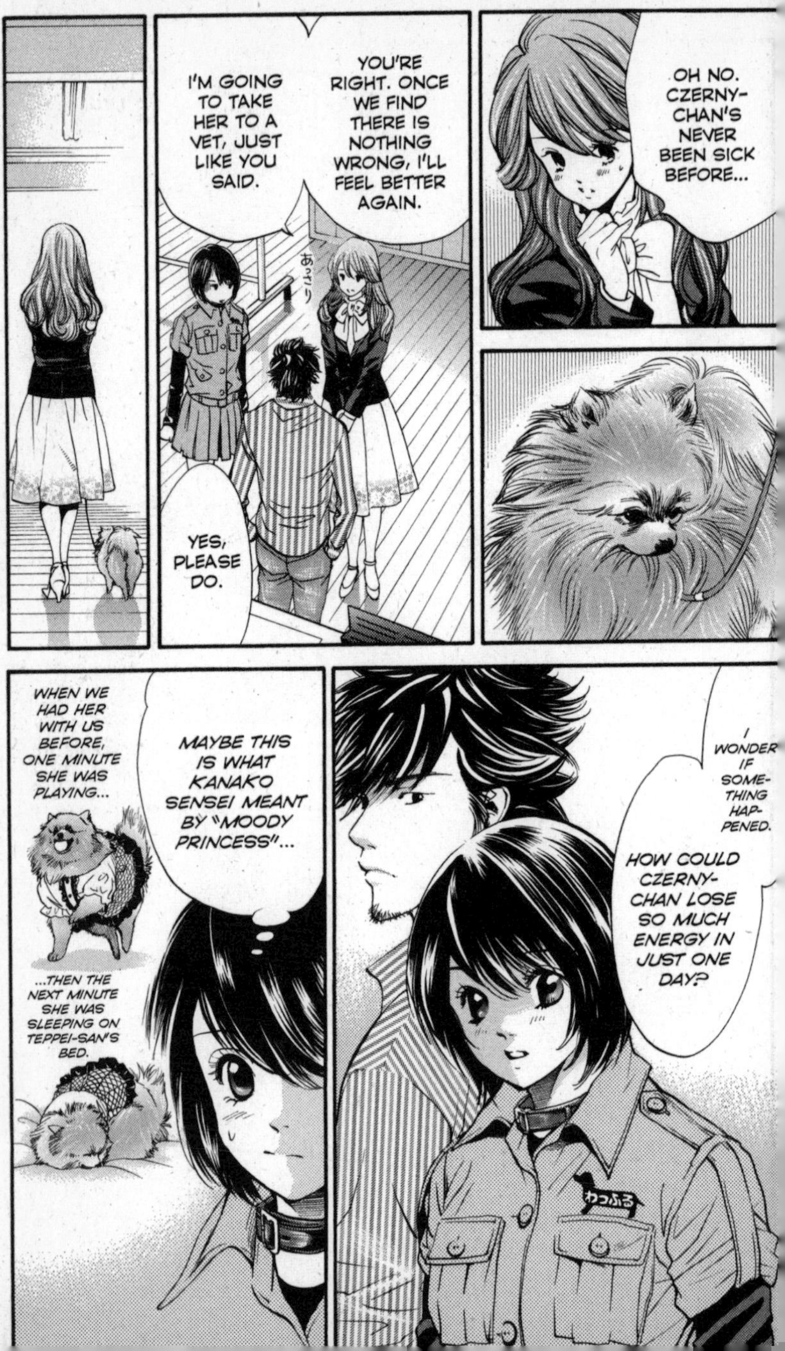
OH NO. CZERNY-CHAN'S NEVER BEEN SICK BEFORE...
YOU'RE RIGHT. ONCE WE FIND THERE IS NOTHING WRONG, I'LL FEEL BETTER AGAIN.
I'M GOING TO TAKE HER TO A VET, JUST LIKE YOU SAID.
あっさり
YES, PLEASE DO.
I WONDER IF SOME-THING HAP-PENED.
HOW COULD CZERNY-CHAN LOSE SO MUCH ENERGY IN JUST ONE DAY?
MAYBE THIS IS WHAT KANAKO SENSEI MEANT BY "MOODY PRINCESS"...
WHEN WE HAD HER WITH US BEFORE, ONE MINUTE SHE WAS PLAYING...
...THEN THE NEXT MINUTE SHE WAS SLEEPING ON TEPPEI-SAN'S BED.
わっふる

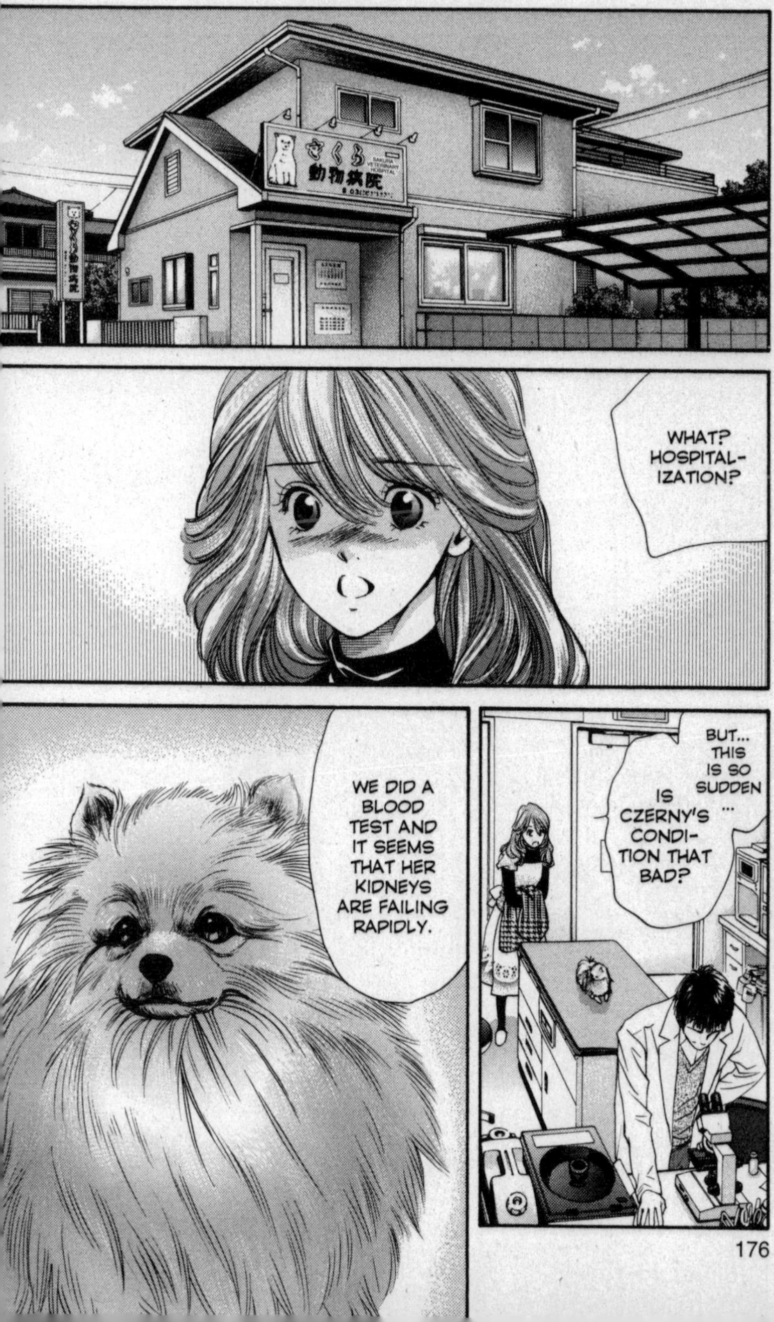
さくら
SAKURA VETERINARY HOSPITAL
動物病院
WHAT? HOSPITALIZATION?
BUT... THIS IS SO SUDDEN...
IS CZERNY'S CONDITION THAT BAD?
WE DID A BLOOD TEST AND IT SEEMS THAT HER KIDNEYS ARE FAILING RAPIDLY.

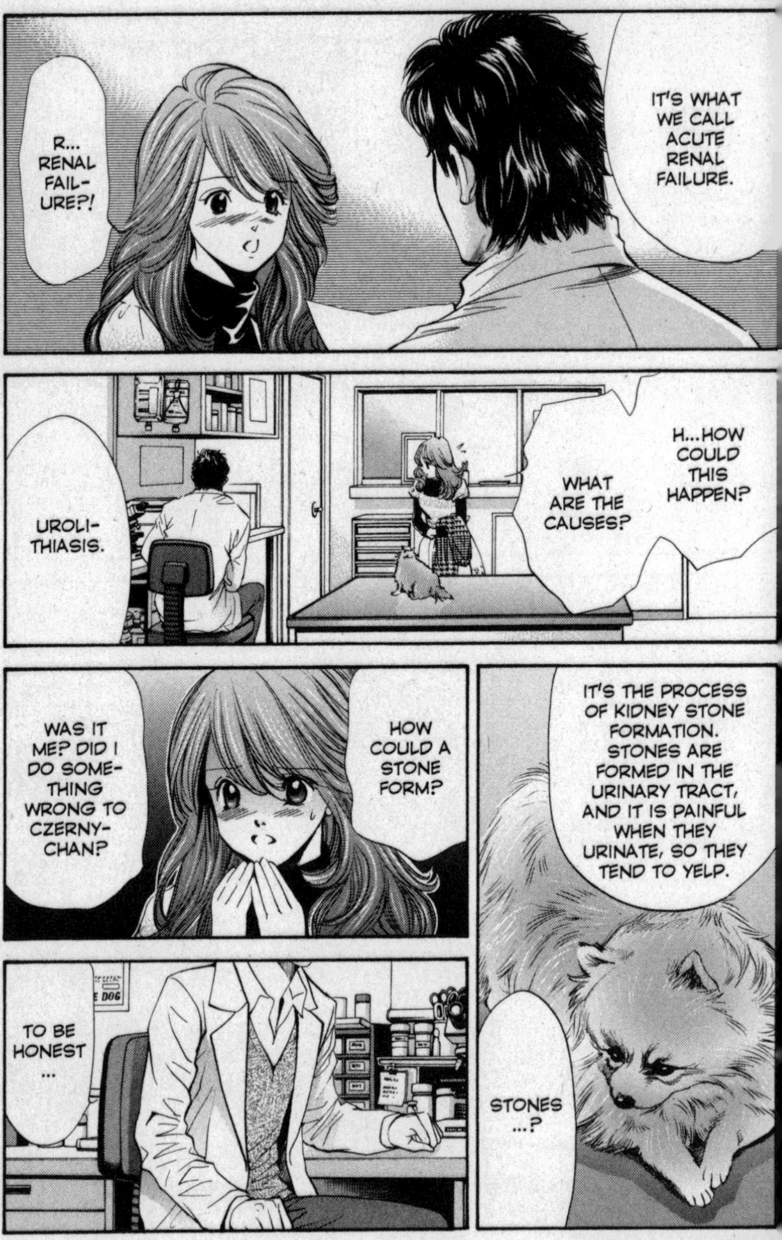
IT'S WHAT WE CALL ACUTE RENAL FAILURE.
R... RENAL FAIL-URE?!
H...HOW COULD THIS HAPPEN?
WHAT ARE THE CAUSES?
UROLI-THIASIS.
IT'S THE PROCESS OF KIDNEY STONE FORMATION. STONES ARE FORMED IN THE URINARY TRACT, AND IT IS PAINFUL WHEN THEY URINATE, SO THEY TEND TO YELP.
STONES ...?
HOW COULD A STONE FORM?
WAS IT ME? DID I DO SOME-THING WRONG TO CZERNY-CHAN?
TO BE HONEST ...

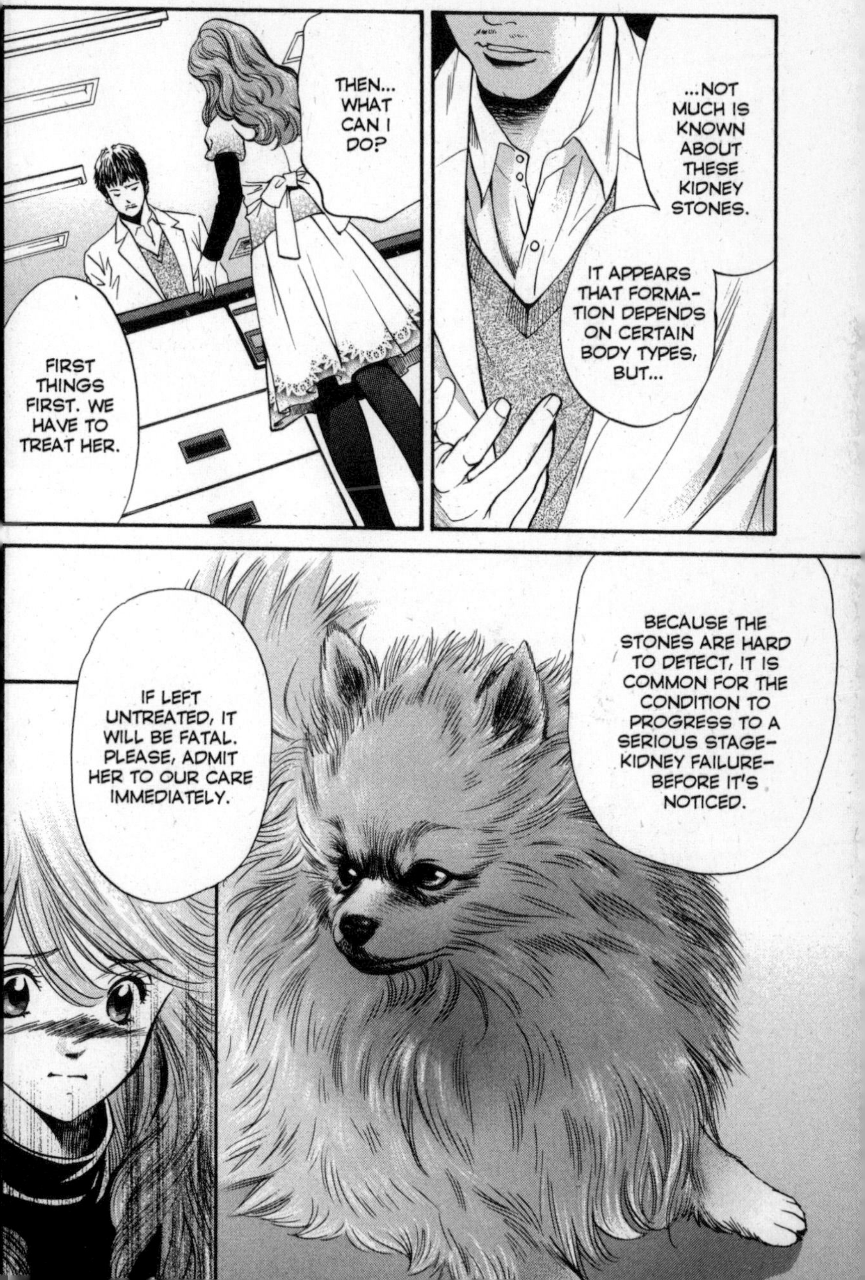
...NOT MUCH IS KNOWN ABOUT THESE KIDNEY STONES.
IT APPEARS THAT FORMATION DEPENDS ON CERTAIN BODY TYPES, BUT...
THEN... WHAT CAN I DO?
FIRST THINGS FIRST. WE HAVE TO TREAT HER.
BECAUSE THE STONES ARE HARD TO DETECT, IT IS COMMON FOR THE CONDITION TO PROGRESS TO A SERIOUS STAGE-KIDNEY FAILURE-BEFORE IT'S NOTICED.
IF LEFT UNTREATED, IT WILL BE FATAL. PLEASE, ADMIT HER TO OUR CARE IMMEDIATELY.

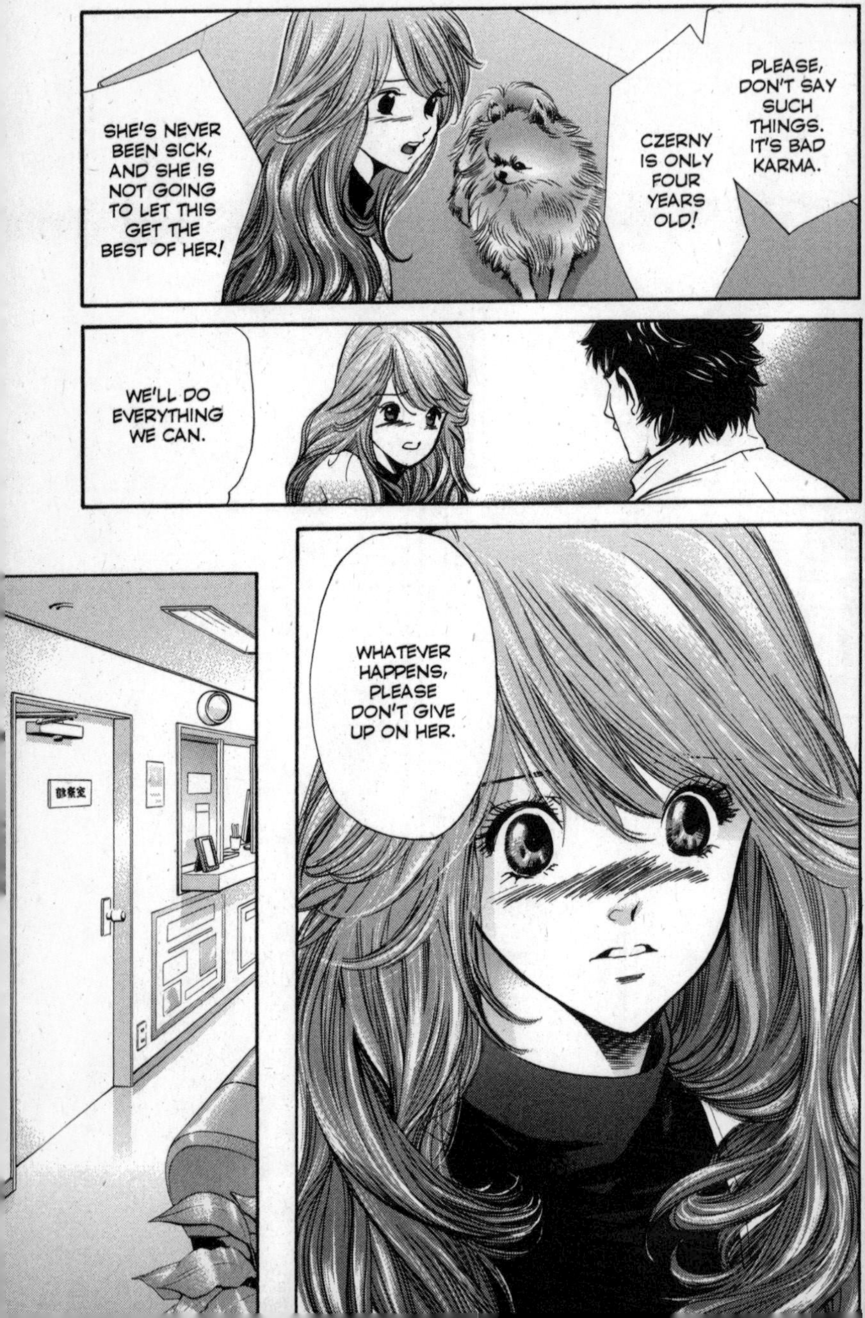
PLEASE, DON'T SAY SUCH THINGS. IT'S BAD KARMA.
CZERNY IS ONLY FOUR YEARS OLD!
SHE'S NEVER BEEN SICK, AND SHE IS NOT GOING TO LET THIS GET THE BEST OF HER!
WE'LL DO EVERYTHING WE CAN.
WHATEVER HAPPENS, PLEASE DON'T GIVE UP ON HER.

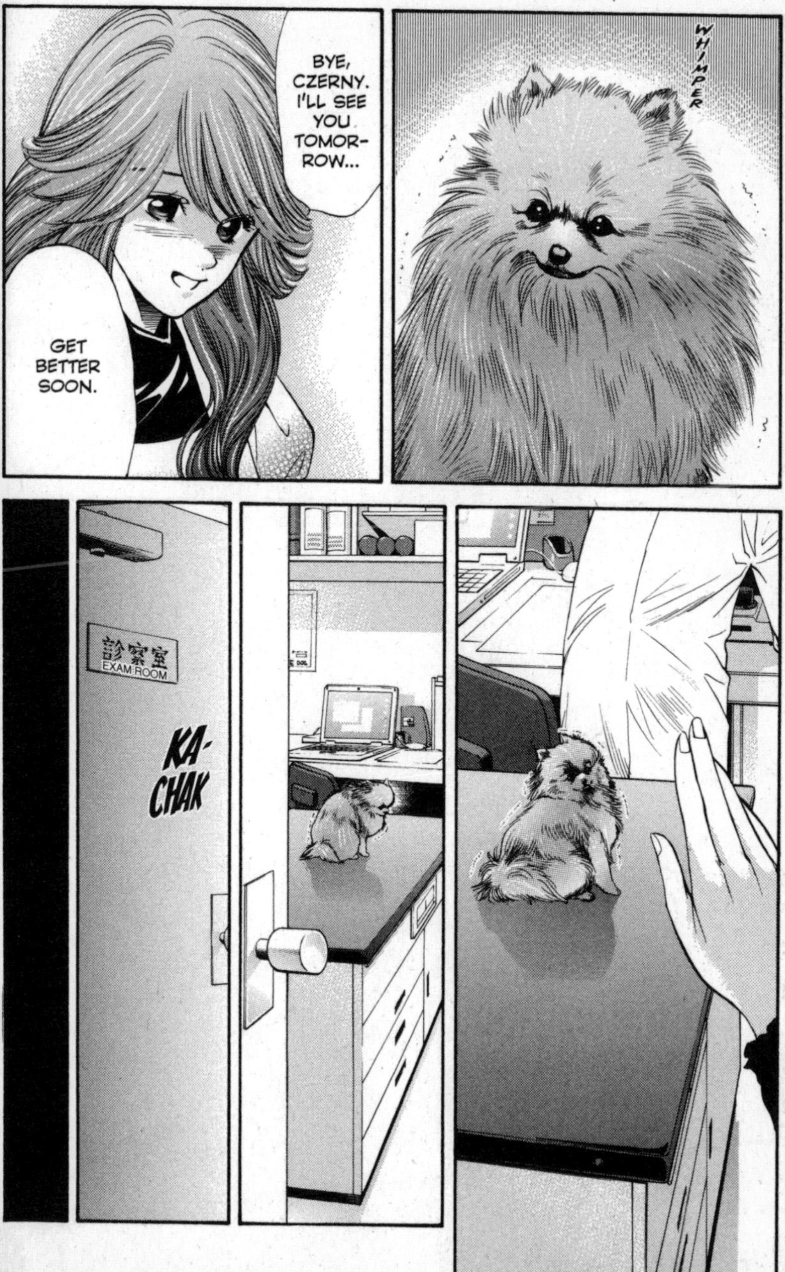
WHIMPER
BYE, CZERNY. I'LL SEE YOU TOMORROW...
GET BETTER SOON.
診察室 EXAM ROOM
KA-CHAK

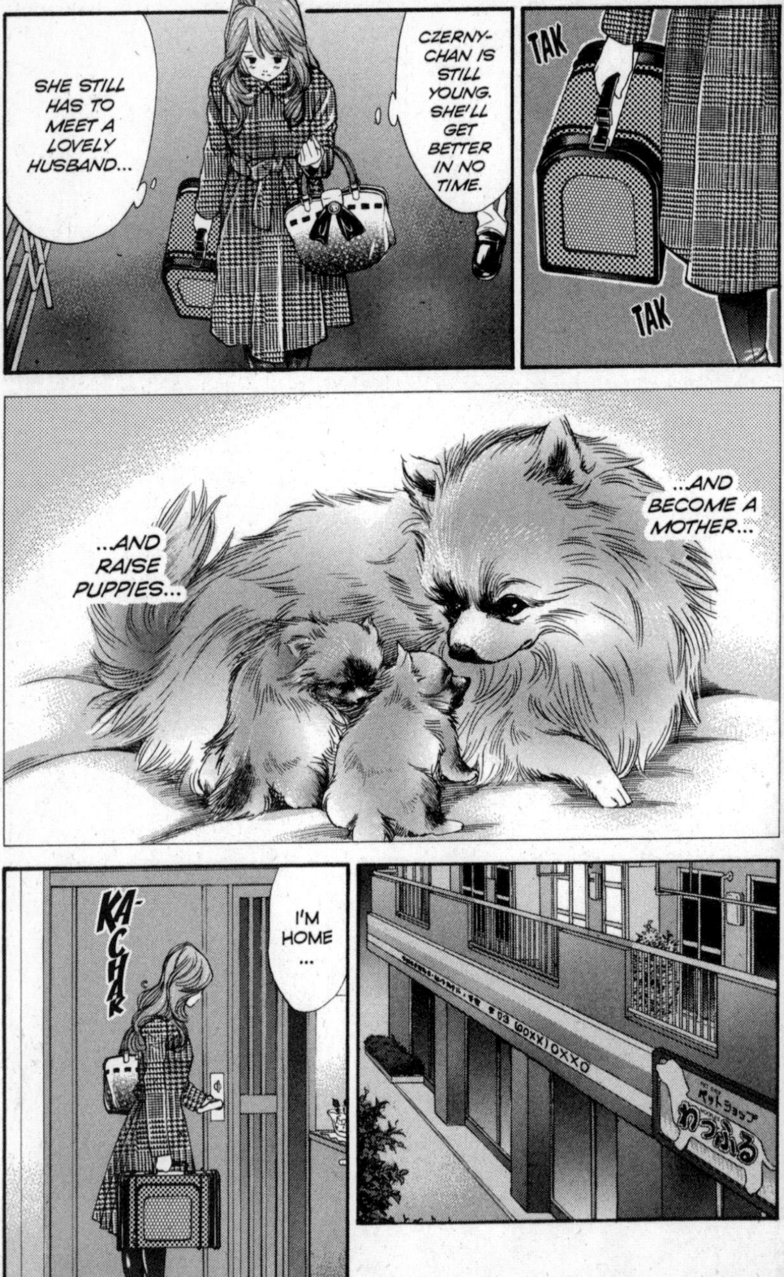
TAK
TAK
CZERNY-CHAN IS STILL YOUNG. SHE'LL GET BETTER IN NO TIME.
SHE STILL HAS TO MEET A LOVELY HUSBAND...
...AND BECOME A MOTHER...
...AND RAISE PUPPIES...
ペットショップ
わっふる
KA-CHAR
I'M HOME ...

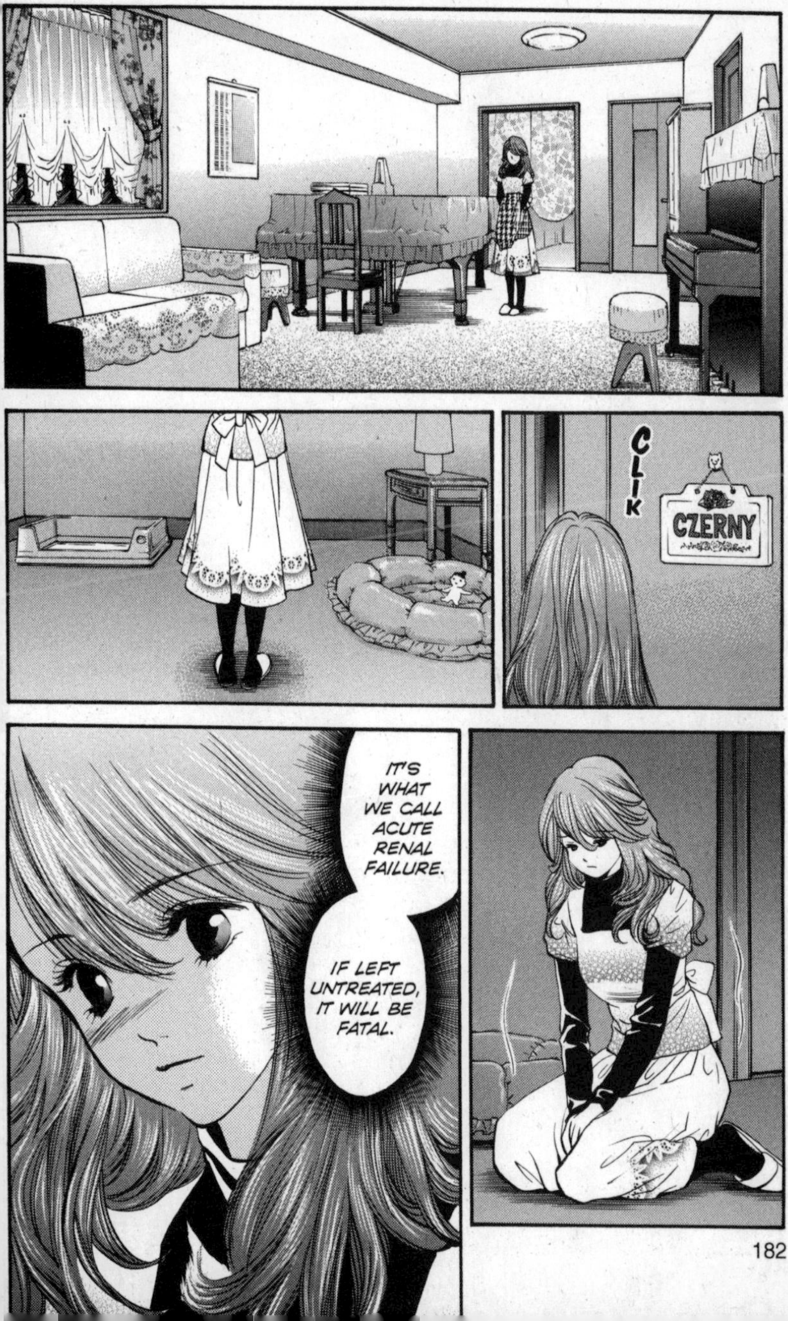
CLIK
CZERNY
IT'S WHAT WE CALL ACUTE RENAL FAILURE.
IF LEFT UNTREATED, IT WILL BE FATAL.

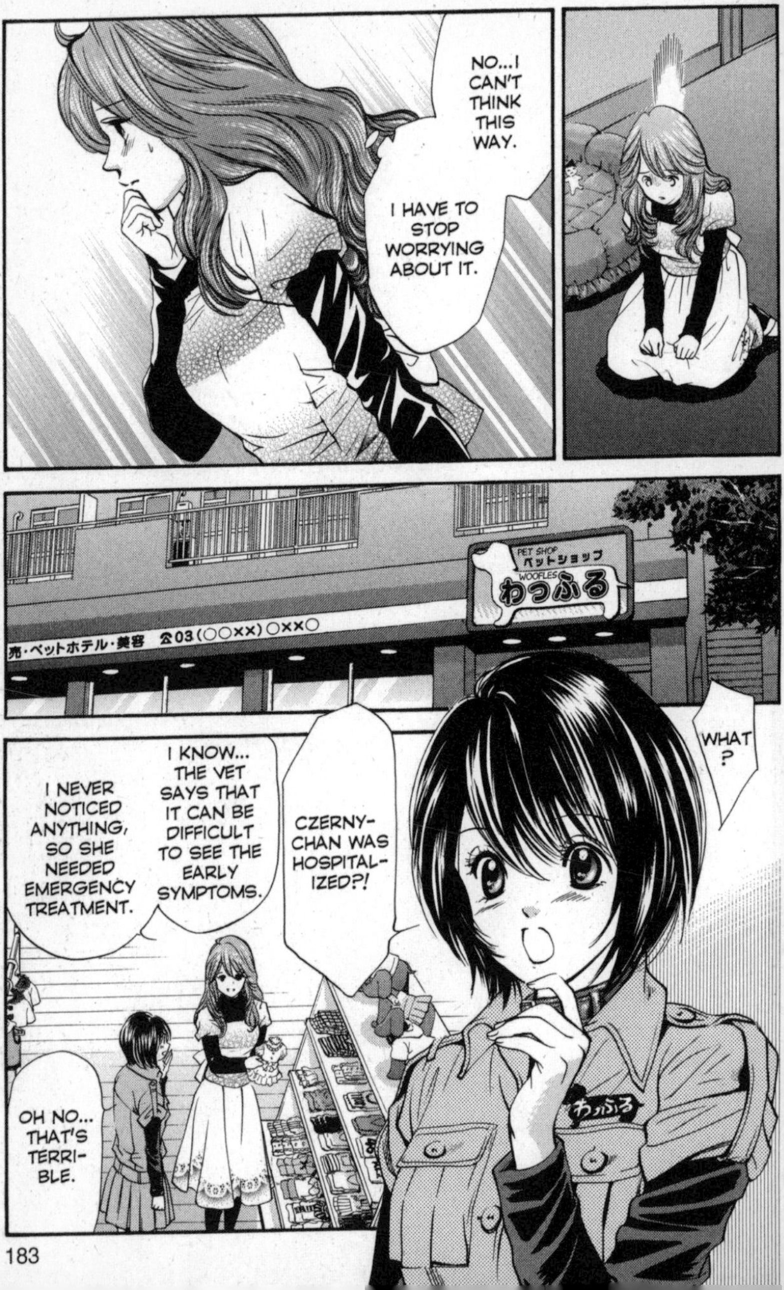
NO...I CAN'T THINK THIS WAY.
I HAVE TO STOP WORRYING ABOUT IT.
PET SHOP ペットショップ
WOOFLES わっふる
ペットホテル・美容 ☎03(○○××)○××○
WHAT?
CZERNY-CHAN WAS HOSPITALIZED?!
わっふる
I KNOW... THE VET SAYS THAT IT CAN BE DIFFICULT TO SEE THE EARLY SYMPTOMS.
I NEVER NOTICED ANYTHING, SO SHE NEEDED EMERGENCY TREATMENT.
OH NO... THAT'S TERRIBLE.

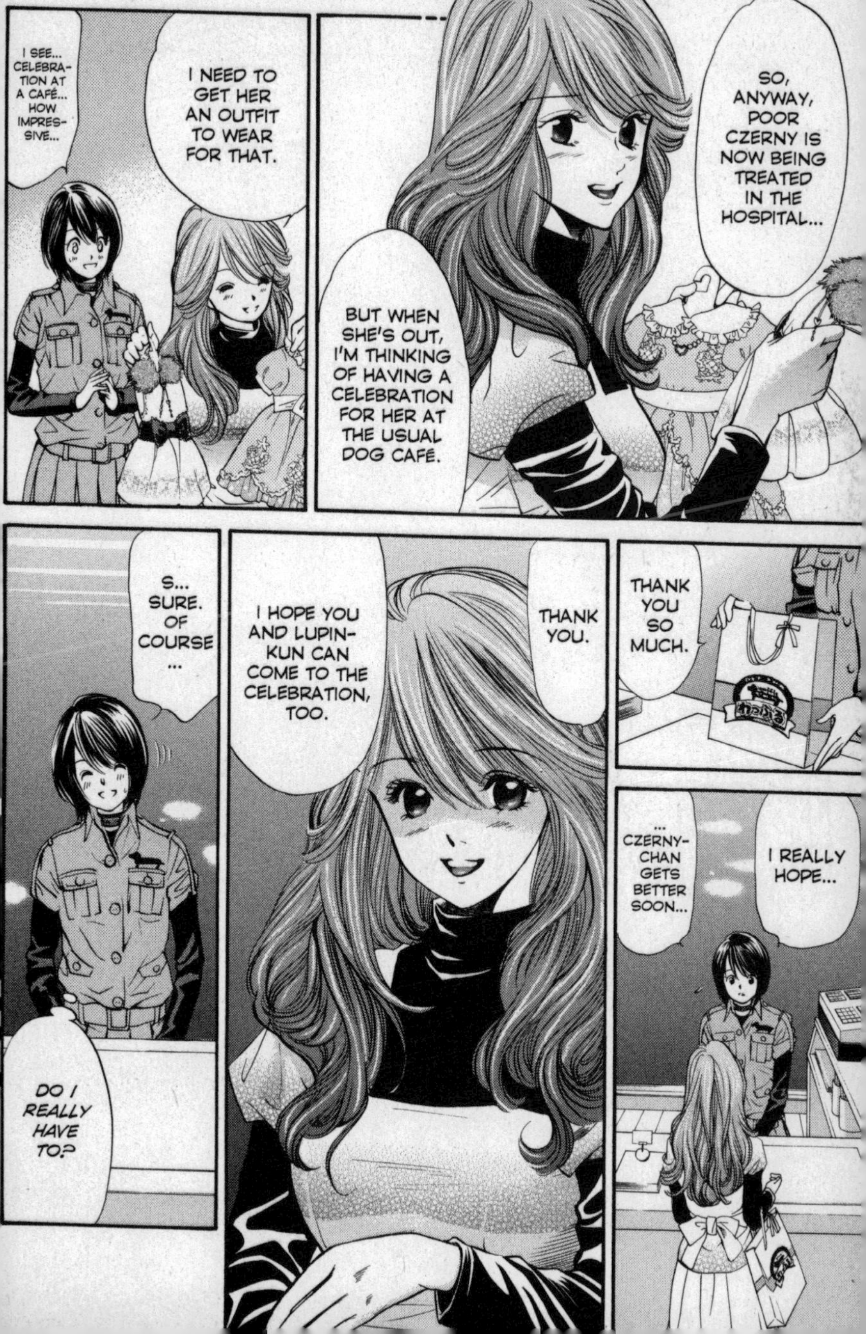
SO, ANYWAY, POOR CZERNY IS NOW BEING TREATED IN THE HOSPITAL...
BUT WHEN SHE'S OUT, I'M THINKING OF HAVING A CELEBRATION FOR HER AT THE USUAL DOG CAFÉ.
I NEED TO GET HER AN OUTFIT TO WEAR FOR THAT.
I SEE... CELEBRATION AT A CAFÉ... HOW IMPRESSIVE...
THANK YOU SO MUCH.
I REALLY HOPE...
...CZERNY-CHAN GETS BETTER SOON...
THANK YOU.
I HOPE YOU AND LUPIN-KUN CAN COME TO THE CELEBRATION, TOO.
S... SURE. OF COURSE...
DO I REALLY HAVE TO?

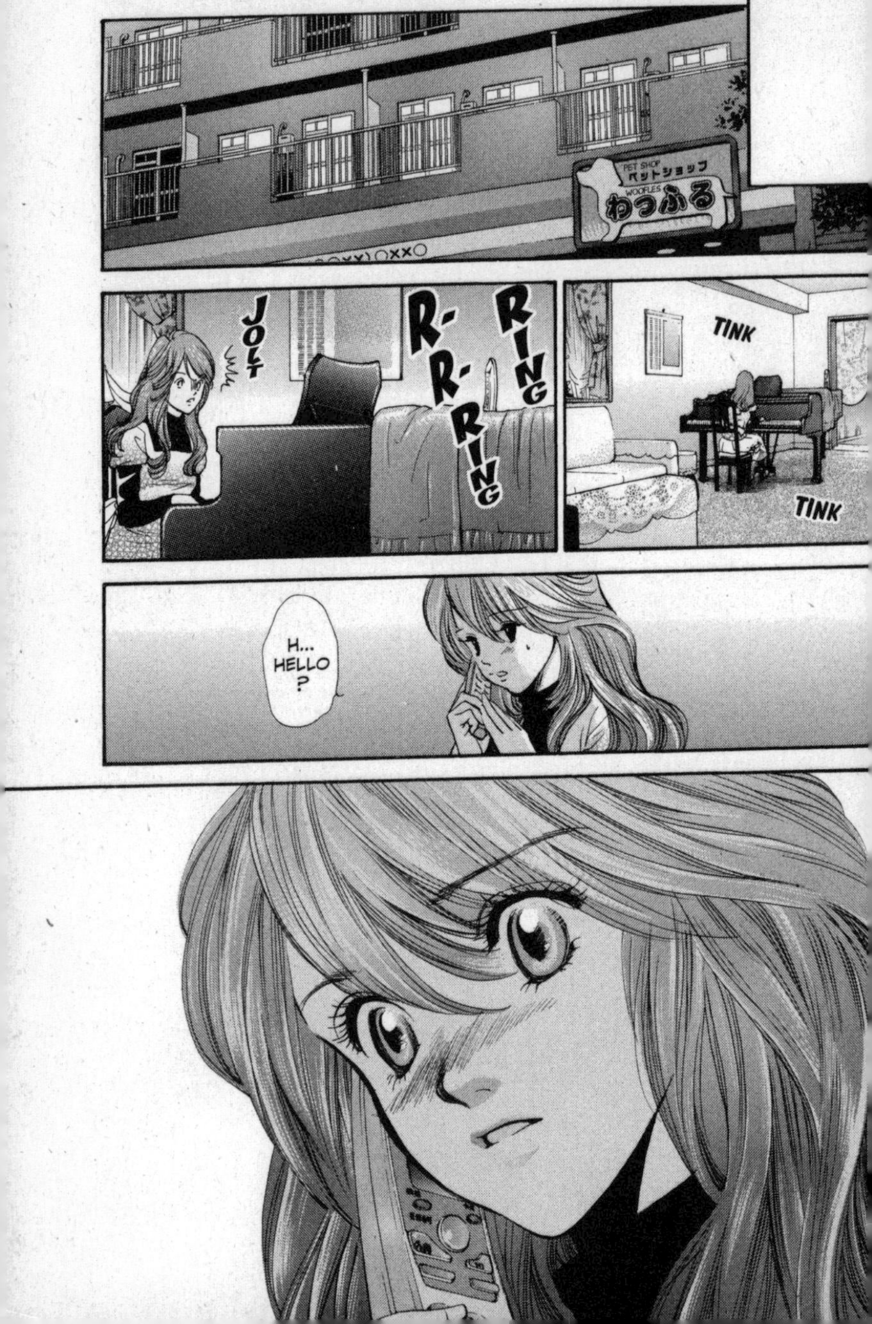
PET SHOP
ペットショップ
WOOFLES
わつふる
TINK
TINK
R-R-RING RING
JOLT
H... HELLO ?

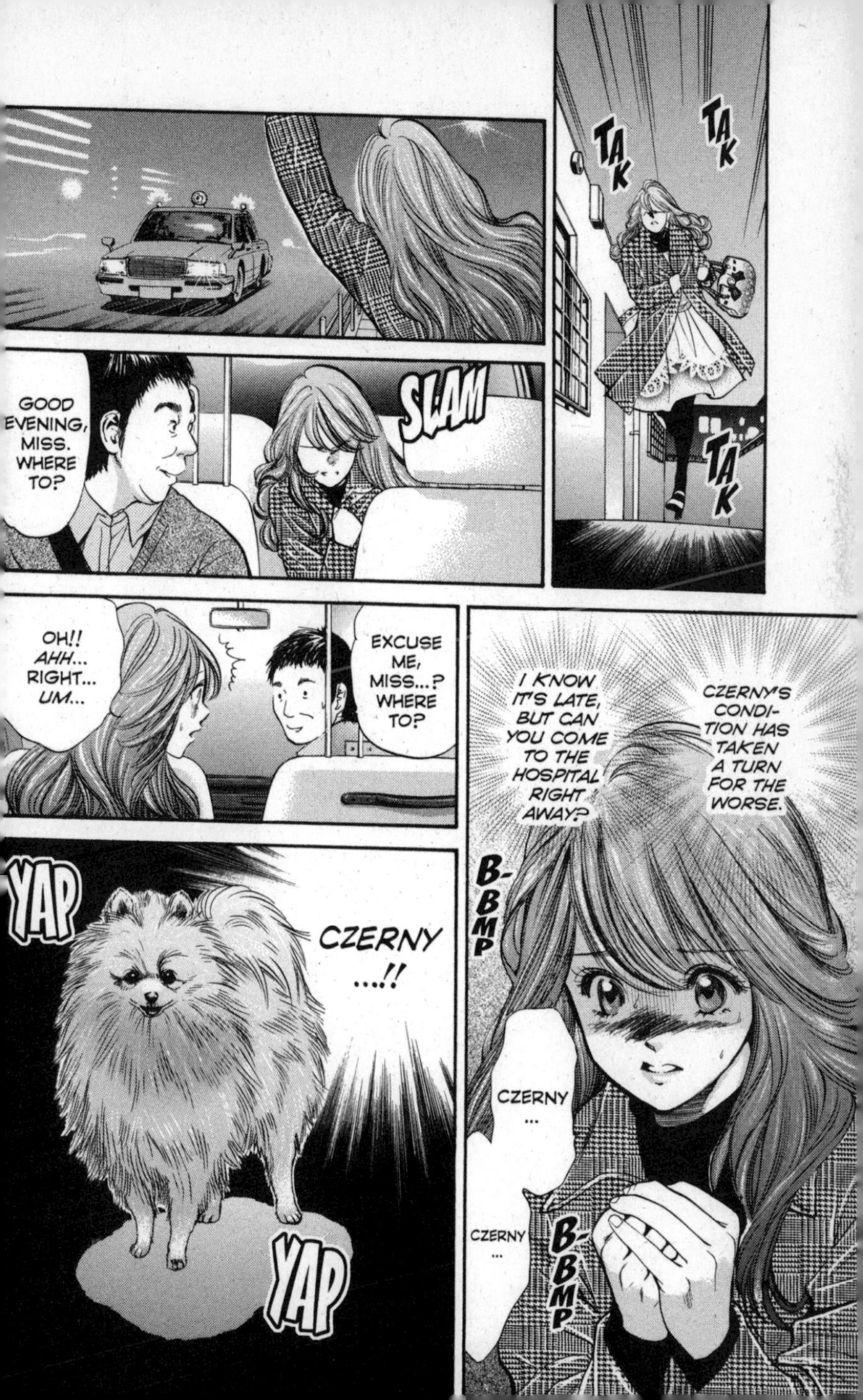
TAK
TAK
TAK
TAK
SLAM
GOOD EVENING, MISS. WHERE TO?
CZERNY'S CONDITION HAS TAKEN A TURN FOR THE WORSE.
I KNOW IT'S LATE, BUT CAN YOU COME TO THE HOSPITAL RIGHT AWAY?
B-BBMP
CZERNY ...
CZERNY ...
B-BBMP
EXCUSE ME, MISS...? WHERE TO?
OH!! AHH... RIGHT... UM...
CZERNY ...!!
YAP
YAP

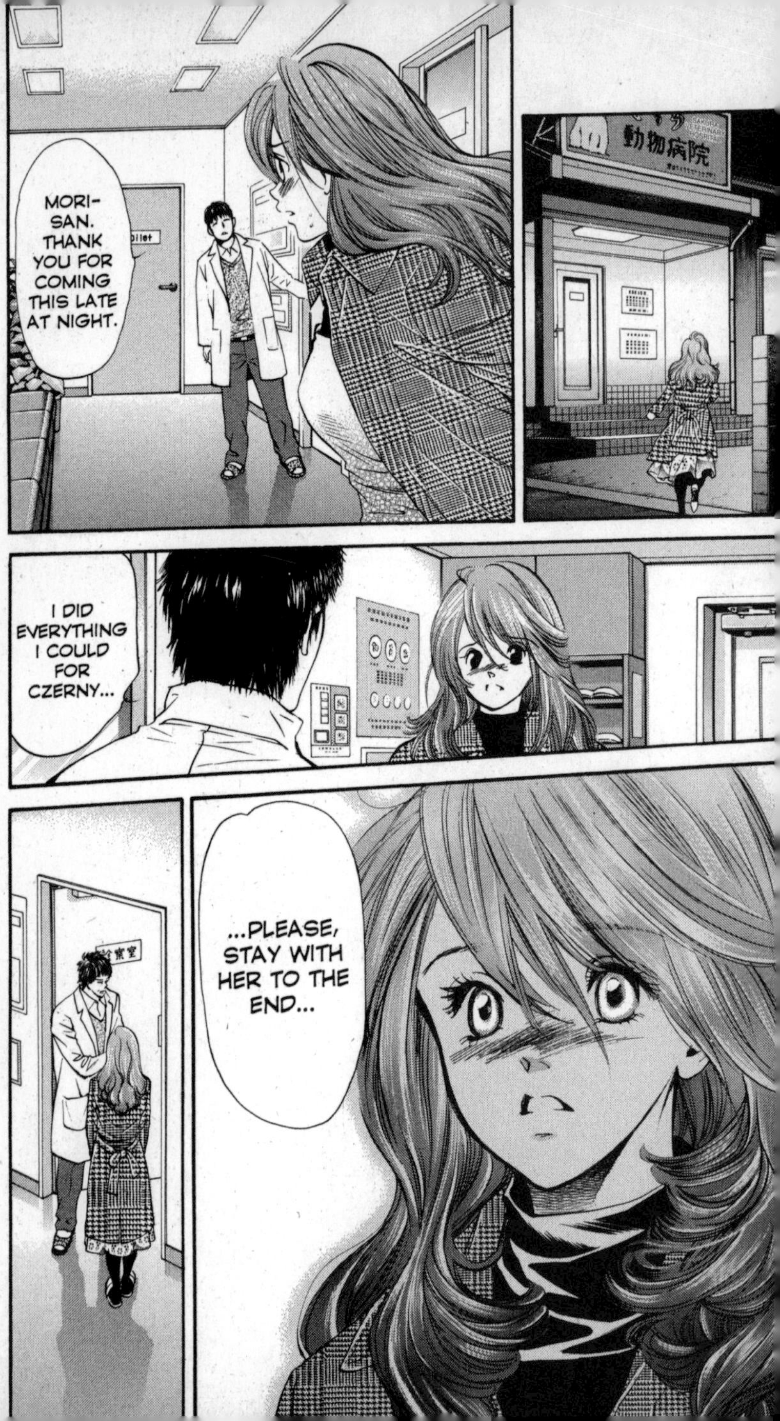
動物病院
MORI-SAN. THANK YOU FOR COMING THIS LATE AT NIGHT.
I DID EVERYTHING I COULD FOR CZERNY...
...PLEASE, STAY WITH HER TO THE END...

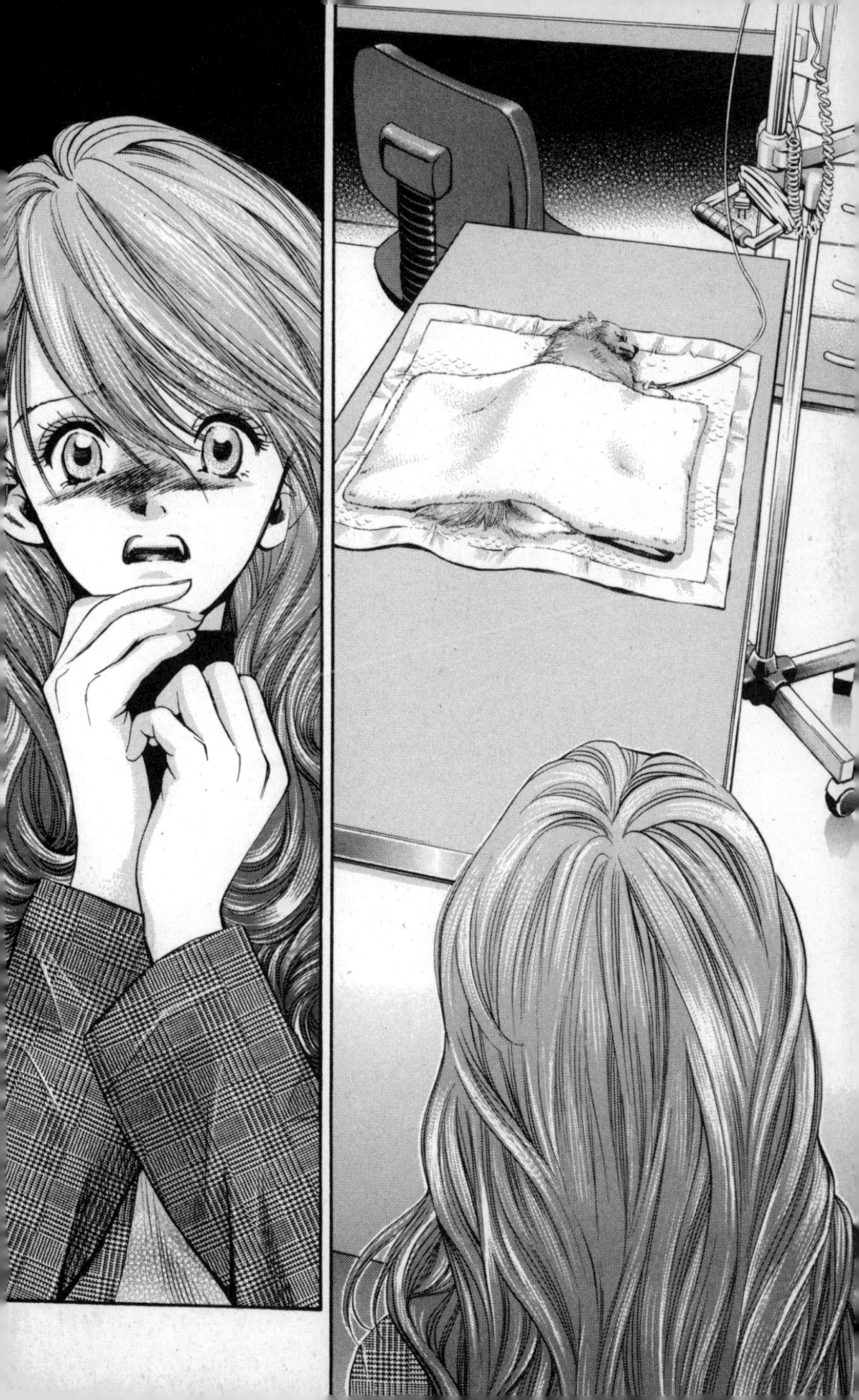

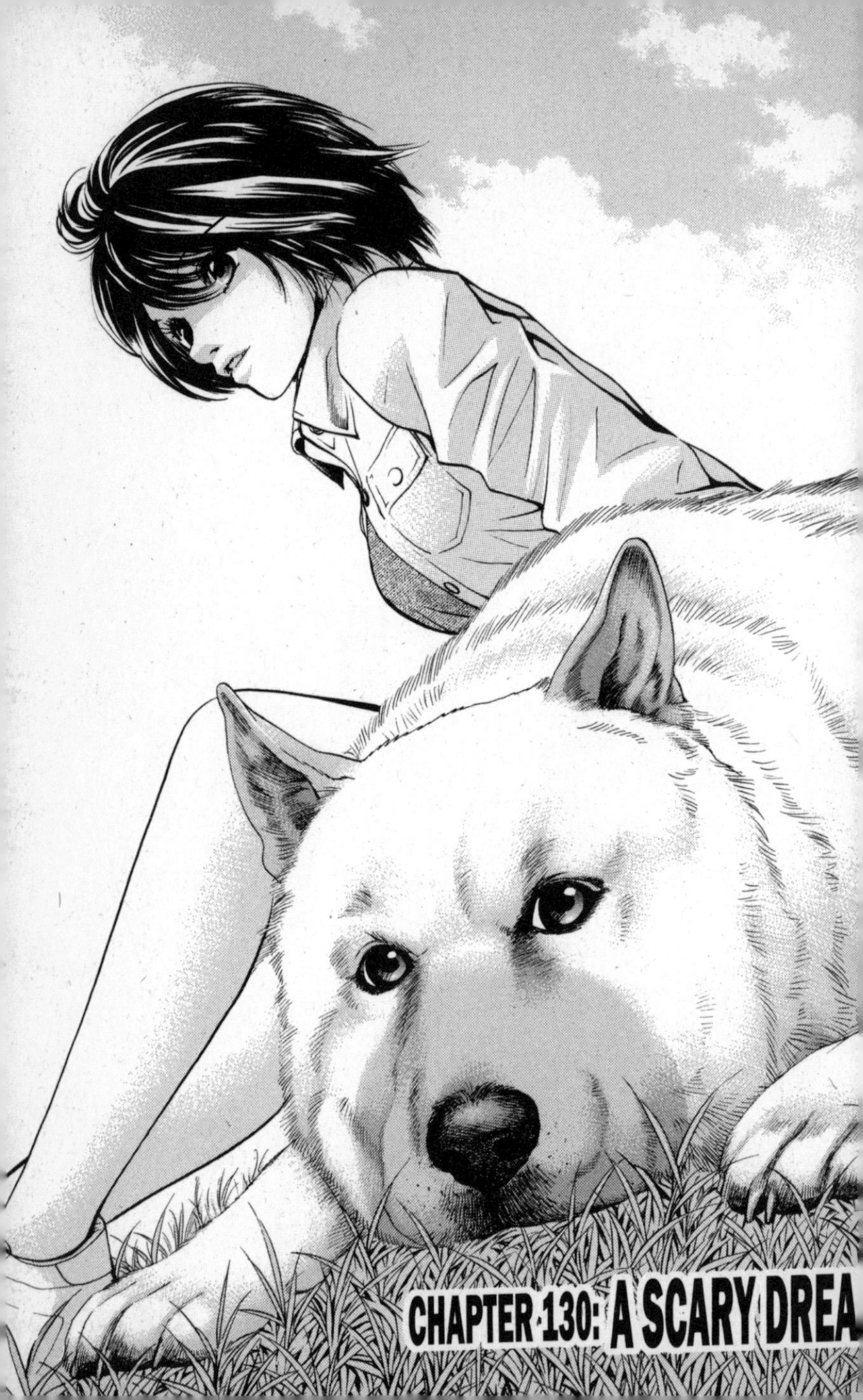
CHAPTER 130: A SCARY DREA

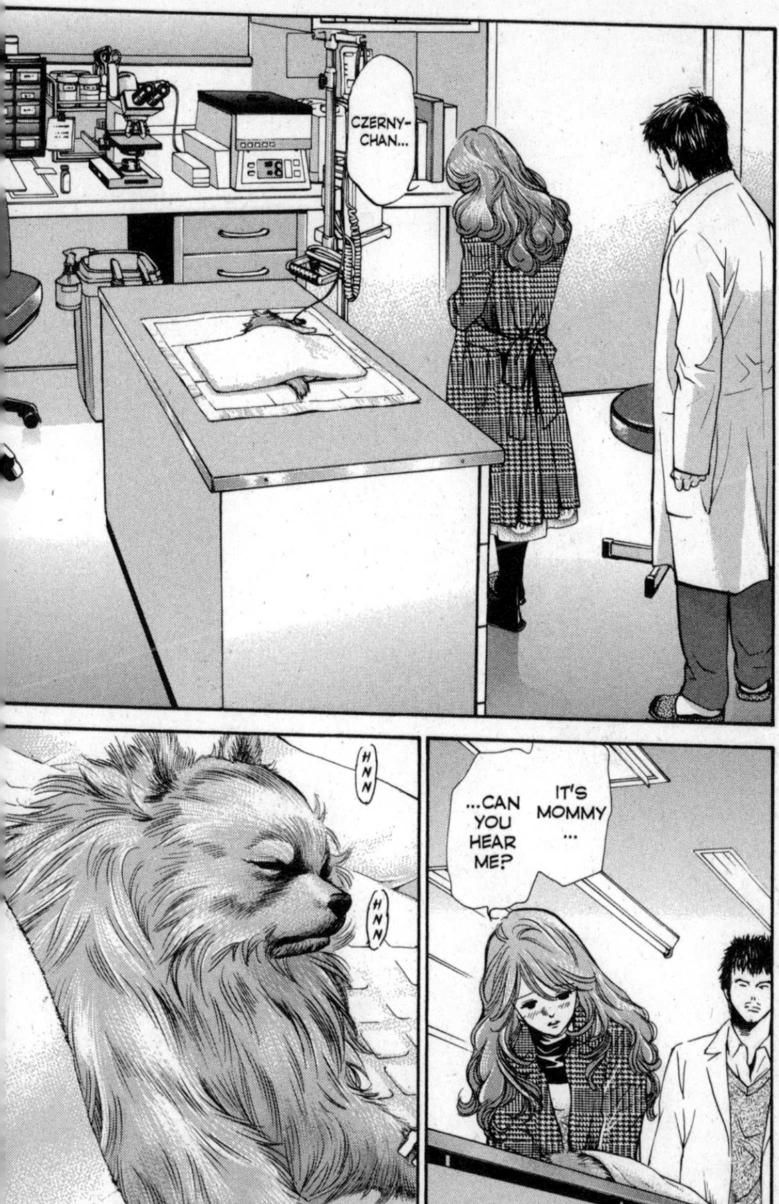
CZERNY-CHAN...
IT'S MOMMY...
...CAN YOU HEAR ME?
HNN
HNN

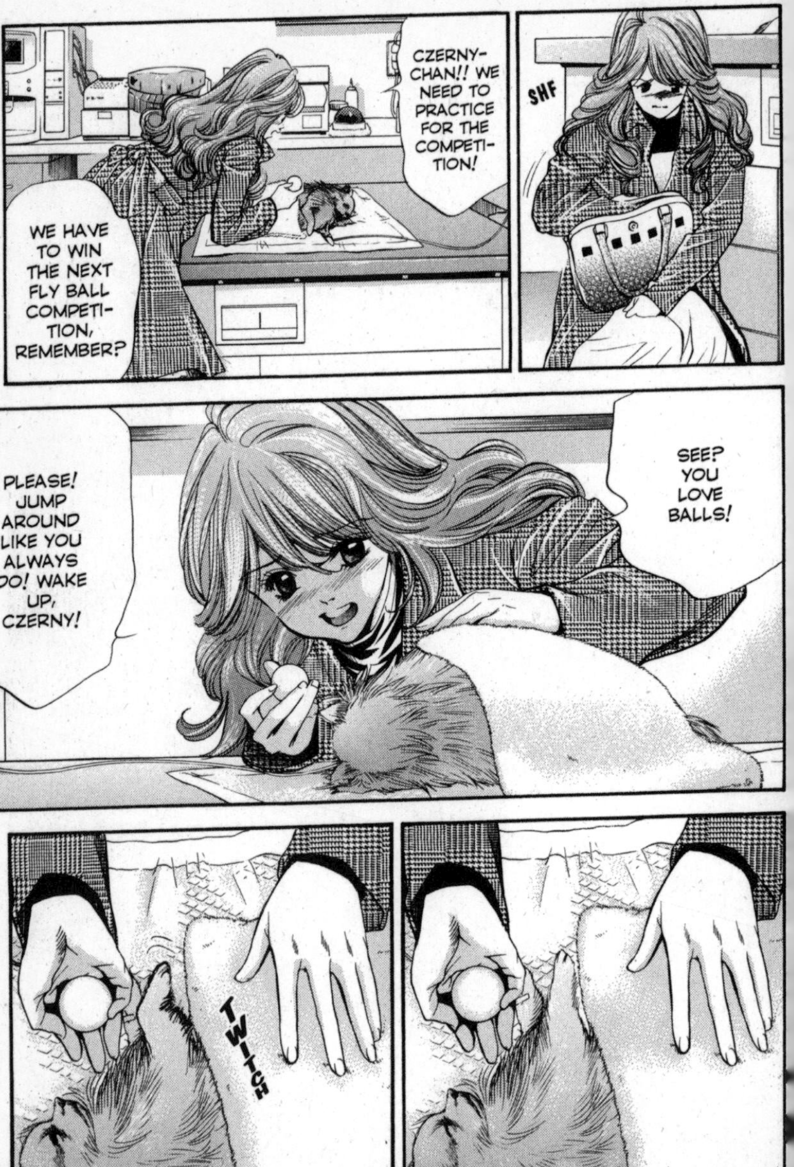
SHF
CZERNY-CHAN!! WE NEED TO PRACTICE FOR THE COMPETITION!
WE HAVE TO WIN THE NEXT FLY BALL COMPETITION, REMEMBER?
SEE? YOU LOVE BALLS!
PLEASE! JUMP AROUND LIKE YOU ALWAYS DO! WAKE UP, CZERNY!
TWITCH

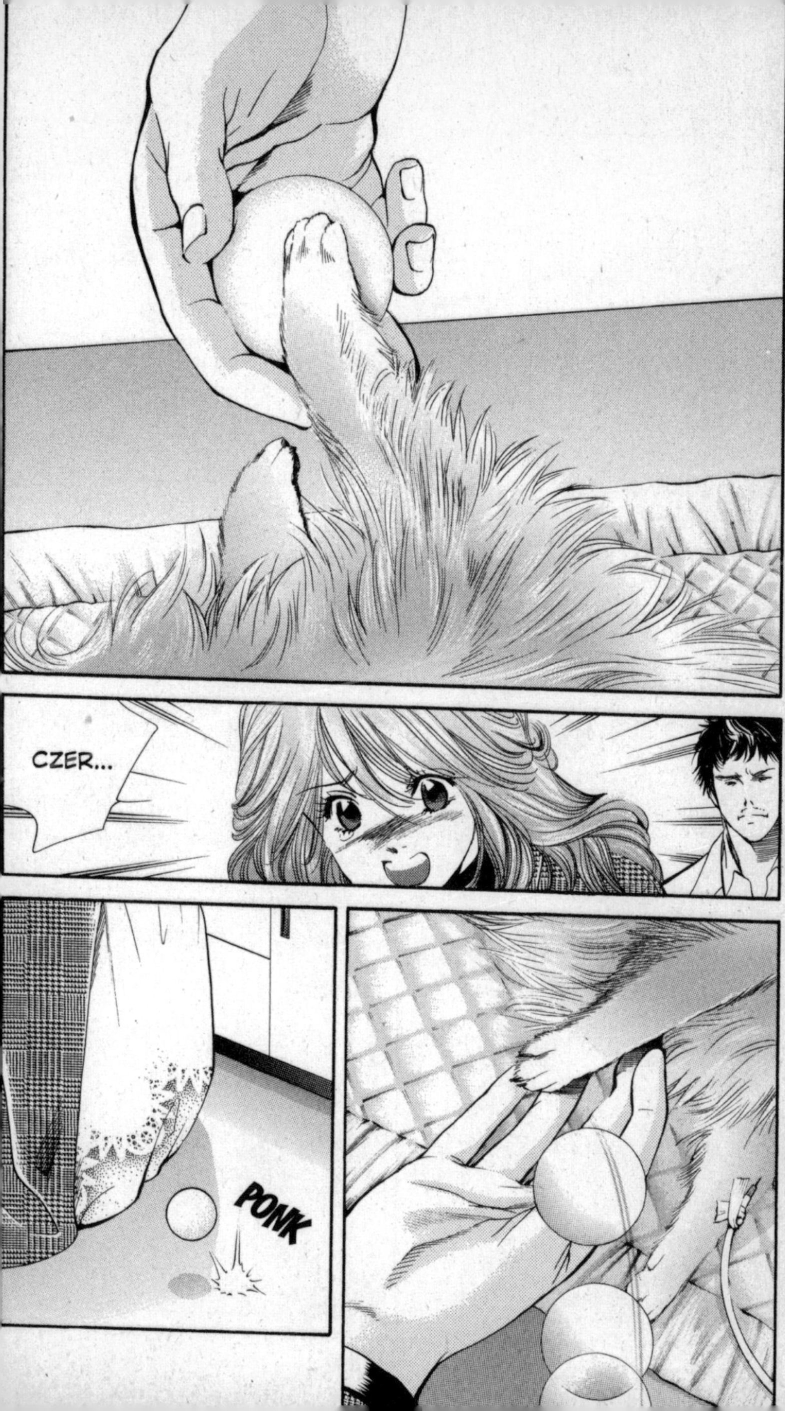
CZER...
PONK

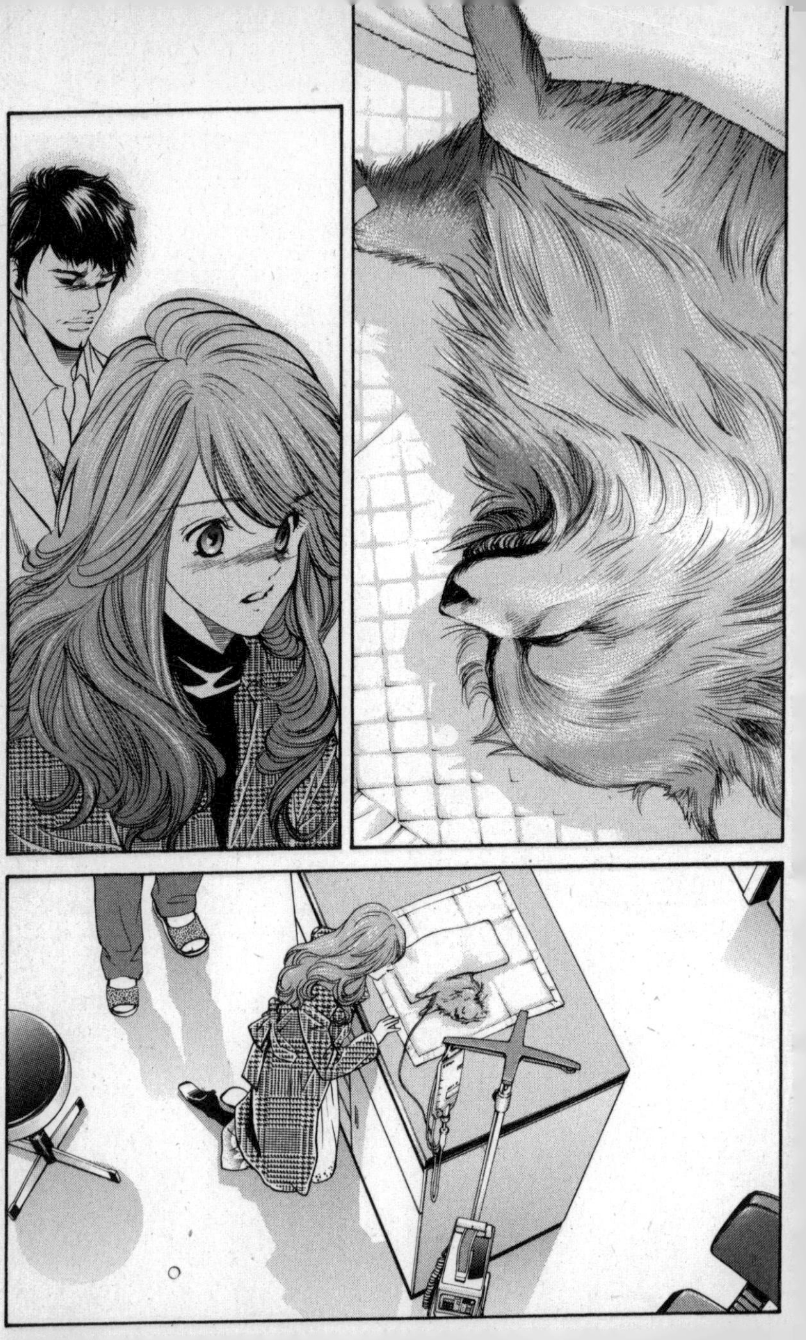

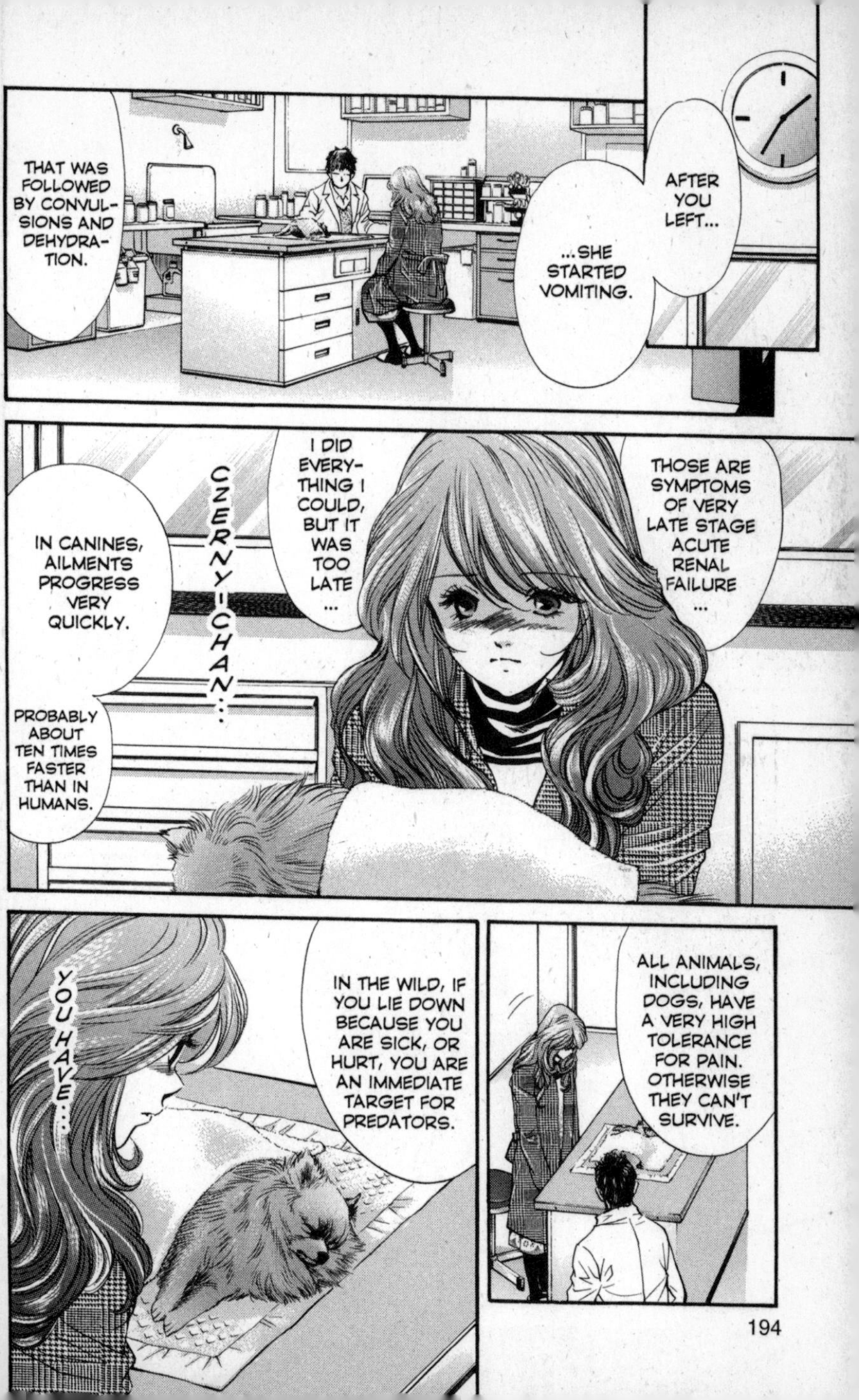
AFTER YOU LEFT...
...SHE STARTED VOMITING.
THAT WAS FOLLOWED BY CONVULSIONS AND DEHYDRATION.
THOSE ARE SYMPTOMS OF VERY LATE STAGE ACUTE RENAL FAILURE...
I DID EVERYTHING I COULD, BUT IT WAS TOO LATE...
CZERNY-CHAN...
IN CANINES, AILMENTS PROGRESS VERY QUICKLY.
PROBABLY ABOUT TEN TIMES FASTER THAN IN HUMANS.
ALL ANIMALS, INCLUDING DOGS, HAVE A VERY HIGH TOLERANCE FOR PAIN. OTHERWISE THEY CAN'T SURVIVE.
IN THE WILD, IF YOU LIE DOWN BECAUSE YOU ARE SICK, OR HURT, YOU ARE AN IMMEDIATE TARGET FOR PREDATORS.
YOU HAVE...

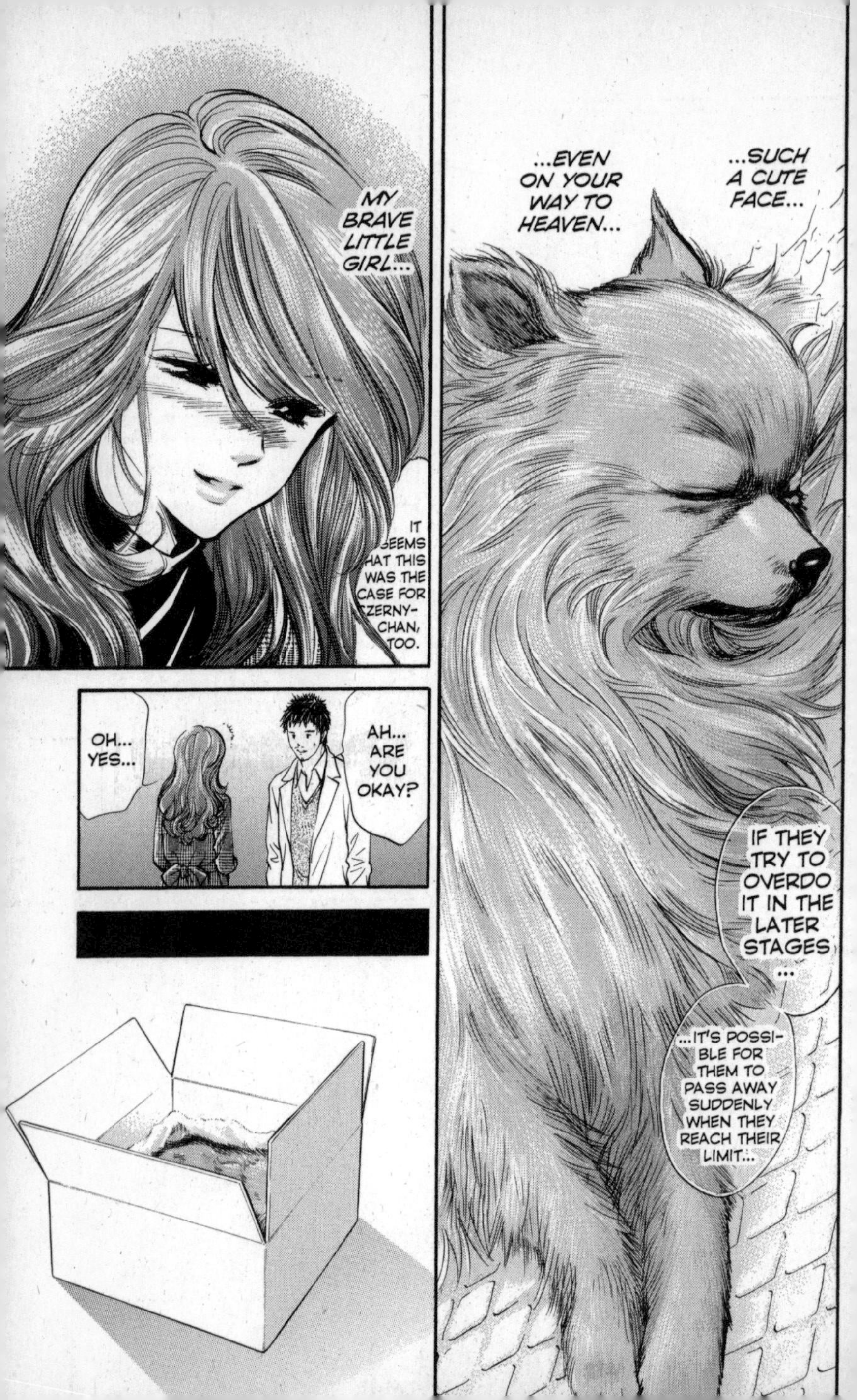
...SUCH A CUTE FACE...
...EVEN ON YOUR WAY TO HEAVEN...
IF THEY TRY TO OVERDO IT IN THE LATER STAGES ...
...IT'S POSSIBLE FOR THEM TO PASS AWAY SUDDENLY WHEN THEY REACH THEIR LIMIT...
MY BRAVE LITTLE GIRL...
IT SEEMS THAT THIS WAS THE CASE FOR CZERNY-CHAN, TOO.
AH... ARE YOU OKAY?
OH... YES...

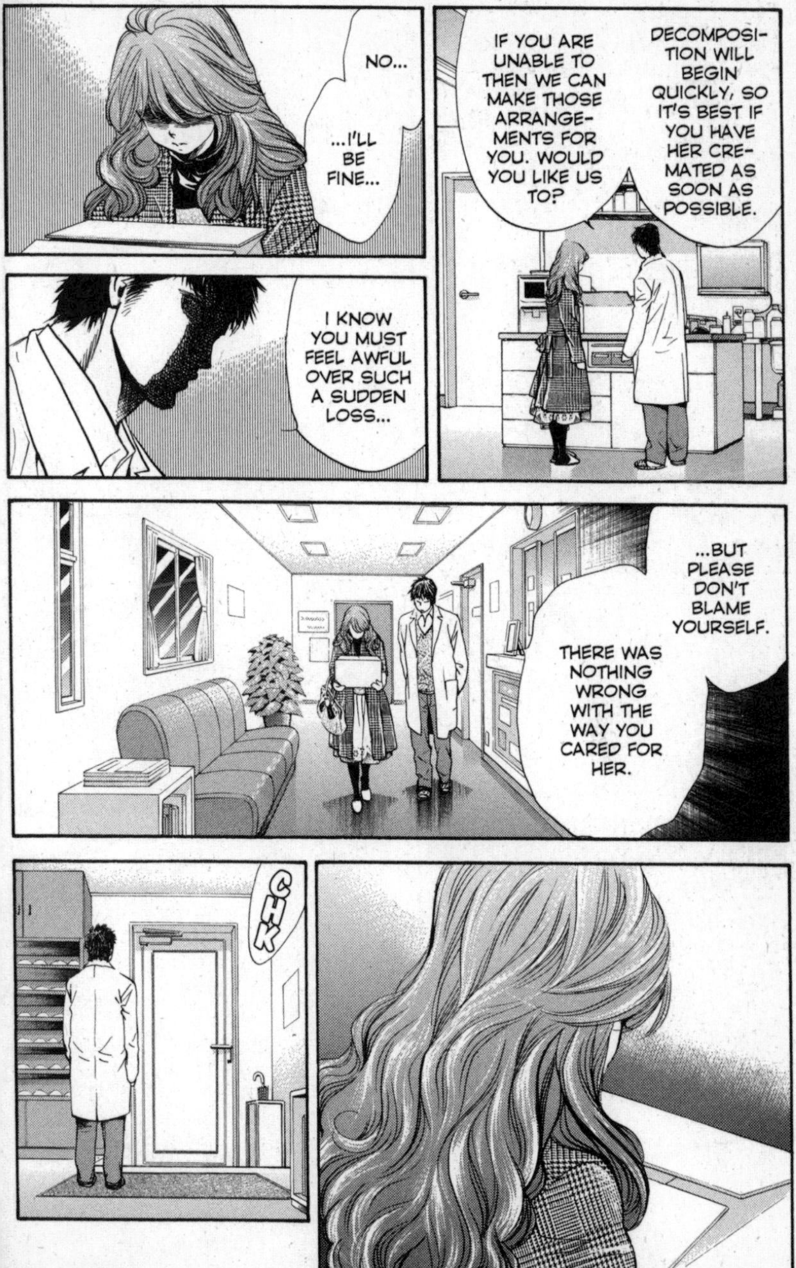
DECOMPOSITION WILL BEGIN QUICKLY, SO IT'S BEST IF YOU HAVE HER CREMATED AS SOON AS POSSIBLE.
IF YOU ARE UNABLE TO THEN WE CAN MAKE THOSE ARRANGEMENTS FOR YOU. WOULD YOU LIKE US TO?
NO...
...I'LL BE FINE...
I KNOW YOU MUST FEEL AWFUL OVER SUCH A SUDDEN LOSS...
...BUT PLEASE DON'T BLAME YOURSELF.
THERE WAS NOTHING WRONG WITH THE WAY YOU CARED FOR HER.
CHK

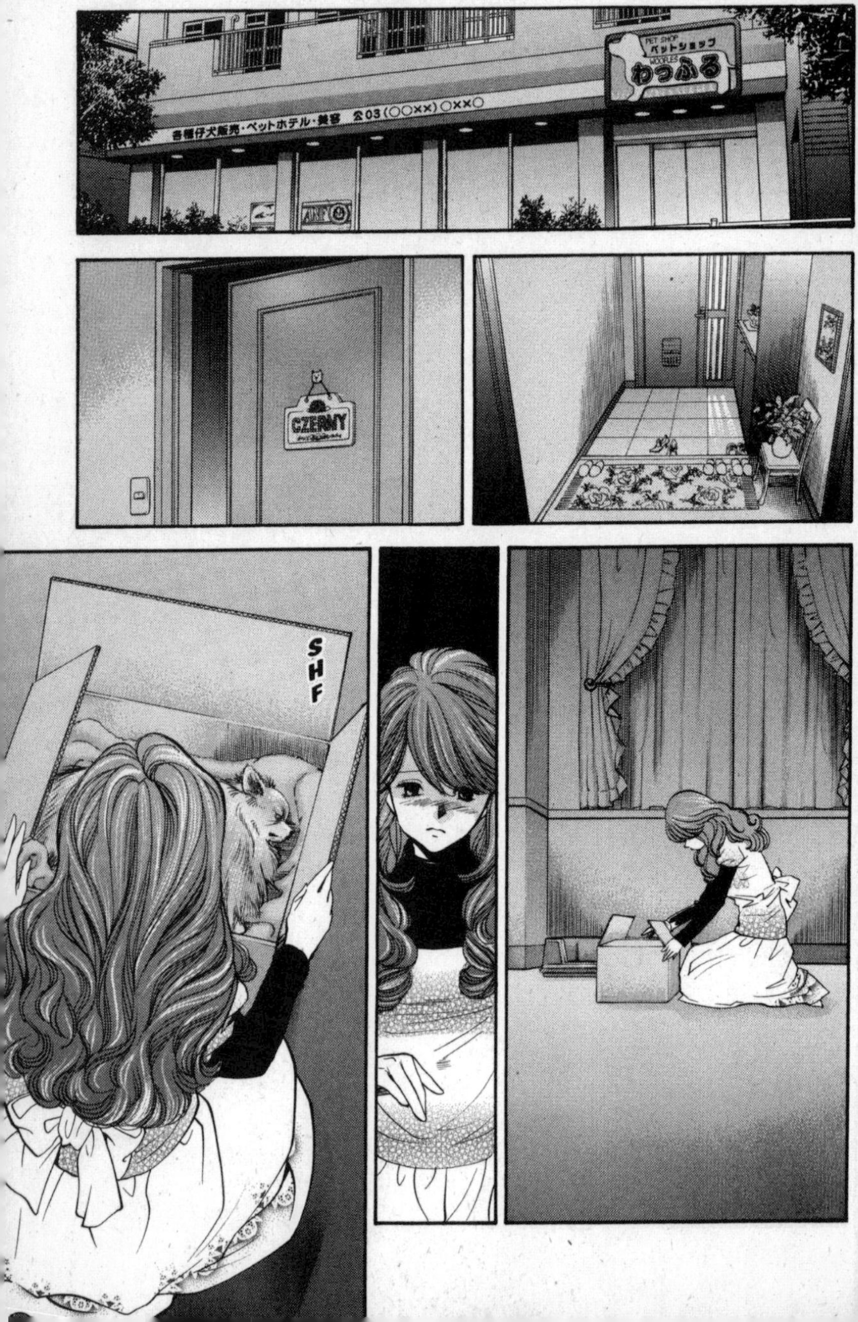
PET SHOP
ペットショップ
WOOFLES
わっふる
各種仔犬販売・ペットホテル・美容 ☎03(○○××)○××○
CZERNY
SHF

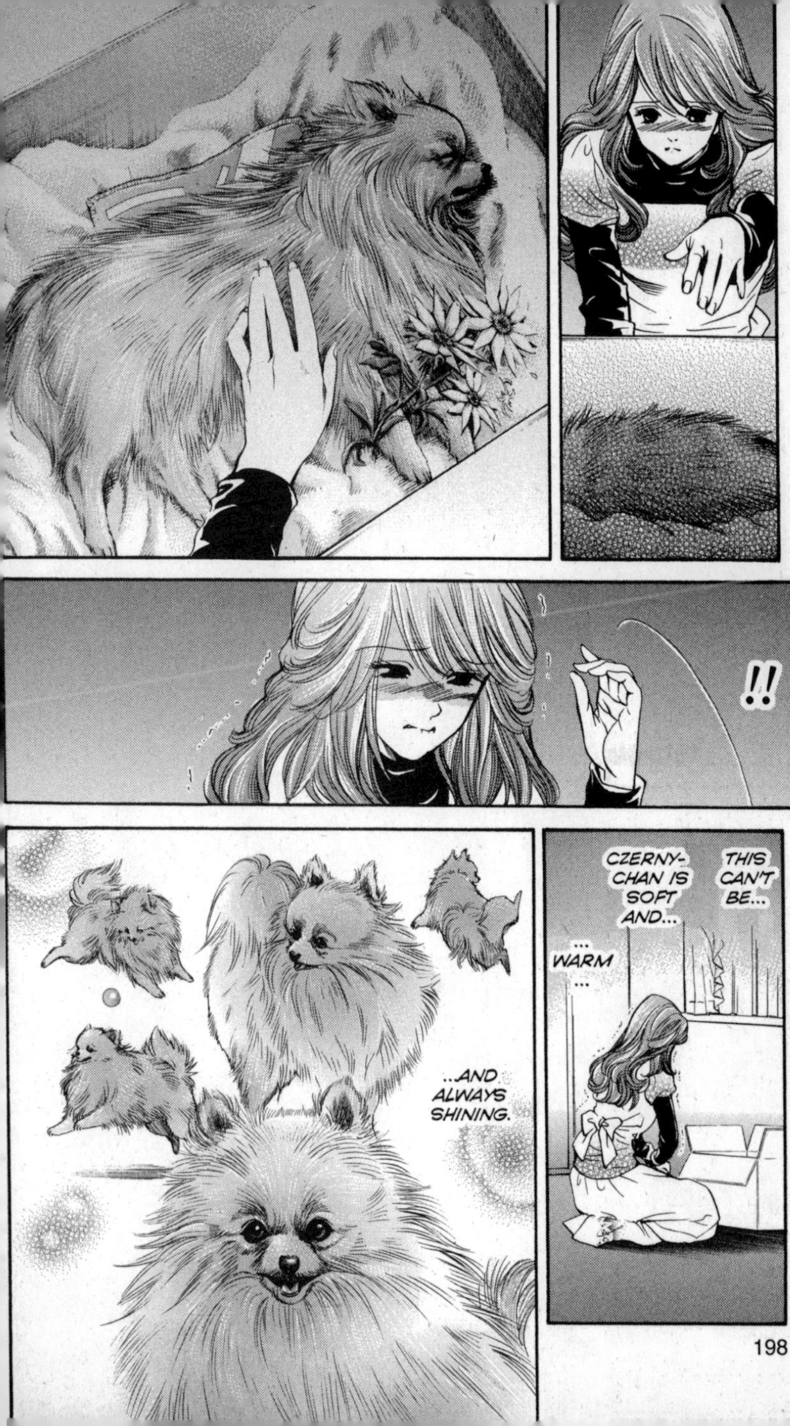
!!
THIS CAN'T BE...
CZERNY-CHAN IS SOFT AND...
...WARM...
...AND ALWAYS SHINING.

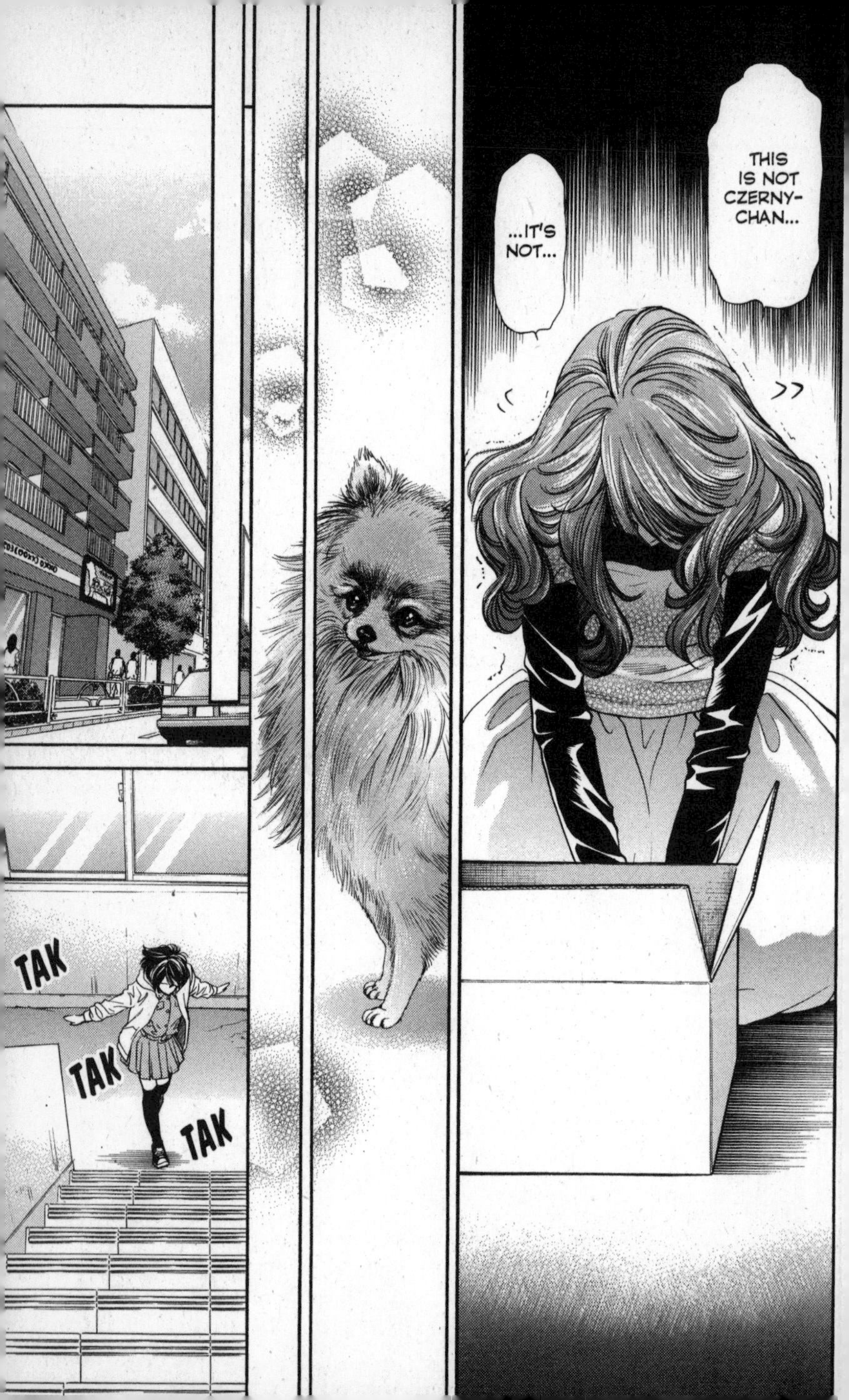
THIS IS NOT CZERNY-CHAN...
...IT'S NOT...
TAK
TAK
TAK

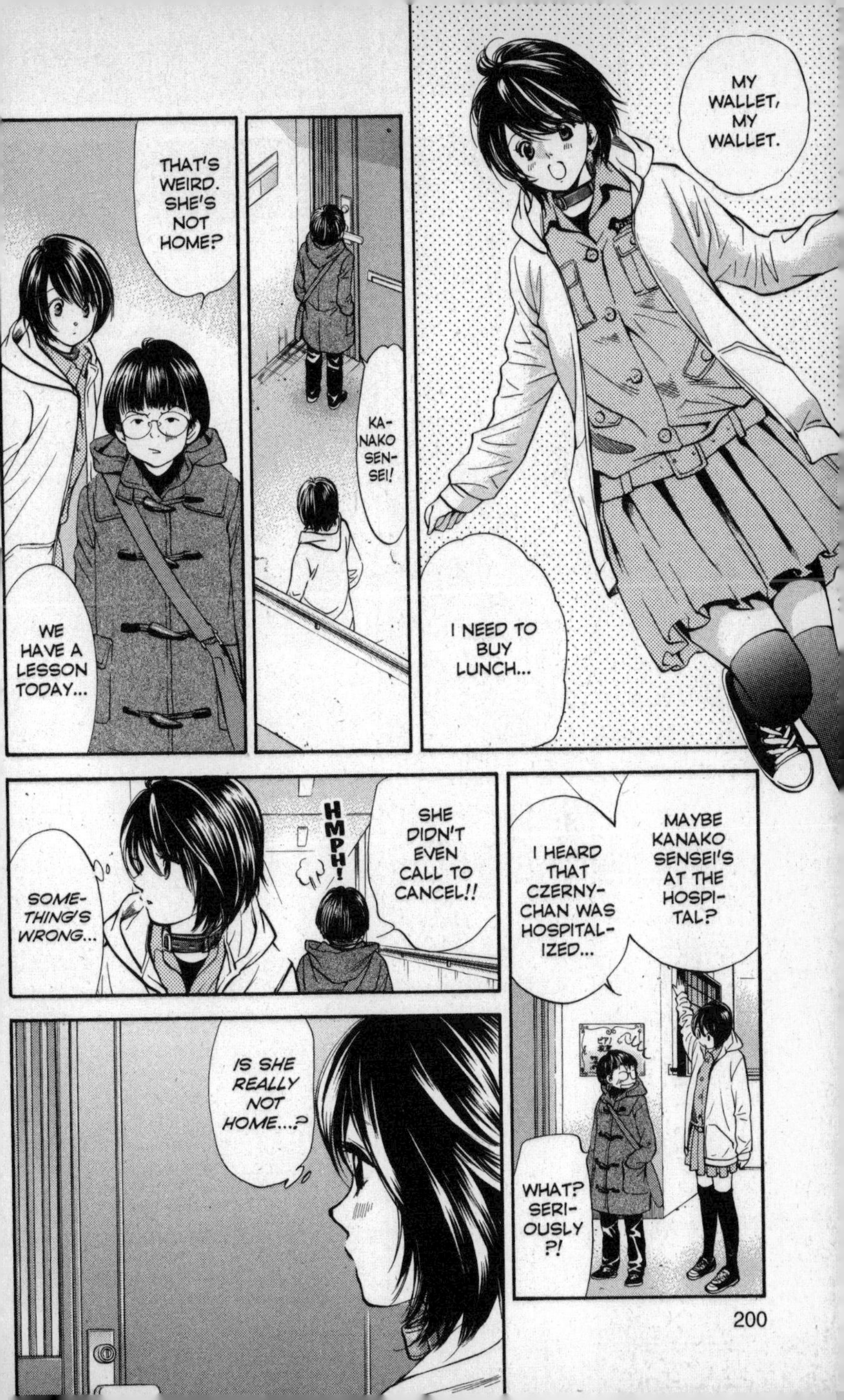
MY WALLET, MY WALLET.
I NEED TO BUY LUNCH...
KA-NAKO SEN-SEI!
THAT'S WEIRD. SHE'S NOT HOME?
WE HAVE A LESSON TODAY...
MAYBE KANAKO SENSEI'S AT THE HOSPI-TAL?
I HEARD THAT CZERNY-CHAN WAS HOSPITAL-IZED...
WHAT? SERI-OUSLY ?!
SHE DIDN'T EVEN CALL TO CANCEL!!
HMPH!
SOME-THING'S WRONG...
IS SHE REALLY NOT HOME...?

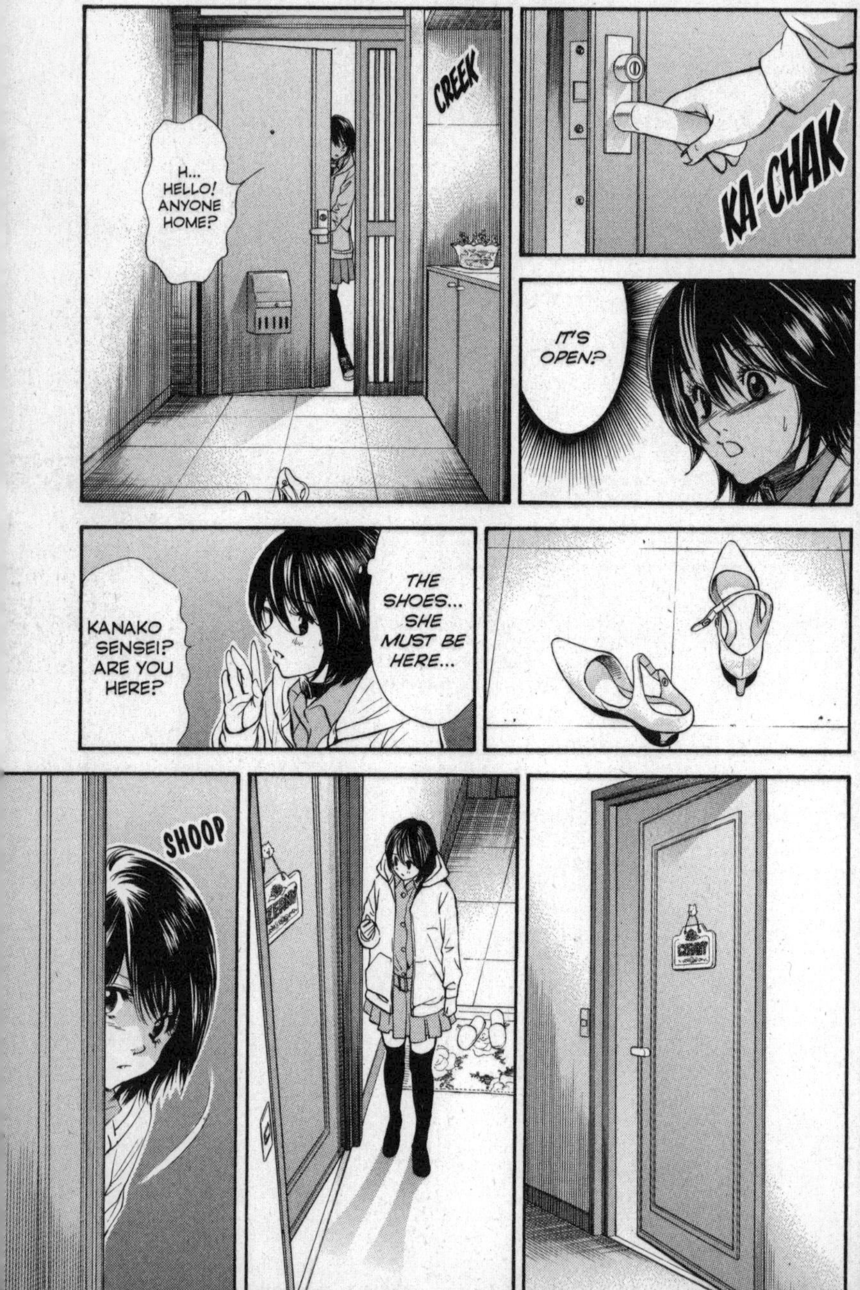
KA-CHAK
IT'S OPEN?
CREEK
H... HELLO! ANYONE HOME?
THE SHOES... SHE MUST BE HERE...
KANAKO SENSEI? ARE YOU HERE?
SHOOP

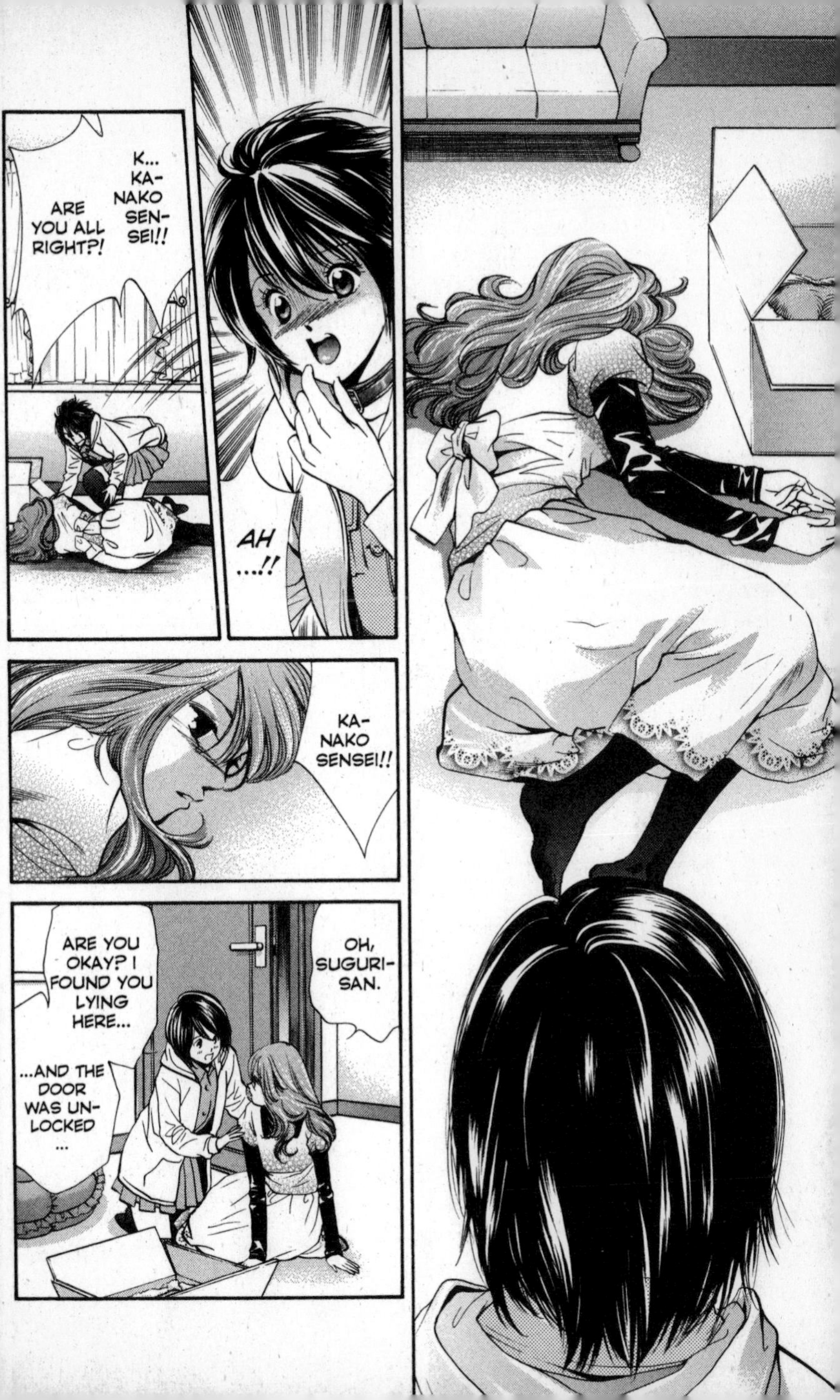
AH ...!!
K... KA-NAKO SEN-SEI!!
ARE YOU ALL RIGHT?!
KA-NAKO SENSEI!!
OH, SUGURI-SAN.
ARE YOU OKAY? I FOUND YOU LYING HERE...
...AND THE DOOR WAS UN-LOCKED ...

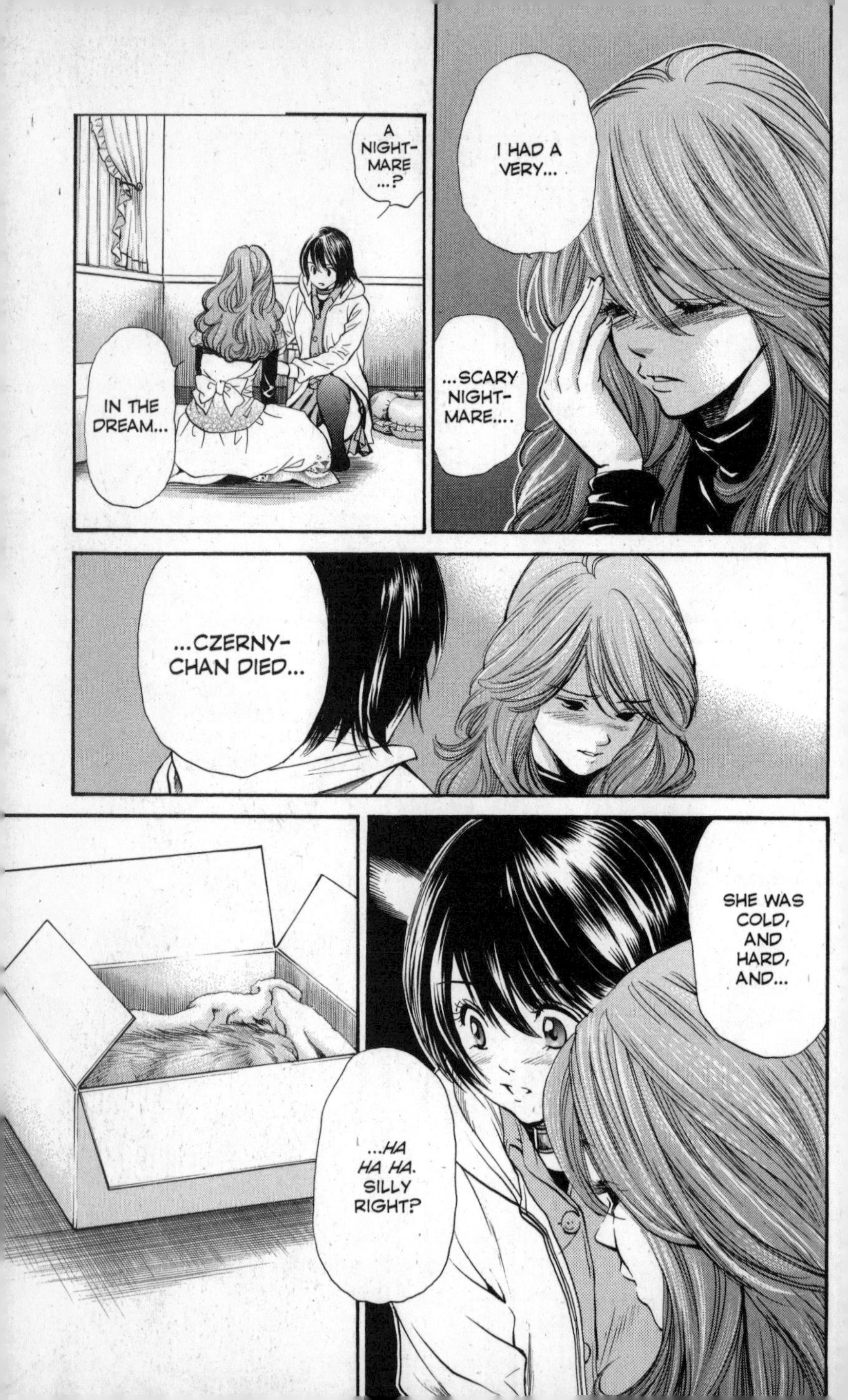
I HAD A VERY...
...SCARY NIGHT-MARE....
A NIGHT-MARE ...?
IN THE DREAM...
...CZERNY-CHAN DIED...
SHE WAS COLD, AND HARD, AND...
...HA HA HA. SILLY RIGHT?

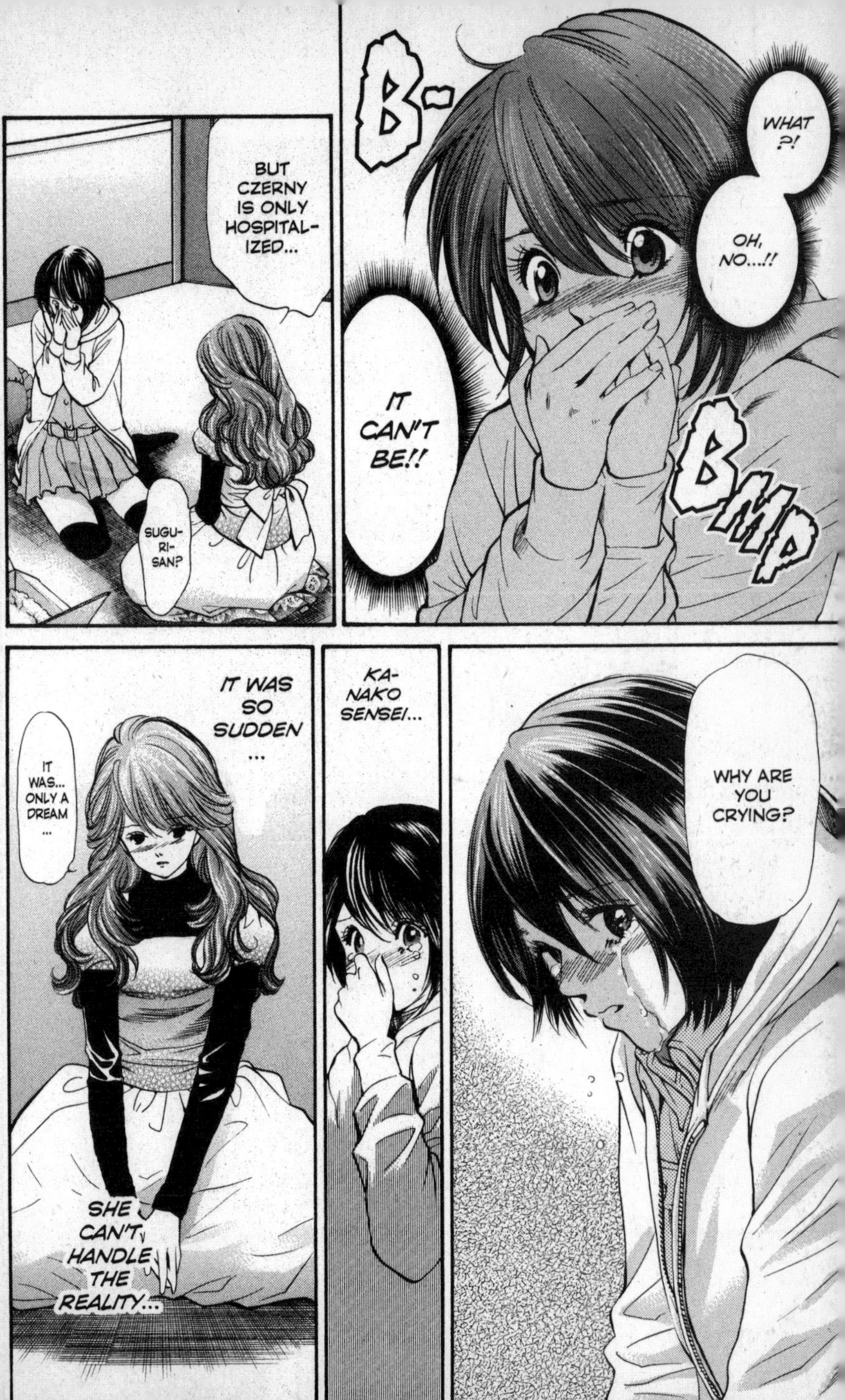
WHAT?!
OH, NO...!!
B-
IT CAN'T BE!!
BMP
BUT CZERNY IS ONLY HOSPITAL-IZED...
SUGU-RI-SAN?
WHY ARE YOU CRYING?
KA-NAKO SENSEI...
IT WAS SO SUDDEN...
IT WAS... ONLY A DREAM...
SHE CAN'T HANDLE THE REALITY...

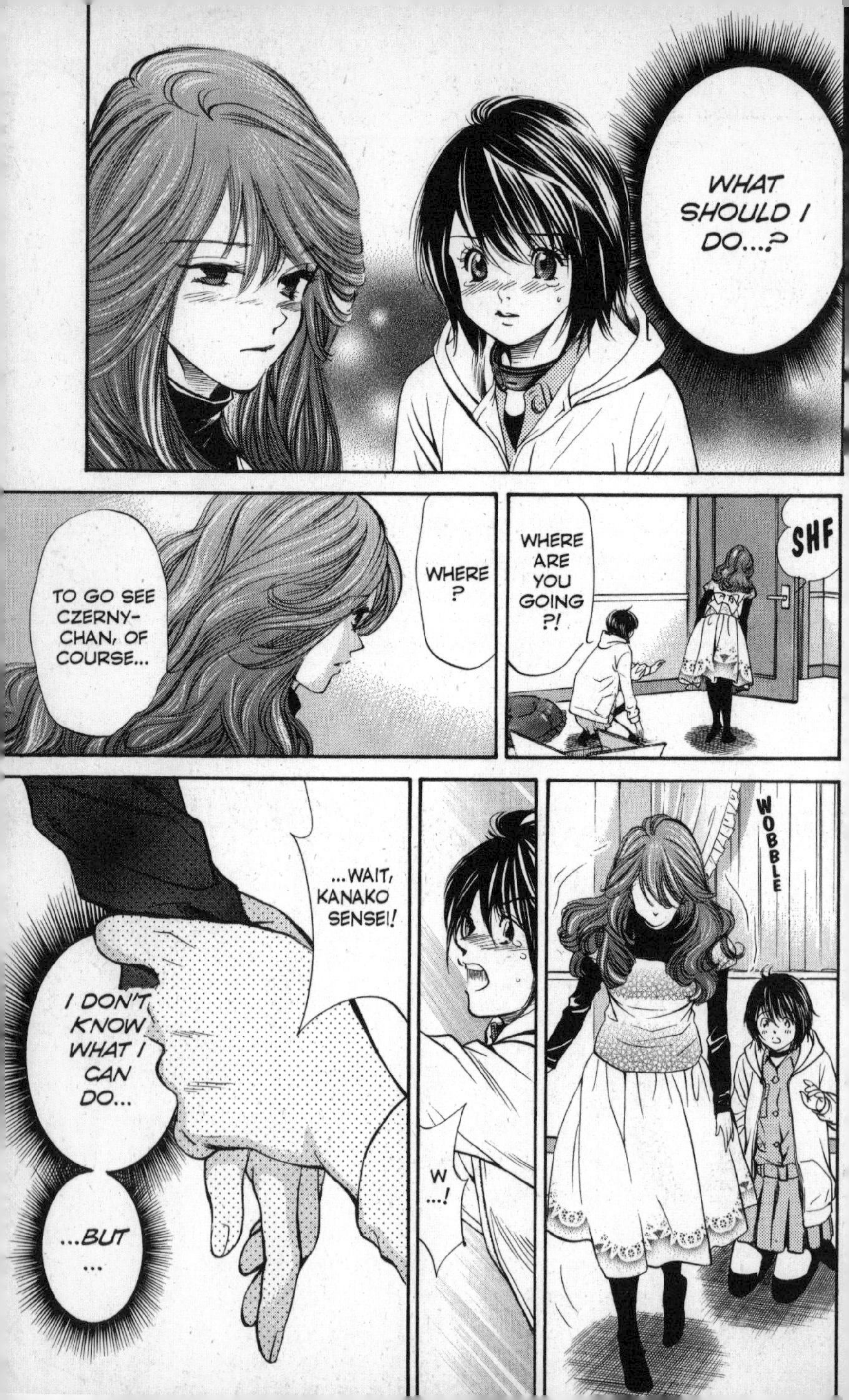
WHAT SHOULD I DO...?
SHF
WHERE ARE YOU GOING?!
WHERE?
TO GO SEE CZERNY-CHAN, OF COURSE...
WOBBLE
...WAIT, KANAKO SENSEI!
W...!
I DON'T KNOW WHAT I CAN DO...
...BUT...

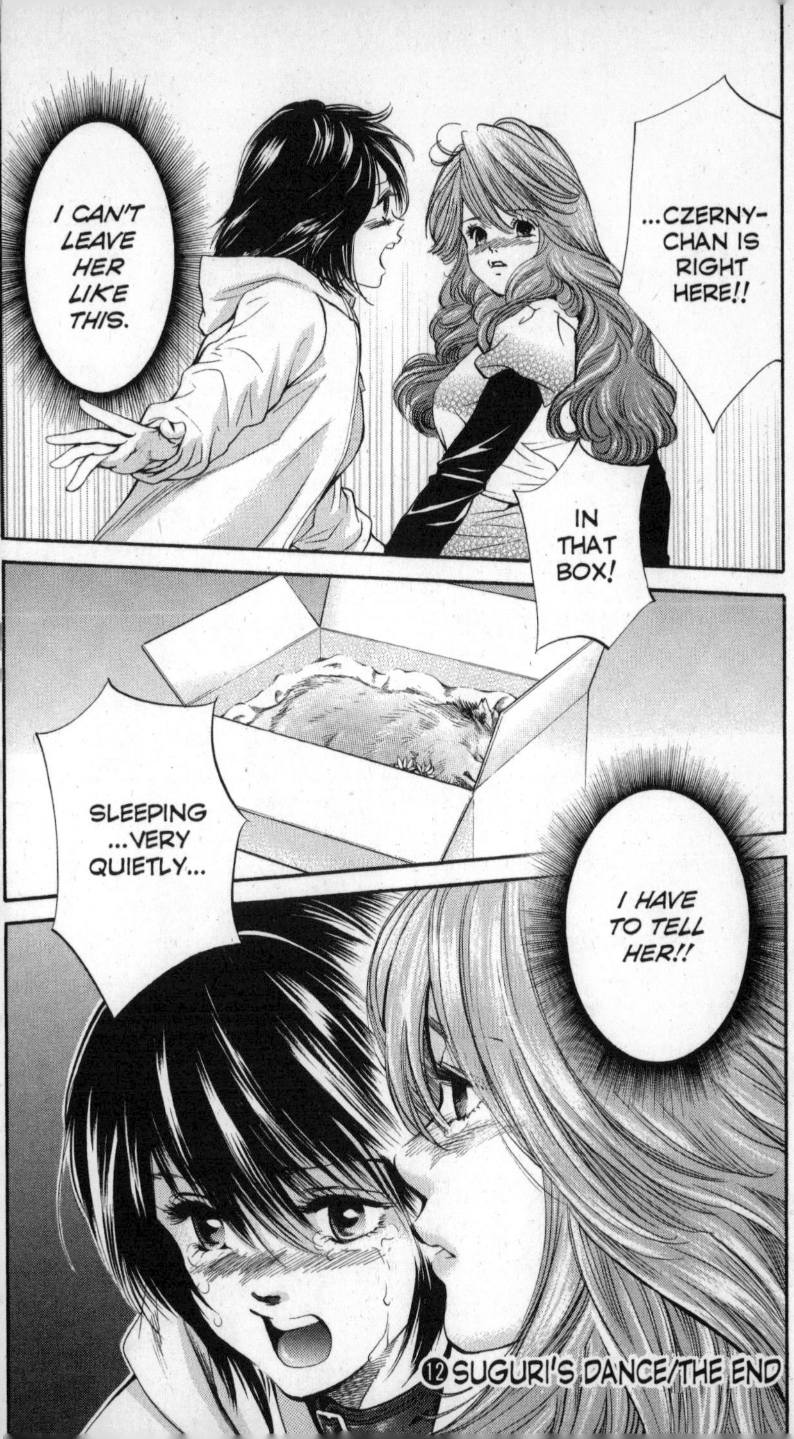
...CZERNY-CHAN IS RIGHT HERE!!
I CAN'T LEAVE HER LIKE THIS.
IN THAT BOX!
SLEEPING ...VERY QUIETLY...
I HAVE TO TELL HER!!
12 SUGURI'S DANCE/THE END

INUBAKA

# INUBAKA

## Everybody's Crazy for Dogs!

**From Bu-ko Takasaka-san in Chiba Prefecture**

### 🐾 Leo-kun and Momo-chan (Papillon)

*With the two of them, the living room is like a dog-run. That's how energetic they are. With their shots taken care of, I bet they are running around together outside now...? Don't catch a cold. ☆*

**Yukiya Sakuragi**

You must be excited to see their butterfly ears develop as they get older. I wonder if Momo-chan is going to be Leo-kun's bride. When we have two dogs, our living room turns into a wrestling ring too.

**From Yamaguchi-san in Fukuoka Prefecture**

### 🐾 Goemon-kun

*Goemon loves to go out more than he loves his food. He especially loves to go driving. He looks pretty sharp taking command of the wheel too! Nice!*

**Yukiya Sakuragi**

It's like he's saying, "Welcome to Goemon Taxi!" (lol) It's really fun going out on a drive with your dog. My Blanc has finally gotten used to cars.

**From Akatsuka-san in Chiba Prefecture**

### ✄ Nana-chan (Toy poodle)

*Apparently she is very energetic in the house, but one step out the door and she becomes really shy. But when you look at her in this picture, you can't help but love her, no matter how she acts.*

**Yukiya Sakuragi**

Yes, yes. I know those types (lol). A friend of ours, Jetta the shih tzu, is the same. At home, he's the boss and jumps on Blanc, but one step outside and he gets quiet all of a sudden. You may never know which one is the true character, but they are cute either way.

**From Chi-san in Osaka**

### ✄ (from the right) Luke-kun, Komomo-chan, Mowa-kun, Anzu-chan, and Fine-kun (Toy poodle)

*They've always played together, but now they can finally stand in line together for a picture. We hope you five siblings stay good to each other. Love the matching outfits!*

**Yukiya Sakuragi**

What a handsome and fashionable group! They look just like stuffed animals! It's amazing they can stand there together so still! One of them must be a strong leader. I wonder who's the boss…

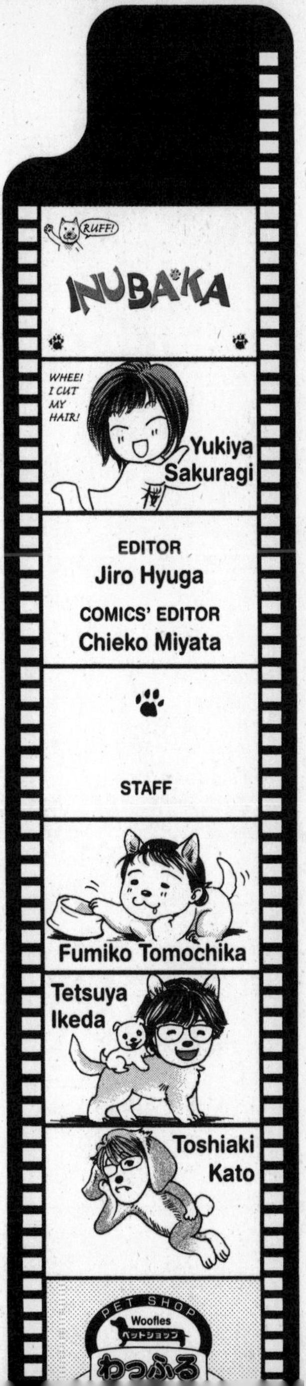
RUFF!
INUBAKA
WHEE! I CUT MY HAIR!
Yukiya Sakuragi
EDITOR
Jiro Hyuga
COMICS' EDITOR
Chieko Miyata
STAFF
Fumiko Tomochika
Tetsuya Ikeda
Toshiaki Kato
PET SHOP
Woofles
ペットショップ
わっふる

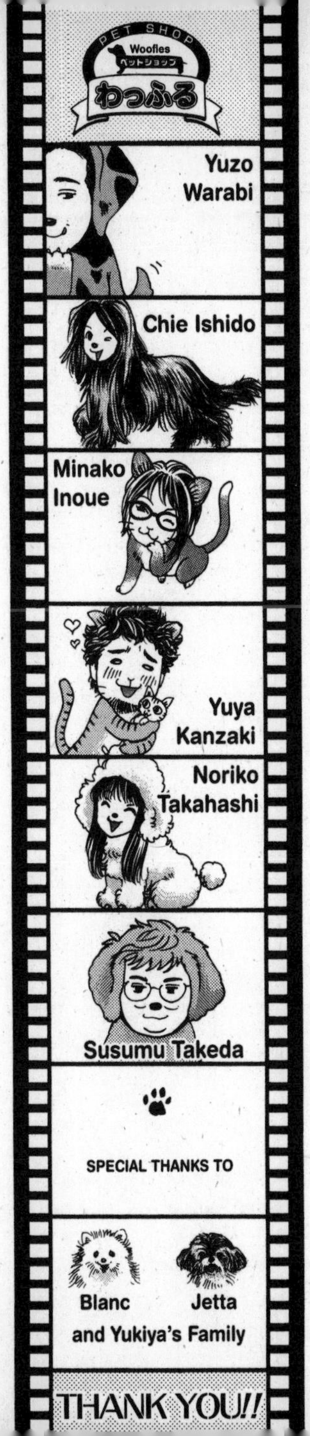
PET SHOP
Woofles
ペットショップ
わっふる
Yuzo Warabi
Chie Ishido
Minako Inoue
Yuya Kanzaki
Noriko Takahashi
Susumu Takeda
SPECIAL THANKS TO
Blanc
Jetta
and Yukiya's Family
THANK YOU!!

# Inubaka
## Crazy for Dogs
### Vol. #12
### VIZ Media Edition

## Story and Art by
## Yukiya Sakuragi

Translation/ Maya Robinson, HC Language Solutions, Inc.
English Adaptation/Ian Reid, HC Language Solutions, Inc.
Touch-up Art & Lettering/Kelle Hahn
Cover & Interior Design/Hidemi Dunn
Editor/Ian Robertson

Editor in Chief, Books/Alvin Lu
Editor in Chief, Magazines/Marc Weidenbaum
VP, Publishing Licensing/Rika Inouye
VP, Sales & Product Marketing/Gonzalo Ferreyra
VP, Creative/Linda Espinosa
Publisher/Hyoe Narita

INUBAKA © 2004 by Yukiya Sakuragi
All rights reserved. First published in Japan in 2004 by SHUEISHA Inc., Tokyo.
English translation rights arranged by SHUEISHA Inc.

Printed in the U.S.A.

Published by VIZ Media, LLC
P.O. Box 77010
San Francisco, CA 94107

10 9 8 7 6 5 4 3 2 1
First printing, April 2009

www.viz.com
store.viz.com

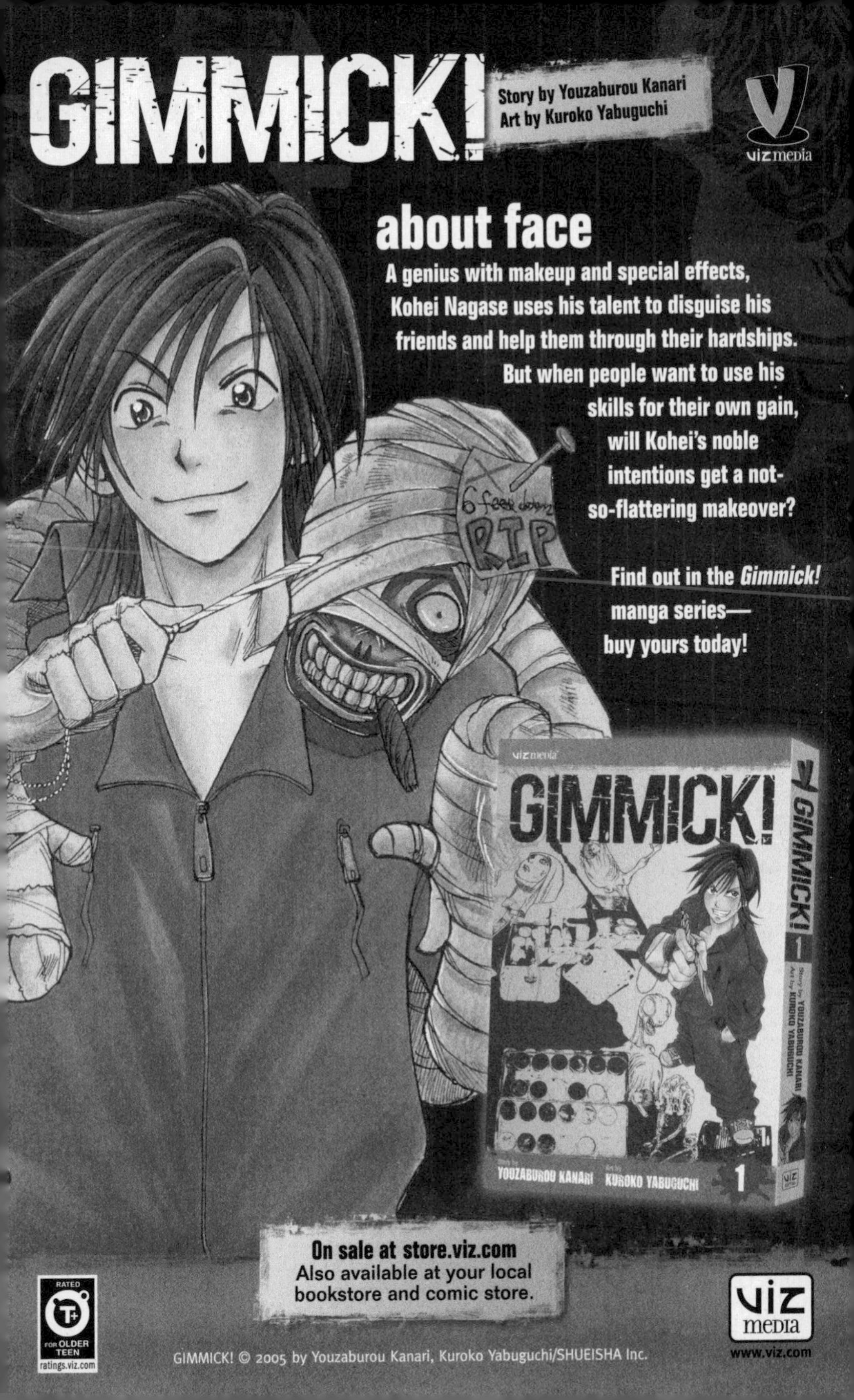
GIMMICK!
Story by Youzaburou Kanari
Art by Kuroko Yabuguchi
VIZ media
about face
A genius with makeup and special effects, Kohei Nagase uses his talent to disguise his friends and help them through their hardships. But when people want to use his skills for their own gain, will Kohei's noble intentions get a not-so-flattering makeover?
Find out in the Gimmick! manga series—buy yours today!
6 feet down
RIP
VIZ media
GIMMICK!
1
YOUZABUROU KANARI
KUROKO YABUGUCHI
On sale at store.viz.com
Also available at your local bookstore and comic store.
RATED T+ FOR OLDER TEEN
ratings.viz.com
GIMMICK! © 2005 by Youzaburou Kanari, Kuroko Yabuguchi/SHUEISHA Inc.
VIZ MEDIA
www.viz.com

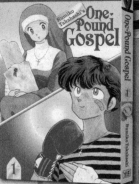

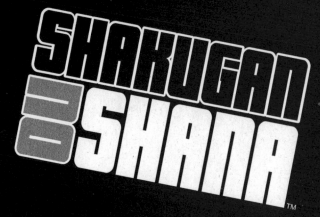
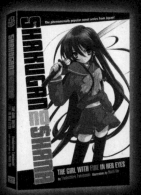
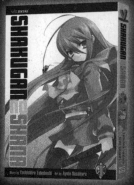

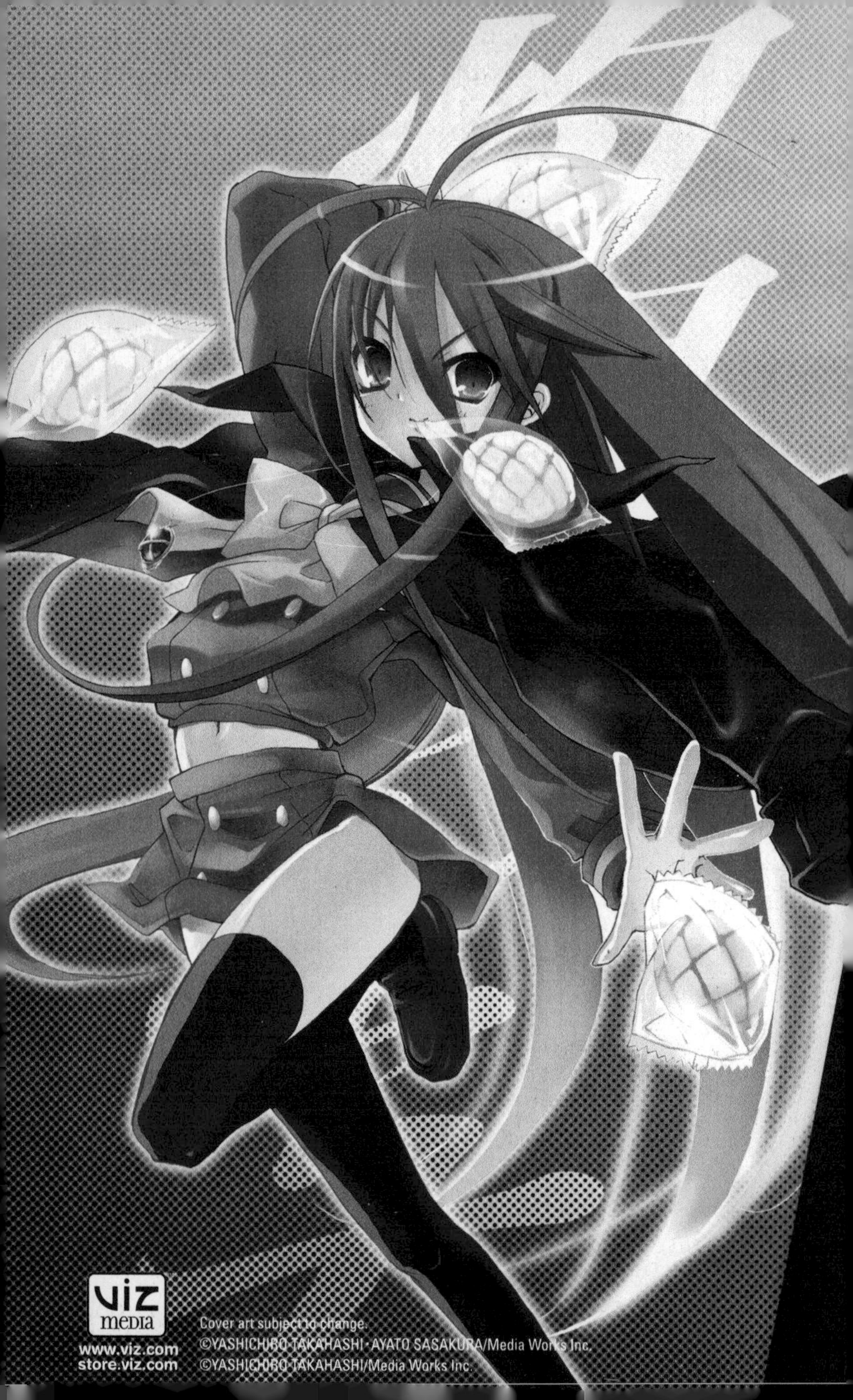

# LOVE MA
## LET US KNOW W

OUR MANGA SURVEY IS NOW AVAILABLE ONLINE. PLEASE VISIT: VIZ.COM/MANGASURVEY

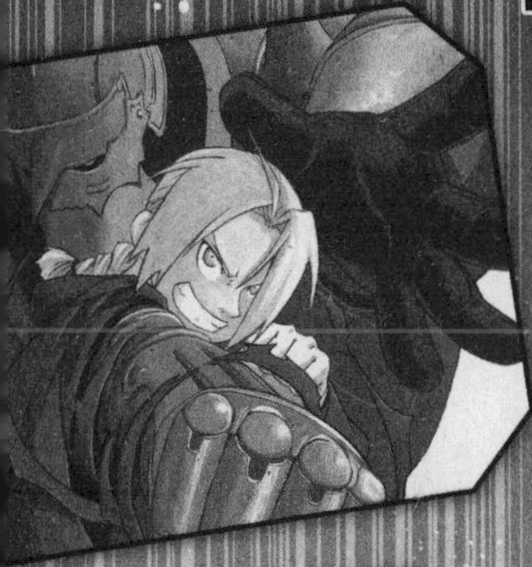

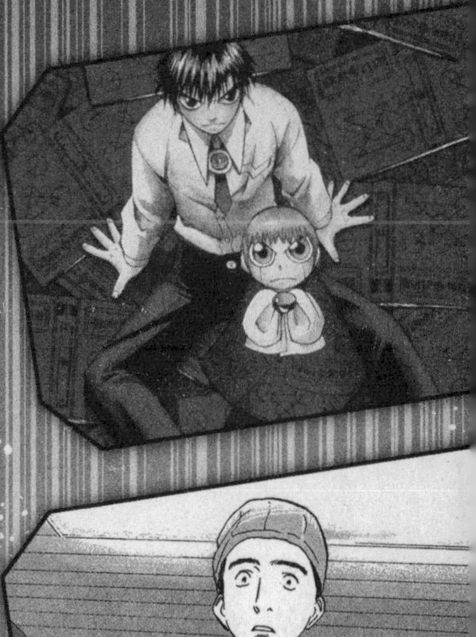

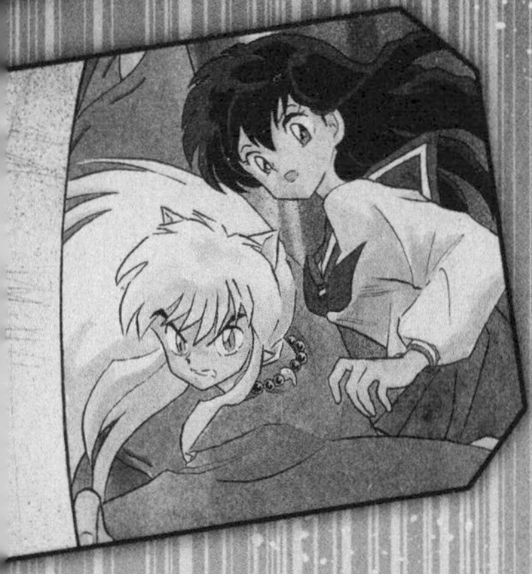

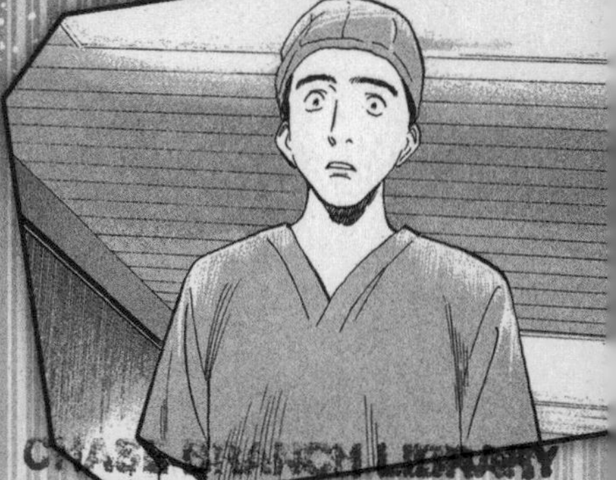



## HELP US MAKE THE MANGA YOU LOVE BETTER!